"Dr. Charles Hodges and other eminently qualified Christian medical professionals have combined together to provide an invaluable resource for counselors. This book should be an excellent resource for every Christian counselor who desires to be wise in making decisions of how best to counsel both body and soul. I highly recommend this wonderful resource."

John D. Street, Chair, Graduate Studies in Biblical Counseling, The Master's University & Seminary; board president, Association of Certified Biblical Counselors (ACBC)

"This book helps counselors think holistically about caring for embodied souls. Each chapter reviews the current medical understanding of common counseling issues and then skillfully applies God's Word to the disruptive, disheartening, and often perplexing problems people experience. If you provide one-another care—whether formally or informally—reading this resource is well worth your time."

Christine Chappell, Author of *Help! I've Been Diagnosed with a Mental Disorder*; outreach director and *Hope + Help Podcast* host, Institute for Biblical Counseling & Discipleship; certified biblical counselor

"Congregants, students, and counselees regularly ask me questions about medical issues, psychology, psychotropic medications, and how all those things connect with respect to God. In the first edition of this book, Dr. Robert Smith wisely provided us help in these areas. In this second edition, a new set of qualified counselors help us wisely serve those striving to honor God through some of life's toughest pressures. Each chapter carefully connects life's sufferings with God's Word while providing practical solutions for living."

Kevin Carson, Pastor, Sonrise Baptist Church, Ozark, MO; professor, Baptist Bible College and Theological Seminary, Springfield, MO

"*The Christian Counselor's Medical Desk Reference* is a very practical resource for the counselor who desires to serve well but is untrained in medical issues. The chapters address common issues counselors face and give scriptural and medical information which will improve their counseling advice. I will use this book and will highly recommend it to others."

Caroline Newheiser, Assistant Coordinator for Women's Counseling, Reformed Theological Seminary, Charlotte, NC

"Dr. Charles Hodges has performed a marvelous service to biblical counselors by assembling a tremendous team to address key issues that may require medical intervention. I look forward to having a copy of this book on my shelf for reference whenever I am trying to determine whether it would be wise to consult a medical doctor, so my counsel to others is as compassionate and comprehensive as possible."

Steve Viars, Senior Pastor, Faith Church, Lafayette, IN

"This is a book every pastor and Christian counselor needs to own and to which they will often refer. The authors combine the wealth of their extensive medical training and experience with their commitment to and knowledge of God's Word. The case studies in each chapter effectively help the reader to better understand medical issues that often come up in counseling and the potential approaches to offer help. Difficult issues are dealt with humbly and carefully. I will encourage every one of my students to buy and use this book."

Jim Newheiser, Professor of Counseling and Pastoral Theology, Reformed Theological Seminary, Charlotte, NC; executive director, The Institute for Biblical Counseling and Discipleship (IBCD); board member of the Biblical Counseling Coalition (BCC) and the Association of Certified Biblical Counselors (ACBC)

"This medical reference book is an important resource for biblical counselors, showing the wisdom of caring for both the body and soul. Charles Hodges and the other contributors provide medical and biblical perspectives that are informative and readable. Around twenty years ago, I used the first edition as a biblical counseling student, and I look forward to sharing the second edition with my students."

Lilly Park, Associate Professor of Biblical Counseling, Southwestern Baptist Theological Seminary

"Since its inception, the modern biblical counseling movement has cared deeply for the physical body and its interaction with the soul. Dr. Hodges and his team provide a fresh reference work for those who counsel and those who train counselors. Their choice of topics, their medical details in lay language, and their counseling implications make this a valuable resource."

Robert D. Jones, Associate Professor of Biblical Counseling, The Southern Baptist Theological Seminary; author of *Pursuing Peace* and *Uprooting Anger*; coauthor of *The Gospel for Disordered Lives: An Introduction to Christ-Centered Biblical Counseling*

THE CHRISTIAN COUNSELOR'S
MEDICAL DESK REFERENCE

THE CHRISTIAN COUNSELOR'S MEDICAL DESK REFERENCE

. . . .

2ND EDITION

. . . .

CHARLES D. HODGES JR., MD,
EDITOR

New
Growth
Press

newgrowthpress.com

New Growth Press, Greensboro, NC 27401
newgrowthpress.com

The names used in this book have been altered for patient/client privacy.

Cover Design: Faceout Books, faceoutstudio.com
Interior Typesetting and eBook: Lisa Parnell, lparnellbookservices.com

ISBN 978-1-64507-231-7 (Print)
ISBN 978-1-64507-232-4 (eBook)

Library of Congress Cataloging-in-Publication Data on file
Names: Hodges, Charles D., Jr., editor.
Title: The Christian counselor's medical desk reference / Charles D. Hodges
   Jr., editor.
Description: 2nd edition. | Greensboro, NC : New Growth Press, [2023] |
   First edition published by Timeless Texts, c2000. | Includes
   bibliographic references. | Summary: "Dr. Charles Hodges and a team of
   contributing physicians set out to answer questions and offer solid
   biblical principles for counseling those with medical issues"-- Provided
   by publisher.
Identifiers: LCCN 2022049848 (print) | LCCN 2022049849 (ebook) | ISBN
   9781645072317 (paperback) | ISBN 9781645072324 (ebook)
Subjects: LCSH: Church work with the sick. | Medicine--Religious
   aspects--Christianity. | Pastoral counseling.
Classification: LCC BV4335 .C48 2023 (print) | LCC BV4335 (ebook) | DDC
   259/.4--dc23/eng/20221130
LC record available at https://lccn.loc.gov/2022049848
LC ebook record available at https://lccn.loc.gov/2022049849

Printed in India
30 29 28 27 26 25 24 23   2 3 4 5 6

Dedication

To Robert Smith MD:

In the first edition of *The Christian Counselor's Medical Desk Reference* (CCMDR), Dr. Smith dedicated the book to two of his friends. In it, "Doc," as we all called him, commended Jay Adams and Bill Goode as godly men who pioneered biblical counseling as we know it today. They were his dear friends and encouragers, and Doc was certain that God had changed his life through the ministry of those two men.

As editor of the second edition, I dedicate this book to the man who more than any other changed my thinking about counseling—Dr. Robert Smith. He was a godly man and a partner with his two friends in returning the care of souls to the church, where it is meant to be. All of these men played a vital part in that enterprise.

I knew all three, but the one who had the most profound and lasting effect on my life was Doc. Like Doc, I had practiced medicine and studied counseling for fifteen years, and I too was unimpressed with the benefit either gave to those who were struggling with worry and depression. In 1998, I traveled to Lafayette, Indiana, where Doc was the director of Faith Biblical Counseling Ministries. From day one, he recruited me to stay and learn how to counsel. And I did. It was one of the most important decisions I made in my life.

Doc was the elder father physician who would change the way I viewed the cause and cure of the worry and depression that has gripped our nation. From the time I took his introductory counseling course to the days that he directly supervised my counseling, he was my mentor, colleague, and dear friend.

Dr. Smith asked me to be the general editor for the second edition of CCMDR. While we were in the process of working on this book, his health was declining. I kept him aware of the progress we were making. On March 27, 2021, he went home to be with the Lord and his precious Leona. Doc was full of great quotes, so time and space won't allow me to relate them all, but I do want to share one.

Doc often said that if a counselee is sick, dying, and fearful, teach them about heaven. In his words, "Heaven will be better!" I am certain that Doc is now enjoying the reality of those words.

Charles D. Hodges Jr.

Contents

· · · ·

INTRODUCTION
Charles D. Hodges Jr., MD

"How blessed is the man who does not walk in the counsel of the wicked, Nor stand in the path of sinners, Nor sit in the seat of scoffers! But his delight is in the law of the LORD, And in His law he meditates day and night" (Psalm 1:1–2). One of the most important choices we will make in life will be who we consult when we are in need of "counsel." Psalm 1 is just one of many passages of Scripture that admonish us to be careful about where we go when we are struggling and in need of direction.

This is particularly true today, when we face the redefinition of inconvenient or difficult behavior as disease. In the last thirty years, we have witnessed the conversion of normal sadness over loss in life into the disease of depression. The question becomes, "Where do we go for help if we struggle with depression or any of the over 400 acronym labels in the fifth edition of the *Diagnostic and Statistical Manual of Mental Disorders* (DSM-5)?"

The biblical counseling movement as we know it today was born in the 1970s to answer that question. There were three general streams of thought at the time. The prominent societal answer was "go see your doctor." On the opposite pole was the beginning of biblical counseling. In the middle were those trying to merge both ends.

Dr. Robert Smith was solidly among those who believed that the answers to the emotional struggles of life could be found in the inspired, inerrant, and sufficient Scriptures. He unapologetically counseled from the principles he found in the Bible any and all who came to the counseling center. He taught thousands of us to do the same.

Over the course of those years, Dr. Smith and I discussed the unique advantage we shared of being physicians who were also biblical counselors. We felt that our advantage was in being able to identify the effects that medical illness could have on the emotions, thoughts, and behaviors of those we counseled. It helped us counsel the individual with an overactive thyroid in a different manner than we would have if her insomnia and weight loss were simply due to worry.

As Dr. Smith worked his way through a more than 50-year career in medicine and counseling, it became obvious to many of us that it would be very helpful if a book could be written to extend some of his medical knowledge to the rest of us in biblical counseling. The result was the first edition of the CCMDR. It has proven to be a help to many.

The first and second edition of the CCMDR were both written with the intention that they could be used as a reference and a guide for counseling individuals with medical problems. In his original foreword, Dr. Smith recounted that he was often presented with the following scenario: "Doctor, I have a counselee who has been diagnosed with _____." Whatever filled in the blank was supposed to be the cause for the behaviors, thoughts, and emotions that were disrupting the life of the counselee and those around him or her.

It was Doc's intent to help counselors, counselees, and the family and friends of these struggling saints. As Doc explained, "This book is intended for use as an aid for the biblical counselor in dealing with the numerous medical problems that arise in conjunctions with counseling . . . and to remove the intimidation biblical counselors often experience when a disease diagnosis is given."

Our goal is to continue to offer that aid in the second edition and to bring the medical science up to date. The CCMDR was published twenty-two years ago and met a great need in biblical counseling at that time. Many have expressed to me that the book helped them overcome their fear of counseling those who were also being treated for a medical disease or had been labeled with a psychiatric diagnosis. We intend for the second edition to do the same. And, while the primary audience of this book is biblical counselors, we also hope that this book can encourage counselees and their loved ones.

The first section of this book deals with general principles that can be used to help frame your thinking about counseling those with a medical problem. While each chapter is written to stand alone, reading these first chapters will help you in understanding and applying the principles found in later chapters.

In the twenty-five years that I have been involved in counseling, one of the significant areas of controversy has been the relationship between medical science and Scripture. One of the foundational principles of the biblical counseling movement is that we believe that Scripture is sufficient in all matters of faith and practice. As the apostle Peter told us, "Grace and peace be multiplied to you in the knowledge of God and of Jesus our Lord; seeing that His divine power has granted to us everything pertaining to life and godliness, through the true knowledge of Him who called us by His own glory and excellence" (2 Peter 1:2–3).

Dr. Smith believed there were biblical principles that applied to every struggle we face. He believed that those principles would be sufficient for counseling problems that accompanied medical disease. While he did not view the Bible as a medical textbook, he reminded us that Scripture had sufficient principles to guide our response to any illness. That is our aim in this section.

The second section consists of chapters that deal with a specific medical or psychiatric diagnosis. Each chapter will examine how that medical disease or a DSM-5 label impacts the counseling process. The chapters will also offer biblical principles that may be applied in order to help in these situations.

As I considered the subjects that we might put in this second edition, I chose subjects that were uniquely medical. The list includes medical problems that were often the reason people came to our counseling center for help. As the list came together, one thing became obvious. It would take more than one medical writer with a biblical counseling background to cover all the subjects.

Thankfully, there were a number of medical professionals who agreed to help with this project. The group consists of ten physicians, two nurses, a pharmacist, and a social worker. Their bios are included in the back of the book. All of them have a part in the biblical counseling movement.

Space and time would not allow us to include every subject that might be considered. We thought these subjects will be a helpful addition to the biblical counseling literature. It is also our goal with this book to help the reader avoid counseling individuals by the labels they have been assigned (by themselves or others). We live in a day when individuals become their label. Instead of approaching people as the owner of an acronym such as MDD (Major Depressive Disorder) or GAD (Generalized Anxiety Disorder), we should see them as individuals who are struggling and suffering with their thoughts, emotions, and behaviors. And we should recognize that we can offer them the hope that is found in Scripture.

In the first edition, Dr. Smith issued a warning that is as important today as it was twenty years ago. Reading this book will not transform a biblical counselor into a physician. It will give you a reasonable understanding of medical issues that will help you avoid providing unhelpful counsel like Job's friends. In my years as a physician and a counselor, I have found that my understanding of a medical problem helps me to avoid jumping to conclusions about the behaviors, thoughts, and emotions of my counselees. It is my hope that this background knowledge will similarly inform the counsel you provide.

However, as Dr. Smith put it, this book is not meant to help you become an "amateur diagnostician."

At no time should you use the information to make a diagnosis or attempt to influence a physician's diagnosis. The information in this book will not make you a diagnostician

. . . So how are you to use this book? It is your guide to help people who already have various medical diagnoses . . . If you suspect that a medical problem may be at the root of a counselee's problem, you should urge your counselee to get a complete physical examination soon.

Dr. Smith never intended this book to be a substitute for good health care. He intended it to be a useful tool in the process of helping those who struggle and are looking for hope. In his own words, "My prayer is that it will be a blessing to the reader." It is my prayer that the second edition will be the same.

CHAPTER 1

. . . .

WHAT IS MEDICAL
ABOUT MENTAL ILLNESS?

Charles D. Hodges Jr., MD

Across my desk is a young couple who have come for counseling because they are having a real struggle with their four-year-old son. For reasons that are beyond their understanding, their boy has begun eating dirt. They have done everything they know to convince him that eating dirt is not at all good for him, but whenever they are not around, he goes right back to it.

They are concerned that this could be due to childhood rebellion and that maybe he decided to have his terrible twos in his fourth year instead. They have instructed, corrected, admonished, and disciplined the boy to no avail. They are looking for help and biblical principles to apply to helping their son.

Compare that to another couple who have come for a similar situation. Their darling daughter is single-handedly wrecking the tranquility of their lives. This child's favorite behavioral tool is often seen in the local grocery store. When the mother takes her along to purchase needed food items, the girl will at some point in the trip demand that either candy or a toy be purchased for her. If the mother declines, the child begins a meltdown.

First, she whines, then she cries, while screaming that her mother doesn't love her and never buys her anything. Eventually she is on the floor kicking and screaming until Mom abandons the trip or gives in and buys what the child wants. Both parents are very concerned and have taken the child to their pediatrician, who has told them that their daughter has DMDD (Dysfunctional Mood Dysregulation Disorder) and perhaps a hint of ODD (Oppositional Defiant Disorder). These parents are also looking for help and biblical principles that apply.

These two families illustrate important questions that all Christian counselors face. What part of these behaviors, thoughts, and emotions could be due to a medical problem? What part is due to their own sin? And what part is due to the suffering this person has experienced? Humanity's fall recorded in Genesis 3 encompasses each of these areas.

These are vitally important questions because how we answer them will determine what we do about the problem. No one wants to counsel someone as though they're simply struggling with sinful worry when in reality they are sleepless, anxious, and losing weight and hair because they have hyperthyroidism. This disease results in an abnormally high thyroid hormone running their body 50 percent faster than it should. It can result in symptoms that look a lot like anxiety. Nor do we want to counsel another person on how to fight their laziness when the primary reason they struggle to do their work is because their thyroid has shut down, leaving them tired, weak, thinking slowly, and gaining weight. We want to be able to answer the question, "What part of this is medical, and what part is not?"

This is an ongoing question for biblical counselors, both for personal reflection (to ensure we are offering wise counsel) and for direct discussion with our counselees. Many counselees may come in for counsel and say that the reason they struggle is their DSM-5 diagnosis. They will say they cannot change because they have been labeled with bipolar disorder, borderline personality disorder, panic disorder, or any of the 300-plus DSM-5 diagnoses used to describe humanity's thoughts, emotions, and behaviors.

So how can we as biblical counselors avoid making errant conclusions about the cause and cure of these kinds of problems? What biblical principles can we bring to bear for the child who is eating dirt? A good place to start is in the gospel of Mark, where we see Jesus healing the sick.

In the first chapters of Mark's gospel, we see Jesus healing the sick and calling disciples. Jesus calls a tax collector to follow him; Levi follows, and he became known as Matthew. That evening, Jesus goes to Matthew's house and eats dinner with him and other "tax collectors, and sinners" (Mark 2:16).

The Pharisees grumble about this, and Jesus hears them and responds: "It is not those who are healthy who need a physician, but those who are sick; I did not come to call the righteous, but sinners" (v. 17). Our Lord is drawing a parallel for us between the real need that those who are physically sick have for a doctor, and the real need that all of us sinners have for Jesus. Sinners need a Savior! And at the same time, he directly acknowledges that the sick need a physician. With this comparison, Jesus helps us understand how to engage with both the dirt eater and the child labeled with DMDD.

Disobedience or Biology?

The first assignment that I give to new counselees who have not recently seen a physician is to make arrangements for an appropriate medical workup. It did strike me as strange that anyone would continually choose to eat dirt, which seemed to indicate that there could be more to the problem than simple childhood rebellion.

The parents made arrangements to see their doctor, who also listened to the story and ordered a couple of laboratory tests. One test showed that the child was anemic and that his anemia was due to a shortage of iron. No other abnormality was found. The doctor assured the parents that once the iron deficiency and anemia were corrected, it was likely the child would stop eating dirt. A daily iron prescription was given, and with time, the anemia was corrected. And just as the doctor said, their boy stopped eating dirt.

This child was ill, and the biblical principal that applied was the words Jesus said at dinner. The sick child needed a physician. As Dr.

Robert Smith once said, "Not every medical problem will have biblical implications."[1] Consider if, instead, I had counseled the family as though they were only dealing with a disobedient child. Would that have been helpful at all? While it may have helped their family life in some ways, it would not have been helpful in addressing the presenting problem because the child's dirt-eating had a clear biological cause, not a spiritual one.

DMDD or Parental Training?

The second child had a much different story, and yet the words Jesus spoke at the dinner party also yield important insights for this situation. This child saw a physician who did a complete workup, and there was no physical, objective finding to support the idea that this child had an illness causing the behavior. The label she was given was simply a description of her behavior. This child's situation did not require a physician because she was not sick. Counseling led to the conclusion that changes could be made in the way the parents were responding to the child. Biblical principles were applied to their parenting, and the chaos in the family's life ceased. Both parents and the child found hope in Scripture.

Dr. Smith also said, "Not every biblical counseling problem will have medical implications."[2] This was certainly true for this child. Medical treatment would not have been useful.

These two situations represent two ends of a continuum, but many counseling situations will live somewhere in the middle. In the subsequent chapters of this book, we will discuss a variety of medical problems that have an impact on our behaviors, thoughts, and emotions. At the same time, individuals affected by these conditions can choose to respond with or without the principles of Scripture. At both

---

1. Dr. Robert Smith, 2019. The statement was made to me while we were discussing the issue of the sufficiency of Scripture and how medical science interacts with it.
2. Smith, 2019.

ends of the spectrum and in this middle ground, "a response that is informed by Scripture will always be superior to one that is not."[3]

How to Sort Out the Labels

During the last thirty years of counseling, I have developed three general guidelines that have helped me deal with the myriad of DSM-5 labels. Having these guidelines in mind will be helpful when individuals come to counseling saying that they have xyz disorder and attributing thoughts, feelings, and actions to the disorder.

The Bible Takes Precedence

I will never call anything a disease that the Bible identifies as sin. This is an important divider of diagnoses. So much of what the DSM-5 calls disease is simply inconvenient or disagreeable behavior. And, in a good number of cases, that behavior is defined in the Bible as sin.

There are many examples, but a clear one is the current diagnosis of substance use disorder for alcohol use. The Bible clearly defines the habitual pursuit of intoxication as sin. Paul says in Ephesians 5:18, "And do not get drunk with wine, for that is dissipation, but be filled with the Spirit." This is a clear prohibition against drunkenness.

This raises an opportunity for a useful dispute. The apostle Paul, under the inspiration of the Holy Spirit, has told the Ephesians and by extension all believers that we are not to get drunk. He does not tell us not to drink wine, but he tells us not to get drunk. Getting drunk is identified as a sin. Many dispute this. They would cite medical information that says that addiction (a word they do not like to use) or substance use disorder is a physical illness that is in some measure genetically influenced.

The difficulty in sorting this out is that habitual sin often results in physical illness. While it may be true that some individuals have a

---

3. Smith, 2019.

genetic predisposition that makes it more likely for them to become trapped in habitual alcohol use, no one makes anyone take that first drink or the second. It is absolutely true that habitual drunkenness will lead to multiple medical problems, some of which are catastrophic. These include liver failure, heart disease, hypertension, cancer, seizures, and cognitive decline. Eventually, substantial, regular use leads to physical dependence, and if stopped suddenly, can result in serious withdrawal problems.

On the other side of the argument, the Bible clearly calls drunkenness a sin, and it is a behavior that at the outset we can choose not to participate in or we can choose to stop. If as a counselor, I agree with the DSM-5 and call this a disease, what do I do next? From this perspective, I appear to be obligated to send the diseased individual to the health care system, which to date has a troubled success rate with rehabilitation of substance use disorder.[4]

Or we could say that this individual is drunk and committing the sin of drunkenness. There will be criticism from all corners for using the word the Bible does in describing the person enslaved by choice to alcohol or some other substance. However, if we choose to identify their actions as sin, something really good can come from it. That individual can, by the grace of God, repent of the sin and escape its control.

In the sixth chapter in his letter to the Roman Christians, Paul asks, "What shall we say then? Are we to continue in sin so that grace may increase? May it never be! How shall we who died to sin still live in it?" (Romans 6:1–2). In this passage, Paul makes it clear that believers should not intentionally persist in sin. Indeed, he tells us to "Even so consider yourselves to be dead to sin, but alive to God in Christ Jesus" (Romans 6:11). Furthermore, he says we get to choose:

---

4. Statistics vary on effectiveness; as high as 60 percent of those treated may relapse. National Institute on Drug Abuse, How Effective Is Drug Addiction Treatment? Principles of Drug Addiction Treatment: A Research-Based Guide (Third Edition), January 2018, https://nida.nih.gov/publications/principles-drug-addiction-treatment-research-based-guide-third-edition/preface.

"Do you not know that when you present yourselves to someone as slaves for obedience, you are slaves of the one whom you obey, either of sin resulting in death, or of obedience resulting in righteousness?" (v. 16).

If I tell the counselee that he has substance use disorder, his only resource is the health care system, which will not address the underlying reasons why he began and continues to drink to excess. If I identify his behavior as the sin of drunkenness, then he has the opportunity to repent. So I refuse to call anything a disease that the Bible calls sin. This is in the best interest of the counselee because it keeps the path of repentance and change open.

Call It Sin Only if the Bible Clearly Calls It Sin

This seems so obvious until you spend your youth growing up among truly wonderful people who seem attracted to the idea that making extrabiblical rules would be good for all of us. In their conversations, they would often discuss important ideas. At the same time, a good number of issues such as the length of a man's hair, bell bottom pants, amusements, and other clearly Romans 14 Christian liberty concerns were dragged into the mix. Soon, we had a set of rules that would rival those of the Pharisees of Jesus's day.

So my second rule is simple: Unless the Bible calls something sin very specifically, I am not going to do so. While this is simple, it becomes very important. The blind man in John 9 serves to illustrate the point. When we do not know the cause for a problem, we may be tempted to jump to the conclusion the disciples did that day. "As He passed by, He saw a man blind from birth. And His disciples asked Him, 'Rabbi, who sinned, this man or his parents, that he would be born blind?' Jesus answered, 'It was neither that this man sinned, nor his parents; but it was so that the works of God might be displayed in him'" (John 9:1–3). When the diagnosis is uncertain, and the facts are not entirely known, and Scripture does not identify the behavior as sin, it is best to withhold judgment.

Always Look for Pathologic Evidence

As a physician, if I am going to identify something as a disease, I aim to understand the changes occurring at the cell level that are causing the change in function. In biblical counseling, to be confident that the thoughts, emotions, and behaviors of the individual are due to a disease, I like to have some assurance that there is a pathological explanation (change at the cell level) that could explain it. However, we must acknowledge that this is not always going to be possible in medicine because at times our technology is limited.

A good example is the migraine headache. My wife has them, and our daughter, who looks just like her, has them. To this date, we do not entirely understand the pathology that causes them. However, no one in medicine would say that migraine headaches are not a disease problem.

We ought to always remember that just because pathology has not been discovered or demonstrated, it does not mean that no disease is present. A favorite phrase that I hear in medicine in the context of biopsy procedures is that "the absence of evidence is not always evidence of absence." So, as we approach the suffering struggler whose situation does not give us a clear diagnosis, we should not jump to conclusions as Job's friends did.

If we are going to do a good job helping individuals who come with various labels, we have to be good listeners. As I teach counseling, one of the most important things I tell students is that being a good listener is required in counseling. Similarly, as a physician, I spend a great deal of time listening to patient stories. It is my job to gather facts and sort them in order to arrive at a diagnosis.

One of the best physicians in United States' medical history was William Osler. He made lots of important observations about the doctor-patient relationship. One of them was, "if you let the patient talk long enough, they will tell what is wrong." I think that statement is just as important to counselors faced with sorting out normal sadness from the disordered sadness of depression. If we are going to successfully navigate the hundreds of DSM-5 diagnoses, careful listening will always be useful.

Do Not Counsel According to Labels

In our current psycho-social state of affairs, any number of counselees will come with a DSM-5 label. Many of them will sincerely believe that their lives are controlled by the disorder the label represents, and I do not engage in disputes with them about it. But I do not allow the labels to decide the course of counseling.

Instead, I listen to their story and then set their thinking, emotions, and behavior next to the Scriptures. What follows is a careful application of the principles of Scripture to their heartaches, their thinking, and their actions. It is not our job to prove their label wrong, but it is our job to apply the principles of Scripture to their situation.

In this process, it is vitally important that we start with a view of the counselee as a sufferer. It is easy to jump to a conclusion and aim for a quick solution to the individual's struggles. The labels they bring represent real problems and suffering for them. The key is not in persuading them that their label is not a real problem. It is in finding a biblical solution to the thoughts, behaviors, and emotions that the label is attempting to describe.

Maintain Humility

As we encounter individuals with significant problems, some will present diagnoses that fall into an area where medical science does not have clear evidence for a disease process. At the same time, their behaviors, thoughts, and emotions might not meet the biblical criteria for sin. In situations like this, when we cannot say for certain what we are dealing with, humility will always be useful.

Let's look at a past counseling case that can illustrate the importance of humility when neither medicine nor counseling seems to clearly address the problem: A young man who struggled with medical problems that kept him from meeting his responsibilities at work and home came to counseling because he wondered if his problem was a spiritual issue and not medical. The man had several physicians working to help him, but without much success. He asked our counseling physician whether a disease or a spiritual/sin problem was causing his struggle and whether he could get better.

The counselor worked through the case, looking for a spiritual or physical source for his struggles. After a while, he concluded that there really was no obvious spiritual concern. His suggestion was to obtain another medical opinion from a physician who had not participated in his care. The result was a considerable reduction in medication, and resolution of the young man's problems. I have always thought that the counselor/physician's willingness to extend that humble "benefit of the doubt" made all the difference in getting to a solution for the counselee.

It was a classic case of no clear medical diagnosis and no clear indication of a spiritual/sin issue. At such times, Proverbs 18:13 encourages us to respond with humility. "He who gives an answer before he hears, it is folly and shame to him." When we cannot know for certain that a problem is either medical or spiritual, we should be humble enough to withhold judgment.

In subsequent chapters, this book aims to examine a number of medical diagnoses from this viewpoint. Some will be the kind of problem that does not have a clear medical definition, while others will. And some will fall in between. We hope to give the reader guidance that will be both medically accurate and biblically sound to deal with these kinds of issues. In the next chapter, we will examine the relationship between what we know of medicine and the doctrine of the sufficiency of Scripture.

CHAPTER 2

. . . .

THE SCRIPTURES ARE SUFFICIENT

Charles D. Hodges Jr., MD

The purpose of this chapter is to explore the relationship between medicine and the sufficiency of Scripture. A clear understanding of this relationship should reduce concerns about counseling those with medical/DSM-5 labels.

It would be difficult to pick just one doctrine from Scripture on which biblical counseling rests. Most of us would say that it requires the "whole counsel of God" from Genesis to Revelation. There is no biblical doctrine that we can safely ignore or dismiss.

If, on the other hand, you asked which doctrine is most often attacked or abused, I would answer, the sufficiency of Scripture. The source texts for this doctrine are found in many places in Scripture. The one I learned first was 2 Peter 1:2–3. It isn't complicated; Peter reveals the doctrine as he tells us the good news of our position in Jesus Christ.

> Grace and peace be multiplied to you in the knowledge of God and of Jesus our Lord; seeing that His divine power has granted to us everything pertaining to life and godliness, through the true knowledge of Him who called us by His own glory and excellence. For by these He has granted to us His precious and magnificent promises, so that by them you may become partakers of the divine nature, having escaped the corruption that is in the world by lust. (2 Peter 1:2–4)

The idea that Scripture contains all the words and knowledge we need in order to live a godly life that glorifies our Father seems obvious. Many have written attesting to this, including Jay Adams,[1] John Frame,[2] and Heath Lambert.[3] What becomes less obvious to many is how this applies to counseling issues that are difficult and those that carry a DSM-5 label. Most counselors have met with counselees who inform us that the reason why they think, feel, and behave as they do is because of their medical or psychiatric label. That disease label may also be offered up as the reason why they cannot change. They believe that Scripture may be sufficient for "spiritual" issues, but not those identified as medical.

Two Ends of the Spectrum

I have often been questioned about the validity of diagnoses such as schizophrenia and the mania of bipolar disorder 1. Some try to explain away the existence of these and other similar diagnoses by appealing to events in the lives of biblical characters. They use the ravings of Saul, David's feigned madness, Jonah's mood swings over the fate of a plant, and Nebuchadnezzar's episode that resembled psychosis to argue that these biblical examples point to the fact that DSM-5 diagnoses for schizophrenia and bipolar disorder are not describing brain-based, psychological diseases.

It is not likely that any of this quartet had a brain disease. Saul was struggling with his continued unrepentant sin. David was feigning madness to avoid being killed. Jonah was simply selfish, and Nebuchadnezzar's problems came as a direct act of God in response to his hubris.

Some have reasoned that because these similar episodes look like schizophrenia or bipolar mania and were not, the same could be said

1. Jay Adams, *Theology of Christian Counseling* (Grand Rapids: Zondervan, 1979), 1–6.
2. John Frame, *The Doctrine of the Word of God* (Phillipsburg, NJ: P&R), 221.
3. Heath Lambert, *A Theology of Biblical Counseling: The Doctrinal Foundations of Counseling Ministry* (Grand Rapids: Zondervan Academic, 2016), 37–54.

of similar problems today. The reasoning continues that since the quartet's problems could have been resolved with the principles of Scripture, biblical counseling should be sufficient for the same kind of problems today. To disagree would mean that we do not agree with the doctrine of the sufficiency of Scripture.

On the other hand, some would say that Scripture does not contain adequate direction to help those who have complicated counseling problems. While mild worry and sadness may be the province of biblical counselors, those who struggle with serious problems need help beyond what is found in Scripture. Diagnoses such as serious depression, obsessive-compulsive disorder, PTSD, and complex trauma need the care that only secularly trained counselors can deliver.

As a physician and biblical counselor, I've spent the last two decades between these two extremes and being criticized by those on either side. The issue is not whether or not Scripture is sufficient, for it certainly is. At the same time, as Dr. Bob Smith frequently said, "not all medical problems are biblical counseling issues."

The solution for those who are on both ends of this spectrum is found in the interplay between three doctrines and medical science. Common grace, the noetic effect of sin, and the sufficiency of Scripture can together help us navigate the questions that the interaction between medicine and biblical counseling raise.

Sufficiency

Many have written about sufficiency. I have chosen John Frame's definition because I think it gets to the heart of the medical question. Frame's definition follows below:

> Christians sometimes say that Scripture is sufficient for religion, or preaching or theology, but not for auto repairs, plumbing, animal husbandry, dentistry, and the like. And of course, many argue that it is not sufficient for science, philosophy, or even ethics. That is to miss an important point.

Certainly, Scripture contains more specific information relevant to theology than to dentistry. But sufficiency in the present context is not sufficiency of specific information but sufficiency of divine words. Scripture contains divine words sufficient for all of life. It has all the divine words that the plumber needs, and all the divine words that the theologian needs. So, it is just as sufficient for plumbing as it is for theology. And in that sense, it is sufficient for science and ethics as well.[4]

When Frame says that Scripture is sufficient for plumbing and dentistry, I wish he had added medicine at the end. Scripture is just as sufficient for medicine as it is for plumbing and dentistry. The Bible contains all the words that a doctor needs in order to be a godly physician. The Scriptures may not tell us how to build a magnetic resonance imaging scanner or how to plug a leaky pipe, but they do tell us how to do both of those tasks in a godly manner that glorifies and honors our heavenly Father.

The Bible does not tell us all I need to know about how to treat a sore throat, a failing heart, or a diseased gall bladder. Medical science gives us that information. As a friend of mine once said, "The Bible tells us how to deal with worry, but it does not tell us the physiology of anxiety."

In the same way, the Bible contains all the words a counselor needs in order to help a depressed, obsessive, or traumatized counselee. This will be true for the individual labeled with any of the hundreds of labels found in the DSM-5. When Jesus tells us to come unto him and find rest, it is not an idle promise. But does this mean that medicine has nothing to offer us for helping those who struggle?

---

4. Frame, *Doctrine of the Word*, 221.

Common Grace

Common grace is the doctrine that says God grants many blessings to both the saved and unsaved alike. Whether we believe God or not, we all breathe the same air, and without it, we could not live. God "causes His sun to rise on the evil and the good, and sends rain on the righteous and the unrighteous" (Matthew 5:45). The crops of Christians and non-Christians grow because of common grace.

This common grace extends to things we can know. God allows all of us, regenerate or not, to know things that are true. This aspect of common grace allows us to drive cars, use cell phones, fly in airplanes, and take medicine that cures cancer. It extends to the observations that physicians and psychologists make about the struggles people have with their thoughts, behaviors, and emotions.

Heath Lambert, in his book *A Theology of Biblical Counseling*, extends this common grace to medical knowledge and describes how it can aid our work as biblical counselors. He writes,

> Contributions from unbelievers can inform the work of biblical counseling. One obvious example of this helpfulness is medical knowledge. Because human beings have a body as well as a soul, and because the Bible is not sufficient for medical knowledge, physicians are a crucial adjunct to biblical counselors. Our counseling is far inferior when we cannot pair our work with the medical competencies of physicians.[5]

A considerable portion of medical research can provide us with helpful insights into the thoughts, behaviors, and emotions of those to whom we minister—this is a common grace gift. As Lambert said, our biblical counseling will be impoverished if we do not make use of the common grace gifts that God provides. At the same time, while this is true, there is a limiting factor.

---

5. Lambert, *A Theology of Biblical Counseling*, 79, Kindle Ed.

The Noetic Effect of Sin

While we should avail ourselves of common grace knowledge, we must also guard against the simplistic notion that medical professionals' interpretation of the facts they find is always correct. The reason for this takes us into another important doctrine, the noetic effect of sin.

If you've never heard this phrase before, you're not alone! When I first encountered it, I wondered what Noah and the ark might have to do with our sin. *The Merriam-Webster Online Dictionary* defines it as "of, relating to, or based on the intellect." It also explains the origins of the word thus: "*Noetic* derives from the Greek adjective *noētikos*, meaning 'intellectual,' from the verb *noein* ('to think') and ultimately from the noun *nous*, meaning 'mind.'"[6] Thus, the word noetic is not confined to biblical counseling—it refers to all areas of thought.

Thus, when we talk about the noetic effect of sin, we're referring to the change that occurred in our minds as a result of the fall. We do not perceive, think, process information, respond emotionally, and make choices in the same way we might have had Adam and Eve not chosen to disobey. As a result, when we look at scientific facts, we are always vulnerable to interpreting them incorrectly. Because of that, we need to be cautious of not only our interpretation of the facts, but also the interpretation of others, even professionals who seem completely objective in their presentation of the information. In the words of John Frame, "There are no 'brute facts,' facts that are devoid of interpretation. All facts are what they are by virtue of God's interpretation of them. And just as facts are inseparable from God's interpretation of them, so our understanding of facts is inseparable from our interpretation of them. Stating a fact and interpreting it are the same activity."[7] For interesting examples of how data is manipulated in research to prove "our" point, I would point the reader to the

---

6. "Noetic," *Merriam-Webster Online Dictionary*, https://www.merriam-webster.com/dictionary/noetic.

7. John M. Frame, *The Doctrine of the Knowledge of God* (Phillipsburg, NJ: P&R, 1987), 140.

book by Stuart Ritchie, *Science Fictions: How Fraud, Bias, Negligence and Hype Undermine the Search for Truth.*[8]

As believers, we remain capable of arriving at wrong conclusions. Despite the presence of the indwelling Holy Spirit, our minds are still subject to the effects of the fall. Paul says as much in his letter to the Romans: "For the good that I want, I do not do, but I practice the very evil that I do not want. But if I am doing the very thing I do not want, I am no longer the one doing it, but sin which dwells in me" (Romans 7:19–20). We all want to arrive at correct conclusions, but at times our nature frustrates it.

We interpret objective information from any source in accordance with our worldview. The evolutionist looks at the Grand Canyon and sees a little trickle of water and billions of years. The young earth creationist looks at the same Grand Canyon and sees a flood. The objective evidence before them is the same, but the interpretation is amazingly different.

The same thing occurs with the common grace information that comes from medicine. It will be interpreted by the reader/observer according to their presuppositions. This is true for the secular counselor, the integrationist Christian counselor, and the biblical counselor. One will look at the medical information we have about obsessive–compulsive disorder and say, "There is nothing religious here. This is a medical issue that requires medication and cognitive behavior therapy." Another may look at the same set of facts and declare it to be "a completely spiritual issue" and believe that the medical "facts" are irrelevant.

Depending on your presuppositions, it could be said that neither position is entirely correct. So how can we sort through this for the benefit of counselees? What conclusion can we arrive at when the Scriptures are sufficient, medical information is a matter of common grace, and not all the interpretations of medical information can be

---

8. Stuart Ritchie, *Science Fictions: How Fraud, Bias, Negligence, and Hype Undermine the Search for Truth* (New York: Metropolitan Books, 2020).

trusted? A couple of case histories can help us in the process. As we seek to apply both Scripture and common grace knowledge, we must remember that humility is an absolute necessity.

Two Case Studies

Across the desk from me sits a young lady who has multiple concerns and struggles. She has been told by her physician that she has depression and anxiety, and she is being treated for them medically without a great deal of improvement. Her physician referred her to a licensed counselor who agreed with the labels she had been given and also added borderline personality disorder (BPD).

Her life has been marked with many disappointments. Her parents did not pay attention to her "needs." Her boyfriend does not seem to understand that his main mission in life is to marry her. The more she reminds him, the further from her goal he seems to move. Her friends seem to understand her need for their undivided attention at first, but eventually they are exhausted by it. Then they disappear.

As if all of this wasn't bad enough, after she was given the borderline personality diagnosis, she went home and had a consult with Dr. Google and learned that many consider BPD to be incurable! She is devastated as she considers that her situation might not change. She came to my office looking for hope that seemed so out of reach everywhere else. Her situation illustrates one end of a spectrum that is useful to understand.

At the other end of that spectrum is a case history of a patient that I did not see, but has been published and widely read. The account can be found in Susannah Cahalan's book *Brain on Fire: My Month of Madness*.[9] Cahalan was well on her way to a career in journalism when she was interrupted by episodes of hallucinations and delusions. Initially she was seen by a prominent neurologist in New York who

---

9. Susannah Cahalan, *Brain on Fire: My Month of Madness* (London: Simon & Schuster, 2013).

was convinced that she was suffering from alcohol withdrawal. She had been drinking a fair amount, but the symptoms and the story did not add up to that conclusion. As I read it, my medical mind wandered from bipolar mania to schizophrenia, and I would have been wrong as well. Over a thirty-day period, Cahalan descended from hallucinations to a nearly catatonic state in which she was incapable of taking care of herself. She was hospitalized multiple times and prescribed medications that did not help her any more than they helped the patient in our first case study.

Eventually she found her way once more to an emergency room and the care of another physician who had never seen or heard her story. She would soon see another neurologist. They believed that something more was going on in her case and did every test known to mankind, including an examination of her spinal fluid by a spinal tap. That test made all the difference.

Inflammatory white cells were found in the fluid, but no bacteria, which led to a brain biopsy. It revealed an inflammatory disease that has since been named anti-NMDA receptor autoimmune encephalitis. This patient was not suffering from alcohol withdrawal, and she was not schizophrenic, although until recently she might have been labeled as such. She had a pathologically defined inflammatory disease of the brain. She was treated with steroids, immune globulin, and her blood plasma was filtered to remove the offending antibodies. Her immune system literally had mistaken her brain for being foreign and was setting out to kill it.

Unlike our first patient, this young woman really had something wrong going on in her body. She survived because at least a couple of physicians would not be satisfied with an easy answer to her problem. They kept looking until they found the pathology. She was cured, and her life was saved.

These two cases are similar to those in chapter 1 because both had the potential to be misdiagnosed and mistreated. Cahalan was accused of a biblically defined sin, that of chronic drunkenness. Her accuser was a well-respected and experienced neurologist. And, although he was not wrong that she had committed this sin, he was wrong in his diagnosis of it as the cause of her current mental and physical problems. Had subsequent physicians agreed, she would have perished. Sin was not the source of her problem.

These two cases give us the opportunity to work through the important triad of the truth of Scripture, the quality of the medical information, and the trustworthiness of the interpretation. Starting with the first case, what can we say about the quality of the medical information? From a medical viewpoint, it is not compelling.

The current literature does not offer any explanation for the cause of BPD: "The cause of borderline personality disorder (BPD) is not known. Most hypotheses suggest that BPD is due to a combination of genetic, neurobiologic, and psychosocial factors."[10] Without a clear physiological cause, the diagnosis of BPD seems to be primarily a description of human behavior.

The behaviors used to diagnose BPD include struggles maintaining relationships, a sense of emptiness, moods swings, anger, strong fear of the loss of friends, and self-harm. BPD did not exist as a medical diagnosis prior to 1980. That does not mean that these behaviors did not exist; they certainly did. They had just never before been grouped together and identified as a disease.

So given that the primary facts of BPD are really a description of a cluster of human behaviors occurring together, what is the trustworthiness of the interpretation of these facts? While psychiatry and secular psychologists today would say that BPD is a disease, this interpretation is not well supported by objective evidence. It would appear that this common grace medical information is not likely to be helpful.

How then should we as biblical counselors view the diagnosis, and how should we respond to it? The deciding factor, as always, is

---

10. Andrew Skodol, "Borderline Personality Disorder: Epidemiology, Pathogenesis, Clinical features, Course, Assessment, and Diagnosis," UpToDate, https://www.uptodate.com/contents/borderline-personality-disorder-epidemiology-pathogenesis-clinical-features-course-assessment-and-diagnosis/print, updated June 24, 2021.

the sufficient Scriptures. As stated in the first chapter, I would never call anything a disease that the Bible clearly identifies as sin. The Bible describes as sin most of the behaviors in the list of symptoms used to call BPD a disease.

As we counsel, we should approach strugglers with the attitude that Paul spoke of in his letter to the Galatians. "Brethren, even if anyone is caught in any trespass, you who are spiritual, restore such a one in a spirit of gentleness; each one looking to yourself, so that you too will not be tempted" (Galatians 6:1).

As we look into the lives of other believers, we must do so with humility and care. We must avoid identifying behavior as sin that the Bible does not clearly identify. However, if we are going to be much help to those labeled with poorly supported diagnoses, we will have to compare their thinking and actions to Scripture. And when their behavior is identified as sin, we serve them best as we share the truth of Scripture. Paul did this without hesitation in his letters to the Corinthians and Ephesians.

At the same time, it is important to remember that these individuals suffer. Many of those diagnosed with BPD have a history of childhood abuse or neglect. Their desire for stable relationships is understandable. We should approach them as sufferers first. But, in doing so, we should offer them the hope that the Bible offers them.

The Bible has a description and a superior solution to the behaviors, emotions, and thoughts described as BPD. The young woman in this case study was spending all of her time seeking to have others serve her needs and fulfill her wants. Paul dealt with this issue at length in his letter to the Philippians: "Do nothing from selfishness or empty conceit, but with humility of mind regard one another as more important than yourselves; do not merely look out for your own personal interests, but also for the interests of others. Have this attitude in yourselves which was also in Christ Jesus" (Philippians 2:3–5).

At the very heart of her struggle was a long-practiced, deeply ingrained self-interest. And, by God's grace, that could change. It would mean that she would have to change the main goal of her living. Instead of having others meet her needs, she would have to make glorifying God the main goal of living (1 Corinthians 10:31).

Over time and with counseling from the Scriptures, this young woman changed. Paul is clear that change is part of the Christian life: "Therefore if anyone is in Christ, he is a new creature; the old things passed away; behold, new things have come" (2 Corinthians 5:17). As believers, we are commanded to change and enabled to do so (Ephesians 4:22–24; Philippians 2:12–13).

Because there is no clear medical cause or treatment for BPD, we should put the diagnosis aside and go straight to the heart issues that are present. The medical information lacks the credibility required to qualify as common grace. It appears instead to be a faulty interpretation of human behavior. In doing so with humility and compassion, we offer the counselee real hope for her real problems.

The second case is different. The validity of the medical information concerning anti-NMDA receptor autoimmune encephalitis is well established today, although it was not as widely understood at the time of the patient's illness.[11] The fact that the medical information we do have about this illness has been discovered is an amazing common grace benefit. The case illustrates well the risks associated with interpreting medical facts. The initial neurologist wrongly interpreted the facts of Cahalan's case, and if she had stopped seeking further treatment at that point, she would no longer be alive.

This case is a cautionary tale for those of us in biblical counseling. It would have been easy enough to fall in with the first neurologist and jump to a conclusion about Cahalan's situation based on her prior behavior. When we encounter counselees whose story does not give a clear conclusion, we should humbly withhold judgment.

There will be times when a counselee presents with behavior, thinking, and emotions that seem to support a conclusion that sin is the source, but don't quite add up. One lady came to the office

---

11. Joseph Dalmau and Myrna R. Rosenfeld, "Paraneoplastic and Autoimmune Encephalitis," UpToDate, https://www.uptodate.com/contents/paraneoplastic-and-autoimmune-encephalitis/print, updated November 3, 2021.

looking for help with anxiety, insomnia, and a rapid irregular heart-beat. Her life was complicated and several aspects of it spoke of poor stewardship on her part. If we approached her situation in a hurry, we could have arrived at the conclusion that repentance, confession, and a change in behavior were the ultimate solution. Instead a thorough history revealed that her use of decongestants and supplements were the source of her troubles. Many similar situations in medicine and counseling require a Proverbs 18:13 willingness on our part to hear the whole of the matter before giving an answer.

The sufficient Scriptures do offer important guidance in situations such as these. As we have said before, the sick need a physician (Mark 2:17). Beyond that, Scripture is rich with direction for the way we as believers should respond to the burden of illness. This discussion goes beyond the scope of this chapter, and will be dealt with in the chapter "Counseling Those with a Medical Illness," by Dan Gannon, MD.

These two patients/counselees illustrate how to apply the doctrines of common grace, the noetic effect of sin, and the sufficiency of Scripture. They are at opposite ends of a spectrum, and as this book continues, we will encounter counselees and medical diagnoses that fit more in the middle. The principles still work, but they will require humility and wisdom as we apply them.

CHAPTER 3

. . . .

COUNSELING PEOPLE
WITH A MEDICAL ILLNESS

Daniel M. Gannon, MD

Julie Gossack loved running, skiing, biking, hiking, and exploring all that God's creation had to offer. At forty-four years old, she was a physically fit, happily married mother of three boys, residing in Bozeman, Montana. Along with her family, she loved God deeply and was active in a variety of church ministries. Life was good. Then, on her twenty-fifth wedding anniversary, she began to experience abdominal pain. After medical tests and scans, abdominal surgery was performed. The pathology report stunned everyone: poorly differentiated, signet ring cell, primary appendiceal adenocarcinoma. In other words, Julie was diagnosed with a rare aggressive cancer of the appendix that had spread throughout her abdominal cavity and metastasized to her lung tissue.

Soon after this initial shock, decisions had to be made about treatment. Julie started intravenous chemotherapy locally, then traveled to a specialized cancer treatment center to undergo HIPEC abdominal surgery. This procedure entails infusion of heated chemotherapy to the entire abdominal cavity, causing subsequent residual pain and many difficult side effects. Julie experienced complications of neuropathy and repeated episodes of collapsed lung that required a total of four chest tube placements. The cancer seemed controlled for eighteen months, then sadly it reemerged. This meant more chemo and a repeat HIPEC surgery. Following this second surgery, the pain management catheter failed. Julie endured severe pain from thermal and chemical burns to her abdominal cavity, which required large doses of opioid painkillers. These drugs led to addiction and difficulty weaning. Julie was diagnosed with pain-induced PTS(D).

After many difficult months, a CT scan showed that the cancer had recurred a third time. She, along with her oncology team, family, friends, and pastor, decided against further treatment. Julie died at age 49.

Because we live in a sin-cursed world, you probably already know people like Julie who are facing a life-threatening illness with an uncertain outcome. We will all face the physical problems of illness, pain, and death, until our Lord returns. How can biblical counselors come alongside those suffering physical illness to best help them, their families, and caregivers in the midst of their struggle? Our goal should be to care deeply for them with the love of Christ, by offering comfort, encouragement, perspective, and a path to honor God as they walk through their trial.

A Spectrum of Disease

Figure 1
A Spectrum of Disease

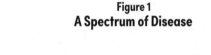

Spiritual  Organic

It is encouraging to know that no matter where a diagnosis falls on a spectrum between spiritual and organic issues, the Word of God is sufficient to comfort, encourage, give perspective, and offer a path for honoring God. On one end of this spectrum, a disease diagnosis might seem to be mostly attributed to spiritual issues, such as substance abuse. However, a person may be prescribed a painkiller and become addicted, as happened to Julie. Or substance abuse that begins as a spiritual issue may over time take on a physical dimension so that even when a person is fighting it spiritually, their body is very much involved.

On the other end of the spectrum, those with terminal cancer seem to have only a physical component to their disease—but of course it impacts them spiritually as well. God's Word is vital in guiding the individual's response to that disease.

Since the Bible has much to say regarding both ends of this spectrum of disease, it follows that God's Word is also relevant to all illnesses in between. Individuals with maladies that include components of *both* spiritual and physical causes are also helped by bringing God's Word to bear on their struggles. Examples include eating disorders, self-harm, anxiety, panic attacks, chronic fatigue, irritable bowel, fibromyalgia, depression, bipolar disorder, schizophrenia, etc.

A medical degree is not necessary in order to counsel those with a medical issue. Using various resources, we can educate ourselves adequately about a disease. Biblical counselors should avoid getting caught up in the argument of whether these issues are mostly spiritual or mostly physical; we need not be intimidated by complex-sounding labels and the argument of causation. The medical community can address those issues, while biblical counselors concentrate on issues of the heart, offering comfort and wisdom from God's Word.

Comfort

In 2 Corinthians 1:3–4, God is called, "the Father of compassion and the God of all comfort, who comforts us in all our troubles . . ." (NIV). As biblical counselors, we desire to offer the comfort of God's precious Word to those suffering with illness or injury. The comfort from God's Word is powerful.

This heartfelt care includes listening with compassion and taking their suffering seriously, for Romans 12:15 tells us to "weep with those who weep" (ESV). Let those you counsel know they are not alone; you will walk through the valley of suffering with them. Listen carefully as they pour out their struggles. Upon hearing of the medical diagnosis, we should not immediately assume that we know the individual's specific problems. Rather, we should ask the person about his or her difficulties, which may be logistical, physical, financial, relational, or spiritual, and could be quite different from what we anticipated.

As we listen with compassion, we will focus on and work to discern heart issues. In his excellent book *Blame It on the Brain*, Dr. Ed Welch emphasizes the importance of distinguishing between physical suffering and sin.[1] We counsel those with these conditions differently. Suffering requires endurance, while sin requires repentance. Being honest about suffering and difficulty is not sinful but is rather encouraged in the Bible—consider the lament Psalms (10, 13, 25, 37, 40, 46, 73, 77, among many others) or the book of Lamentations. A right response to trial involves the honest expression of pain while going to God with our sorrows, and then remembering and acting on God's truth. However, it would be sinful for them to harbor anger against God's sovereign choice or to live completely in despair, for example. In any situation, our goal is to encourage the counselee to turn to the Lord, yield all things to him, grow near to him, and apply the principles found in his Word.

As biblical counselors, we should be careful not to offer false reassurances, such as "Don't worry, it will turn out fine"; "You can beat this if you fight hard enough"; "You will be healed if you just have enough faith." These statements are misleading because we can't guarantee the outcome of their struggle with illness. It is quite possible that the Lord has chosen that the individual will not recover from his or her illness and that it may lead to a chronic ailment or even to

---

1. Ed Welch, *Blame It on the Brain* (Phillipsburg, NJ: P&R, 1998), 69.

death. In all cases, we take great comfort in the Lord's sovereignty, his character, and his going before us in suffering. Because Jesus was "a man of sorrows and acquainted with grief" (Isaiah 53:3), who suffered and died to purchase our eternal life, we can promise to those who are suffering that nothing and no one "shall separate us from the love of Christ" (Romans 8:35 NIV).

Encouragement

When we are physically miserable, it is understandably easy for us to get "tunnel vision." At times, all we can see are the difficulties of our situation. As counselors, we can help others by broadening their view beyond the present difficulty to what God is doing in their illness. We can encourage a suffering believer to see their physical trials in light of the gospel and the promises of God.

- Your Father chose you and is for you (Ephesians 1:4; see also John 15:17; 2 Corinthians 5:17).
- Jesus empathizes with you as a faithful High Priest (Hebrews 2:18; 4:1–16).
- God is your ever-present comfort and refuge (Psalm 46; 2 Corinthians 1:3–11).
- God will pour out his grace sufficient for the trial (2 Corinthians 12:9; Hebrews 4:16).
- The extent of this suffering is not comparable to future glory (Romans 8:17–18; 2 Corinthians 4).

In particular, counselors can remind sufferers that these promises of God are especially encouraging to reflect upon when facing illness.

We learn from 1 Corinthians 10:13 that we are not suffering uniquely, even when it feels as if we are. Illness and injury are part of our fallen world. Point counselees to Christ, who suffered physically, emotionally, and spiritually. Encourage them to read and even memorize Isaiah 53. Jesus knows our struggle intimately, and he is able to help us. God is faithful. We can depend on him for ultimate victory over sin and death. This trial will not be beyond our ability to endure as we depend on God for the strength he promises. It may certainly feel that way, but God is aware of the degree to which we are suffering. He wants us to draw near to him, and he will draw near to us (James 4:8). As we cry out to him for help, God will provide the way of escape for us to endure, persevere, and bear suffering.

In John 16:33 (NIV), Jesus says, "I have told you these things, so that in me you may have peace. In this world you will have trouble. But take heart! I have overcome the world." Jesus's victory over this world gives believers otherworldly peace in Christ that is deeper than our confusion, fear, and anxiety. We live securely in God's care, even with all that this world throws at us.

God is with us in every trial. We will never face this without his help. Through Isaiah, God gives us these precious words: "So do not fear, for I am with you; do not be dismayed, for I am your God. I will strengthen you and help you; I will uphold you with my righteous right hand" (Isaiah 41:10 NIV).

Finally, heaven is certain for the believer. Jesus tells us, "Do not let your hearts be troubled. You believe in God; believe also in me. My Father's house has many rooms; if that were not so, would I have told you that I am going there to prepare a place for you? And if I go and prepare a place for you, I will come back and take you to be with me that you also may be where I am. You know the way to the place where I am going" (John 14:1–4 NIV). As they face a medical illness, encourage your counselees to grieve with hope (1 Thessalonians 4:13). Biblical hope is a confident expectation based upon God's character and his promises. We can confidently anticipate our future life in heaven, where all the trials of this life will have disappeared (Revelation 21:4).

Perspective

People struggling physically need not only hope and encouragement, but also a biblical perspective on what is happening. Many people who suffer with illness are unaware of important principles from God's

Word that bear on their situation. We can bring helpful perspective in key areas of possible confusion regarding health and illness: We know from Genesis 3:15–19 that all health problems are a result of the fall of man into sin, resulting in the curse on creation. Now physical illness and death is universal. Human mortality rate is 100 percent. Barring the Lord's return, every person will die, most of some illness.[2]

We also know that some sickness is a consequence of a particular sin, either as a natural result of our behavior (drunkenness leads to liver disease, for example), or as a discipline from the Lord (see 1 Corinthians 11:29–30 where people were sick as a result of taking communion in an unworthy manner; see also Psalm 38:3–11; 32:3–5). God can use sickness to discipline and sanctify us. Illness can be an opportunity to examine your heart to see if anything is hindering your relationship to the Lord.[3]

But we must also be clear that not all sickness is due to a particular sin. For example, in John 9:1–3, we find that the disciples saw a blind man and asked Jesus the reason for his blindness, assuming it to be the result of someone's sin. Instead, Jesus reveals that it was not due to anyone's particular sin. He answered, ". . . so that the works of God might be displayed in him."[4]

Whenever people undergo trials of any kind, they may be tempted to express, either inwardly or outwardly, a furious outburst of anger: Why did God allow this? Why now? Does he even care about me? Is God really good? We must be prepared to help the sufferer go to God with their why questions.[5] The Scripture invites us to turn to God and cry out to him, to express our thoughts and emotions: "Trust in him at all times, O people; pour out your heart before him; God is a refuge for us" (Psalm 62:8 ESV).

---

2. Robert Smith, *The Christian Counselor's Medical Desk Reference* (Stanley, NC: Timeless Texts, 2000), 53.

3. Smith, 54.

4. Smith, 56.

5. Pamela Gannon, "Compassionate Answers to Why Questions," Biblical Counseling Coalition, July 13, 2017, https://www.biblicalcounselingcoalition.org/2017/07/13/compassionate-answers-to-why-questions/.

In dealing with physical illness, we must accept that it is okay to not know exactly "why." There are "secret things" that belong to the Lord alone (Deuteronomy 29:29). For example, Job did not know why he was going through many trials. And his counselor friends actually did well with helping Job for several days . . . until they opened their mouths and spoke!

Our minds are finite, unable to completely understand the mysteries of God's ways (Isaiah 55:8–9; Romans 11:33). Humility lives with unanswered questions (Isaiah 45:9). However, although there are things we cannot know, there are things we do know. Scripture tells us that God has given us all we need to know in order to respond to illness in God-honoring ways (2 Peter 1:3–4). Our souls should be anchored in what Scripture plainly reveals about the character and ways of God.

Ultimately, we know that God is sovereign over our health and illness. Yet, Christians should seek appropriate medical care for proper stewardship of their bodies. To refuse reasonable and available medical care and instead only pray for (and demand) God's healing is to presume upon him. Essentially, this heart attitude reveals that we believe we can control God by expecting him to heal us, according to our terms and expectations. Of course, it is right to cry out to God and pray for healing, and he may choose to heal us. But we cannot demand healing from God.

During the course of one's illness, there may be a time in which it is appropriate to discontinue seeking medical care. For example, if the illness is terminal and further medical care falls into the realm of only experimental, one must weigh the pros and cons of treatment. My own mother declined a six-month trial protocol for advanced kidney cancer because it would have required her to spend most of that time traveling back and forth to the university oncology center for chemotherapy and many monitoring studies, limiting her from visiting loved ones. Even with such a treatment, her outcome was far from certain. She declined that protocol and instead chose to spend the next six months visiting family and friends. She then died at age 80. I think she made the right choice.

A Path to Honor God

I have my own personal experience with cancer. In May of 2021, my wife and I received the call from the surgical pathologist. It was not the benign tumor in my chest wall that I had expected; instead, it was MPAL—an extremely rare presentation of two cell strains of aggressive leukemia. With that call, my wife and I were thrust into a major disruption of life and health that continues as of this writing. We moved to Rochester, Minnesota, for the next ten months, for treatment at the Mayo clinic. I became a patient, rather than the physician. Treatment involved four months of chemotherapy, followed by bone marrow transplant and, finally, radiation therapy. During the course of treatment, there were complications of clotting, bleeding, liver, nerve and kidney damage, fever and gastrointestinal mucositis. I became very weak and lost 35 pounds. I am now considered to be in remission as I recover back at home, but recurrence is probable and further treatment options are limited. All of the material in this chapter became immediately personally relevant because I needed God's comfort, encouragement, perspective, and a path to honor him in this new situation.

What elements would be most important in formulating a plan to honor God in physical illness? As a biblical counselor I have often been overwhelmed by the convoluted, complex, and seemingly impossible counseling scenarios put before me. What should I say? Where should I turn? I have no idea. I have no persuasive argument to offer, based upon my personal wisdom, with which to provide a "home-run" conclusive statement that will bring people to Christ. I feel stuck. I can't do this. I need to go to another conference, read another book, or refer this counselee to someone else. And now I was in my own complicated situation.

A Useful Tool for the Counselor

When the going gets complicated, I go simple. I place all of the Bible and biblical counseling into a simple four-part formula (see Figure 1). This "quadratic formula" can be found within Philippians 4:8–9 (NIV): "Finally, brothers and sisters, whatever is true, whatever is noble, whatever is right, whatever is pure, whatever is lovely, whatever is admirable—if anything is excellent or praiseworthy—think about such things. Whatever you have learned or received or heard from me, or seen in me—put into practice. And the God of peace will be with you."

Figure 2
Quadratic Formula

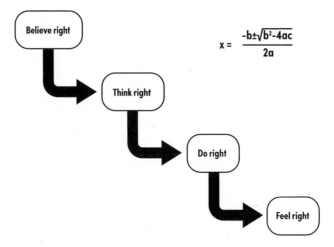

This "formula" is a simple guideline, a tool which can help the counselor discern where a sufferer's heart needs instruction and change. Which specific aspects of their lives are out of step with the Scriptures? Are there errors in their beliefs about God that are leading them astray in their response to their condition? Are they struggling to put their professed beliefs into practice? Biblical counselors minister the Word to help the sufferer apply the biblical truth they know, in order to honor God in their illness.

Believe Right

Today's secular counseling methodologies tend to focus on simply helping a suffering person to feel better. Instead, biblical counselors directly address beliefs and attitudes of the heart. For physically suffering believers, we can help them reestablish a vertical focus on the truths of who God is, the gospel, salvation through Christ, our purpose in life, the certainty of heaven, and the eternal inheritance for the believer. We need to remind others, as well as ourselves, to believe what is right because, at times, those who are ill and in pain can lose a godward focus. Peter reminds us that our faith is of greater worth than gold and is refined by our sufferings (1 Peter 1:7). As we live by faith through illness, God promises to be near, and as we turn to him our faith will grow.

At the right time in the counseling process, turn to the beautiful truth found in Romans 8:28–29. Here the Bible teaches that God uses all things, including the suffering his children experience, for our ultimate good. In a helpful lecture, Robert D. Jones talks about several ways that God uses suffering for good. I have paraphrased some of his thoughts below. God uses our physical misery to

- Remind us of our weakness and dependence, and his sufficient power (2 Corinthians 12:9).
- Test our faith and produce endurance and maturity (James 1:1–4).
- Equip us for compassionate ministry, as we share his comfort with others (2 Corinthians 1:3–6).
- Expose remaining sin and discipline us as beloved children (Hebrews 12:1–15).
- Deepen our relationship with the Lord (Philippians 3:10).
- Wean us from this world, that we hope in him and heaven (1 Peter 1:6–7, 13).[6]

---

6. Robert Jones, "When Hardships Hit: 7 Ways God Uses Suffering to Make Us Like Jesus," conference message, Association of Certified Biblical Counselors, https://biblical-counseling.com/product/hardships-hit-7-ways-god-uses-suffering-make-us-like-jesus/, accessed May 12, 2022.

We can assure our counselees and ourselves that our physical illness will not be wasted by the Lord—it is not useless, meaningless difficulty. In God's goodness, he will make it useful for his good purposes in our lives. In the words of my pastor, Dr. Bryan Hughes:

> Joy is the gladness of heart that comes from the deep assurance that God is in complete control of our circumstances, and He uses those circumstances for our good and His glory. The basis for our joy is not our changing circumstances. The basis for our joy is the unchanging character of God. The fullness of our joy is directly related to our view of God. If [we] see God as sovereign and good, then [we] can rejoice always.[7]

Especially for those with a chronic or terminal illness, a vital truth is that biblical victory is possible even if there is no physical cure or relief available for their ailment (Romans 8:35; 1 Corinthians 15:54, 57; 2 Corinthians 4:8–9). Biblical victory in illness means glorifying God by imitating Christ in yielding everything to his will. Facing great suffering, Jesus prayed, "Father, if you are willing, take this cup from me; yet not my will, but yours be done" (Luke 22:42 NIV). Likewise, we are to, "offer our bodies as a living sacrifice" (Romans 12:1). Victory is demonstrated by growing in endurance and serving others. Christ exemplified this attitude in the midst of enduring great suffering on the cross, as he humbly submitted to his Father, and as he continued to serve others—the Roman guard, John, Mary, the thief next to him, and all of us—by staying on the cross until death.

Sacrificing our lives completely to the Lord contrasts with the view of the secular world. In the world's perspective, life is random and belongs to each individual, which gives them the right to decide when to end their life. However, the Bible teaches that God created us. Our lives belong to him; they are not ours to own or decide when

---

7. Bryan Hughes, "Grace Bible Church Members Newsletter," Grace Bible Church, Bozeman, Montana, February 19, 2021.

to end. God has fashioned our days, and in his hand is held the life and breath of mankind (Job 12:10; Psalm 139:16). It would be foolish to lean on our own understanding and not entrust our final breaths to the sovereign God of the universe (Proverbs 3:5–7).

While the Christian has freedom to utilize modern hospice services to minimize unnecessary suffering, physician-assisted suicide should not be considered even if empathetic people may suggest that a peaceful suicide is better than prolonged agony for the sufferer and their families. With euthanasia or physician-assisted suicide, someone administers a lethal drug to the patient. Some states and countries have legalized this practice, sometimes known as "assisted dying" or "death and dignity" statutes. (Notice the effort to remove the word *suicide* from this title in an effort to rationalize its use.) Even if the practice is not technically legalized in a particular state, physicians are not usually prosecuted if they facilitate a person's death. For example, legal medications can be prescribed in large doses and the patient is told that such doses could be lethal. Then that individual decides whether or not to self-administer that medication.

Think Right

We can believe all these things, yet not think right at times. Thinking more about the misery than about the Lord may bring discouragement and apathy—"This is too hard; I give up." Those suffering with illness will most likely need coaching to remind themselves who God is and what he is doing. "I recall this to my mind, therefore I wait," Jeremiah says (Lamentations 3:21). That sounds as though the author is reminding himself of something, but it is more than that. He is training his mind and molding his thinking. He is choosing to focus on right beliefs about God despite life's difficult circumstances. As a Christian, I find that I must frequently train my mind to think right, directed by believing right about the truths of God and the good news of Jesus Christ—what he accomplished on the cross and through his resurrection from the dead. This thinking is in direct contrast to our typical focus on the malady itself.

Our counselees can actually think about illness as an opportunity to glorify God. John Piper has written a short but powerful booklet entitled *Don't Waste Your Cancer*.[8] Piper enumerates in the booklet how to use by our illness to grow more like Christ and be a platform for witnessing. (We could substitute any medical diagnosis, as in "Don't waste your fibromyalgia," "Don't waste your hip fracture," "Don't waste your COVID-19 diagnosis," etc.) In several ways, Julie exemplified John Piper's message. "She Was Alive When She Died."[9] These words are inscribed on a gravestone that Julie learned of through a friend. The two friends reflected upon what that inscription might mean to Julie regarding the short time she had left on this earth. The illness and treatments had left her weak, nauseated, in pain, wanting to give up and to withdraw from life prior to the Lord's calling her home. But Julie's friend repeatedly encouraged her to finish life's race well: "Make sure you are alive when you die!" Keep loving, growing, and serving the Lord until the day he takes you home. They realized that the diagnosis of terminal cancer provided a unique position, an opportunity, a "gift" to be used for God's glory. Julie's words would now have more credibility when she met with others and shared her testimony. Boldly she shared the gospel at the gym, at the grocery store, at every doctor's appointment, in the chemotherapy chair, everywhere. She authored two excellent booklets, which are helpful resources for anyone dealing with illness, whatever the diagnosis or prognosis. In her last days, Julie did not waste her cancer.

If physical illness progresses to the point of impending death, many emotions will result. In our weakness as humans, we may experience significant fear. We may fear for the people we leave behind on this earth when we pass into heaven—spouses, friends, children. We may think that our lives are indispensable to them. Yet we experience God's peace when we "recall to our minds" that if they are believers, God will provide for them. He will give them the grace they need as

---

8. John Piper, *Don't Waste Your Cancer* (Wheaton, IL: Crossway, 2011).
9. Julie Gossack, *Whether by Life or by Death: Reflections for the Terminally Ill* (Bemidji, MN: Focus Publishing, 2018), 27.

they mourn. When we fear the process of physical illness and death, we should call to our minds that we belong to Jesus and he is faithful. He will be with us through it all. When we have placed our faith in Christ as Lord and Savior, we need not fear what will happen to our soul, but we might struggle with this fear in times of weakness. As we reflect on the truths and promises of God, our fears will be quieted.

Do Right

Obedience flows from a heart focused on Jesus. As we depend on him by faith, we can live out of the truths of the gospel. Physical illness does not cause us to sin or excuse our sin, but it does bring about many temptations to sin. Our hearts are squeezed by the trial, which may expose self-focus, self-pity, complaining, anger, fear, irritability, and many other issues. Praise God for the gospel! When we confess and repent of these things, he forgives and helps us grow. Jesus tells us how to develop fruit from our trial rather than thorns. He says in John 15, "If you remain in me and I in you, you will bear much fruit; apart from me you can do nothing" (v. 5 NIV). As we think on Christ and meditate on truth (remain in him), we are empowered by grace to follow him in doing what is right, bearing fruit and proving to be his disciples (John 15:5, 8).

It could be said that the believer in Christ should strive to be a "Christian oyster." An oyster does something extraordinary with an irritant, a foreign body such as a piece of sand. It makes something of value from it—a pearl, which is beautiful, long-lasting, and valuable. The pearl brings joy and inspiration to others. But the oyster without irritants will never produce this beautiful pearl.

"And be thankful" (Colossians 3:15b). It is perhaps hard to imagine being thankful in the midst of feeling physically terrible. During my eight months of intensive treatment, I had to train my mind toward gratitude rather than complaint. Hebrews 12:28 (NIV) says, "Therefore, since we are receiving a kingdom that cannot be shaken, let us be thankful, and so worship God acceptably with reverence and awe." And 1 Thessalonians 5:16–18 reminded me to "Rejoice always, pray continually, give thanks in all circumstances; for this is God's will for you in Christ Jesus." Many other passages can be used in counseling to help sufferers toward gratitude: Acts 24:3; 1 Corinthians 10:30; Ephesians 5:20; Colossians 1:3; 2:7; 3:15–17; 4:2; and 1 Timothy 4:4.

In my situation, I grew to be thankful for many things: for the ability to receive excellent medical care, for the doctors and nurses, for the body of Christ and how they sacrificially served us, for the hope of the gospel, for our family's encouragement, for each day's blessings, for how God was working in my life. And for the opportunities to spread the seeds of the gospel to those we met in the hospital and in our extended-stay hotel.

When I was initially diagnosed, I thought about keeping it quiet. However, it became evident that we should be willing to make our journey with illness a group project. Although it may seem noble to keep our sickness to ourselves to avoid adding misery to the lives of others, that approach deprives them of an opportunity to pray and serve and love and grow. We needed to be wrapped in the arms of the body of Christ, using their varied giftedness to meet practical and spiritual essentials. When the church body functions as it should, with every part doing its share, the body "grows and builds itself up in love" (Ephesians 4:16 NIV). God is glorified as brothers and sisters in Christ unify to meet needs (John 17:22–23).

In the case of terminal illness, leaving a legacy can be a blessing to many. I remember attending a funeral of a Christian who had arranged to have a videotape played at his service. During his last days on this earth, he recorded what he wanted to share about his life, his successes and failures, what was important, and his testimony of faith in Jesus. There were many non-believers in attendance, and they heard the gospel. This recording might be used many times again in the lives of future family members, perhaps even those not yet born.

Feel Right

When Cain was angry that God had not accepted his sacrifice, God told Cain, "If you do well, will not your countenance be lifted up?" (Genesis 4:7). Or consider that after Jesus instructed his disciples to wash one another's feet, he said, "Now that you know these things, you will be blessed [happy] if you do them" (John 13:17 NIV). These passages imply that experiencing emotional stability through physical suffering is connected to following Christ. While feeling right (good, happy) is not the Christian's primary goal in life, we can affirm that genuine contentment and even joy can come when our heart chooses obedience. Perhaps it is also important to note that "feeling right" might mean sorrow over the brokenness of the world or grief over loss. In other words, feeling right doesn't always mean being happy; it means having feelings appropriate to the situation.

Children with Disease

All these principles are applicable to children as well, adapted to their level of understanding. Amy Baker edited an excellent resource titled *Caring for the Souls of Children*. Chapter 14, written by Joni and Friends, brings particular sensitivity about counseling children with a disease, along with their parents.[10]

A Word to the Counselor

As you think about how to help those you counsel, remember that Philippians 4:8–9 (NIV) is preceded by verses 4–6: "Rejoice in the Lord always. I will say it again: Rejoice! Let your gentleness be evident to all. The Lord is near. Do not be anxious about anything, but in every situation, by prayer and petition, with thanksgiving, present your requests to God." As you guide your counselees to think

---

10. Amy Baker, *Caring for the Souls of Children* (Greensboro, NC: New Growth Press, 2020).

biblically about their suffering, begin with "the Lord is near" and then encourage them to pray to the God who is near as they encounter the troubles of each day. Philippians 4:8–9 will come alive to them as they go to God each day for the help and hope they need.

Each of us will face aging and decay, if the Lord tarries. Since we ourselves are likely to face illness, it is prudent for each of us to plan ahead for how we will react when we receive a diagnosis, perhaps one of cancer. How will we use that diagnosis to glorify God? Let's think about ways to show the joy of our salvation to medical personnel, to neighbors, to family, even to those we might not like!

To those currently suffering physically, biblical counselors need to offer comfort, encouragement, the perspective of biblical truth and godly principles, and a plan to help them endure the trials of physical illness. We can help those who are suffering by pointing them to the promises of God and encouraging them to fulfill the goal of all Christians: to glorify God and become more like Christ. God's Word is always practical and helpful in all types of illness. Help your counselees to look at physical maladies as an opportunity to glorify God and to see that victory is possible even without a cure. Help them to maintain a vertical perspective when illness befalls. They will gain comfort from a proper view of this fragile earthly life compared to the certainty of heaven for all the saints. They can be thankful for the gift of life that God has given, both our earthly life and our eternal life.

A Word to Those Suffering with Illness

During the last years of Julie's life, she experienced many physical, emotional, and spiritual struggles. It was tempting for her to give up, to become resentful, to despair. Instead, Julie lived out the principles of the quadratic formula. She recalled the wonderful truths and promises of God. She directed her mind to think rightly about the difficult circumstances of her cancer. She chose obedience, serving and glorifying God to the very end of her days on earth. Julie experienced contentment and perhaps even smiled, knowing that she was alive when she died. I hope to follow her example.

Let's Pray

Lord, thank you for who you are, your attributes of perfection, your promises, for what Jesus accomplished on the cross for us. Therefore, we have certain hope of eternity in heaven with you—praising you in our new bodies! But, Lord, now for a while, this thorn in our flesh is hard for us. Give us strength to endure; make a pearl from this thorn so that our lives will make your glory evident to others. We long to be with all the saints in heaven and to see Jesus . . . oh, what joy!

Additional Resources

Baker, Amy. *Caring for the Souls of Children*. Greensboro, NC: New Growth Press, 2020.

Bridges, Jerry. *Trusting God*. Carol Stream, IL: NavPress, Reprint ed., 2017.

Gossack, Julie. *The Fear of Death and the Promises of God*. Bemidji, MN: Focus Publishing, 2019.

Gossack, Julie. *Whether by Life or by Death: Reflections for the Terminally Ill*. Bemidji, MN: Focus Publishing, 2018.

Hughes, Bryan. Grace Bible Church Members Newsletter, Bozeman Montana, February 19, 2021.

Piper, John. *Don't Waste Your Cancer*. Wheaton, IL: Crossway, 2011. (Additionally, see the John Piper article "Don't Waste Your Cancer," *Desiring God*, February 15, 2006, https://www.desiringgod.org/articles/dont-waste-your-cancer.)

Piper, John, ed. *Suffering and the Sovereignty of God*. Wheaton, IL: Crossway, 2006.

Smith, Robert. *The Christian Counselor's Medical Desk Reference*. Stanley, NC: Timeless Texts, 2000.

Tada, Joni Eareckson and Steve Estes. *When God Weeps*. Grand Rapids: Zondervan, 2000.

Tripp, Paul David. *Suffering: Eternity Makes a Difference*. Resources for Changing Lives. Phillipsburg, NJ: P & R Publishing, 2001.

Viars, Steve. *Suffering. Audio series*. Lafayette, IN: Faith Resources, https://store.faithlafayette.org/browse-by-topic/christian-life-and-growth/grief-death/suffering-mp3-series-six-audio-sessions/.

Welch, Ed. *Blame It on the Brain*. Phillipsburg, NJ: P&R Publishing, 1998.

CHAPTER 4

. . . .

WHEN SHOULD A BIBLICAL COUNSELOR CONSULT A DOCTOR?

Martha Peace, RN

Over my thirty-two years of being a NANC/ACBC counselor, there have been many times that I have consulted with or referred a counselee to their doctor. Often, it was their primary care physician, but sometimes it was their psychiatrist. In fact, I have even gone with a counselee the first two visits to see her new psychiatrist, due to the fact that she was frightened, had asked me to go, and her case was complicated. In that incident, it was very helpful for me as well as the doctor because I shared my observations, and he explained to me his diagnosis and basis for prescribing her medicine. I have often longed for all biblical counseling ministries to have an ACBC certified physician serving in partnership with them because there are so many counselees with additional medical problems and counselees taking medications with complicated side effects. So far, that has not happened, but it would be great if it did.

An Example of Referring to a Physician

Early on in my counseling ministry, I received a telephone call from a husband who was desperate to seek help for his wife. Kevin was a pastor and had recently learned about biblical counseling. He and his wife, Pam, had recently had their third child. Pam began to have panic attacks and could not sleep at night. After a few days of not sleeping, she was really struggling due to having panic attacks, crying spells, and the inability to cope with her newborn baby and her other children. I knew if she did not get some sleep soon she could undergo a psychotic break, and she might harm herself or someone else. A psychotic break is "a fundamental mental derangement characterized by defective or lost contact with reality."[1]

Providentially, I answered the telephone that Monday morning at the Atlanta Biblical Counseling Center[2] where I was counseling women. I had an opening in my schedule that afternoon, and Kevin agreed to bring her. When they arrived, they both looked like they were at their wits' end. She had been afraid to get into the car, but he had insisted. At the time, I was a fairly new counselor, and I was at my wits' end too! However, I did not tell them that, and I pretended this was routine. Her husband stayed with her throughout the session and listened intensely to everything I told her. He was the nicest pastor, but it made me nervous with him being there because I was so new to counseling. When I thought of a Scripture to use, he would help me out by telling me where it was located. After a few sessions with the both of them, I figured out that her husband was my own personal Bible concordance.

At the time, I really thought she should be in a psychiatric hospital so they could give her something for sleep. Pam was adamant she did not want to go into the hospital. One very encouraging factor was that this couple really loved the Lord and really loved each other. In between counseling sessions, her husband would pray with her, take care of the baby and the other children, remind her of the Scriptures that I had used (and he likely added more Scripture than I had used), and he would give her hope. Still, she could not sleep and was moving closer and closer to a psychotic break.

---

1. *The Merriam-Webster Dictionary* (Boston: G.K. Hall and Co., 1977), 733.
2. The Atlanta Biblical Counseling Center was started by Dr. Howard Eyrich and later overseen by Lou Priolo. It is no longer in operation.

Early on in one of the sessions, I suggested that she contact her doctor to see if he would give her a small amount of a mild tranquilizer that she could take when the panic was the worst. My hope was that the medicine would relax her enough so that she could get some sleep. The doctor did call in the prescription, they picked it up, but she would not take it because she did not want to be addicted. However, one time she did give in and take it, and her comment was, "Now I know why people love this medicine!" That was the one and only time she took that pill, but Pam and Kevin had a few minutes of blessed relief.

After several counseling sessions, Pam got better, mainly due to the fact that she loved the Lord so much and began to trust him with her future by biblically addressing her anxiety throughout the counseling process. Upon questioning her further, I learned that she had been a worrier since she was a little girl. That long-standing *sinful* habit pattern, coupled with new baby hormone changes, resulted in adrenaline surges in her body and panic attacks. Following the first panic attack, she continued to have more.

Slowly, with counseling and her husband's reminders of the Scriptures and what I was telling her, she began to stabilize and get some sleep. I have kept in touch with this couple for years. In fact, I was recently at their church to speak at a women's conference, and we reminisced over those early counseling sessions. Their baby is an adult now and married. Kevin pursued biblical counseling, and he is a beloved counselor to his people and to those in their community. All three of us saw the power of God, his Word, and that one tiny little tranquilizer to help her through what really was a nightmare.

Why do I share this story? I want to reassure you that doctors are not our enemy. Modern medicine is a grace gift from God to us, and we should be prepared to professionally communicate with the counselee's doctors if necessary. In fact, the doctor may want to speak to you or have regular reports from you about how their patient is progressing. In this chapter, I want to cover how to obtain permission to talk to the counselee's doctor if needed, how to refer to a doctor in an emergency (such as suicide ideation or anorexia), and when to refer your counselee to their doctor for a specific complaint (to rule out physical causes of their symptoms).

Let's begin with how to obtain permission to talk to their doctor.

Obtaining Permission to Talk to Your Counselee's Doctor

Obtaining permission to talk to their doctor begins with the counselee. This is rare, but sometimes needed. If you think it is necessary, talk to your counselee about the possibility. He or she will need to give written permission to you as the counselor, as well as to their doctor, for communication to take place. Normally this is not necessary, but when it is, it is important. For example, there are many physical issues that can contribute to depression. Those need to be ruled out and, if possible, corrected by their physician early on in counseling.

Most of the time when you recommend your counselee see their medical doctor for a physical, you will not need to communicate directly with the doctor. You can simply depend on the verbal report that your counselee gives you. However, there are times when it is needful for you and the doctor to communicate, such as when the counselee is anorexic, very emotionally unstable, or they need their physician's help in withdrawing from alcohol or illegal drugs. In cases like those, I would not agree to counsel someone who would *not* give me permission to talk to their doctor.

It is possible that their doctor will request periodic updates on how the counseling is progressing. For example, the doctor may want to know your assessment of his patient's emotional stability and progress, such as his or her desire to commit suicide. Often simply giving your counselee a boatload of hope from Scripture helps them to stabilize emotionally. As an aside, your assessment may actually help the doctor. If so, put it on your calendar and give professional updates as requested. Updates in general should be professional short summary critiques, not a lengthy detailed letter.

If your counselee is not stable and if they have an appointment with a psychiatrist, I recommend they have an advocate go with them. An advocate is someone who comes with them to counseling and can also go see the psychiatrist with them. An advocate could be a friend or family member who is aware that they are receiving biblical counsel and can remind them of what the doctor says in case they become confused or feel overwhelmed. Otherwise, if your counselee is doing well, they certainly can go alone to doctor's appointments.

If the counselee continues to go to counseling with you *and* with some other therapist, such as a psychologist, then my personal conviction is I will not counsel them. Secular or integrationist counseling will be contrary to biblical counseling and likely confuse the counselee. If they are a new counselee to me, I will gradually and kindly address the issue of telling them that they need to decide one way or the other, but only after I have developed a relationship with them. The counselee will have to decide whether they want biblical or secular counseling. The two do not mix. (If your counselee routinely sees a psychiatrist, encourage them to keep their appointments.)

Be wise and listen carefully when your counselee's doctor does consult with you. Assume the doctor has a good motive of desiring to help their patient. They certainly have a lot of experience with treating patients with medical issues. In the case that you do not agree with the doctor, be careful how you express that to your counselee. The counselee has freedom in the Lord to continue on with their doctor, to seek a second opinion, or to change doctors. We are not at war with doctors. Their training and expertise is a grace gift from God to us and to our counselees. Be wise in when to consult with their doctor. Ask God for wisdom, and ask in faith. He will give it to you. He promises. "But if any of you lacks wisdom, let him ask of God, who gives to all generously and without reproach, and it will be given to him. But he must ask in faith without any doubting, for the one who doubts is like the surf of the sea, driven and tossed by the wind" (James 1:5–6).

Consulting in Emergencies

Another time when a biblical counselor should consult with their counselee's physician is in emergency or semi-emergency situations. The situations that come to my mind are anorexia, suicide threats, psychotic breaks, and counselees that are very emotionally unstable.

Someone who is in the middle of a psychotic break usually needs the help of a psychiatrist. They can be a danger to themselves and to those around them. If this has never happened to the person before, it is very frightening to the counselee and to the family. Depending on the situation, if they are threatening to harm themselves or someone else, and if they will not voluntarily go for a psychiatric evaluation, you may need to call the police because what they are threatening to do is illegal. The police and/or emergency medical personnel will take them to an emergency room for an evaluation. Depending on the outcome of the evaluation, they will then be transported to a psychiatric hospital. Most states have a mandatory time that the patient can be confined against their will. In Georgia where I live it is seventy-two hours. If the counselee will voluntarily go to a psychiatric hospital for evaluation, they will have the option of voluntarily checking themselves out. However, if they refuse to go voluntarily, they *can* be hospitalized against their will.

Certainly their family will need to be informed on what is happening and hopefully be involved with the solution. When I agree to confidentiality, I make it clear that in cases like threatening self-harm, harm to others, or acute psychotic breaks, I will tell the appropriate persons—such as family or possibly even the police—to help protect my counselee.

When I have a new counselee who is struggling with anorexia, I consider that a life-threatening situation. So I require they receive a complete physical exam from their doctor, tell that medical professional the truth about their anorexia, receive a target ideal weight from the doctor, arrange to be weighed every week in the doctor's office, and give the doctor permission to talk to me as their counselor.

Because anorexia *is* life-threatening, I will not take on the responsibility of counseling without a doctor's professional guidance.

So far, the psychiatric community has not found a medication that is helpful with anorexia. I doubt that they ever will. So I see no reason to refer my counselee to a psychiatrist. I also require my counselee to have an advocate with her at each counseling session. The advocate needs to be someone who loves the Lord, loves my counselee, and will speak truth to her between counseling sessions.

Now we turn to the issue of suicide. I take all suicide threats seriously. I never think, *They are simply trying to get attention and they won't do it.* There is no way we can know. Obviously, if they have no plan, they are less likely to carry it out, but it still can happen. Gather data and question your counselee about any previous suicide desires, attempts, or psychiatric admissions. When someone has had a psychiatric admission, I want to know what their diagnosis was upon discharge. That tells me something about their previous thinking and behavior. I don't give them a negative lecture about psychiatry or psychology. I am simply gathering data.

Giving biblical hope can turn a suicidal counselee around—sometimes quickly—but regardless, their family needs to know and take responsibility to keep close watch on their loved one and/or take them for a psychiatric evaluation if deemed necessary. Suicide threats are scary and obviously can be acted on. I have sent several counselees who were threatening suicide for a psychiatric evaluation (accompanied by their family). Most times, they were admitted to the hospital for several days. I have even gone with one counselee's husband when he took his wife for a psychiatric evaluation. This is certainly not required of a counselor, but there have been a few times that it was helpful to my counselee and her family for me to go along beside them. It is a judgment call. Pray for wisdom.

This leads us to the issue of depression that is not accompanied by suicide threats.

Considering Depression

What causes depression? That is a good question, and it takes time to figure out what is causing depression. When gathering data, I like to question my counselee in four areas: physical causes, circumstantial causes, bitterness, and other sin issues.

As biblical counselors, we know how to help our counselees with their circumstances, bitterness, and sin. We know how to hold them accountable for their schedules and come up with a practical biblical plan to help them overcome (with the Lord's help) their sin issues such as negative thinking and self-pity. However, we need their doctor to deal with their physical issues and to correct them when possible.

It begins with a thorough, complete physical examination. It is possible that one or more of the contributing factors in their depression is purely physical. An example is hypothyroidism. I have known people who did not know that their thyroid levels were low and once that was corrected by their doctor, they perked up.

Another, sometimes major, example of medical issues contributing to depression are the side effects of medicine. For example, someone who is on seizure medicine often will feel "down." It is the nature of the medicine, and more often than not, their medicine is life-changing for them and sometimes even life-saving. Another medication that can result in the patient feeling down is steroids. Most times, patients are on steroids for a short period of time, but some diseases—such as Addison's disease—render steroids necessary for life. Other medicines that have a side effect of depression are some blood pressure medicines and hormone therapy such as birth control pills.

As a counselor, I usually check the side effects of my counselee's medicines on the internet. This is not necessarily to tell them what I learned, but if something is obvious, I might explain that a side-effect could possibly be a contributing factor to how they feel.

Most medicines that contribute to depression are necessary for your counselee for more pressing reasons. Their doctor can certainly help figure that out. In the event that the medicine is necessary, the counselee will need to "fight" the sadness by honoring God and continuing to "pray without ceasing; [and] in everything give thanks [remembering] this is the will of God in Christ Jesus concerning [them] (1 Thessalonians 5:17–18, adaptation mine). You, as the counselor, can help the counselee figure that out. In other words, help them "set [their] mind on the things above, not on the things that are on the earth" (Colossians 3:2, adaptation mine).

Considering PMS

PMS is another issue that causes women physical and emotional pain. PMS is premenstrual syndrome. It causes miserable emotional symptoms, such as anxiety, feeling down, and often outbursts of anger. It confuses the people around them. There are more details in my book, *Damsels in Distress*, but suffice it to say that PMS occurs several days *prior* to a woman's period starting. Once the PMS days are over and her menstrual period begins, the emotional issues will improve, but she may subsequently experience some physical issues such as cramping and inordinate bleeding. If that is the case, refer your counselee to a physician to check for physical issues that can and should be medically dealt with.

If a woman has a problem with anxiety, anger, or self-pity, those issues will be exaggerated during her PMS time each month. Gynecologists have said that if she will go off caffeine during those days and does mild simple aerobic exercise daily, such as taking a walk in the neighborhood, she will likely get through that time much easier than otherwise. Because medicines such as birth control pills and antidepressants usually do not help very much,[3] I recommend trying simple remedies first. It may also greatly help her to read the PMS chapter in the book *Damsels in Distress*.[4]

This leads us to another issue—anxiety and panic attacks.

3. J. E. Daugherty, "Treatment Strategies for Premenstrual Syndrome," *American Family Physician* 58, no. 1 (July 1998): 183.
4. Martha Peace, *Damsels in Distress: Biblical Solutions for Problems Women Face* (Phillipsburg, NJ: P&R, 2006), 103.

Considering Panic Attacks

Panic attacks are a miserable and frightening experience. I have often said I would rather have a baby than have a panic attack. It seems that once a counselee has a panic attack, they have others. Many times they cannot sleep at night and, very often, the panic attack comes because they are so anxious and worried about their life that eventually adrenaline surges throughout their body and causes the panic. The fear of having another attack becomes the fear. Emergency Rooms see patients who are having panic attacks because the patient believes they are having a heart attack. Of course, the heart attack has to be ruled out, but many times, they are in a panic with acute worry and fear that is not being handled biblically.

Therefore, a doctor and a complete physical is a necessity for your counselee. Two physical diseases that cause panic attacks are hyper-thyroidism and an increased cortisol level. Their doctor can certainly either diagnose those maladies or rule them out. Of course there are many more examples of underlying behavioral or mental-emotional symptoms that should be ruled out by a physician. The examples given here are not exhaustive. Often, you should refer your counselee to a physician for a routine physical, especially if they have not had one in the last few months or even a year.

Understanding That a Sin-Cursed Body Is a Reality for All of Us

As a counselor, pray for wisdom and help your counselee think true, God-honoring thoughts to cope with their physical illness. We live in a sin-cursed world and put up with a sin-cursed body. The older I get, the more I am *certain* that my body is sin-cursed, and I look forward to being with the Lord, where there will be no more pain, sorrow, tears, surgery, and death. People do have symptoms, and the symptoms may indicate disease whether the doctor can figure it out or not. Doctor Bob Smith, in his book *The Christian Counselor's Medical Desk*

Reference (the book that is the inspiration for this new version) tells an interesting story about a patient he treated who was struggling with heart pain. It is worth repeating here.

Years ago a man in my practice had developed heart disease. He was a young man with a family, but his disease was so severe he was unable to work. This was before the days of the treadmill, coronary care units, monitors, cardiac surgery, and so on. We did not have a good test to evaluate the exact nature of a person's heart disease. Whenever I did an electrocardiogram, or EKG (which was always in a resting condition), his heart was normal. Yet when he tried to work he had significant symptoms that prevented his holding of a job. When coronary catheterization became available, I sent him for this test. In my mind, this would reveal the nature of his disease or show that he was having "psychosomatic" symptoms. The test revealed that all three of his major heart vessels were severely blocked. So he then had bypass surgery. Within a few years, his body had blocked the bypass vessels the same as the original vessels. We didn't know this at that time, nor did we know the body would continue doing his. We also did not know about the effects of cholesterol on heart disease. When the symptoms returned, he was sent for another exam, and the bypasses were found to be blocked. This meant another surgery to replace the old bypasses. Months after this second surgery when his surgery wound was completely healed, he came to the office complaining of chest pain. God made certain he was the last patient of the day so that I would have the time for another and important kind of "heart" work. I ran another EKG and could see no changes. I asked him what bothered him about the pain. He replied that he was concerned it might be his heart. I informed him I could not tell him if his heart was okay. He had had heart surgery twice, and the pain might be from where his breastbone had been divided for the surgical procedure. The EKG did not show any changes, but that did not mean the heart was not having a problem. Then I asked what bothered him about the possibility of it being his heart. He replied that he was concerned it might stop. I told him that was a possibility, and I couldn't say for certain that it would not. But when I asked what concerned him about the possibility of it stopping he replied, "I don't know what will happen to me then." When the door is open, it is best to drive the gospel truck through—which I did, and he was saved that day. His disease and my concern for his spiritual condition made it possible for me to use his disease and fear of death as a means of presenting the gospel. He lived another seven years, became a leader in his church, and now is in Heaven free from all heart diseases. My patient's heart disease was the result of sin's effect on the human body.[5]

What an amazing providence of God that Doctor Smith was that man's doctor and that Doctor Smith was a Christian and a NANC/ACBC counselor. Would it be that God would give us all a doctor to refer to like Doctor Bob Smith! But, obviously, that is not the case for almost all of us. But whether the counselees' doctor is a Christian or not, or whether he has the courage and insight to give gospel truth to his patient, we *can* and *should* nevertheless refer to doctors, communicate with them, and work alongside them to help our counselees.

Conclusion

Doctors are not our enemy. We need them to help our counselees recover from diseases, if possible, and tolerate, as best they can, noncurable symptoms. Modern medicine is a kindness from God, a gift as it were. We should thank him for it.

---

5. Robert D. Smith, MD, *The Christian Counselor's Medical Desk Reference* (Stanley, NC: Timeless Texts, 2000), 53–54.

When should a counselor refer their counselee to a doctor? Probably more often than not. If needed, your counselee should give you and their doctor permission to communicate with each other. Especially in cases like suicide, anorexia, or psychotic breaks. Even if you never talk to their doctor or communicate with them in some way, though, your counselee's doctor can be an amazing blessing from God to them.

CHAPTER 5

. . . .

DEPRESSION:
MEDICAL BACKGROUND AND BIBLICAL HOPE

Charles D. Hodges Jr., MD

In the last thirty years, the word *depression* has taken a new place in the language of medicine and counseling. Prior to 1980 and the third revision of the *Diagnostic Statistical Manual of Mental Disorders*, the word was generally reserved for individuals with a sad mood that lacked a well-defined cause. Those who had a reason to be sad were said to be grieving or struggling to adjust. Those changes, coupled with the introduction of the SSRI antidepressant Prozac in 1988, changed how we use the word.[1]

Four decades later, we live in a society that has replaced the word *sadness* with the word *depression*. And depression of all sorts is defined as a medical disorder requiring medication to correct. We might think this is medical progress, just as we view ten days of penicillin for strep throat as a cure for the disease. Instead, we have increasing numbers of individuals diagnosed with depression and a growing number of patients being diagnosed and treated for a lifetime.

A lifetime of medication might be a reasonable model of care for high blood pressure or diabetes, where the diagnosis can be certain

---

1. Alan Horwitz concludes that the rapid rise in the diagnosis of depression was explained by changes in the criteria, page 51 in "Creating an Age of Depression: The Social Construction and Consequences of the Major Depression Diagnosis," *Society and Mental Health* 1, no. 1, 2011: 41–54.

and the treatment has been shown to be beneficial and effective. However, the diagnosis and treatment of depression is not nearly as certain or beneficial as many other medical diagnoses. This presents those of us in biblical counseling with both responsibility and opportunity. We have a responsibility to understand how the diagnosis is made and how reliable it is. We are responsible to listen carefully to the stories our counselees bring.

The opportunity before us is to help those who come to us suffering with sadness to identify the source of their struggle and offer the encouragement that comes from Scripture. In order to do this, it will be useful to understand the current societal definition of depression and its treatment. Then we can help counselees understand the difference between normal grieving and disordered sadness. Let's consider three different cases that might be labeled depression.

A Connection Between Sadness and Circumstances

Fred was a new patient to my family medicine office.[2] He came because it was time for his annual adult health exam, and he wanted to discuss whether he should take medication for depression. As we discussed his medical history, we came to the topic of depression. I asked him when it began and what had been going on in his life at the time.

Fred was one of many people who suffered from the COVID-19 pandemic. Shortly after the outbreak in February 2020, he found himself locked down, working from home with children who were attempting to study virtually and with a wife who struggled with having her family underfoot. Around six months into it all, the job he loved was eliminated by his company, which was struggling to survive. Suddenly, he was a man adrift, and his mood began to sink. Sleep escaped him, along with any enjoyment that he had previously

---

2. The patients described in this chapter are composites and represent no specific individuals in order to protect the privacy of my patients' information. Rather, they represent three distinct populations I have worked with that have been diagnosed as depressed.

experienced from hobbies such as running. He just wasn't in the mood to tie on his Nikes and hit the road. His appetite left him. Nothing tasted good.

Fred was a Christian who had prayed and read his Bible daily, but now he seemed to be letting himself drift. The church he had regularly attended and served in had been reduced to a one hour livestream. There were no smiling faces, encouraging words, firm handshakes, or sincere hugs to be had.

Life began to seem like a long trip in a small camper in the middle of a hot summer. There was very little space and little to no privacy. The family thought Fred was a bomb waiting to be ignited by a spark, so his children gave him a wide berth. He and his wife lost interest in each other. Eventually, family and friends suggested he see a doctor because they believed that he was suffering from depression. He made the appointment, and his main question was "Do I have depression and can I get better?"

I have counseled many people like Fred who begin to experience prolonged sadness after suffering a significant loss in life. However, his experience is not the only path to a diagnosis of depression. Evelyn's case was different.

The Incidental Diagnosis

Evelyn came to my office with a complicated medical history, starting with things like generalized aches, pains, and fatigue. At first her diagnoses had begun with things like chronic fatigue syndrome and fibromyalgia, but later she was also diagnosed with multiple autoimmune disorders, including lupus and thyroid disease.

As the number of disease diagnoses increased, her mood began to sink under the burden. Along the way, one of her many physicians added a diagnosis of depression to the mix. What followed was a succession of different medications that were intended to address her sad mood but seemed to add side effects instead of improving her mood.

Like Fred, she was a believer in the redemption found in confessing Christ as her risen Savior and Lord. Her aches and pains had not kept her from church, but it did seem to take some of the joy out of it for her. They did not keep her from her Bible or prayer, but her pursuit of feeling better seemed to consume her time.

After several years in doctors' offices and taking medications with the hope of feeling better—but never quite getting there—Evelyn decided it was time to take a different approach. Her questions were as simple as her medication list was long. It began with: How many of these medications can I do without? What can I do to improve my health and my mood without adding another prescription?

Evelyn was questioning which of her diagnoses were real. In particular, she wondered if the diagnosis of depression was added because there was no good explanation for her discomfort. She wondered if her life had become one never-ending medical misadventure.

In the months that followed, she worked through a process of withdrawing much of the medication with medical supervision. She improved her diet and increased her activity by walking. At the end of the process, Evelyn believed that she felt better. She still had some of the aches and pains that she started with, but they seemed less of a problem than the side effects of the multiple medications she had been taking. She doubted that her aches and pains had anything to do with depression.

Another Look at a Sad Mood

Mike also experienced depression. However, unlike Fred—who had a clear connection between his life circumstances and his sad mood—and Evelyn—who was diagnosed as a complication of her search to find an answer to her many medical problems—Mike's depression didn't appear to be connected to his circumstances. It didn't seem connected to anything.

Mike came to my office because he had been told by his pastor that I was a biblical counselor and a physician. He had been living with episodes of sad moods for decades, and he had attempted to deal with them in many ways. He searched for help in counseling, therapy, exercise, meditation, and medication. None of these tools had offered him much relief. Mike, like Fred and Evelyn, testified to his belief in salvation by the grace of God through faith in Christ. But his faith had not insulated him from his sad mood.

Mike's family and friends observed his struggle and endeavored to help him as he faced the successive waves of sadness, anger, and worry. He had received many diagnostic labels over the years, but he was not currently taking medications and didn't really think they made much difference. When one of his dark moods would come, he would simply stop talking to people. His family felt rejected, and his friends struggled to understand him at these times. Mike wanted to know what he should call this struggle. He was looking for a better way to respond to it.

These three individuals illustrate different aspects of the large group of patients who are diagnosed with and treated for depression every year in the United States. Not everyone who has been labeled with depression is facing the same problem. It is important to listen carefully to each counselee's story, rather than focus on a diagnostic label. If we understand the thoughts and actions that accompany their mood, we will be better able to direct them to biblical principles that will be helpful to them.

What Is Depression?

Before we can discuss biblical responses to depression, we need to understand how our society defines it. Depression today is a relatively new phenomenon, at least at the levels we are seeing it diagnosed. Currently the prevalence of depression in the United States is 8.4 percent.[3] It ranges from 6.2 percent for men to 10.5 percent for women

---

3. Major Depression, National Institute of Mental Health, https://www.nimh.nih.gov/health/statistics/major-depression, accessed July 23, 2022.

and can reach 17.5 percent for those between the ages of eighteen and twenty-five.[4] Records indicate that the rate was 5 percent or less in 1950.[5]

There are many explanations for the increase, but the mostly likely culprit is the ever-changing *Diagnostic and Statistical Manual of Mental Disorders* (*DSM*). We used to make a distinction between grief that came from a loss in life such as the death of a loved one or the loss of a job and sadness without a cause. Prior to 1980, we would have been less likely to identify someone as depressed who could tell us why they were sad. The changes that started in 1980 and in subsequent revisions, removed that distinction.[6] As it stands, those who struggle with a sad mood can be diagnosed with depression without regard to the cause and in as little as two weeks.

To be diagnosed with depression, the DSM (now in its fifth edition) states that the person must experience one of the first two symptoms listed below and at least five of the nine total symptoms.[7] The following is a summation of the full list found in the DSM.

1. A depressed mood most of the day, every day
2. Loss of interest or enjoyment in most all activities
3. Either too little or too much sleep
4. Significant weight loss or weight gain with a decrease or increase in appetite
5. Responses with physical and mental agitation or slowness
6. Complaints of fatigue or loss of energy
7. Decreased ability to concentrate, think, or make decisions
8. Thoughts of worthlessness or excessive or inappropriate guilt

4. Major Depression, NIMH.

5. Allan V. Horwitz, "How an Age of Anxiety Became an Age of Depression," *The Millbank Quarterly* 88, no. 1 (2010): 114, doi:10.1111/j.1468-0009.2010.00591.x.

6. Allan V. Horwitz, "Creating an Age of Depression: The Social Construction and Consequences of the Major Depression Diagnosis," *Society and Mental Health* 1, no. 1 (March 1, 2011): 51, doi:10.1177/2156869310393986.

7. American Psychiatric Association, *Diagnostic and Statistical Manual of Mental Disorders*, 5th Edition, Text Revision: DSM-5 TR (Arlington, VA: American Psychiatric Association, 2022), 155.

9. Recurrent thoughts of death or suicidal ideation, or a suicide attempt

A person can be diagnosed with depression if they have been experiencing these symptoms for at least two weeks. The problem with diagnosing someone with depression is that the process is completely subjective.[8] There are no current, readily available tests that can confirm or deny the presence of depression. The result is that some people who are simply sad over losing something important to them might be incorrectly diagnosed as having depression. It is likely that 90 percent of those diagnosed with depression are grieving a loss and do not have any medical disease.[9] Simply meeting these criteria does not mean that a disease is present. All three of my patients met the criteria for depression, but their problems were really very different. While diagnosing each of them as depressed might seem reasonable, it would likely result in none of them receiving the help they needed.

Current Treatments for Depression

Patients who seek care for depression today will generally receive a thorough physical exam and laboratory testing to determine whether there are treatable physical causes for their mood disturbance.[10] If no specific medical cause is found, a patient will most likely be offered medication, some form of psychotherapy, or both.

Medications

Selective serotonin reuptake inhibitors (SSRIs) such as fluoxetine, sertraline, and escitalopram are commonly prescribed as first-line medications. Medicines such as duloxetine and venlafaxine are in a similar category and widely used in depression. A third group of older

---

8. American Psychiatric Association, *DSM-5 TR*, 155.

9. Jerome Wakefield, Allan Horwitz et al., "Extending the Bereavement Exclusion for Major Depression to Other Losses," *Archives of General Psychiatry* 64 (April 2007): 438.

10. Jeffrey M. Lyness, Peter P. Roy-Byrne, and David Solomon, "Unipolar Depression in Adults: Assessment and Diagnosis," UpToDate, updated May 9, 2022, https://www.uptodate.com/contents/unipolar-depression-in-adults-assessment-and-diagnosis/print#!.

antidepressant medications called tricyclics is used less often today because of side effects and potential hazards.

There are many other antidepressants that do not fit neatly into one category. These medications are called atypical and include bupropion and mirtazapine. Drugs in this class are often used for other indications such as insomnia or to improve appetite.

Another class of medication is being promoted as a supplemental drug for individuals who do not respond completely to their first medication. These medications include antipsychotics such as quetiapine, aripiprazole, and lurasidone, which were first manufactured for use in problems such as schizophrenia. They have significant side effects that limit their use.

Since I am both a practicing physician and a biblical counselor, I am often asked what I think about the role of medication in the care of those who face sadness and depression. My response as a biblical counselor is that the question of whether or not to take medication for depression falls within the realm of Christian liberty (Romans 14; 1 Corinthians 8). Not much is said in Scripture about it. Thus, Christians have the privilege of making the choice themselves within the confines of the rest of Scripture and taking into account how their choice will affect others.

As a physician, I would say that we all should be good medical consumers. There is not an absolute consensus that current medications work much better than counseling. There are concerns about side effects. I suggest anyone who would take medicine for any condition have a thorough conversation with their physician and discuss the benefits and risks of the medicine.

Research published this year makes the question of side effects versus benefits even more important. The chemical imbalance or serotonergic theory of depression that was the foundation for research for decades has proven to be false. "Our comprehensive review of the major strands of research on serotonin shows there is no convincing evidence that depression is associated with, or caused by, lower serotonin concentrations or activity. Most studies found no evidence of reduced serotonin activity in people with depression compared to people without . . ."[11] Without a good understanding of how these medicines work for those diagnosed with depression, it is wise to be cautious when considering taking them.

Psychotherapy and Other Treatments

I have often said that even if we disagree about the cause of depression and how to care for those who suffer from it, doing nothing about it is not a viable strategy. Patients who are offered the opportunity to talk with someone about their depression typically profit from it. Studies that have compared the effect of psychotherapy to medication in treating depression have found the differences in outcome to be small.[12]

Of the many forms of therapy, cognitive behavioral therapy (CBT) is the most commonly used. It has been reported to be nearly as effective as medication for mild to moderate depression in the short run. In the long run, the improvement seen in counselees seems to be more enduring than the effect of medication.

Other useful things border on common sense but are very helpful to many. One of the most important questions I ask a patient or counselee who is struggling with a sad mood is, how are you sleeping? Inadequate rest will eventually lead to struggles with worry and a sad mood. Many sleep issues can and should be corrected and may result in resolution of mood problems.

Exercise has been repeatedly shown to help those who are diagnosed with depression. In some studies, it equals the effect of medication. The "runner's high" has long been identified as the emotional lift that runners get from the release of endorphins during their

---

11. Joanna Moncrieff et al. "The Serotonin Theory of Depression: a Systematic Umbrella Review of the Evidence," *Molecular Psychiatry* (July 20, 2022), https://doi.org/10.1038/s41380-022-01661-0

12. A. John Rush, Peter P. Roy-Byrne, David Solomon, "Unipolar Major Depression in Adults: Choosing Initial Treatment," Uptodate.com, https://www.uptodate.com/contents/unipolar-major-depression-in-adults-choosing-initial-treatment?search=depression&topicRef=90154&source=see_link, accessed July 22, 2022.

vigorous aerobic exercise. That endorphin response can be a help to those dealing with a depressed mood.

Finding social support from family, friends, and organizations such as church and service clubs is thought to be important in dealing with depression. Those struggling with a sad mood will often isolate themselves from friends and loved ones. Restoring connections is considered useful to those seeking to escape a sad mood.

Other treatments are used today for those who are diagnosed as severely depressed. Time and space do not allow full consideration of medications such as ketamine[13] and electroconvulsive therapy (ECT). Both are thought to have some benefit, but carry significant side effects.[14] I do not recommend ECT for that reason. Transcranial magnetic stimulation of the brain has been shown to benefit some of those who have failed to improve with other treatments.[15] It has no more side effects than a magnetic resonance imaging (MRI) brain scan. Time will tell if it provides any long-lasting benefits.

There is something missing here! While the current care for depression offers some relief to those who pursue it, at times recovery rates run close to placebo care.[16] And, complete resolution of the problem escapes many. If we are going to help those who struggle with a sad mood by using means that go beyond secular resources, it will require us to identify the gaps in the current model of care.

Perhaps the most significant gap has to do with the way we have decided what depression is and who has it. Horwitz and Wakefield made a good case for their contention that the majority

---

13. Michael Thase and K. Ryan Connolly, "Ketamine and Esketamine for Treating Unipolar Depression in Adults: Administration, Efficacy, and Adverse Effects," Uptodate .com, https://www.uptodate.com/contents/ketamine-and-esketamine-for-treating-unipolar-depression-in-adults-administration-efficacy-and-adverse-effects, accessed July 24, 2022.

14. Charles Kellner, "Overview of Electroconvulsive Therapy (ECT) for Adults," Uptodate.com, https://www.uptodate.com/contents/overview-of-electroconvulsive-therapy-ect-for-adults, accessed July 24, 2022.

15. L. De Risio et al., "Recovering from depression with repetitive transcranial magnetic stimulation (rTMS): a systematic review and meta-analysis of preclinical studies," *Translational Psychiatry* 10, no. 1 (November 10, 2020):393, doi: 10.1038/s41398-020-01055-2.

16. Rush, Roy-Byrne, and Solomon, "Unipolar Major Depression in Adults: Choosing Initial Treatment."

of the diagnoses of depression made in the United States are cases of normal sadness, which they distinguish from disordered sadness or depression.[17] Normal sadness has a beginning and is connected to a significant loss. The depth of the sadness is determined by the seriousness of the loss, and it lasts until what was lost has been recovered or the individual comes to a resolution in their thinking.

Disordered sadness is different. It is what was described as depression when I was in medical school. We would not have labeled an individual with "major depression" if they could tell us why they felt sad and when it started. Generally, we would have said they were grieving a loss.

This distinction is absent from the DSM-5 today, so after two weeks of meeting the criteria listed therein, any of us could be labeled as depressed. The grief associated with significant losses in life can last much longer than two weeks, which puts many people in jeopardy of being misdiagnosed and receiving unnecessary medical treatments.

In contrast, biblical counseling can offer an accurate assessment through good data gathering. Simply asking the counselee when their sadness began and what happened can reveal whether they're suffering from normal or disordered sadness. This also opens the door for counseling from the Scriptures, which address how to respond to and make sense of our losses in life.

All three of my patients would benefit from identifying the source and duration of their sad mood. Fred would perhaps benefit the most. It is unlikely that he has a disease called depression. He certainly had significant losses that left him adrift and grieving. Recognizing the impact of his experiences would provide opportunities to also offer him the hope of Scripture.

Evelyn would benefit from reviewing her medical diagnoses with her physician and reconsidering the diagnosis of depression. It would help her to change her goal of feeling better to finding a biblical

---

17. Alan Horwitz and Jerome Wakefield, *The Loss of Sadness: How Psychiatry Transformed Normal Sorrow into Depressive Disorder* (New York: Oxford University Press, 2007), Chapter 1, Location 143.

response to discomfort. As Dr. Robert Smith used to say to me, "We need to be God's best patient." Evelyn found a new way to look at her aches and pains.

Mike had no discernible loss that preceded his inexplicable sad mood. He had no particular behavior that made it come or go. And his response seemed to only complicate his life. Medication, CBT, and a host of other things had not measurably improved his situation. What could Scripture offer Mike, Fred, and Evelyn?

A Biblical Counseling Approach to Depression

The apostle Paul told us to "Rejoice with those who rejoice, and weep with those who weep" (Romans 12:15). Among the most important things biblical counselors can offer to those experiencing depression is a careful listening ear that is attuned to their suffering. And, yes, they suffer. We can take them to the Savior who invites them to "Come to Me, all who are weary and heavy-laden, and I will give you rest. Take My yoke upon you and learn from Me, for I am gentle and humble in heart, and you will find rest for your souls. For My yoke is easy and My burden is light" (Matthew 11:28–30).

In the process, we can help these individuals see the burden that weighs them down and exchange it for the lighter one of which our Savior spoke. There is a considerable difference between an office visit that ends with a prescription and the principles of Scripture that lead to change. As Paul said, "For whatever was written in earlier times was written for our instruction, so that through perseverance and the encouragement of the Scriptures we might have hope" (Romans 15:4). And hope was exactly the thing that Fred, Evelyn, and Mike were seeking.

Finding New Purpose by Abandoning Loss Recovery Mode

Fred, Evelyn, and Mike had one thing in common: they were all intent on feeling better. Of course, feeling better is not a bad goal on its own. However, when feeling better is our primary reason for living, it becomes a problem. I describe this state as being in "loss recovery mode," and for many it can be all-consuming.

Fred had lost many things, and he spent a great deal of time mourning his losses and plotting ways to get them back. Evelyn faced the same problem with her aches and pains that made life inconvenient and uncomfortable. She would love to feel as good as she had ten years earlier. Mike would like to find a way to avoid another episode of his dark mood. For all three, loss recovery drove their behavior.

The one thing that was missing in the care that they had received was a reason or a purpose that would move their focus from their goal of feeling better to something that would better occupy their time. Since all were Christians, the most important purpose I could suggest was found in 2 Corinthians 5:9. As Paul said, "Therefore we also have as our ambition, whether at home or absent, to be pleasing to Him."

I suggested that all three learn a sentence that I've taught counselees for a couple of decades that derives from the verse: "I want to glorify God with my life more than I want to breathe." Living this way requires the Christian to love God as Jesus said: "with all your heart, and with all your soul, and with all your mind. . . ." and "love your neighbor as yourself" (Matthew 22:37–39). The result of this love should drive the believer to obey God's Word and serve others (John 13; 14:21).

Fred could go through his long list of real losses and see that they had chained him to his sad mood. Evelyn could see how her discomfort had come to occupy most of her effort and attention. By default, her medical concerns had squeezed out time for setting her mind on Christ and serving others. And Mike's dark mood consumed all of his attention. The goal for all three was to turn their thinking away from their distressing circumstances to how they might serve and worship God in the middle of their circumstances. Glorifying God with their lives would give them purpose, no matter what their mood might be.

Understanding the Relationship Between Depression and Emotional Responses to Life

There are many ways to develop a sad mood in life, but two stand out: anger and worry. The psalmist describes the process well:

> Do not fret because of evildoers,
> Be not envious toward wrongdoers.
> For they will wither quickly like the grass
> And fade like the green herb.
> Trust in the LORD and do good;
> Dwell in the land and cultivate faithfulness.
> Delight yourself in the LORD;
> And He will give you the desires of your heart.
> Commit your way to the LORD,
> Trust also in Him, and He will do it.
> He will bring forth your righteousness as the light
> And your judgment as the noonday.
>
> Rest in the LORD and wait patiently for Him;
> Do not fret because of him who prospers in his way,
> Because of the man who carries out wicked schemes.
> Cease from anger and forsake wrath;
> Do not fret; it leads only to evildoing.
> For evildoers will be cut off,
> But those who wait for the LORD, they will inherit the land.
>   (Psalm 37:1–9)

Fret is a good old English word, which mostly means to worry in such a way that the worry consumes the worrier. The psalmist tells us that we should not worry about what others are doing, including how much better they seem to be doing than us or about how wickedly they behave. This kind of worry often leads to anger toward those who have what we want. The writer wisely admonishes us to cease from anger, wrath, and worrying as these thoughts lead to evildoing. Those who do evil, along with their evil deeds, will not last. Instead, we are to trust and delight in the Lord and commit our way to him as we faithfully live and work where he has planted us.

Scripture offers examples of those whose worry and anger resulted in a sad mood—Cain, Elijah, Ahab, and Jonah are just a few. Scripture also offers good solutions to both problems that are beyond the scope of this chapter. Fred struggled with both worry and anger throughout his year of discontent, as did Evelyn. They were helped by learning how to change their goal and deal with their anger/worry over their losses.

Mike was also dealing with anger and worry. He worried that his dark mood would return. At times he was angry that neither medicine nor therapy could offer an explanation or a cure. That anger and worry was poured out on those around him. Mike was helped considerably as he found purpose outside of fixing his mood.

Finding Hope

The major shift from loss recovery mode to a 2 Corinthians 5:9 view of life can be daunting for the believer, but there is real hope in the biblical approach to change. No Christian is ever called to reorder their lives on their own. Paul shared with the Philippians some of the most hopeful news for believers who need to make a change: "work out your salvation with fear and trembling; for it is God who is at work in you, both to will and to work for His good pleasure" (Philippians 2:12b–13).

We are not called to work "for" our salvation, but to work "out" our salvation. Indeed, the change that occurs in our lives on conversion means that "the old things passed away; behold, new things have come" (2 Corinthians 5:17). The hope is found when we realize that it is God working in us so that we want to do his will, and he is enabling us to do his good pleasure! Our Father is at work shaping our will, and then he empowers us to make whatever change he desires in our lives.

Abandoning loss recovery and living to glorify God ceases to be an insurmountable task. Instead, we discover what Paul meant when he said, "I can do all things through Him who strengthens me" (Philippians 4:13). Holding on to these truths gave hope to Fred, Evelyn, and Mike.

Choosing Gratitude

One important change that believers need to "work out" is how to find their way to thankfulness. Choosing gratitude changes our attitude and our emotional responses to life. An excellent book on this topic is Nancy Leigh DeMoss's *Choosing Gratitude: Your Journey to Joy*. It is helpful to those who are struggling to be thankful.[18]

From prison in Rome, Paul commanded the church at Ephesus to "be filled with the Spirit, speaking to one another in psalms and hymns and spiritual songs, singing and making melody with your heart to the Lord; always giving thanks for all things in the name of our Lord Jesus Christ to God, even the Father" (Ephesians 5:18b–20). If anyone had reason to complain about life, it was Paul. Instead, he tells us to do all things without murmuring and complaining (Philippians 2:14). Paul knew from experience that in difficulties, we face a choice no one can make for us. We can choose to worship our Lord in the middle of our struggles or we can complain. Choosing to worship God through gratitude will always leave us in a better mood.

Fred was faced with a choice. He could sink under the weight of his multiplied losses, or he could choose to see his adversity in the same way as Paul. Few of us would be critical of his sadness in light of the losses he had sustained, but at the same time, leaving him to wallow in his sadness would provide no help or hope.

Instead, I encouraged him to do what Paul did as he sat in prison. "But whatever things were gain to me, those things I have counted as loss for the sake of Christ. More than that, I count all things to be loss in view of the surpassing value of knowing Christ Jesus my Lord, for whom I have suffered the loss of all things, and count them but

---

18. Nancy Leigh DeMoss, *Choosing Gratitude: Your Journey to Joy* (Chicago: Moody Publishers, 2009), Kindle Edition.

rubbish so that I may gain Christ" (Philippians 3:7–8). Fred would benefit from putting a greater value on what he gained in Christ than on his losses.

Paul provided real insight when he said, "Be anxious for nothing, but in everything by prayer and supplication with thanksgiving let your requests be made known to God" (Philippians 4:6). Fred could, like Paul, ask for a solution to his problems, while thanking God for his care as he faced them. Evelyn and Mike would be helped by doing the same.

This does not mean that we should not mourn our losses. Any number of Psalms would say otherwise. In Psalm 13:1, the writer asks, "How long, O Lord?" How long will my suffering continue? God expects us to bring our suffering to him. But at some point each of us has the option to choose to thank God for what he does for us when we suffer. And when we choose gratitude, we will be better for it.

Returning to Service

Paul gives us another tool in his letter to the worried Philippians: "The things you have learned and received and heard and seen in me, practice these things" (Philippians 4:9a). While in prison and in the middle of suffering, Paul reminds the Philippians to remember how he lived among them and to do those things. I have taken this verse to mean that most of us who struggle with worry or sadness can benefit greatly from getting back to the normal routine of life, and in particular, getting back to serving others.

Fred, Evelyn, and Mike needed to get back to the normal things of life. As is often the case with those who struggle with their mood, they had neglected many things. They needed to return to their responsibilities in the home, at work, and at church. They also needed to resume the spiritual priorities of Bible reading, Bible study, and prayer. Social engagements and fellowship with friends, family, and the church needed to be resumed as well. At the same time, it is important for depressed people to return to these normal activities of daily living gradually.

In addition to resuming the normal activities, it is important for Christians to return to Christian service. All three of my patients were assigned to find someone worse off than they were and provide needed help. They could not be paid for the work, and it could not be for a relative. They had to do it for at least two hours a week. This forced them to take their eyes off their own problems, to look into the lives of others, and to serve them. They all benefited from doing these good deeds.

Persevering Over the Long Haul

All three of my patients found hope and help in counseling. Of the three, Fred seemed to make the quickest progress. As he made the adjustments in his heart attitude and his actions, his circumstances changed as well. As restrictions with the pandemic lifted, his job returned. His children returned to school, and he and his wife remembered what it was like to be married before the great pandemic. They resumed serving each other together in their respective biblical roles.

Evelyn took a bit longer to adjust her heart attitude and thinking so that she could put her health issues in biblical perspective. Her losses and suffering were real. Instead of being stuck in sadness, she began to count her present suffering as not worthy to be compared to the glory that is coming (Romans 8:18). As she disengaged her life from the pursuit of health, she found joy in living to glorify God with her every breath.

Mike faced a different situation, but the remedy was similar. While there wasn't a discernible reason for his sadness, his former way of responding caused him as much trouble as his sad mood. Instead of walling himself off from family, friends, and loved ones, Mike developed a biblically informed response and began to follow it. His new response pattern did not prevent his sad mood, but it did keep him from being trapped by it.

Words of Encouragement

For the counselee: Do you have someone to talk with if you have a persistent sad mood? Start with your pastor. Research tells us that those who seek counseling for their mood struggles will do much better than those who do not!

For the counselor: Good data gathering and listening may be the most important first thing you do to give hope and help to those who struggle with sadness and depression. As counselors helping those who have been given a diagnostic label of depression, we can then help the counselee understand the difference between normal sadness over loss and our societal definition of depression. There is biblical help for both.

CHAPTER 6

. . . .

LIFE-ALTERING ANXIETY:
MEDICAL BACKGROUND AND BIBLICAL COUNSELING APPROACH

Gordon "Chip" Phillips, MD

Do not be anxious about anything, but in everything by prayer
and supplication with thanksgiving let your requests be made known
to God. And the peace of God, which surpasses all understanding,
will guard your hearts and your minds in Christ Jesus.
(Philippians 4:6–7 ESV)

Jenna held one-year-old Michael in her arms and rocked, seemingly trying to comfort herself as much as the baby. All she wanted was a quiet, peaceful life, but that ship sailed a long time ago. She met Jake in high school, and they started dating. Not long after she became pregnant, and he moved into her parents' home. They married a few months later, before the baby was born.

While Jenna was pregnant, Jake started working as a ride-share driver. Everything seemed fine until he started going out with some new friends. After a few months, Jenna began to hear rumors that his friends were involved with drugs, but Jake denied any involvement in illegal activity. But whenever he left for work, she wondered, *What is Jake up to? Is he safe?*

She did her best to put those thoughts out of her mind, especially as her delivery neared. The nausea she felt at the beginning of her pregnancy returned, and she started to feel a burning sensation in her stomach at night. It helped to eat, drink some milk, and keep occupied with preparations for the new arrival. She looked forward to the joy a new baby would bring into her life.

However, as her delivery approached, she noted that Jake was staying out later. He paid less attention to her, and she feared he no longer found her attractive. She continually thought, *Is Jake out because he found someone else?* Her stomach would churn, and she quelled the feeling with more food. She began to worry not only about herself but also about the baby, thinking. *How will I pay the bills if Jack leaves me?*

For Jenna, the happiness of the birth of their little boy Michael was short-lived. As she held him and spent hours nursing and caring for him, her mind kept wandering to Jake and what he might be doing. Caring for Michael became a burden. She became irritable with her parents and fought with Jake. A number of times she became short of breath and felt her heart racing for no apparent reason. Once her mom called 911, but by the time the medics arrived, Jenna was back to normal and did not go to the hospital. She began to neglect the housecleaning and often forgot to help with meal preparation. Her mother picked up the slack, but she began to complain about Jenna's low functioning. Wondering if Jenna might be ill, her mother suggested she see a doctor.

Jenna went to her family physician, who ordered some screening tests. He noted that she was overweight but found nothing else wrong. When he asked about stresses in her life, she mentioned the possibility of Jake's leaving and doubts about how she would care for the new baby without him. "We can calm these reactions down with medications," said Jenna's physician. He suggested that she take some antianxiety pills, but she was reluctant to take medication while breastfeeding.

Jenna and her physician decided that she should see a psychologist. The therapist was personable, and Jenna liked her. Just having someone to talk to made her feel better. The therapist gave her helpful information about how to talk more effectively with Jake, how to calm herself down when she felt anxious, and how to adjust her bedtime habits so she could sleep better. What a relief!

However, Jake did not change, and Jenna's anxiety continued. The helpful suggestions from the therapist began to lose their effectiveness. Jenna again found herself up at night, staring at Michael and wondering, *What is happening to me? Why can't I get my life under control?*

One Saturday, Jenna heard a biblical counselor on the radio and listened as the speaker talked about anxiety. It resonated with her that what began as simple apprehension had grown to control her life. The problem went deeper than just her reactions to the situations she encountered. She decided to call and set up an appointment.

The Effects of Anxiety

Anxious people like Jenna are truly suffering and desperately seek relief. Studies on anxiety have shown it to be common and chronic.[1, 2] Our bodies have a normal mechanism to deal with emergencies and dangerous situations, often called a flight-or-fight response. Chemicals such as adrenaline and cortisol are released into the blood, the sympathetic nervous system is stimulated, and blood is diverted from maintenance areas to parts of the body needed to address a crisis. In the short-term, this increases alertness, strength, and the ability to react quickly. But with anxiety and chronic worry this reaction is continuously triggered, creating physical problems. Muscle stimulation can produce jitteriness, generalized aches, and

---

1. R. Lieb, E. Becker, and C. Altamura, "The Epidemiology of Generalized Anxiety Disorder in Europe," *Eur Neuropsychopharmacol*, no. 15 (2005): 445.

2. "Lifetime Prevalence and Age-of-Onset Distribution of DSM-IV Disorders in the National Comorbidity Survey Replication," *Arch Gen Psychiatry*, no. 51 (2005): 8.

tension headaches. Diversion of blood from the gut can produce "butterflies," nausea, stomachaches, and diarrhea. The heart and blood pressure system can present with chest pain, palpitations, and high blood pressure. Alterations of blood flow in the brain can even provoke dizziness, headaches, and feelings of doom or depression. Breathing can become more rapid as well. How are these physical reactions calmed?

Current medical care starts by determining whether treatment is needed. While some forms of anxiety can be helpful, such as with the heightened awareness that accompanies a firefighter as he anxiously enters a burning building, others have no apparent benefit, as when a parent waits up for a teen to return home from an evening out with friends. Deciding whether anxiety needs treatment is subjective and based upon feelings of distress in the individual and any associated difficulty in performing routine or necessary activities. The American Psychiatric Association has attempted to provide guidance for this determination in the *Diagnostic and Statistical Manual of Mental Disorders*. The outline that follows gives the requirements for an anxiety diagnosis:

Generalized Anxiety Disorder (GAD) as described in the DSM-5[3]

A. Excessive anxiety and worry (apprehensive expectation), occurring more days than not for at least six months, about a number of events or activities (such as work or school performance).

B. The individual finds it difficult to control the worry.

C. The anxiety and worry are associated with three (or more) of the following six symptoms (with at least some symptoms having been present for more days than not for the past six months):

Note: Only one item is required in children.

1. Restlessness or feeling keyed up or on edge
2. Being easily fatigued

---

3. *Diagnostic and Statistical Manual of Mental Disorders*, 5th ed. (Arlington, VA: American Psychiatric Association, 2013).

    3. Difficulty concentrating or mind going blank

    4. Irritability

    5. Muscle tension

    6. Sleep disturbance (difficulty falling or staying asleep, or restless, unsatisfying sleep)

D. The anxiety, worry, or physical symptoms cause clinically significant distress or impairment in social, occupational, or other important areas of functioning.

E. The disturbance is not attributable to the physiological effects of a substance (e.g., a drug of abuse, a medication) or another medical condition (e.g., hyperthyroidism).

F. The disturbance is not better explained by another mental disorder.

Secular Treatment Options

When a person is deemed to need an intervention, two general secular treatment modalities are recognized to be effective: cognitive behavioral therapy (CBT) and medication. Comparison studies have not shown one to be significantly better than the other, and the choice of modality is often based upon what is locally available and the patient's preference.[4] CBT aims to help an individual control their thinking, calm physical reactions, and modify behavioral responses to the anxiety-producing stimulus.

Medications focus on improving the person's sense of well-being by diminishing episodes of panic, improving sleep, and stabilizing emotional highs and lows. Below is an overview of typical medications that are currently being used to treat anxiety.

---

4. Pim Cuijpers et al., "The efficacy of psychotherapy and pharmacotherapy in treating depressive and anxiety disorders: a meta-analysis of direct comparisons," *World Psychiatry* 12, no. 2 (2103):137–148.

TABLE 1	Common Medications Used to Treat Anxiety[5]		
Class	**Subclass**	**Generic/Trade name**	**Common side effects**
Serotonin reuptake inhibitors (SRI)	Selective serotonin reuptake inhibitors (SSRI)	Paroxetine (Paxil) Sertraline (Zoloft) Citalopram (Celexa) Escitalopram (Lexapro) Fluoxetine (Prozac) Fluvoxamine (Luvox)	Sexual dysfunction, nausea/diarrhea, insomnia, withdrawal on discontinuation, weight gain, agitation/hyperactivation
	Serotonin-norepinephrine reuptake inhibitors (SNRI)	Venlafaxine (Effexor) Duloxetine (Cymbalta)	Nausea, dizziness, insomnia, sedation, constipation, sweating
Benzodiazepines		Lorazepam (Ativan) Diazepam (Valium) Temazepam (Resporil) Triazolam (Halcion) Clonazepam (Klonopin)	High potential for abuse, quicker action, impaired coordination, amnesia, rebound anxiety after short-term therapy
Azapirones		Buspirone (Buspar)	Insomnia, agitation, nausea
Pregabalin		Pregabalin (Lyrica)	Sedation, dizziness
Tricyclic Antidepressant (TCA)		Imipramine (Tofranil) Amitriptyline (Elavil)	Dry mouth, blurry vision, urinary retention, constipation, agitation
Antipsychotics		Quetiapine (Seroquel)	Sedation, extrapyramidal symptoms, tardive dyskinesia
Antihistamine	H1 antagonist	Hydroxyzine (Atarax)	Sedation

While some medications, such as the benzodiazepines, are immediately effective and preferred in crisis situations, they have a higher potential for abuse and are prone to rebound anxiety when discontinued. The serotonergic reuptake inhibitors (SRIs) are generally preferred for long-term treatment, which typically lasts six to twelve months or longer. Unfortunately, these medications require four to six weeks of treatment before the person will notice a clinical difference.

5. Adapted from Alexander Bystritsky, "Pharmacotherapy for generalized anxiety disorder in adults," UTD Pharmacotherapy, November 2020, www.uptodate.com/contents/pharmacoltherapy-for-generalized-anxiety-disorder-in-adults (physician access only).

A Biblical Approach to Treating Anxiety

The distress from anxiety is profound and like the secular therapist, the biblical counselor desires to relieve suffering. However, the approach is fundamentally different. While therapists generally view themselves as well people who are helping ill individuals, biblical counselors come alongside the anxious individual as fellow sufferers. The counselor functions as a tool that the Holy Spirit uses to help counselees understand and apply biblical truth to their lives so that the anxious sufferer can find comfort in Christ.

Related to this distinction is the fact that although secular counselors may personally hold a theistic worldview, their approach to the client is naturalistic. They limit their focus to the physical and thus miss essential aspects for a holistic treatment of anxiety. Following the emphasis of their particular training, they aim to lessen the manifestations of anxiety. The Scriptures, however, teach that every person is a union of physical and spiritual parts, a material/immaterial union created in God's likeness (Genesis 1:27; 1 Thessalonians 5:23). For this reason, all counselees with anxiety should be referred to a physician to verify there is not a physical illness responsible for the person's symptoms. The biblical counselor focuses on the heart, where the primary cause of anxiety normally resides.

All anxiety has a significant spiritual component. People's relationship with God impacts their reactions to life's challenges. They question what should or should not occur and express doubts about why something was "allowed to occur." The Scriptures teach us that worry or anxiety is a common problem. When Peter became afraid for his safety, Jesus calmed him by saying, "Take heart; it is I. Do not be afraid" (Matthew 14:27 ESV). Jesus addressed Peter's heart, directing him to trust God in faith.

The biblical counselor can share with anxious people how the Bible defines anxiety and guide them to resolve anxiety at its root by turning to the Lord, asking him for help, and learning to apply biblical truth through the power of the indwelling Holy Spirit. At the heart of the struggle will be the issue of worship.[6] What we worship determines what we love most and what our goals in life will be. Jenna's goal was tightly focused on Jake's becoming the kind of husband she hoped to have. Because Jake was not cooperating with that goal she was constantly worried and anxious. She needed to be reminded that God is sovereign, good, and active in the lives of his children.

To help Jenna, a significant change would have to occur in the realms of motive, goal, and worship. Instead of making changes in Jake's behavior her main concern, Jenna would need to make glorifying God with her life her primary goal. In order to do that, she would need to love God with all her heart, soul, and mind and then love others (Matthew 22:37–39). Her love for God would need to be demonstrated by living according to His commands (John 14:21). This would have to be the starting point for meaningful change in her anxiety. How could this happen for Jenna? She needed a wise biblical counselor to point her to Jesus and his love, care, forgiveness, and help.

Biblical Solutions for Jenna

Shortly after Jenna called the church, she was scheduled to meet with Cathy, a lady who had specific training to use the Bible to help people who suffer with problems like anxiety. In their first session, Cathy listened intently and asked many questions, reassuring Jenna when she was reluctant to share personal details and explaining that she didn't want to give an answer before hearing the details, as Proverbs 18:13 says, "If one gives an answer before he hears, it is his folly and shame" (ESV). Jenna could understand that, and Cathy's gentle spirit helped her to open up and share.

---

6. Greg Gifford has a helpful presentation of how the heart and worship affect our motivations in *Heart and Habits: How We Change for Good* (The Woodlands, Texas: Kress Biblical Resources, 2021), 30–37.

Cathy explained that the Bible talks about anxiety in both positive and negative terms. Paul states that a married person may be anxious to please a spouse (1 Corinthians 7:33) and that he himself was anxious to visit Timothy (2 Timothy 1:4), indicating good, expectant desires. Jesus addressed a different type of anxiety when he said, "Therefore do not be anxious about tomorrow, for tomorrow will be anxious for itself. Sufficient for the day is its own trouble" (Matthew 6:34 ESV). Although it is a common human response to living in a world where things can and do go wrong, this kind of anxiety is harmful and destructive and robs the anxious person of the abundant life Jesus came to give (John 10:10). During their initial session, Cathy also inquired about common physical responses to anxiety and was encouraged to learn that Jenna had already seen her physician to rule out medical conditions such as thyroid or parathyroid dysfunction, heart arrhythmias, adrenal or endocrine tumors, a blood pressure crisis, or early menopause that might mimic the physical symptoms of anxiety.

As counseling progressed, Jenna began to learn that God cared for her and desired her to have a fulfilling life. Anxiety is one of many ways that people suffer because they try to live life separated from the Creator who cares about them (Isaiah 59:2; Ephesians 2:12). Cathy explained that, by nature, everyone desires to make their own decisions and live independently of God (Isaiah 53:6; Ephesians 2:3). Yet God loves the world and desires that we be reconciled to him through repentance from sin and belief in Christ's death and resurrection (John 3:16–17, 36; Romans 5:8; 6:23; 10:9–10). Those who recognize him as Lord become his children, but the Bible also states that God will judge those who don't turn to him in faith (John 1:12; 3:36).

Cathy showed Jenna how God uses the problems that bring us anxiety to show us the true nature of our hearts (Deuteronomy 8:2–5; Mark 7:20–23). Jenna considered her thoughts and actions as she had become more and more anxious, and realized that she had hurt others, become angry with God, and mainly focused on what she thought would be best for her. She became convicted of her sinful heart attitude and prayed, asking God to forgive her and show her how to live a life that would please him. Cathy next showed Jenna that as God's child, she was empowered by the Holy Spirit to please God and do everything that his Word called her to do. Now Jenna was ready to hear how the Scriptures could give her victory over anxiety.

Understanding How the Bible Describes Anxiety

To help Jenna understand anxiety, Cathy asked her to read Jesus's teaching on anxiety in Matthew 6:25–34. Together they identified eight truths about anxiety:

1. Anxious fear always has an object. The anxious person is worried about specific problems, such as being able to pay a bill, remain safe, have adequate housing, and so on (v. 25).

2. The anxious person does not consider God's love and care ("are you not more valuable than they?") and how it might apply to their situation (vv. 26–27).

3. God knows and cares about the same things the person is worried about (v. 30).

4. Anxiety can focus on a possible, future event (worry) or a current, present problem (fear) (v. 27).

5. Believers who worry are living as unbelievers who do not have a Father who loves them and cares for them in their lives (v. 32).

6. The believer is precious to God, and he promises to care for his needs (v. 33).

7. God desires that we focus on what we do today, not what may occur in the future (v. 34).

8. God desires that every day we focus on him, his power, his kingdom, and his care for his children (v. 33).

Together, Cathy and Jenna contemplated Jenna's situation considering these truths. Jenna's anxiety focused on Jake's possible illegal activities and the possibility of Jake's leaving and how that might hurt her and her baby. She had been distraught at her inability to "fix" Jake and thought constantly about what he might be doing and the harm it could bring. She certainly had not considered God's role in the matter. But as she read Jesus's words, she began to see that God was involved and interested in her life. He used her anxiety to show her a selfish side to her thinking that she had not appreciated. She found it comforting to think of God as a loving father who was caring for her. But did this really change anything?

Jenna noted, "Cathy, it is comforting to think about God's taking care of me, but I don't see how this really helps. What if Jake leaves me? Michael and I would still be destitute."

Focusing Believers' Thoughts

"Yes, your *circumstances* have not changed," said Cathy, "but consider how your *situation* has changed since becoming a child of God. Understanding that is the first step to getting past your anxiety." Cathy realized that Jenna needed to understand her new relationship with God before she could fully address her anxiety. Cathy had Jenna read 2 Corinthians 5:17. There Jenna learned that she had become a new creation in Christ. Not only had her relationship with God changed, but she became spiritually alive and the Holy Spirit began to empower her to live for and with God as her Father, which is the gateway to an abundant and peaceful life (John 10:10; 14:27).

Cathy suggested that when we are anxious we focus our thoughts on problems or threats that *might* occur in the future. When we ignore God, there is no underlying significance to life's events, and the best we can hope for in treatment is to learn to control our reactions to life's unpredictable circumstances. The Scriptures paint a totally different picture. God is active in human history and in every person's individual life (Proverbs 21:1; Romans 8:28–30). Cathy continued, "The Scriptures can give you hope because you now have concrete reasons upon which to base a life filled with joy and contentment rather than anxiety and fear" (Romans 15:4).

Jenna appeared skeptical and asked, "Isn't this just the power of positive thinking? The therapist who helped me before taught me techniques to help me feel better. But it didn't last." Cathy replied, "I can see why you might think that, but the truth is that God has a plan for your life." Cathy explained that a believer who is anxious has lost sight of the fact that God is both sovereign and good. Jenna remembered Jesus's teaching that God already knows our needs and has promised to take care of them (Matthew 6:25–34). He is a loving Father who only gives good gifts to his children (Luke 11:11–13; James 1:17). Most anxious individuals do not say they doubt God's goodness or his ability to care for them, but their anxiety points to the truth that they do not trust God or believe he is in control. Cathy went on to teach Jenna that this was the first of four common themes in the life of an anxious person. These themes are

1. A low view of God's sovereignty and goodness.
2. A misconception of God's plan for the believer's life.
3. A lack of biblical love in the sufferer's life.
4. An inadequate control of one's thinking.

Jenna learned about God's plan for her life in Romans 8:28–29, "And we know that for those who love God all things work together for good, for those who are called according to his purpose. For those whom he foreknew he also predestined to be conformed to the image of his Son, in order that he might be the firstborn among many brothers" (ESV). Cathy explained that not all things that happen to us are good, but God uses all things—even our problems—for the believer's good. Then Cathy asked, "What do these verses say is God's plan for you as a believer?" Jenna noted that God wanted her to become like Jesus.

Jenna's overwhelming desire had been for protection and feeling secure, but God's plan had been to use her vulnerable situation to help her become like Jesus. She began to understand that while her focus had been on avoiding a painful or threatening situation, God desired to use these very circumstances to help her to grow in Christlikeness (Romans 5:3–5; James 1:2–4). Cathy noted that this is the way God dealt with the nation of Israel as they worried about food and water during their forty years of desert wanderings (Deuteronomy 8:2–9).

After Jenna understood how God was working in her life for her good and his glory, Cathy began to teach her about the importance of biblical love in dealing with anxiety and fear. They looked at 1 John 4:18: "There is no fear in love, but perfect love casts out fear" (ESV). As they studied the context of these verses, Jenna observed that fear in this passage is fear of punishment. Her new loving relationship with the Father has removed any fear of punishment because Jesus was punished on her behalf (1 Peter 3:18).

Cathy went on to note that the incompatibility of love and fear is broader than just a fear of punishment. Another far-reaching aspect involves the application of love in the life of the anxious sufferer. Since fear and love are incompatible, they cannot coexist. So as Jenna learned to love, her worry and fear would abate.

Cathy explained that when we are anxious, we concentrate all our energies and thoughts on ourselves and our circumstances. But God desires that every believer be an agent of his love and care for others just as he promises to do for us (2 Corinthians 1:4; 5:14–15). Jenna began to appreciate that when her life was characterized by fear and anxiety, this was rooted in her desires and thoughts, not in her external circumstances. When Jenna concentrated her thoughts and energy on her desire for security, she became more and more self-centered. Her passion for security seduced her to believe she could find peace by controlling the future through micromanaging the circumstances of her life and Jake's. She thought she could avoid harm by being alert enough, supportive enough, protective enough or good enough. However, her constant focus on herself and her actions overshadowed thinking about the needs of others. Subsequently, her close relationships became strained. To help Jenna understand how love and fear/anxiety were incompatible, Cathy showed her several biblical passages and together they made the following chart.

TABLE 2	Love–Fear Dynamic	
Love	**Fear–Anxiety**	**Text**
Focuses on others -I care about you	Focuses on self -I care about me	Philippians 2:3–4
Serves others	Protects oneself	Ephesians 4:28
Reaches out to others	Isolates oneself	Galatians 6:1–3 Proverbs 18:1
Forgives, covers other's faults	Hypocritical, hides one's faults	Psalm 32:1–5 Psalm 103:1–14 Colossians 3:13
Compassionate, merciful	Unkind, critical	Psalm 51:1–19; 71:4–6 Proverbs 12:10
Learn from God as we ask him for help	The result of Adam and Eve listening to Satan instead of God	Genesis 3:1–6 John 3:16 Romans 5:8
Jesus's example as the new Adam	Natural inclination as an old Adam	1 John 4:7–12
Consequence of restoration/grace	Consequence of sin	1 John 4:17–21 Hebrews 2:12–14
Grateful	Angry/ feels deprived	Hebrews 12:28
Content	Grumbling	1 Timothy 6:4–8
Merciful, humble attitude	Condemning, proud attitude	Romans 8:1 Luke 18:9–14
God's protection is sufficient	My protection is inadequate	Psalm 91:4–6 Matthew 6:27–32 1 Corinthians 10:13

Retraining Believers' Thinking

Jenna needs to address her anxious thoughts in order to learn how to turn to God in her anxiety. A common theme for anxious individuals is a tendency to allow their thoughts to run away with them. The Scripture teaches that believers are to grow in controlling their thoughts because their spiritual battle is in their mind (2 Corinthians 10:4–5). Paul instructs believers to train their minds not to drift toward worrisome, unwholesome thoughts, but instead, to focus on thoughts that are true, pure, lovely, and excellent (Philippians 4:8–10).

Consider trusting God

To help Jenna grow in her ability to gain victory over anxiety, Cathy directed her to Philippians 4:1–10, where Paul presents several truths that can help believers avoid worry and have the peace of God in their lives. First, Jenna noted that Paul directs Euodia and Syntyche to "agree in the Lord" (4:2 ESV). He uses a similar Greek expression in Philippians 2:5 where he encourages believers to "have the same attitude" that Christ had. Although fully God, Jesus humbled himself like a human servant and willingly obeyed the Father even though this led to suffering and death (2:6–11). Like Jesus, Jenna needed to learn humble reliance on a loving Father as an initial step in overcoming her anxiety, even when life "goes bad."

Consider rejoicing

Next, Paul calls the Philippians to rejoice always (4:4). Jenna felt that her circumstances had robbed her of joy, but she was not a hapless victim of her circumstances. She had a loving heavenly Father who was always with her and who used every circumstance to help her become more like Christ in attitude and action. God is by nature full of joy and blessing (1 Timothy 1:11). When anxious people recognize God's goodness, they become grateful and joyful even though they face difficult situations where the outcome is unsure. Thus, rejoicing is a reflection of contentment and confidence in God's faithfulness and providence. MacArthur notes that contentment is the result of learning that God is sovereign in both his supernatural acts as well as the common events of our lives.[7]

Consider praying

Paul goes on to encourage the Philippians to replace worry and anxiety with praying—with going to their loving heavenly Father and pouring out all their troubles. The key that unlocks the door to a peaceful heart is prayer (4:5–7). It's important to help anxious people

---

7. John MacArthur, *Anxiety Attacked*, MacArthur Study Series (Wheaton, IL: Victor Books, 1993), 112.

turn to God in faith with all of their troubles and encourage them to trust him. Cathy showed Jenna that many psalms reflect this truth. The following are some examples:

- Psalm 3:4–6—"I cried aloud to the LORD, and he answered me from his holy hill. I lay down and slept; I woke again; for the LORD sustained me. I will not be afraid of many thousands of people who have set themselves against me all around" (ESV).
- Psalm 34:4—"I sought the LORD, and he answered me and delivered me from all my fears" (ESV).
- Psalm 118:5–6—"Out of my distress I called on the LORD; the LORD answered me and set me free. The LORD is on my side; I will not fear; What can man do to me?" (ESV).

Cathy encouraged Jenna to openly express her concerns and fears to God. Rather than viewing God as subject to her every whim and demand, Jenna needed to see God as her loving Father who was in control and was looking out for her best interests. Even when she faced seemingly impossible situations, she could follow Jesus's example of seeking the Father's guidance and resting in the assurance that his good plan was in motion (Matthew 26:36–46). His love allowed her to pray with anticipation of the good that he was doing in her and through her.

Consider redirecting

Paul instructs the Philippians to fill their minds with godly thoughts and their lives with godly actions (4:8–9). A fundamental aspect of biblical counseling is helping the counselee replace old manners of living with godly ones (Ephesians 4:22–24). Since anxiety grows when we concentrate our thinking on perceived injustices, worry about things that may not be true, consider the worst motivations for others' behaviors, or anticipate how others could cause us harm, Jenna would need to do the hard work of retraining her thinking.

Cathy helped Jenna make a list of specific fears and next to each one they noted one or two verses with biblical promises for Jenna to memorize. When she was tempted to worry about something she would pray, thank God for his active care of her life, and recite the verse. Jenna related to Cathy that at first this was tedious and tiring, but soon, her thinking began to shift. Initially, her fears over finances were almost nonstop. She must have quoted Philippians 4:19 (NIV)— "And my God will meet all your needs according to the riches of his glory in Christ Jesus"—thirty times a day. But then she began to notice that the verse would come to mind before she felt anxious, and it started to serve as a hedge against anxiety.

Cathy also mentioned that growth in Christlikeness is like taking a bath in running water (Ephesians 5:26). The Holy Spirit uses the Word to renew our minds, direct and teach us (Colossians 3:15–17; 2 Timothy 3:16). Jenna began to read through the Psalms and write down each time the psalmist expressed worry or fear and identify how he came to appreciate and trust in the promise of God's presence and protection. She also started an anxiety journal and cataloged the places and situations where she struggled most with anxiety. In addition, they considered places of serenity where Jenna could go and meditate on God's goodness. She began to look forward to a daily walk with Michael around the lake in a nearby township park. Together they made a plan for how Jenna could approach anxiety-provoking situations with a heart already prepared to be thankful and trusting in God.

Jenna's improvement was not automatic, nor quick. Cathy needed to remind her that although God promised her victory against anxiety, she needed to persevere and work each day to follow Christ in her thinking and actions (Luke 9:23; 2 Corinthians 10:4–6). Cathy stressed the need for Jenna to persist even when she did not feel motivated because—opposite of what many expect—a peaceful life free from anxiety is the result of godly thinking and actions, not the motivation for them (John 13:17).

Final Words to the Counselor

Remember that the counselee's initial focus will be on symptom relief. Do not be distracted by this and give into the temptation to pursue a secular approach that focuses on helping the counselee to simply feel or function better. Have the counselee seek a medical evaluation to verify there are no physical causes for the anxiety, and then focus on the heart.

While not losing sight of the benefits of a sense of emotional well-being and a productive, functional life, the biblical counselor must focus on addressing the underlying cause of anxiety. This is addressed by helping counselees examine their hearts' desires and worship. The stress of an anxiety-provoking situation is designed by God to show what their hearts love and where they put their trust. Remind your counselees that God is with them and cares greatly for them.

TABLE 3	Passages for Counseling the Anxious Person
Verse	**Approach**
Genesis 3:10 Proverbs 18:1	Hiding and isolation are common but going to the Lord and others will bring hope and help.
Proverbs 10:24	Self-fulfilling nature of anxiety. It tends to grow.
Joshua 1:9 Proverbs 29:25 Philippians 2:12–13	Anxiety from the fear of man is a trap that is countered by the fear of God (trusting in his sovereignty and goodness).
Isaiah 41:8–13; 43:5	"Fear not" for God is present with his children and he cares for them.
Matthew 6:25–34	Jesus's teaching about anxiety, God's sovereignty, and trusting God.
Matthew 10:26–31 Matthew 13:13–14 John 16:21 2 Corinthians 5:10	Focus should be on eternal, not temporal consequences. Pain and suffering now can have greater eternal rewards. Anxiety focuses on avoiding pain now, God focuses on growth.
2 Corinthians 5:14–15	Christ's love motivates the believer to love others, not self.
2 Timothy 1:7	God has given us his Spirit of power, love, and self-control, not fear.
Hebrews 2:14–15	Although fragile flesh and blood, we are not slaves to fear.
1 Peter 3:6, 13–14	God desires godly lives, not ones motived by fear and self-centeredness.
1 John 4:16–18	Love is the antidote for fear.

CHAPTER 7

ADHD:

Essential Medical Background and Biblical Counseling Guidelines

Pamela Gannon, RN

It was a typical Sunday morning. As soon as the Pastor said, "Amen," wiggly little four-year-old Tommy jumped out of the pew, ran down the church aisle toward the front, and began climbing the platform. He jumped off and then ran back, as his mom Louise ineffectually called to him, "Don't run in church!" He began climbing over the back of each pew, teetering on the edge and then jumping to the next. His exasperated mother grabbed him midair, and the family departed.

Tommy had always been an active child. His dad, Ralph, loved his son's energy and didn't see it as problematic, but stay-at-home mom Louise was becoming overwhelmed as the little guy zoomed about the house, seemingly oblivious to her instructions. She was relieved when Tommy started pre-Kindergarten at age five.

That relief was short-lived, however. Tommy's teacher soon reported behavioral problems; if Tommy was told to do something that required focus and concentration, he would run around the room and climb on the tables. He consistently disregarded instructions to sit and play quietly. Ralph and Louise bought some parenting books to learn skills to help Tommy with school, and they did make some progress. But by the end of first grade, Tommy was struggling with reading, despite testing that showed excellent aptitude. He complained that he couldn't listen because of all the noises in the classroom.

As the years progressed, Tommy's behavior became more reckless and disruptive. His constant talking and interrupting was exhausting to his family. In school, he would interrupt his teacher to spout forth his own opinions on unrelated topics. One friend commented that Tommy was "always talking and he thinks he knows everything." Tommy's demeanor was impulsive; even a simple walk to the store brought chaos as Tommy climbed on every tree, rock, or snow pile. He didn't seem to comprehend the effect he had on others, and he often blurted out unkind things toward his siblings. Ralph believed that Louise's inconsistent discipline was the problem, but she argued that Tommy hated being in trouble all the time—he was often grounded and barred from his favorite activities. Besides, she was weary from the rigors of parenting this difficult child.

At school, Tommy had a hard time keeping quiet in class. He struggled to get his work done. He would squirm at his desk for an hour and only finish two math problems. Yet his inability to concentrate was not universally poor; at home, he was a Nintendo champion and he could play for long periods of time. Gaming was exciting and fast-paced while math was not.

Tommy was halfway through the third grade when his teacher asked to meet with his parents. She shared that his failure to complete class assignments and his messy homework was being reflected in poor grades. Tommy's teacher suggested that he be evaluated by his pediatrician.

After the findings of a thorough physical examination came back as normal, the doctor suggested a possible diagnosis of attention deficit hyperactivity disorder (ADHD). She handed Tommy's parents a pamphlet that delineated ADHD diagnostic criteria. As they paged through the literature that described inattention and hyperactivity, Ralph and Louise both agreed: "Yeah, that's our child. This describes Tommy perfectly!"

The pediatrician also suggested that Tommy could be treated with stimulant medication. She explained that stimulants such as Ritalin or Adderall have a paradoxical effect on people diagnosed with ADHD—instead of increasing energy, they have a calming effect.

Ralph, who had also struggled in school and frequently been in trouble as a youngster, was reluctant to consider medications. But Louise was anxious to do anything that might help. They compromised and agreed to try biblical counseling through the church's counseling ministry before making the medication decision.

Many of us can relate to Ralph and Louise. When homeschooling our two boys, I would often read to them while they ran around the living room doing cartwheels and summersaults. Yet when I tested them on the material, they could accurately explain the concepts. Some children *are* different; they have difficulties with inattention and hyperactivity to a significantly greater degree than other kids their age. They learn differently than others. For these kids, allowing some sort of movement can often help them to focus and concentrate.[1] Unfortunately, today's typical school classroom can be agonizing to them. It is not to their advantage to require complete cessation of movement.

What Is ADHD?

ADHD is one of the syndromes described in the *Diagnostic and Statistical Manual of Mental Disorders* (DSM). In the DSM-5, it is described as a neuro-developmental disorder with a persistent behavioral pattern of severe inattention and/or hyperactivity/impulsivity.[2] The behaviors must be uncharacteristic for the developmental age of the child, be manifest in different settings (for example at home and at school), have started before age twelve, be present for at least

---

1. T. A. Hartanto et al., "A Trial-by-Trial Analysis Reveals More Intense Physical Activity Is Associated with Better Cognitive Control Performance in Attention-Deficit/Hyperactivity Disorder," *Child Neuropsychology* 22, no. 5 (2016): 618–626, https://doi.org/10.1080/09 297049.2015.1044511.

2. American Psychiatric Association, "Diagnostic Criteria (ADHD)."

six months, and interfere with social and academic performance.[3] Severity is rated as mild, moderate, or severe.

The diagnosis requires a persistent pattern of inattention and/or hyperactivity–impulsivity that interferes with functioning or development.

1. Inattention: Six (or more) of the following symptoms have persisted for at least six months to a degree that is inconsistent with developmental level and that negatively impacts social and academic/occupational activities.

- a. Often fails to give close attention to details or makes careless mistakes in schoolwork, at work, or during other activities (overlooks or misses details, work is inaccurate).
- b. Often has difficulty sustaining attention in tasks or play activities (difficulty remaining focused during lectures, conversations, or lengthy reading).
- c. Often does not seem to listen when spoken to directly (mind seems elsewhere).
- d. Often does not follow through on instructions and fails to finish schoolwork, chores, or duties in the workplace (starts tasks but quickly loses focus and is easily sidetracked).
- e. Often has difficulty organizing tasks and activities (difficulty managing sequential tasks; difficulty keeping materials and belongings in order; messy, disorganized work; poor time management; fails to meet deadlines).
- f. Often avoids, dislikes, or is reluctant to engage in tasks that require sustained mental effort (schoolwork or homework).
- g. Often loses things necessary for tasks or activities (school materials, pencils, books, tools, wallets, keys, paperwork, eyeglasses, mobile telephones).
- h. Is often easily distracted by extraneous stimuli.
- i. Is often forgetful in daily activities (doing chores, running errands).

---

3. Sanne te Meerman et al., "ADHD: A Critical Update for Educational Professionals," *International Journal of Qualitative Studies on Health and Well-Being* 12, no. 1 (2017), https://doi.org/10.1080/17482631.2017.1298267.

2. Hyperactivity and impulsivity:

a. Often fidgets with or taps hands or feet or squirms in seat.

b. Often leaves seat in situations when remaining seated is expected (in the classroom).

c. Often runs about or climbs in situations where it is inappropriate.

d. Often unable to play or engage in leisure activities quietly.

e. Is often "on the go," acting as if "driven by a motor" (uncomfortable being still for extended time; restless or difficult to keep up with).

f. Often talks excessively.

g. Often blurts out an answer before a question has been completed (completes people's sentences; cannot wait for turn in conversation).

h. Often has difficulty waiting his or her turn (while waiting in line).

i. Often interrupts or intrudes on others (butts into conversations, games, or activities; using people's things without asking permission).[4]

Attention deficit disorder (ADD) and ADHD were once considered different disorders. If a child showed inattention, they were diagnosed with ADD. If they showed hyperactivity or impulsivity, they were labeled ADHD. Now they are considered different variations of the same disorder (ADHD), falling into one of three categories:

- Predominantly inattentive—This was formerly known as ADD. A child mostly displays signs of inattention, but isn't hyperactive or impulsive.

- Predominantly hyperactive-impulsive—A child can focus and pay attention, but shows mostly signs of hyperactivity and impulsivity.

---

4. American Psychiatric Association, "Diagnostic Criteria Attention-Deficit/Hyperactivity Disorder (ADHD) 314.0X (F90.X)," in *Diagnostic and Statistical Manual of Mental Disorders*, 5th ed. (Washington, DC: APA, 2013).

- Combined—Most children with ADHD have symptoms from both sides of the disorder.

As you can see from the behavioral patterns listed, no particular cause for these behaviors is implied. The diagnosis describes what a child is doing, but not why they are doing it.

The estimated number of children diagnosed with ADHD, according to a national 2016 parent survey, is 6.1 million (9.4 percent of all children).[5] This number has increased dramatically since 1994, when it stood at 3 percent.[6] In approximately 80 percent of children given the diagnosis of ADHD, symptoms persist into adolescence and may even continue into adulthood.[7] Adults can also be diagnosed with ADHD if their behavior meets similar criteria, that is, they exhibit five or more symptoms of inattention and /or hyperactivity/impulsivity that have persisted for six months or longer, they had symptoms before the age of twelve, they have symptoms in more than two settings, and their symptoms clearly interfere with social, academic, or occupational functioning.[8]

This chapter will focus on ADHD in children because they are being more frequently diagnosed. Biblical counselors are more likely to see children and their parents coming for counseling to help with the ADHD diagnosis.

Diagnosis

Teachers and other school personnel are often the first to suggest the diagnosis of ADHD in a child, as in Tommy's situation. ADHD can be diagnosed by a psychiatrist, psychologist, pediatrician, family

---

5. Melissa L. Danielson et al., "Prevalence of Parent-Reported ADHD Diagnosis and Associated Treatment Among U.S. Children and Adolescents," *Journal of Clinical Child and Adolescent Psychology* 47, no. 2 (2018): 199–212, https://doi.org/10.1080/15374416.2017.1417860.

6. te Meerman et al., "ADHD: A Critical Update for Educational Professionals."

7. Stephen V. Faraone et al., "The Worldwide Prevalence of ADHD: Is It an American Condition?," *World Psychiatry* 2, no. 2 (2003): 104–113.

8. American Psychiatric Assoc. Attention-deficit and disruptive behavior disorders. In *Diagnostic and Statistical Manual of Mental Disorders*, 5th ed. (Arlington, VA: American Psychiatric Association, 2013).

doctor, nurse practitioner, neurologist, master's-level counselor, social worker, or even by parents themselves. Relative age compared to peers seems to be a significant factor in ADHD diagnosis. In other words, "the youngest children in class are twice as likely as their classmates to receive a diagnosis of ADHD and be medicated for it. Apparently, health care professionals and teachers tend to classify relative immaturity as ADHD."[9]

Other problems, such as anxiety and depression, are commonly diagnosed along with ADHD. These must be ruled out as the cause of the child's behavior. In addition, undetected physical problems such as seizures, middle ear infection causing diminished hearing, other hearing or vision problems, and learning disabilities need to be ruled out.

Medical Perspective on Cause

In extensive medical research, no measurable biological markers have been discovered, and no objective tests have been established to detect the presence or absence of ADHD. The diagnosis is made based on subjective assessment of behaviors.

Since these behavioral symptoms tend to run in families, it was thought that there was genetic influence; however, in genetic association studies, genes show very small effects.[10] High-resolution magnetic resonance imaging (MRI) and computed tomography (CAT) scan brain studies are also inconclusive, not revealing any innate brain defect. Case-control studies, which compare groups of children with and without a diagnosis of ADHD, show insignificant differences in terms of brain anatomy.[11]

---

9. Te Meerman et al., "ADHD: A Critical Update for Educational Professionals."

10. Anthony Dillon and Rhonda G. Craven, "Examining the Genetic Contribution to ADHD," *Ethical Human Psychology and Psychiatry* 16, no. 1 (2014): 20–28, https://doi.org/10.1891/1559-4343.16.1.20.

11. Elizabeth R. Sowell et al., "Cortical Abnormalities in Children and Adolescents with Attention-Deficit Hyperactivity Disorder," *Lancet* 362, no. 9397 (2003): 1699–1707, https://doi.org/10.1016/S0140-6736(03)14842-8.

Studies have shown various factors associated with higher rates of ADHD. They range from divorce, poverty, parenting styles, low maternal education, lone parenthood, reception of social welfare, sexual abuse, lack of sleep, heritability, perinatal issues, eczema, artificial food additives, and growing up in areas with minimal sunlight. All these factors may influence a particular child who shows inattention or hyperactive/impulsive behaviors. However, none of these factors were found to be a determinative cause.[12]

Secular Treatment

Treatment generally includes medications and therapy, such as behavior management therapy. There is general consensus in the secular psychiatric/psychological community that ADHD is both overdiagnosed and overmedicated.[13] Over half of children given the diagnosis of ADHD are treated with stimulant drugs such as Ritalin or amphetamines (including Adderall), among other medications. It is unknown how a stimulant medication has the paradoxical effect of calming a high energy, distractible child. Medication is used pragmatically; that is, it is prescribed because it alleviates symptoms, not because it treats a known physical problem. The benefit of these medications is short-lived; in follow-up studies at three years and eight years, no significant benefit could be seen when comparing medicated and unmedicated children.[14] Children taking these medications often experience side effects such as trouble sleeping, decreased appetite (which may hinder growth), and irritability. The following table lists some of the more common medications used for ADHD. It is helpful to be aware that

---

12. Te Meerman et al., "ADHD: A Critical Update for Educational Professionals."

13. Christopher Lane, "ADHD Is Now Widely Overdiagnosed and for Multiple Reasons," *Psychology Today*, blog, October 20, 2017, https://www.psychologytoday.com/us/blog/side-effects/201710/adhd-is-now-widely-overdiagnosed-and-multiple-reasons.

14. Brooke S. G. Molina et al., "The MTA at 8 Years: Prospective Follow-Up of Children Treated for Combined-Type ADHD in a Multisite Study," *Journal of the American Academy of Child and Adolescent Psychiatry* 48, no. 5 (2009): 484–500, https://doi.org/10.1097/CHI.0b013e31819c23d0.

if your counselee is taking any of these, the side effects may influence their behaviors. If the side effects are troublesome, encourage the parents to inform the prescribing physician.

ADHD Stimulant Medication List

Stimulant medications are used to treat moderate and severe ADHD. Some stimulants are approved for use in children over age three. Side effects include loss of appetite, weight loss, sleep problems, crankiness, and tics. The Food and Drug Administration (FDA) warns about the risk of drug abuse with amphetamine stimulants. FDA safety advisers are concerned that all amphetamine and methylphenidate stimulants may make heart and psychiatric problems more likely.

Drug Name	Brand Name	Duration
Dextroamphetamine	Dexedrine	4–6 hours
Dextroamphetamine and amphetamine	Adderal or Adderal XR	4–6 hours
Dexmethylphenidate	Focalin or Focalin XR	4–6 hours
Methylphenidate	Methylin, Ritalin, Concerta or Ritalin LA	3–4 hours
Amphetamine Sulfate	Dyanaval	13 hours
Lisdexamfetamine	Vyvanse	14 hours

ADHD Non-Stimulant Medication List

In cases where stimulants are ineffective or cause unpleasant side effects, non-stimulants might be used. Some non-stimulant medications may raise the risk of suicidal thoughts and death by suicide in teens. The FDA warns that anyone taking atomoxetine (Strattera) should be monitored for suicidal thoughts, especially during the first few weeks. Common side effects of these drugs include fatigue, upset stomach, dry mouth, and nausea.

Drug Name	Brand Name	Duration	Side Effects
Atomoxetine	Strattera	24 hours	Sleep problems, anxiety, fatigue, upset stomach, dizziness, dry mouth. Although rare, can cause liver damage. Higher risk of suicide in adults ages 18-24.
Clonidine	Catapres	4-6 hours	Fatigue, dizziness, dry mouth, crankiness, behavior problems, low blood pressure. Stopping this medicine suddenly can result in high blood pressure.
Guanfacine	Intuniv	24 hours	Fatigue, dizziness, dry mouth, crankiness, behavior problems, low blood pressure. Stopping this medicine suddenly can result in high blood pressure.
Viloxazine	Qelbree	12 Hours	Tiredness, sleepiness, nausea, vomiting, sleeplessness, irritability, decreased appetite.

ADHD Antidepressant Medication List

People diagnosed with ADHD may also be treated for depression or anxiety and take an antidepressant along with a stimulant for ADHD.[15]

Drug Name	Brand Name	Side Effects
Bupropion	Wellbutrin	Headaches. Although rare, may make users more likely to experience seizures.
Desipramine	Norpramin	Not recommended for children. Associated with rare cases of fatal heart problems.
Imipramine	Tofranil	Anxiety, fatigue, upset stomach, dizziness, dry mouth, high heart rate, risk of heart arrhythmias.
Nortriptyline	Aventyl, Pamelor	Anxiety, fatigue, upset stomach, dizziness, dry mouth, higher heart rate, risk of heart arrhythmias.

The American Academy of Pediatrics (AAP) advises structure, organization, and simplification as tools for managing ADHD behavior. For example, parents should create a routine, organize the child's things, limit choices, and control the child's environment. Parents may choose not to attend events where they cannot control the environment or may be embarrassed by the child's rambunctious behavior. The AAP also suggest that parents find ways for the child

---

15. Hansa D. Bhargava, "ADHD Medications and Side Effects," WebMD, last updated March 9, 2021, https://www.webmd.com/add-adhd/adhd-medication-chart.

to be regularly physically active because lively play can improve mood and help regulate sleep. In schools, smaller classrooms seem to benefit the child due to fewer distractions.

Biblical Counseling for Parents or Caregivers of Children with ADHD

As we peruse the symptom lists that describe the behaviors labeled ADHD, we may think of people who perfectly fit into this description, as Ralph and Louise did. Maybe even ourselves! It's true that at some point, every single child (and many adults) occasionally show ADHD symptoms.

Many of these behaviors are disruptive—even embarrassing—but, generally, children are exhibiting normal behaviors for a child their age. This is why many even in secular communities are concerned that the diagnosis of ADHD is being applied too frequently to children who are on the far end of the "normal for age" behavioral spectrum.

However, some children are a great deal more energetic, active, and distractible than others of their age, as we have previously noted. The qualifier "often" fits them (often interrupts, often loses things, etc.). Their body seems to run ahead of their thinking. Parents trying to keep up with these children become exasperated and exhausted. There is good news—parents and caregivers can do much to help these little bodies and minds grow in wisdom and favor with God and others (Luke 2:52) by using God's Word.

In counseling caregivers, it is useful to have a general outline of direction. In his book, *Blame It on the Brain*, Ed Welch gives such an outline.[16] Dr. Welch points out that these steps are appropriate for any psychiatric diagnosis, including ADHD. I've adapted them here:

1. Get information. Gain an understanding of the specific ADHD experience for both the child and their caregivers.

---

16. Edward T. Welch, *Blame It on the Brain* (Phillipsburg, NJ: P & R, 1998), 132.

Ralph and Louise's experience with Tommy was typical, but each situation has unique features that need to be addressed in counseling.

2. Help caregivers distinguish between physical and spiritual symptoms.

Physical Symptoms

Children diagnosed with ADHD often have several physical strengths and abilities: high energy, gregarious personality, creativity, and enthusiasm. These children are not timid! They tend to be risk-takers, which, when rightly directed, allows them to conquer many challenges. Help caregivers think in terms of maximizing physical strengths and remedying weaknesses.

Ralph and Louise were encouraged to find appropriate outlets for Tommy's physical strengths. His high energy was channeled into age-appropriate seasonal sports: running on a cross-country team, swimming on a team, and climbing at the local gym. These activities built Tommy's coordination and focus, as well as allowing him to competitively excel. His teammates also enjoyed his outgoing personality and energetic enthusiasm!

Physical weaknesses can be addressed with training—reduced short-term memory, difficulty sequencing (doing several tasks in a row), and trouble screening out irrelevant stimuli. These things are not necessarily a moral violation of God's law. Care must be taken not to call something sinful that is more accurately called physical weakness.

Spiritual Symptoms

In the same way, care must be taken not to treat a behavior issue as a physical weakness when it actually transgresses God's law. Any physical weaknesses that might be present in the child do not cause his/her sin. Sin comes from the heart of the child. We are all sinners, by birth, by nature, by choice, and by practice. To be equipped to wisely treat the actual problem, we need to call sin what it is. A child's sin can be addressed with nurture and admonition: discipline, confession, repentance, and forgiveness. If sinful behavior is incorrectly treated as merely physical weakness, sin is excused rather than addressed. For example, one boy grabs a toy that another boy is playing with, but his mom excuses this as an impulsive symptom of his disorder. This confuses the child because their conscience and guilty feelings tell them they have done something wrong. To deal with that guilt biblically is a blessing to the child.

In trying to discern between physical limitations and spiritual (heart) issues, the main question for parents is, considering the context of this situation, am I confident that the child is doing something that the Bible clearly forbids? If so, this is a spiritual issue of sin. Help caregivers address the heart with spiritual instruction and encouragement.

First, the counselor can assess and address the following general principles of godly parenting:

Understand the importance of inner convictions and external control

Children need to be taught inner convictions, and they need to be externally controlled in behavior until they develop self-control. "Fathers, do not provoke your children to anger, but bring them up in the discipline and instruction of the Lord" (Ephesians 6:4 ESV). In 2 Timothy 3:16, God tells us that the Word is profitable for teaching, reproof, correction, and training in righteousness that the man of God may be equipped for every good work. God gives us wise ways to teach, reprove, correct, and train.

Teach to the biblical standard

God has given parents the responsibility to display Christ to their children. Teach children by word and example that our goal in life is found in 1 Corinthians 10:31 and 2 Corinthians 5:9—to glorify God, to please the Lord in whatever we do. As the adage says, "Just two choices on the shelf, pleasing God or pleasing self."

Believe that change is possible

We need to believe that our children can put off sinful thoughts and behaviors, change their thinking by renewing their mind, and put on God's ways (Ephesians 4:22–24). If the child is not a believer, teaching to that standard can open the door for the gospel by leading them to see their need for Christ and his righteousness.

Train for accountability

Teach parents that before bringing correction to hold a child responsible for a particular behavior, the parent must be sure (a) the child has the *ability* to hear and understand (process) your instructions and (b) the child is *aware* of your expectations and has *practiced* the specific concrete steps of the behavior.

In other words, make sure your child is set up to be *accountable* for their behavior. When determining whether we should hold a child accountable for their behavior, it is helpful to consider the difference between childishness and foolishness. Childishness is innocent immaturity—making childish mistakes. But foolishness is rebellious intent—defiance. Overt rebellion is quite obvious when the child deliberately crosses a well-drawn line. But passive rebellion can be subtler: "I didn't hear you," "I forgot," silliness, whining, sulking, and pouting. This takes training. Parents must train before they can expect a behavior. Tell the child what is expected, explain it to them, then have them explain it back. Give the child examples of how to do or say something. Have them practice it. Parents can then be sure the child has owned the awareness of what the parents expect. Let me illustrate these concepts with an example: "the morality of spilled milk."

Scenario 1

Tommy puts his drinking glass near the edge of the counter, wiggles around as he eats, turns quickly, and knocks his cup of milk over with his elbow. Sin? No, this is childishness. He had not been trained in being careful not to spill the milk. Help him clean up the mess.

Scenario 2

Knowing Tommy's propensity for spilling milk with his elbows, you tell Tommy to put the glass farther away from the edge. You show him where. You have him show you where. You tell him why (we please God when we are careful with the things he has given to us). You have him tell you why. You practice it a few times. You watch the first time after the instruction and remind him of what you have discussed (you give a warning). You give him about a week of grace, reminding him each time he does not do it that it needs to change, and you have him clean up the spilled milk. You tell him the consequences for disobeying the behavior, which will start on a specified day. You catch him placing the glass where you showed him, and you praise him! You talk through scenarios that may make it more difficult to obey (distractions, visitors, etc.), to help him gain awareness of possible temptations. Now Tommy is accountable. After the specified day, if he does not put the milk in the correct place, it is sin, and you bring the agreed upon consequences.

Choosing appropriate consequences for specific behaviors is a wisdom issue, in which several factors need to be considered. The frequency of the offense, the age of the child, the context of the moment, and the overall character of the child will help determine appropriate consequences. A parent should make it clear to the child what the consequences will be so that the child is aware of the consequence they are choosing when they choose the behavior. This also guards the parent from being either too lenient or too harsh, depending on their whim at the moment.

Pre-teaching for challenging situations can be very helpful. This simply means reminding the child of expected behaviors (that have already been taught) prior to an activity. Dialogue with the child. Gain eye contact, and ask them to repeat what you've said. For Tommy, that might mean staying with the family at church and not climbing on pews after the service. For example, Louise could ask before church, "Tommy, what did Mommy say for you to do right after church is done today?" Praise him when he remembers. Re-instruct if it is a new requirement that he doesn't remember.

These are general principles for parenting any child, but parents can also use them to address many of the behaviors that fall under the ADHD umbrella. In addition, there are ways to specifically adapt biblical instruction for areas of distractibility and high energy. Let's see what more we can do to help Tommy and his parents.

Biblical Counseling for the Person with ADHD

You may recall that the two main categories of behavioral problems involved in the diagnosis of ADHD were inattention and hyperactivity-impulsivity (with more specific descriptions listed under each). We also previously mentioned that an important skill for both parents and counselors is to distinguish physical weakness issues from heart issues so that we can address both wisely. In the following plan for Tommy, the counselors helped his parents add training tools to increase success in thought processing and intentionality and biblical truths to address the heart.

Possible biblical heart issues underlying these behaviors include disobedience, laziness, self-centeredness/selfishness, anger, disrespect, lack of perseverance, and poor self-control.[17] These heart issues are not unique to children so the counseling principles for children who struggle with ADHD symptoms can be adapted to work with an adult who struggles in similar ways.

Tommy was often described by his parents and caregivers as being "out of control." Therefore, the counselor and Tommy's parents agreed that developing self-control was the overall goal. Ralph and Louise were encouraged to initially increase external control of Tommy's behavior, with the goal of helping him develop internal self-control with God's help and for God's glory.

---

17. Marshall Asher and Mary Asher, *The Christian's Guide to Psychological Terms*, 2nd ed. (Bemidji, MN: Focus Publishing, 2014), 17.

Ralph and Louise created a parenting plan in which they chose which behaviors (in biblical terms) were most troublesome and prioritized which issues to work on first, second, and so on. The counselor pointed out that by focusing on only one issue at a time, Tommy could experience some success before being required to make additional changes.

Throughout counseling, Tommy's parents were greatly helped by learning the wisdom in the book of Proverbs. They also found many Old Testament stories and several New Testament passages to be applicable to behaviors within the diagnosis of ADHD.[18] After finding relevant biblical truth, they developed practical applications for their particular child. First, they worked on issues of inattention.

Inattention

Much biblical instruction is given surrounding this issue. Some examples are in Proverbs, which tells us repeatedly to *listen* and *pay attention* to gain understanding and knowledge. Consider the following verses:

- "But he who listens to me shall live securely and will be at ease from the dread of evil" (1:33).
- "Hear, O sons, the instruction of a father, and give attention that you may gain understanding" (4:1).
- "Listen, for I will speak noble things; And the opening of my lips will reveal right things" (8:6).
- "Now therefore, O sons, listen to me, for blessed are they who keep my ways" (8:32).
- "He whose ear listens to the life-giving reproof will dwell among the wise" (15:31).
- "He who gives attention to the word will find good, and blessed is he who trusts in the LORD" (16:20).

---

18. Pam Forster, *For Instruction in Righteousness: A Topical Guide for Biblical Child-Training* (Gaston, OR: Doorposts, 1995).

- "Listen to counsel and accept discipline, that you may be wise the rest of your days" (19:20).
- "Listen, my son, and be wise, and direct your heart in the way" (23:19).

Jesus's story in Matthew 7:24–27 speaks of a wise builder who hears and acts and is then compared to a foolish builder who hears but does not pay attention to the instruction and act on it. The consequences of each are clear—the house stands in the storm or it falls catastrophically.

Galatians 6:7–9 teaches us to persevere to finish well: "Do not be deceived, God is not mocked; for whatever a man sows, this he will also reap. For the one who sows to his own flesh will from the flesh reap corruption, but the one who sows to the Spirit will from the Spirit reap eternal life. Let us not lose heart in doing good, for in due time we will reap if we do not grow weary."

Philippians 4:4–9 addresses right thinking and behavior, and verse 13 encourages us that Christ's strength is enough to help.

The story of creation in Genesis 1 tells us that God makes order out of chaos.

So when a child is not paying attention to the things in their environment that they know are important to those in authority, both the child's heart and physical ability are the target of training with biblical principles. Address the heart by finding out what is more important to that little heart than heeding their current responsibility. What do they want more than obedience in that moment? Pleasure? Ease? Excitement? What should they want? According to Proverbs, they should want to listen and pay close attention to gain wisdom and to use their minds the way God instructs them to. They should also desire not to be self-focused, but to please God by obeying. Parents can lead them to put off desires of the flesh, renew their minds, and put on obedience to the task at hand. Skills training comes into play to address the bodily weakness.

It is good news that God's instructions always come with enabling grace as we set our hearts to obey (2 Corinthians 12:9). That means that even an energetic child is able to learn to listen and give attention!

The Bible also includes practical application. First, God is a God of order (1 Corinthians 14:40), so one main training tool for Ralph and Louise was to add structure and order to their home life. Tommy's parents learned to give him clear, simple, step-by-step written rules for the home and for his schoolwork. They limited his choices to a narrow range of options for food or desired activities. They developed a schedule for him from morning to evening in order to establish regular routines that he could follow. This schedule included a specific daily time for vigorous physical activity. They helped him organize all of his things so that everything had a place. They worked over several weeks to train him to put things away in the correct place, with reminders and loads of encouragement when they caught him doing the right thing. After accountability was established, appropriate, consistent, predetermined consequences for infractions were brought to bear.

After teaching God's commands about paying attention, they wanted to help Tommy expand his attention span. They set about making the training a positive experience. First, they chose a fun activity and, using a timer, started with just a few minutes and increased the time each day. They charted the progress Tommy was making.

They also wanted to help Tommy pay attention to them when they spoke. To initially catch his attention, they made themselves obvious—they stood in front of him, called his name, turned off distractions, etc. Then, using reminders and praise, they taught Tommy to say, "Yes, Mom," or "Yes, Dad" when spoken to. They gave point-by-point instructions and asked Tommy to repeat what they had said. Tommy was required to follow through on their instructions right away. Initially the required behavior was done together, and later the parents supervised to ensure success.

The next things on the parenting plan included working on helping Tommy be more controlled in his speech (indoor and outdoor
voice, as well as kindness—Proverbs 21:23), to not be easily distracted
(what is important to God is important to me—Deuteronomy 4:9),
to exercise good stewardship of his things (1 Corinthians 4:2), and to
persevere when his work was difficult (James 1:12).

Ralph and Louise were realizing how much work it is to train a
child, but they began seeing some promising changes in Tommy over
the first several weeks. They, like Tommy, had to learn to persevere
in doing good because God promises we will reap in due time if we
do not give up. They, like Tommy, had to learn that "hard" does not
mean impossible—hard is not bad, it is just hard. Obeying in the
hard things teaches us to rely on the Lord for help.

Hyperactivity-Impulsivity

As the process of training Tommy with biblical instruction continued, the daily scheduled physical activity helped with Tommy's
seemingly constant movement, but more needed to be done to address
his heart. He needed the gospel. And he needed to present his body
to the Lord in obedience (Romans 12:1–2). Ralph and Louise learned
to pre-teach for times when staying put was going to be expected. In
order to love others, Tommy had to learn to be obedient even when he
didn't feel like it (Matthew 26:39; Colossians 3:20). He had to learn
to think about others before acting or speaking (Philippians 2:3–4).
Tommy had to learn patience (don't we all!?) because life is full of
times we must wait (1 Corinthians 13:4; James 5:8). He needed to
learn to be an encourager to others (Matthew 5:9; Ephesians 4:29).

The family also worked on practical application. They began to
role-play social situations and how to wisely navigate them. "So, let's
say your teacher wants you to sit quietly at your desk and you want to
get up and run or talk. But to obey your teacher and love/serve others
(Mark 10:43–45; Philippians 2:3–4), you want to stay in your seat
and not disturb them. So instead of running around, you stay in your
seat and quietly focus on your work or what the teacher is saying. Let's

practice that. I'll be the teacher . . ." (They read Proverbs 10:8, 19; 13:3.) Tommy learned "the interrupt rule," because love is not rude (1 Corinthians 13:5). This means that if he had something he urgently wanted to say while others were conversing, instead of interrupting them, he was taught to place his hand gently on his parent's arm and wait for them to attend to him. Tommy also wrote out a list of ways to encourage others. He was challenged to see how many he could do each day.

Tommy's parents had been so focused on containing Tommy's behavior that they had not developed the habit of praising him for good behavior. During counseling, they learned to encourage him more consistently. They praised him for waiting, for encouraging others, for using the interrupt rule, for staying seated even when it was hard, etc. Tommy flourished under biblical "nurture and admonition." With biblical truth, consistent correction, and his parent's encouragement, he was gaining confidence and motivation to do the right thing.

A Word to the Counselor

At all times, show compassion for the struggles of both the child and the parents. Parents of energetic children face the judgmental attitudes of others at church, in stores, and in restaurants, etc., even though they may be responsibly parenting their child's behaviors. Parents/caregivers may become weary and discouraged. But there is great hope because God's Word has answers for the behaviors that can lead to the diagnosis of ADHD! None of these problems are too difficult for God's Word to address. God created this person and has a plan for his/her life. Parents can be encouraged to persevere and anticipate God's good fruit from their obedience. We want to caution parents with children on Ritalin or another medication that while the drugs may be effective in suppressing symptoms, it is still important for them to parent their children according to the principles in the Scripture.

A Word to the ADHD Individual

If you are a believer in Christ who struggles with the behaviors that fall under the diagnosis of ADHD, there is great hope! While the struggles are real, as you work on the heart issues and skill issues we've discussed, the Lord has promised to strengthen you. Be encouraged that in all the ways we need to change to be more like Jesus, he who began a good work in you will be faithful to complete it. It is God who works in you both to will and to do. Your energetic constitution can be channeled successfully into great productivity for the kingdom of God! Often, a person with great enthusiasm can motivate others around them to accomplish greater things. As you use your energy to work for the Lord, you will receive the joy it is to glorify him with your life.

When we think about how to approach this difficult diagnosis, our love for these children and parents motivates us to meet them in their struggles and bring the best help we can. Parents and counselors who are dealing with ADHD can receive timeless wisdom from 1 Thessalonians 5:14: "We urge you, brothers and sisters, admonish the unruly, encourage the fainthearted, help the weak, be patient with everyone."

CHAPTER 8

Autism Spectrum Disorder (ASD):

Essential Background Knowledge and Helpful Biblical Principles

Pamela Gannon, RN

Jay was a quiet child. As a newborn, he hardly ever cried. But in the following weeks and months, he failed to thrive. It was as if he wasn't even interested in food. At one year old, he developed rather severe digestive problems. He was unable to absorb food and lost weight. The family worked with a pediatrician to rule out disease or allergies, but there was no discernible cause. These issues continued over the next two years, and finally partially resolved, although he remained nauseated much of the time.

Jay's demeanor was distant, even as a baby. He rarely seemed to notice people. He did not smile or catch his mom's eyes; in fact, he avoided eye contact with everyone. He didn't reach up to be held or take a helping hand. He liked being left alone. He wasn't excited or happy at things one would expect him to be, such as a new toy. He didn't point at things to share what he saw with others. When faced with a change in environment or routine, the reaction was swift—fear or anger. But when something upset him, he did not want to be physically comforted—he would stiffen and arch his back when held.

He lacked typical motor coordination, failing to meet many milestones of physical development. Instead, he engaged in repetitive physical movements. He would rock back and forth, or suddenly jump or twirl without a discernible reason. He would sometimes pace and flap his hands. He wasn't interested in playing with his older brother or imitating anything he did, but he could stare at a ceiling fan for hours. He also loved wheels—any and all wheels. He would line up his little toy cars very carefully—and woe to the one who moved them even a little. He lived in a world of his own that others did not understand.

As young believing parents, Melinda and Bob dealt with each of these issues as well as they knew how; they disciplined for perceived sin and taught right behavior, but they did not understand what these signs might indicate.

By three years old, Jay had spoken only a few words. A speech therapist at his preschool got him to say a few simple sentences. Then it was as if a spigot had been opened—the words came flooding out. He had an amazing vocabulary for one so young. Melinda thought, *He's clearly brilliant.*

However, his use of language was unusual. Jay's words were monotone, almost robotic, and seemingly emotionless. He would repeat phrases over and over. He didn't understand the typical back and forth of conversation, but he would give facts at length about wheels. He didn't understand or use nonverbal communication appropriately; his facial expressions and gestures did not match what was being said. He had to be taught things that typical children naturally pick up, like knowing how to wave goodbye and understanding the meaning of different facial expressions. He responded to his parents' words slowly, as if he was still processing what they said.

Along with these unusual behaviors, he had heightened reactions to smells, textures, sounds, or flashes of light. There were certain clothes that he objected strongly to wearing. He disliked being in the kitchen if his mom was cooking because of the potential for loud noises and strong smells. He would put on earmuffs when she vacuumed. His parents sought help from his speech therapist for some of these sensitivities, and physical therapy helped with his balance and coordination issues.

Melinda and Bob addressed the issues they could. At the suggestion of their pediatrician, they visited a neuropsychologist for testing. The diagnosis was autism spectrum disorder (ASD). They knew nothing about it, but they quickly learned that the things they saw in their son were described by this diagnosis. Melinda caught her breath as she read the following list:

- A child on the autism spectrum might show signs of poor eye contact quite early.
- Autistic kids tend to fixate on certain activities or objects.
- Autistic kids don't understand emotions.
- About 40 percent of kids on the autism spectrum don't talk at all, and about 30 percent develop some language skills but lose them later.
- Autistic kids thrive on order—specific routines or rituals. Change can be terrifying for them in an already confusing world.
- Autism is often accompanied by gastrointestinal issues.
- Autism is often associated with sensory problems—either heightened sensitivity to sensory input or lack of typical responses to sensory information. There can be diminished sensory adaptation.[1] For example, while typical people adapt to smells or clothes, touching them so that the sensations fade over time, an autistic person keeps getting constant sensory input— the smell continues and the feel of the clothing continues.

Autistic kids also frequently engage in "stimming"—repetitive movements that seem to bring comfort. Stimming described Jay's odd movements: rocking, jumping, twirling, pacing, and flapping his hands. Autistic people of any age may "stim" in response to emotions such as excitement, boredom, stress, or anxiety.[2]

---

1. National Institutes of Mental Health, *Autism Spectrum Disorder,* https://www.nimh. nih.gov/health/topics/autism-spectrum-disorders-asd. Accessed March 11, 2022.

2. Lori Smith, MSN, "What is stimming?" *Medical News Today,* Feb 19, 2018, https:// www.medicalnewstoday.com/articles/319714. Accessed March 11, 2022.

Their little boy had all these characteristics, which led to his difficulty interacting and conversing with others. Melinda and Bob grieved, realizing that Jay wanted to have relationships, but he did not know how.

What Is ASD?

What exactly is ASD? ASD is a psychological diagnosis that describes a set of developmental difficulties and differences in communication and behavior. Autism is known as a spectrum disorder because there is wide degree of variation in the type and severity of symptoms that people experience. On one end of the spectrum are those considered "highly skilled," previously considered to have *Asperger syndrome*. (In the fifth edition of the *Diagnostic and Statistical Manual of Mental Disorders* (DSM-5), the American Psychiatric Association merged Asperger's with ASD).[3] These individuals are intelligent and able to perform the life skills necessary to live independently. On the other end of the spectrum are the "severely challenged" persons—those with severe mental disabilities who require substantial support to perform basic activities. Between these extremes are individuals with various abilities and challenges.

How Is ASD Diagnosed?

According to the Centers for Disease Control, ASD affects an estimated one in forty-four children in the United States today.[4] Researchers think it may be possible to identify ASD as early as three months of age by assessing infants' eye contact.[5] About half of parents

---

3. Leanne Tull, BCBA, "Changes to the DSM Autism Diagnostic Criteria," Association for Science in Autism Treatment, https://asatonline.org/research-treatment/resources/topical-articles/changes-to-the-dsm-autism-diagnostic-criteria/.

4. Centers for Disease Control and Prevention, "Data & Statistics on Autism Spectrum Disorder," https://www.cdc.gov/ncbddd/autism/data.html. Accessed March 11, 2022.

5. National Institutes of Health, "Eye Contact Declines in Young Infants with Autism," November 25, 2013, https://www.nih.gov/news-events/nih-research-matters/eye-contact-declines-young-infants-autism.

of autistic children noticed issues by the time their child was a year old, and almost all noticed problems by two years. ASD occurs in every racial and ethnic group and across all socioeconomic levels. However, boys are more likely to develop ASD than girls by a ratio of about 4:1.[6]

Diagnosis often begins with the family physician that regularly assesses children for developmental delays. This doctor may recommend further evaluation by a neurologist or neuropsychologist who will conduct neurological, cognitive, and language testing. ASD is diagnosed according to descriptions in the DSM-5,[7] which includes two main categories:

1. Challenges with communication and social interaction. Difficulty "connecting" with or predicting the reactions of other people, reading social cues, making eye contact, or having a conversation. They might not begin to speak as early as other children do.

2. Restricted and repetitive patterns of behavior. Rocking, repeating phrases, organizing objects. They become upset with change in routine. They're often deeply focused on one subject.

Frequent comorbidities (associated physical issues) include sensory hyperactivity (heightened senses of smell, taste, hearing, touch, and sensitivity to light), lack of coordination (e.g., awkwardness, difficulty writing), gastrointestinal (GI) disorders, seizure disorders, and sleep disorders. In the diagnostic process, other known diseases with similar symptoms will be ruled out, such as lead poisoning and known genetic disorders.[8]

---

6. Centers for Disease Control and Prevention, "Data & Statistics on Autism Spectrum Disorder.

7. *Diagnostic and Statistical Manual of Mental Disorders, Fifth Edition, Text Revision* (Washington, DC: American Psychiatric Association, 2013).

8. David Cawthorpe, "Comprehensive Description of Comorbidity for Autism Spectrum Disorder in a General Population," *Perm J* 21, no. 16-088, 2017. Published online December 23, 2016. doi: 10.7812/TPP/16-088.

What Causes ASD?

The cause of ASD is unknown. While there are many associated physiological abnormalities, none are consistent enough to be deemed causative. Scientists believe that both genetics and environment play a role. Possible environmental contributions to ASD include prenatal exposure to air pollution or chemical pesticides.[9] Studies have identified a number of associated genetic differences that suggest that ASD could result from disruptions in early brain development. Since ASD can be detected early in life, when environmental influence has been minimal, genetic influence is strongly supported.

Risk factors for ASD include the following:[10]

- Having a sibling with ASD
- Having older parents
- Having certain known genetic conditions—people with conditions such as Down syndrome, fragile X syndrome, and Rett syndrome have a higher likelihood of also being diagnosed with ASD
- Having very low birth weight

Do vaccines cause ASD? Multiple studies have shown that vaccination to prevent childhood disease does not increase the risk of ASD in the population. The research is clear that vaccines don't cause ASD.[11]

What Are the Typical Signs or Symptoms of ASD?

No matter what the cause, all individuals on the autism spectrum have similar struggles. One of the great challenges of raising an autistic child is discerning whether these struggles are a moral issue or

9. National Institute of Environmental health services, "Autism," https://www.niehs.nih.gov/health/topics/conditions/autism/index.

10. National Institute of Mental Health, "Autism Spectrum Disorder," https://www.nimh.nih.gov/health/topics/autism-spectrum-disorders-asd.

11. Anders Hviid et al., "Measles, Mumps, Rubella Vaccination and Autism: A Nationwide Cohort Study," *Annals of Internal Medicine*, April 16, 2019, https://www.acpjournals.org/doi/full/10.7326/M18-2101.

a physical issue. What we *can* say is that many of the struggles are nonmoral—that is, clearly not sinful and better termed "physical weakness." Many of the odd behaviors seem to be based on the inability of the brain to naturally function in neurotypical ways.

While caregivers can grow in discerning sin from weakness, let me just say that it is not always easy to figure this out; many issues that seem to be moral also involve bodily weakness or inability; some issues that seem to be arising from physical weakness also include matters of the heart. Remember that the purpose of godly parental discipline is to help children learn and grow; just as the Lord disciplines those he loves, parents are not primarily called to respond to their children's sin as judges meting out just punishments, but as loving shepherds who want to guide their children in learning how to walk in paths of righteousness for their own good and God's glory. Awareness of the following typical physical disabilities can help parents discern whether behavior is inability, lack of training, or sin. However, the differences are not always clearly distinct.

As previously noted, the common thread in ASD is differences in social skills, communication, and behavior patterns compared with neurotypical people. However, there is a range between high-functioning and low-functioning autism.

Characteristics of the Highly Functioning Person with ASD

Toward the highly skilled end, the struggle is with language and social interactions—individuals on this end of the spectrum frequently misunderstand others and are often misunderstood. Below is a list of some of the different components that make communication and social interactions more difficult for people with ASD.

- *Nonverbal communication*—Autistic people have an inability to naturally understand nonverbal forms of communication (such as posture, facial expression, eye gaze, gestures, and tone of voice). Since much of our communication is nonverbal, this can lead to socially awkward behaviors. For example, the person may not understand the concept of a "personal bubble," and as a result may stand too close to people, look over their shoulder, or touch them when it is not desired. They may talk too loudly and use strange gestures. They may misunderstand a sarcastic tone of voice—their tendency to take words literally leads to misinterpretations.

- *Eye contact*—Because of differences in eye contact, an autistic person might be misunderstood in multiple ways. When a person avoids your eyes, you might think they are fearful, rude, disrespectful, lacking confidence, guilty, unfriendly, untrusting, etc. Is it a sin not to make eye contact? Not necessarily. It may stem from perceptual difficulty. Jay, the child from the beginning of the chapter, was able to explain that for him, faces are indistinct from the background and therefore don't attract special attention. However, while making eye contact may not come naturally to the person with ASD, it can be taught. Once the child knows how to make and keep eye contact, if they then fail to do so, it could be disobedience. Even then, context of the behavior matters. For example, if the environment is loud or bright or smelly so that the child's senses are overwhelmed, it would be difficult to focus on making eye contact. Discussion of why they failed to make eye contact will yield insights into what kind of response would be appropriate and beneficial.

- *Sensory overload*—The autistic person often has heightened or continuous sensory input. Their senses don't seem to adapt, or "turn off" as they do in a neurotypical person. Jay described it as having a lack of normal sensory filters. For example, an autistic person who puts on a jacket *feels* it the entire time he wears it, whereas a non-autistic person soon adapts. While smells typically fade from awareness, they continue for the person with ASD. Understanding this helps parents in several areas. For example, a child's reluctance to put on that wool coat that Grandma bought him could be a sensory issue, rather than disobedience or ingratitude. Or resistance to going a certain place could be because the smell or noise is unbearable. A heightened sense of taste may lead to a picky eater. Jay was immediately nauseated by the smell or taste of food that was not absolutely bland. He also wore headphones to block out noise whenever Melinda would vacuum, cook, or have the TV on. Jay found it hard to ignore background noise to focus on a person talking. All noises continually vied for his attention. Another child may dislike having a flash picture taken or going outside in the sun because the light is agonizingly bright for them.

- *Anxiety about changes in routine or schedule*—Repetition and structure are important to many on the spectrum. Autistic kids respond anxiously to schedule changes, even positive ones (like going skiing or getting ice cream). Routine represents stability in a world that feels unstable and chaotic.

Imagine being in a world where you are unable to quiet a constant stimulation to your senses. You hear, see, smell, and feel continually. Add to that the confusion of people speaking and acting in ways you don't understand, and it makes sense that autistic persons are exhausted by being out in the community in stimulating or unfamiliar places.

Characteristics of the Low-Functioning Person with ASD

People with more severe cases of ASD will often exhibit the same characteristics as those with less severe cases, and, in addition, they may never gain the ability to speak or even notice people around them. While higher-functioning persons can often learn to control repetitive movements, the more severely affected may have extreme and seemingly uncontrollable repetitive behaviors (e.g., violent rocking, unending moaning, head-banging). They may also be significantly impaired in cognitive and motor abilities. However, it's still worthwhile to help them achieve, learn, and grow as much as they can within their challenges. In some cases these individuals have been taught to use sign language or a keyboard to communicate. The movie *Rain Man* illustrated some of the characteristics of a person with a more severe case of ASD.

Strengths of People with ASD

Even with all these difficulties, people with ASD have unique strengths. Autistic people are often able to learn things in detail and remember information for long periods of time. Now an adult, Jay's current job requires that he memorize where everything is in the store in order to help customers find things, and he is good at this. People with ASD tend to think "outside the box." Dr. Temple Grandin, a woman who is on the autism spectrum, is famous for her expertise in solving animal behavior issues.

Autonomy Works is a Silicon Valley tech firm that hires many people on the autism spectrum. They are excellent workers because they are punctual, detailed, and innovative. Dave Friedman, the founder of the company, said that Autonomy Works is thriving by tapping into the unique strengths of these employees.[12]

Autistic people tend to be very honest; lying often doesn't make sense to them. Their literal way of thinking helps them avoid deceiving people into thinking something that isn't true. They say what they mean and mean what they say. Their heightened senses could be an asset in certain situations where it is important to notice details. Rather than pitying people with these differences, society and the church can learn ways to accept and benefit from their unique qualities, while also acknowledging and helping them with their weaknesses.

Treatment Options for ASD

Most health care professionals agree that the earlier the intervention, the better. The psychological community believes that there is no cure for ASD. However, speech therapy, physical therapy, occupational

---

12. Anderson Cooper, "Recruiting for Talent on the Autism Spectrum," *CBS News,* October 4, 2020, https://www.cbsnews.com/news/autism-employment-60-minutes-2020-10-04/.

therapy, and structured, skill-oriented education for specific challenges can improve life skills and social function. Jay, who is now thirty-one, was delighted to tell me that a coworker was surprised to find out that he was autistic.

One current popular psychological intervention is called applied behavioral analysis (ABA).[13] This therapy encourages positive behaviors and discourages negative ones (which sounds similar to a secular version of God's timeless wisdom in Ephesians 4:22–24 to put off, renew your mind, and put on). Family counseling for parents and siblings of children with ASD is encouraged to help families learn how to live with and respond to the particular challenges they are facing or will face.

No medication can treat ASD, but some can treat other health issues that frequently accompany ASD. For example, seizures can be treated with anticonvulsant drugs, while digestive problems and nausea can be treated with antacids. There is a necessary caution in terms of treatment: sadly, people seeking fame or financial reward can take advantage of autistic individuals and their families by promoting unproven treatments. Parents, caregivers, and people with ASD should use caution before adopting any unverified treatments.

With this medical background in mind, let's look at wise ways to counsel both the family and the autistic person.

Counseling the Family

When Melinda and Bob first faced the diagnosis of ASD, they had many questions and concerns: How did this happen to my child? Is this a physical or spiritual problem? What can I expect for Jay? How will I care for him? What kind of help will he need? Will he ever go to school, have friends, get married, have a family, or get a job? No matter where a child falls on the spectrum, families will need help

---

13. "Applied Behavior Analysis," Autism Speaks, https://www.autismspeaks.org/applied-behavior-analysis.

to gain a biblical perspective on their situation, and they will need encouragement to persevere in the process of parenting biblically.

Hear Their Cries

Parents of children diagnosed with ASD will likely be faced with grieving the loss of "normal." We all have expectations for how life will go, and when suddenly faced with a life different from what we anticipated, we grieve. It is appropriate to acknowledge the pain and difficulty of living in the brokenness of the world. So hear their cries. Weep with those who weep. Families of autistic children face confusion, discouragement, and fatigue as they endure day-to-day struggles. Caregivers can feel exasperated and rejected by a child who doesn't look at them, enjoy their hugs, or respond to the comfort they offer. And because these children are often unable to communicate what is bothering them, parents may feel that they are "at their wit's end."

Encourage sorrowing parents to cast their cares on the Lord because he cares for them: "Trust in Him at all times, O people; Pour out your heart before Him; God is a refuge for us" (Psalm 62:8). God knows. He understands. He loves the parents. He loves the child. Remind them of these truths. "For we do not have a high priest who cannot sympathize with our weaknesses" (Hebrews 4:15a).

Help Them Surrender to God's Sovereignty

As in any type of suffering, parents may struggle with "why" questions. Bodily disorders, including ASD, are a product of the fall, so in that sense they are not part of God's original design for humanity, but at the same time none of us are a mistake or an accident. God is still king. He reigns over the earth and everything in it. God can use bodies marred by the fall (which includes all of our bodies) to do great things! He causes all things to work for his glory and our good—even ASD. He designed each child for his purposes—the greatest of which is to glorify his name in them (John 9:1–3).

Help grieving parents turn to the Lord for strength and lead them toward yielding to and trusting in God's good purposes for their family. God has entrusted *them* to care for this precious person during this lifetime. We want to help them be able to say, "Lord, I am willing to receive what you give, lack what you withhold, and relinquish what you take."[14]

Steve Viars, in his helpful talk on *Helping Parents of Special Needs Children*, suggests parents of children with disabilities ask themselves these six questions:

1. Is there anything about this situation that is outside of God's control?
2. Could God have prevented this from happening to [our child] and to us if he had chosen to?
3. Will God ever give us more than we can bear (1 Corinthians 10:13)?
4. Can God use this situation for his glory and our good?
5. Has God promised to go with us as we try to raise our [child] for him?
6. Will we accept this responsibility and seek to joyfully submit to his plan for our family?[15]

Each child with ASD is made in the image of the God of the universe, just like any other person. In the eyes of the world, they may be "lowly," but as image-bearers, they are precious to God. Melinda was encouraged by reading truths like 1 Corinthians 1:26–29:

> For consider your calling, brethren, that there were not many wise according to the flesh, not many mighty, not many noble; but God has chosen the foolish things of the world to shame the wise, and God has chosen the weak things of the world to shame the things which are strong, and the base things of the world and the despised God has chosen, the things that

---

14. Jerry Bridges, *Respectable Sins* (Colorado Springs: NavPress, 2007), 75.
15. Steve Viars, "Helping Parents of Special Needs Children," Faith Church Counseling Ministries, https://media.biblicalcounseling.com/wp-content/uploads/2020/09/14083118/SteveViars-HelpingParentsofSpecialNeedsChildren.pdf.

are not, so that He may nullify the things that are, so that no man may boast before God.

Help Them Embrace Their Child's Uniqueness

Jay was high-functioning and quite verbal. But his use of language remained unusual. For example, when Melinda would say "Hi," he said, "low." These ways of communicating come from the autistic tendency to use language in a very literal way. Rather than responding with irritation, Jay's family learned to enjoy his outside-of-the-box responses.

When families embrace God's unique plan for them, they can enjoy the child as the gift that God made them to be. Help families think about the unique opportunities in their situation: to grow spiritually and to understand God's acceptance and care for all his "special needs" children (1 Corinthians 1:26–30). Help them think about distinctive ways that God's glory can shine through their situation.

In an article called "Preaching in the Valley," Pastor Todd Hardin relates an experience that he and his wife had with their youngest son Fletcher. Fletcher is on the "severely affected" end of the spectrum—he has severe ASD and mental disabilities. Todd tells how God has used his son to shape his life as both a father and a Christ-follower:

> Our last "worship service" took place at our local children's hospital where we took Fletcher for an electroencephalogram (EEG). In addition to autism, Fletcher also struggles with epilepsy. We arrived at the hospital at 6:30 a.m. and Fletcher's pensive body language signaled that he had remembered his last trip to the facility. Fletcher's anxiety initially emerged when the admissions person attempted to place the identification bracelet on his wrist. When the lady produced the bracelet, Fletcher buried his face in my side and hugged me like a desperate man hugs a tree in a tornado. The closer the

lady came, the tighter Fletcher clung to his "Dada." In his fear, Fletcher sought refuge in his father. During that moment, Fletcher embodied Psalm 56:3 which states, "When I am afraid, I put my trust in you" (ESV). . . . Fletcher did instinctively what three seminary degrees and a decade of pastoral ministry has still not taught me. When he experienced fear, he clung to his father. As I walk with this red-headed, speechless preacher through the Valley of Autism, I am amazed at how God uses him to preach his Word to me. Hopefully, one day, I will learn to listen.[16]

As Mark Shaw points out, "Aren't we glad that the Bible teaches the eternal worth and dignity of all humans regardless of their function or contributions to society? Being made in the image of God gives every human being value and purpose regardless of what is considered typical or nontypical functioning. Each severely challenged autistic person is an image-bearer of God and has a purpose ordained by him."

Help Them Love Their Child Wisely

Kids on the autism spectrum are sufferers and sinners, just like the rest of us. But because of their weaknesses in communication, they can be difficult to **understand**. As previously mentioned, one challenge is to discern which behaviors are sinful and which are simply an expression of the child's inability or weakness.

Because of these weaknesses, autistic behaviors require creative and individualized applications of biblical principles. For example, a parental command to "go clean your room" can be simply overwhelming to them. And with their poor communication skills, they often can't explain that dilemma or ask for clarification.

---

16. Todd Hardin, "Preaching in the Valley," Biblical Counseling Coalition blog, August 22, 2013, https://www.biblicalcounselingcoalition.org/2013/08/22/preaching-in-the-valley/. Used by permission.

So let's say that you give that direction, and after some time, you go in their room and find them just standing there staring at the wall. In a situation like this, don't assume defiance until you know the child understands what is expected, is capable of what is expected, has no valid reason (physically) not to do what is expected, and has sinfully chosen not to do it. It is important to make sure that behavior you discipline for is truly from a heart of defiance rather than from misunderstanding or inability.

An autistic child is capable of learning obedience within their limitations. Most nurture and admonition for autistic kids involves teaching and reteaching (repeat, repeat, repeat!), modeling, and gently walking their little body through the steps of the behavior you require. If there is resistance, have parents ask ability-appropriate heart questions (i.e., "What makes it hard to do this?" "What are you thinking when you do that?" "What would help you?"). As you can see, biblical principles of parenting don't change, but application is adapted to the needs and capabilities of each child. Faithful, consistent, patient, and loving biblical parenting will be pleasing to God.

Encourage Them to Seek Help

Wise biblical love goes a long way. This is because, most of all, autistic kids have hearts that we want to reach with the gospel. God's Word and his Spirit remain our main source of wisdom and help. Wise people in the body of Christ can encourage parents to stay the course in biblical parenting and pray with them, asking God for the wisdom they will need to raise the precious child he has entrusted to their care. And as with all people, autistic kids *can be* saved by believing the gospel, they *can be* indwelt by the Holy Spirit who will empower them to be more like Christ, and they *can have* spiritual gifts that God will use to minister to others.

In addition to spiritual support and wisdom from the body of Christ, parents may also benefit from engaging appropriate medical help for their child in order to maximize strengths and minimize weaknesses. Melinda and Bob used physical therapy, speech therapy, and occupational therapy providers to mitigate the physical deficits that frequently accompany ASD. Special education workers may also be helpful.

Teach Parents to Beware of Idolizing Their Child's Progress

While it is reasonable to get available help from many sources, there is a balance. It may become a temptation for the primary caregiver (usually the mom) to make an idol out of "fixing" the child. Idolatry could manifest as discontentment with the child's progress or bitterness over his lack of growth. These moms may expect that because they are "doing everything right," the results they want (like a happy, obedient, and appreciative child) are guaranteed. False worship will lead a mom to spend an inordinate amount of time, energy, or finances supporting her autistic child to the point that she neglects other responsibilities to her marriage or her other children. As a result, the marriage and family will suffer. As biblical counselor Robert Jones has said, teach parents "never to fix your hope on something that God has not guaranteed."[17] Lead parents to fix their hope on Jesus Christ and the promises of God (Romans 15:13; 1 Peter 1:13). Lead them to remember their main goal in life is to work and serve for his glory and honor.

Encourage Parents to Exercise Medical Discernment

Help parents avoid the pitfall of errant medical advice that makes unproven claims. In order to avoid unwise courses of action, it is important for families to be "shrewd as serpents and innocent as doves" (Matthew 10:16) in dealing with any potentially false information they may receive from well-meaning people. Current medical research on ASD has not definitively determined a cause or a cure for their condition. So teach a family to graciously but firmly respond in this way to any offered information that claims to know the cause or

---

17. Robert Jones, "Thinking Biblically about Depression," notes from lecture for Faith Bible Seminary, BC 401 (2009), 10.

cure of ASD: "Thank you for your concern. My husband/wife and I have a different opinion or have chosen a different option."

Counseling the Person with ASD

Your ministry to an autistic individual is to offer compassionate care and practical tools for biblical change in a way that the person can best receive and understand. There are several specific ways of relating to a person with ASD that should inform your counseling approach. First, they usually do not want to be treated like a victim or looked on with pity. You don't have to mention the diagnosis of ASD. Labels, especially when used outside of a medical context, can be demeaning, stigmatizing, and condescending, so it is important to use biblical terms to describe behaviors and difficulties. As one young man said, "The label says we are 'lesser.' But we just have different tuning, like stiff vs. soft suspension on brakes. We are not mentally ill; we are just another person with different ways of processing and thinking things through." As with anyone we counsel, we need to treat them with respect.

Be patient when you speak with them. They may hesitate to answer as they think things through. Jay describes it this way: "When I think a thought, it connects with so many other ones that my mind goes into many different, but related, ideas. That's why I am slow to respond in conversations. I'm processing."

Consider short weekly sessions (thirty minutes or less), depending on the abilities of the person you are meeting with. Know that an autistic person can get overwhelmed easily in new environments because a lot of sensory information all at once is exhausting—they may find it hard to ignore sounds, smells, visual stimuli, touch, etc. Distractions should be removed as much as possible so they can reason through the given guidance.

Tailor homework to ability level. They can read or listen to Scripture. If they are believers, they can serve in their giftedness— homework may be just to say a specific encouraging word to someone.

Start small and simple and build from there. If what is assigned is confusing, they may not be able to explain that to you. So take the time to explain and find out if they understand by having them summarize their homework assignment in their own words. If the homework is doable, they tend to be reliable, diligent workers. Also, repeat former lessons frequently until they can verbalize their understanding.

Be knowledgeable about the typical struggles of a person with ASD, many of which we have covered in this chapter. Work hard to understand how this particular autistic person thinks and processes the world—listen carefully and ask good questions. Show interest in their life:

- Ask what they like most in life (to do, eat, read, etc.).
- Ask why they like what they like.
- Ask about how they understand things.
- Ask what motivates them.

One young autistic lady said, "Something has to be important for us to bother spending time on it. I struggle with doing a lot of things because I haven't figured out that they are important." So ask what is important to them and why. Teach them what God says is important, and help them find ways to do what God says we should do in ways that are appropriate for our culture (for example, discuss what it can look like to be kind, encouraging, etc.).

Ask about potential loneliness, anxiety, or sadness. What makes them sad? Most autistic people desire strongly to interact with others; they simply don't have the skill set to do so easily. Jay put it like this: "We start life from an alternate, confusing beginning, without an understanding of neurotypical people. Without a way to learn how and why they think how they do, we become discouraged in relationships, which leads us to distance ourselves from others."

Ask what is most difficult about relationships for them. Jay said that for him, what is most difficult about relationships is "When you get the feeling that you're missing something that everyone else gets. It's like living in a foreign land and you don't understand the language. We know we are different and are frustrated by that. We do try to connect with people by expressing our interests; for example, if I care about batteries, I'll show you I care about you by talking about batteries."

These quotes from individuals with ASD highlight the typical struggles with communication that a person with ASD might experience. These could be summarized simply as the pain that comes from being misunderstood and misunderstanding others. Be aware that these deficits may leave a child or even an adult with ASD vulnerable to being taken advantage of because it is difficult for them to discern evil intent. One autistic lady I counseled had been raped, while one young man had been convinced to steal his father's car for "friends."

While those examples are more extreme, there are multiple, less dramatic misunderstandings in their everyday lives that can cause significant pain or struggle. Mark Shaw describes this experience with a simple illustration: "Imagine how discouraging it would be to be misunderstood by others when you make a statement that you meant in all seriousness, but the crowd of people bursts into laughter thinking you were making a joke, and you are not even sure why they are laughing . . . often the autistic person cannot clearly identify where the communication error occurred."

These counselees need the same biblical truth that we all do, but they are more likely to understand and apply it if it is expressed in ways that are adapted to their particular abilities. So counselors can teach better ways to express thoughts, desires, and emotions with real-life examples. Teach them about the heart, sin, grace, idolatry, and how to change. Use Proverbs to teach relational wisdom and how to discern right from wrong; teach the "one another" passages in the New Testament and then illustrate them with concrete examples of what it looks like to love or encourage or help others. Role-play appropriate responses and conversations. You may also want to bring in helpful resources that teach basic social skills. Don't be afraid to be direct, and keep it simple. If they already know something you are teaching, they will tell you. Remember, they tend to be very honest.

You might have to explain things to them in the counseling session like

- What people's facial expressions and body language means—happy, confused, questioning, etc.
- Why people maintain eye contact.
- How and why people keep personal space.
- The importance of culturally appropriate hygiene as a way to love others.
- How to express emotions righteously. One counselee said, "I have no understanding about emotions; other people's or my own. And I have a hard time remembering how to respond, so sometimes I get that wrong."

While we teach to minimize weaknesses, we also want to maximize strengths. If the person is a believer, how are they gifted? How can their unique abilities and strengths be used to glorify the Lord and love others? One counselee works with elderly people at an extended care facility. She enjoys helping, and they love her! One young man has a wonderful memory, and he helps customers find things in the store where he works. They both unashamedly talk about Jesus in their places of employ.

A Word to the Counselor

The information presented in this chapter is intended to heighten your awareness of what the diagnosis of ASD describes so that when you serve people on the autism spectrum and their families, you will be equipped to give them wise and gentle help and encouragement. It is a call to come alongside them and to learn to love and appreciate those who are different (James 2:1–5). God uniquely created each person with ASD to be exactly as he desired for his own redemptive and glorious purposes. As image-bearers, they deserve our compassion, care, and respect. They have an everlasting soul and need to hear the hope of the gospel just like everyone else. If they are believers, they have the power of the Holy Spirit to change and grow.

One young lady said, "'He is so he is.' Everything changed because that's truth. When I turned to God for life, I saw that I had been dead. Now I have order, hope, a reason to learn to understand others, and something beyond this life. My autistic state was different from others in the family of God, but salvation was similar. We are all members of the King's body, and we share the King's desires." When asked what was the most important thing to her, she said, "That all come to know, learn from, and love him who made them with all their heart, regardless of their mental capabilities; and second, that you love others without prejudice of their mental capabilities, spiritual condition or maturity, physical health, or wealth." That is pretty good advice.

Keep reading and learning about ASD. Help others to better understand the image-bearers who have been diagnosed with ASD. Remember that, despite some unusual behavior, you are more alike than different! As one autistic young lady noted, "It takes a while to understand anybody, but know that it will take a while to get to know an autistic person too. Once you do, you may find you get to like their oddities just as we come to enjoy your strange habits."

A Word to the Individual with ASD

You are precious to God, made by him, for his purpose. He made you exactly as he wanted in order to do what he has planned for you to do. If you already know him, keep getting to know him better by reading or listening to the Bible. Use the gifts you have been given to the best of your ability. Seek counseling when you need help. Be teachable— be willing to learn different ways to do things. Then, seek ways that you can help other people.

If you don't know God yet, you can! God made us and loves us. God is perfectly good. But people are not perfectly good; everyone does wrong things—everyone sins. Our sins separate us from God. But because God loves us and wants us to live with him forever, he made a way for our sins to be wiped away. That way is Jesus. Jesus suffered and died on the cross for us, in our place, so that we don't have to suffer and die for our sins. Jesus died but came to life again on the third day.

Jesus takes our sins away and gives us forgiveness. And that forgiveness allows us be able to live with God forever. If we want to live with God forever, this is what we have to do: be sorry for the wrong things we have done, thank Jesus for dying for us, and ask him to forgive our sins.

Conclusion

As the mom of an autistic son, my desire in writing this chapter is to help other counselors who may not have experience with autism be able to interact with autistic counselees and their parents in helpful ways. Many interactions with ASD sufferers will be awkward—that's okay. My son's advice is apropos here: "We live in [experience] a different world than you do—please be patient."

CHAPTER 9

. . . .

THE BRAIN ON MEDICATION:
AN OVERVIEW OF FOUNDATIONAL CONCEPTS AND STRATEGIES

Craig K. Svensson, PharmD, PhD

The National Center for Health Statistics reports that nearly half of American adults received a prescription drug in the last thirty days, and almost 25 percent received three or more prescription drugs.[1] When this is combined with the fact that 90 percent of Americans regularly consume nonprescription drugs,[2] it is a given that biblical counselors will regularly serve counselees who are consuming one or more medications. Hence, it is helpful for counselors to possess a basic understanding of how drugs may influence thinking and behavior, as well as the ability to receive and respond to counseling. While this need is most apparent with psychotherapeutic drugs (e.g., antidepressants and antianxiety medications), there are many drugs used for non-psychiatric conditions that have subtle or profound effects on the ability of counselees to acquire, process, recall, and act on biblical truth.

---

1. National Center for Health Statistics, "Therapeutic Drug Use," *Centers for Disease Control and Prevention*, last updated October 21, 2021, https://www.cdc.gov/nchs/fastats/drug-use-therapeutic.htm.

2. Troy Trygstad, "Americans Love OTC Medications," OTC Guide 23, no. 1 (July 16, 2019), https://www.pharmacytimes.com/view/americans-love-otc-medications.

Dynamic Interaction Between the Brain, Heart, and Behavior

While we are far more than our chemical selves, it is also clear that events influencing brain activity impact our affections and decisions, which drive our behavior. There is much about this dynamic interaction that we do not understand, but it should be obvious that interactions between the three can influence the outcome of counseling efforts.

Figure 1 illustrates the brain–heart–behavior dynamic. In its biblical usage, the heart represents the core of our being as image-bearers of our Creator. It is the seat of our affections, source of our will, root of our reasoning capacity, driver of our emotions, and locus of our moral convictions. Importantly, the Bible reveals that the heart is both the wellspring of sin and shaped by sin (cf. Matthew 5:19; Hebrews 3:13). As such, it can be deceived and molded by other sinners (John 12:40). While we are warned about the negative influences of sin and sinners on the heart (1 Corinthians 15:33), the heart is also informed and renewed by Scripture (2 Timothy 3:16), guided and comforted by the Spirit (1 Corinthians 2:13), while also refreshed and encouraged by the saints (Philemon 1:7). Understanding the profound influences of these five factors (Figure 1) directs the work of biblical counselors seeking to help counselees. But in doing so, it is imperative to recognize the other elements that both influence the heart and impact the ability of the heart to govern thinking and behavior.

Figure 1: The Brain–Heart–Behavior Dynamic

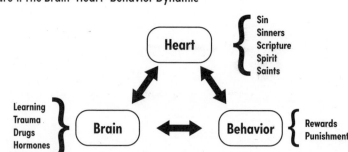

Importantly, there is a three-pound organ encased in our skulls that clearly influences how we think and behave. Neuroscientists have uncovered a fascinating network of physiological changes that occur with the acquisition of new knowledge. There are measurable changes in pathways within the brain when we learn a new skill or develop habitual patterns of behavior. The ability of the brain to rewire connections and modify pathways by which signals are transmitted (which is called neuroplasticity) is essential for learning, recovery after brain injury, and imprinting ways of doing things that become routines that require little conscious thought (e.g., elements of driving or the process of brushing our teeth).[3]

Disruption of normal brain function can have a dramatic, while at other times subtle, impact on normal cognition and emotional expression. For example, traumatic injury to the brain can result in short- or long-term loss of ability to think clearly, recall previously learned knowledge, and even control motor functions. People with a family member suffering from Alzheimer's disease, other forms of dementia, or even brain cancer, can attest to the marked changes in their loved one as a result of brain disease. The impaired ability to think and control one's emotions may be manifested by changes in how a person speaks or responds to various situations. It should not be controversial to assert that trauma- and disease-induced brain damage may dramatically change a person's behavior, which indicates that there are biological determinants behind behavior.

In addition to trauma and disease, drugs and hormones are known to alter brain function in measurable ways, as well as result in observable changes in thinking and behavior. A wide variety of drugs alter brain function in critical regions of the brain associated with pleasure, cognition, wakefulness, and impulse control. Readers presumably have personal experience with the changes brought by prescription and nonprescription drugs on their ability to concentrate,

---

3. Pedro Mateos-Aparicio and Antonio Rodríguez-Moreno, "The Impact of Studying Brain Plasticity," *Frontiers in Cellular Neuroscience* 13, no. 66 (February 27, 2019), doi. org/10.3389/fncel.2019.00066.

perform simple mental tasks, or even stay awake. In addition, whether it is the volatile emotions observed during puberty, the "brain fog" of pregnancy, or emotional swings during menopause, we are all familiar with the power of hormonal surges or dips to make emotional control and clearheaded thinking a challenge. Thus, we should not underestimate the ability of chemical changes in the brain to alter cognitive ability, emotional control, and behavior.

Moreover, it is clear that external factors have a shaping influence on behavior. Even animals will respond to rewards and punishment—they alter their behavior to gain the former and avoid the latter. Parents have long deployed rewards and punishment to mold their child's behavior, perhaps with overconfidence in its impact on the heart. Nonetheless, human experience and formal studies both demonstrate the persuasive power of reinforcing desired behavior and penalizing destructive behavior. Parents, coaches, employers, and others use this knowledge to bring about change in those under their charge. For example, employers increasingly reward employees financially for not smoking or adopting healthy behaviors. In contrast, peer pressure is often a driver in teens' adoption of negative behaviors (e.g., smoking, recreational drug use).

It is also true that persisting in specific patterns of behavior not only imprint networks in the brain, but they also shape the heart, both negatively and positively. Persistent participation in sinful conduct can harden the heart, while habits of devotion and sacrificial service can soften it.[4] For example, King Nebuchadnezzar's reveling in his earthly accomplishments produced a heart hardened by pride, ultimately leading to his chastening by the Lord (see Daniel 4). Romans 1 describes the progressive moral decline, and ultimate abandonment by God, in the lives of those who persist in idolatrous pursuits.

---

4. For an interesting discussion of the shaping power of habit, see Justin Whitmel Earley, *The Common Rule: Habits of Purpose for an Age of Distraction* (Downers Grove, IL: IVP Books, 2019).

Collectively, the observations in the preceding paragraphs make it obvious that drugs that can alter brain activity can also influence the effectiveness of counseling. But how do they alter the brain and, thereby, change a person's ability to benefit from counseling?

How Drugs Alter Brain Activity

Brain activity is not controlled by an on-off switch, but by a dimmer switch. This means that drugs that alter brain processes have a graded effect on brain function. Thus, the degree of impairment created by a drug is determined by how much it dims brain function, which varies with the dose of the drug and an individual's susceptibility to the effects of the drug. This is best illustrated by considering the effects of central nervous system (CNS) depressants, such as alcohol and sedatives (see Figure 2). At low doses, these drugs have subtle effects that may not be recognized by the person taking the drug or those who observe them. These include disinhibition, meaning the person will say or do things that their moral judgment or rational thinking would normally prevent. They may also be less attentive to their surroundings and have a reduced ability to concentrate on important tasks. As the dose is increased, more serious impairment of brain function becomes evident, up to and including the inability to maintain vital functions, such as breathing and blood pressure, which, if left unchecked, leads to death.

Figure 2: Graded Effect of CNS Drugs on Brain Function

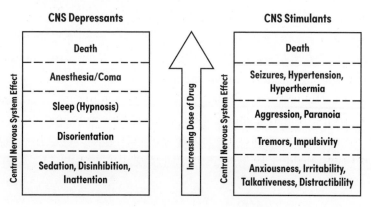

When CNS depression is significant enough to cause disorientation, it becomes clear to others that something is amiss with the person. But lesser levels of impairment may not be readily recognized by those unfamiliar with the person, or even by the person themselves. Nonetheless, mild impairment may have consequences. For example, patients undergoing brief outpatient surgery that involves short-duration anesthesia are commonly given post-surgery instructions that recognize the persistence of anesthetic effects—effects which even the patient may not recognize. These instructions include not driving or operating machinery, as well as not making significant personal or legal decisions for twenty-four hours. This is due to the subtle impairment of cognitive and fine motor abilities that can last for many hours after significant sedation. By the time they are discharged from the ambulatory surgical center, most patients feel alert and don't recognize these subtle degrees of impairment, which is why the warnings are so important.

In addition to impairment resulting from CNS depressant effects, drugs can also induce the opposite effect of CNS stimulation, which results in irritability, aggressiveness, anxiety, and an inability to focus (see Figure 2). As the dose of a stimulant is increased, life-threatening hyperstimulation may occur. Again, low levels of stimulation secondary to the effects of drugs may not be recognized by those unfamiliar with a person. Despite this, these effects can impair the ability of a person to function, including their ability to receive and respond to counseling. Examples of how the impairment produced by both CNS depressants and stimulants alter cognitive processes critical to biblical counseling are discussed later in the chapter.

While many people recognize that psychotherapeutic agents alter brain activity, the array of drugs that cause subtle impairment—and sometimes not-so-subtle impairment—to the CNS is actually quite expansive. Table 1 lists the categories of drugs found to cause some level of CNS impairment. These agents include common over-the-counter medications, prescription drugs, and the most widely socially used drug, alcohol. In fact, at the time of this writing, ten of the top twenty prescription medications sold in the US (by volume) can cause some level of CNS depression or stimulation. Any drug that may cause drowsiness (often marked by a label to this effect on the prescription vial) has the ability to cause some level of altered cognitive ability.

TABLE 1 Medications Known to Cause CNS Impairment	
ADHD Medications	Antihistamines
Alcohol	Antihypertensives
Analgesics	Antimanics
Anesthetics	Antipsychotics
Anorexiants	Anxiolytics
Antiarrhythmic	Migraine medications
Anticonvulsants	Muscle relaxants
Antidepressants	Sedatives
Antidiarrheals	

Another way to think of who might be experiencing CNS impairment due to drug therapy is to consider which diseases are often treated with drugs that may exhibit these effects. Table 2 lists some diseases for which such drugs are commonly prescribed. For example, people receiving drug therapy for seizures may experience significant levels of sedation during the peak effect of the drug after each dose. Family members may note that the person is "not quite themselves" for several hours after their morning dose of medication, but their cognitive capacity seems normal in the afternoon.

TABLE 2 Diseases that Often Require Therapy with Drugs Known to Cause CNS Impairment	
Chronic pain	Cluster headaches
Fibromyalgia	Hypertension
Irritable bowel syndrome	Migraine headaches
Parkinson's disease	Restless leg syndrome
Seasonal allergies	Seizure disorders

Some patients appear to develop a tolerance to the CNS depression of many drugs when they receive them chronically (e.g., sedation due to antihistamines), but others do not. Thus, the impairment may occur for days or weeks after initiating or increasing the drug therapy, and then dissipate. Obviously, short-term impairment is easier to manage than ongoing side effects. In addition, people who receive drug therapy for a limited time period, such as for treatment of seasonal allergy, may only struggle with these effects for a few months (though they may recur annually).

The key areas of minor CNS impairment from medications occur in four domains relevant to the biblical counselor, as illustrated in Figure 3. Importantly, people are affected differently and to different degrees, dependent upon a host of factors. For example, most people who take the common antihistamine diphenhydramine (also known by the brand name Benadryl) will report drowsiness, but the degree will differ from person to person. In addition, if this drug is combined with another sedative (such as any common muscle relaxant), the degree of sedation will be greater. In contrast, the vast majority of people taking the antihistamine loratadine (also known by the brand name Claritin) experience no drowsiness, but it does occur in a small fraction of patients (less than 10 percent). Thus, one should not assume these impairments will be manifested in all or most people consuming drugs that have the potential to cause these effects.

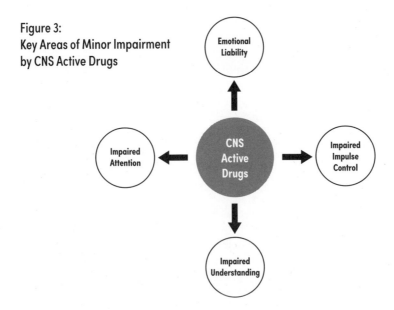

Figure 3:
Key Areas of Minor Impairment
by CNS Active Drugs

Impaired attention may be the most common side effect of drugs that affect the CNS. Impaired attention can arise from either drowsiness or agitation and will make it difficult for counselees to focus their attention on the task at hand. Behavioral pharmacologists who have studied whether people have the ability to overcome these effects by sheer willpower generally conclude that it is not possible to do so.[5] This conclusion is controversial due to the difficulty of studying this phenomenon with proper controls. After all, how do you measure the exertion of willpower? Nevertheless, a counselor and counselee are ill-advised to think drug effects can be decisively dismissed by conscious choice.

A person with impaired attention will find it hard to concentrate during counseling sessions, especially the longer the session continues. A counselee struggling with this drug side effect may appear

5. See S.A. Maisto, et al., "Alcohol and volitional control on affect/sensation, cognitive and perceptual-motor measures" *Current Psychological Research* 1, no. 3-4 (September 15, 1981): 235–249, https://doi.org/10.1007/BF03186734 and C.K. Svensson, "Attenuation of Response to Repeated Drug Administration: A Proposal for Differentiating Tachyphylaxis and Tolerance," *Journal of Pharmacology and Experimental Therapeutics* 381, no. 1 (April 1, 2022): 28-32, https://doi.org/10.1124/jpet.121.000978.

to the counselor to be uninterested in what the counselor is saying, when they are actually struggling with a side effect from medication. Strategies to optimize counseling in the face of impaired attention are discussed in a later section of this chapter.

Cognition is the process of acquiring knowledge, gaining conceptual understanding, engaging in abstract thought, and interpreting both experience and ideas. Cognitive capacity underpins our ability to function in a world that continually stimulates our nine senses (vision, hearing, smell, taste, touch, balance, pain, temperature, and body position). Thus, it follows that impaired cognitive ability due to drug therapy will result in impaired understanding. Importantly, the process of understanding abstract concepts is a higher-order brain function that is more susceptible to subtle changes (and is established later in child development). Hence, in addition to impaired attention, impaired understanding may be the most common manifestation of an altered CNS. For example, one of the earliest signs of dementia (in which cognitive decline eventually becomes severe) is the inability to learn new technology and the loss of ability to operate technology previously used without trouble (such as a smartphone). Those with mild CNS impairment, whether due to drugs or disease, may exhibit difficulty "translating" instructions into action. Again, this is not something that can be overcome by sheer force of will.

A person with cognitive impairment may find abstract biblical concepts difficult to grasp, especially at first presentation. This may require more repetition than normal to comprehend important truths. This impairment may also make Scripture memorization especially difficult. What may appear to the counselor to be an unwillingness to do the work necessary for Scripture memorization may actually be due to cognitive impairment. A simple test may help the counselor differentiate between these two. Ask the counselee to read a short verse, such as the first half of Isaiah 43:5 ("Fear not, for I am with you") five times. Then ask the counselee to close their Bible, wait one minute, and recite the verse. An inability to perform that level of recall would suggest cognitive impairment that will make verse memorization especially difficult.

Disinhibition, or impaired impulse control, is another low-dose effect of drugs that depress the CNS. It is why lapping up alcohol leads to loose lips. People will disregard social norms, demean others with their speech, and act out in uncharacteristic ways. This explains why conflict among people consuming alcohol and other drugs often escalates rapidly. Impaired impulse control is also one reason for an unwritten rule in surgery and recovery units: never repeat what a patient says when going into or coming out of sedation.

Some might think that drug-induced impaired impulse control simply reveals what a person is really like and can, therefore, be a window to the heart. Indeed, this is the basis for using what have been called truth serums. Yet, a person's character is not simply a reflection of what they might be tempted to do or say, but also the level of constraint they exhibit based on their moral judgment. I presume we have all been shocked by thoughts or ideas that pop into our mind from time to time. But moral evaluation quickly turns us from such thoughts and subsequent actions. In a disinhibited state, due to injury or medication, we may not display that moral restraint.

Impaired impulse control as a result of medication can be hard to detect in a person you don't know very well. Perhaps the clearest sign of this is changes observed in a person across the course of a day, something unlikely to be detected by a counselor who only sees a counselee weekly at the same time each week. On the other hand, a counselee who acknowledges struggling to control their response to others, perhaps leading to interpersonal conflict, and is receiving a medication known to cause CNS depression, could be probed to determine whether there is a common time of day when these instances arise. If these times of conflict are commonly associated within the first hour or so after taking their medication, their awareness that the medication may make them more susceptible to impulsive responses may help them be cautious with their words.

For example, I occasionally take a medication to halt an emerging attack from a rare form of colitis. My wife helped me realize that I tend to talk too much after taking the medication (something that is admittedly already a problem for a person employed full-time as a professor). As a consequence, when I need to take this medication, I consciously remind myself of this tendency and work harder at listening more than speaking.

Emotional lability refers to rapid and exaggerated changes in mood, sometimes resulting in seemingly uncontrollable crying or laughter, irritability, or bursts of anger. People with emotional lability due to brain injury, neurodegenerative diseases (e.g., Parkinson's disease or multiple sclerosis), or medication may be able to forestall these reactions by becoming aware of and avoiding triggers, or by taking a break from stressful situations. Displays of emotional lability appear to occur more often during times of fatigue in patients with brain deficits. Counselors should be aware of their own reactions to others' displays of emotional lability (e.g., when they cry or laugh at seemingly inappropriate moments), as such responses can create embarrassment and block communication with the counselee. Compassion, humility, and patience by the counselor will best enable counselors to help people struggling with episodes of emotional lability.

It is not unusual for patients recovering from surgery, who are commonly on potent narcotic analgesics, to express extremes of gratitude or frustration with hospital staff—levels of emotional expression that are out of character for the individual. This is a manifestation of the emotional lability produced by such drugs. In like manner, counselors may observe similar out-of-character emotional expressions in people taking such drugs for short or long terms. For example, when counseling a patient recovering from knee replacement surgery, it is best not to read too much into emotional responses by counselees. Either the trauma of surgery or the medications may be the root cause of such responses.

Drug-Induced Neuropsychiatric Symptoms

Though not widely recognized, drugs may also induce symptoms that mimic neuropsychiatric disorders.[6] Table 3 provides a list of medication-induced symptoms that have been reported in medical literature. If not recognized as drug-induced, interventions to address these symptoms will likely be ineffective. Even worse, the patient may be prescribed long-term psychotherapeutic drugs due to misdiagnosis of the underlying cause of observed symptoms. Unfortunately, neuropsychiatric adverse effects of medications are both underappreciated by clinicians and understudied by researchers. Yet, as shown in Table 4, a variety of drugs and toxins can provoke these adverse effects. If a biblical counselor suspects that a counselee's symptoms may be due (even in part) to a medication, they should encourage their counselee to seek advice from their health care provider.

TABLE 3 Medication-Induced Neuropsychiatric Symptoms	
Agitation	Hallucinations
Anxiety	Mood disorders
Delirium	Psychosis
Delusions/Paranoia	Sleep disturbances

Effect of Psychotherapeutic Drugs on the Brain

Psychotherapeutic drug therapy is initiated with the intent of reducing the primary symptoms of psychiatric disorders (e.g., anxiety, paranoia). Similar to therapy for many other ailments (e.g., Parkinson's disease, hypertension), these drugs neither cure nor remove the underlying causes of observed symptoms. Indeed, it is reasonable to ask whether many of these drugs actually alleviate or

6. D. A. W. Johnson, "Drug-Induced Psychiatric Disorders," Drugs 22, no. 1 (1981): 57–69, https://doi.org/10.2165/00003495-198122010-00004.

simply mask symptoms. For example, some commonly used antipsychotic agents are potent tranquilizers. Indeed, they are sometimes used to calm aggressive patients in emergency rooms. When used for psychiatric disorders, are they treating the underlying cause of the disorder or simply dulling the patient's emotive responses? While the appropriateness of drug therapy for various psychiatric conditions remains controversial within the biblical counseling community and beyond, their widespread use makes it inevitable that biblical counselors will encounter counselees prescribed psychotherapeutic agents. It is, therefore, helpful to possess a basic understanding of the major classes of psychotherapeutic drugs.

TABLE 4 Agents Associated with Drug-Induced Psychosis	
Adrenergics	Cocaine
Alcohol/sedatives	Methamphetamine
Antiarrhythmics	Ecstasy
Antibiotics	Corticosteroids
Anticholinergics	Dextromethorphan
Antihistamines	Heavy metals
Antimalarials	Organophosphates
Antitubercular agents	St. John's wort
Bath salts	Thyroid hormones
Cannabis	

Historically, psychotherapeutic drugs have been grouped by their primary therapeutic indication: antidepressant, antianxiety, antipsychotic, hypnotic, and mood stabilizer. In other words, they were named based on the syndrome they were used to treat. Drugs were sometimes further subclassified by their chemical structure (e.g., tricyclic antidepressants) or unusual features (e.g., atypical antipsychotics). However, numerous agents now have expanded application (beyond their original intent) and are used for multiple disorders. For example, many commonly used drugs for depression are also prescribed for the treatment of anxiety. In addition, some antipsychotic agents are used as combination therapy for patients with depression that have become resistant to standard antidepressants. This increased use of psychotherapeutic drugs for multiple disorders has resulted in the development of a classification system based on the underlying pharmacological effects of the drug, irrespective of a drug's therapeutic application.[7] The current classification is known as the Neuroscience-Based Nomenclature (NBN). While the NBN provides a more informative framework for clinicians with knowledge of pharmacology, the classification may be opaque to those lacking this background. Nevertheless, a conceptual understanding of neurotransmission (how cells in the brain communicate with one another through chemical messengers) can provide enough knowledge to grasp the fundamental basis of the current classification of psychotherapeutic drugs.

Signaling in the CNS can be viewed as a four-step process occurring at the biochemical/molecular level of single neurons (the primary cells of communication in the brain):

Electrical Signal → Neurochemical release → Receptor Binding → Cell Response

Psychotherapeutic drugs act by altering the amounts of neurochemicals (also known as neurotransmitters) available or the binding of these chemicals to proteins (called receptors) expressed on the surface of adjacent neurons. As illustrated in Figure 4, neurochemicals are normally stored in small compartments within the neuron known as vesicles. When an electrical signal arrives, these are released into a region between neurons called the synapse. They can then migrate to an adjacent neuron and bind to specific receptors on the receiving neuron, which activates a cell response. But once the signal is received, there needs to be a means of ending the messaging between neurons.

---

7. Joseph Zohar et al., "A Review of the Current Nomenclature for Psychotropic Agents and an Introduction to the Neuroscience-Based Nomenclature," *European Neuropsychopharmacology* 25, no. 12 (2015): 2318–2325, https://doi.org/10.1016/j.euroneuro.2015.08.019.

After receiving a message via email, you can either delete it or save it in a file for later retrieval. Similarly, our Creator has endowed our bodies with two primary means by which to deal with a chemical message that has been received: breaking down the neurotransmitter (like deleting an email) or taking it back up into the sending neuron for later reuse (like filing a read email). This latter process is called reuptake. Hence, there are enzymes in the synaptic space that can degrade the neurotransmitter, and there are transporters on the sending neuron surface that can retrieve the neurotransmitter.

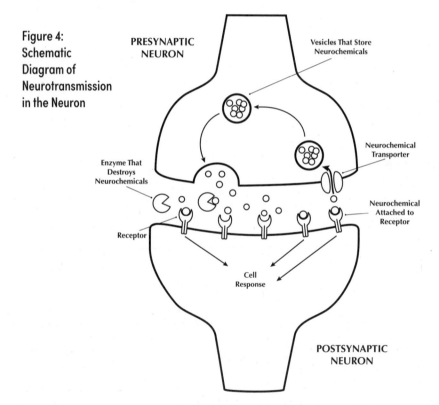

Figure 4: Schematic Diagram of Neurotransmission in the Neuron

PRESYNAPTIC NEURON

Vesicles That Store Neurochemicals

Neurochemical Transporter

Enzyme That Destroys Neurochemicals

Neurochemical Attached to Receptor

Receptor

Cell Response

POSTSYNAPTIC NEURON

Understanding this mechanism of neurotransmission makes it obvious that cell signaling may be enhanced by chemicals that cause the release of the neurotransmitter, inhibit the enzyme that breaks it down, bind to the same receptor as the neurotransmitter, or block the reuptake of the neurotransmitter by the presynaptic neuron. Drugs that bind to the same receptor as the neurotransmitter are referred to as agonists. In contrast, neurotransmission can be decreased by drugs that either reduce the release of neurotransmitters, or increase their degradation, increase their reuptake, or block the receptor to which the neurotransmitter binds. Drugs that block receptors for neurotransmitters are known as antagonists.

The NBN classifies psychotherapeutics based upon which neurochemical they alter and how they change the way the neurochemical is handled by the cell. In the same way that you can use your smartphone to send a message to someone by text, email, or voice, the brain can send signals using different neurochemicals. The primary neurotransmitters of interest in psychotherapeutic drug therapy are dopamine, GABA, glutamate, norepinephrine, and serotonin. As a consequence, drugs are classified using terms that include the names of these neurotransmitters. For example, a serotonin reuptake inhibitor is a drug that enhances cell signaling by inhibiting the reuptake of serotonin into the neuron after it has been released into the synaptic space. In contrast, a serotonin enzyme inhibitor (also known as a monoamine oxidase inhibitor, based on the name of the enzyme) enhances cell signaling by blocking the breakdown of serotonin. Similarly, a dopamine receptor antagonist blocks the effect of the dopamine by occupying the receptor to which dopamine normally binds. In the same manner that tape placed over a keyhole will prevent the key from entering and unlocking a door, an antagonist blocks access to the receptor without stimulating cell signaling.

This mechanistic classification is not without its limitations, because numerous drugs have multiple effects on neurotransmission. When this occurs, the classification expresses this diverse effect by acknowledging similar mechanisms on different transporters or receptors (such as inhibiting reuptake of serotonin and norepinephrine). Other drugs have multiple distinct modes of action, such as receptor agonism and enzyme inhibition. These instances are referred to as multimodal in mechanism. In addition, the pharmacological effects of some drugs are poorly understood. This would include several drugs formerly classified as mood stabilizers. In particular, lithium and valproate appear to enhance glutamate neurotransmission by an unknown mechanism.

Unfortunately, though first introduced in 2014, the NBN has not been uniformly adopted, and older nomenclature remains in use among some clinicians and researchers alike. Though most major medical and scientific journals have adopted the NBN, older terms frequently appear in the literature—even within books edited by some of the founders of the NBN classification system. Thus, Table 5 provides both the indication-based and NBN classification, along with common drugs within these classifications. It is anticipated that the indication-based nomenclature will fall into greater disuse over time.

It should also be recognized that the NBN classifies agents based on their pharmacological mechanisms of action and not the pathophysiological mechanism for psychiatric symptoms or their root causes (which are largely unknown). The link between neurochemical changes in the brain and the distortions individuals display in perceiving the world or shaping their behavioral responses remains an unproven hypothesis.

Brain Adaptation to Chronic Drug Exposure

The process of neurotransmission described above also provides a basis for understanding changes in the brain that occur as a result of chronic drug exposure. Physiologic processes in the body are largely driven to maintain homeostasis, which means they seek to stabilize normal functioning. If your blood pressure drops because you are dehydrated, your heart rate will increase, blood vessels will contract, and kidneys will preserve water to try to maintain normal blood pressure. Similarly, cell signaling in the brain and elsewhere is driven to maintain homeostasis in the long term. When external chemicals provide a continuous activation of cells through receptor engagement, the normal homeostatic mechanisms respond by reducing the expression of receptors on the cell surface. This results in a decrease of the signal. This loss of cell sensitivity is a means by which our bodies have been designed to return to homeostasis.

Studies in subjects who chronically ingest methamphetamine or other stimulants have shown a reduction in the number of dopamine receptors in the brain. This has been cited by some to support the idea that addiction is a disease akin to other diseases, such as diabetes, hypertension, or schizophrenia.[8] However, these changes observed in the brain with chronic recreational drug use are not pathological and actually demonstrate that the brain is functioning as designed.[9] Indeed, when drug ingestion ceases, there is a gradual increase in dopamine receptor expression in the brain. Importantly, alterations in receptor expression can also occur in other organs in the body with chronic drug exposure. For example, chronic use of decongestant nasal spray causes a reduction of receptors in the nose—resulting in a worsening of nasal congestion with continued administration.[10]

These cellular changes in response to chronic drug administration explains some of the adverse effects that can occur with continued use of psychotherapeutic drugs, as the normal release of neurotransmitters will exhibit a blunted effect in the face of reduced cell surface

8. Nora D. Volkow, George F. Kob, and A. Thomas McLellan, "Neurobiological Advances from the Brain Disease Model of Addiction," *New England Journal of Medicine* 374, no. 4 (2016): 363–371, https://doi.org/10.1056/NEJMra1511480.

9. For an in-depth discussion of the shortcomings of the brain disease model of addiction, see Craig K. Svensson, *Breaking the Grip of Addiction: How Is Addiction Started, Sustained, and Stopped?* (West Lafayette, IN: Consilium Publishing, 2022).

10. Sriram Vaidyanathan et al., "Fluticasone Reverses Oxymetazoline-Induced Tachyphylaxis of Response and Rebound Congestion," *American Journal of Respiratory and Critical Care Medicine* 182 (2010): 19–24, https://doi.org/10.1164/rccm.200911-1701OC.

receptors. More importantly, this also reveals why many patients find it extremely difficult to stop using these drugs and why they experience withdrawal symptoms when they do.

Withdrawal Effects of CNS Active Drugs

Essentially all psychotherapeutic drugs can result in a constellation of symptoms upon abrupt withdrawal of therapy. For example, a review of numerous studies concluded that, on average, over 50 percent of patients experience withdrawal symptoms when therapy with reuptake inhibitors of serotonin (a.k.a. SSRI—the most frequently prescribed antidepressants) are stopped.[11] These symptoms generally last for six weeks, but they may last for one year or more in many patients. Figure 5 summarizes the withdrawal symptoms observed with cessation of therapy with these agents. While the array of symptoms that can be provoked by withdrawal is quite broad, dizziness, flu-like symptoms, gastrointestinal symptoms, and mild cognitive impairment appear to be the most commonly observed. In addition, it should be noted that there is an increased risk of suicide attempts and ideation during the withdrawal period. Hence, cessation of drug therapy is not a step to take lightly or without medical supervision.

Unfortunately, many patients do not appear to receive adequate warning of the difficulty of stopping therapy when these drugs are first prescribed. Yet, this knowledge is essential if patients are going to weigh the risks and benefits of drug therapy versus nondrug interventions to manage symptoms of anxiety and depression. If a counselee discloses that they are considering starting an antidepressant or antianxiety medication, it may be advisable to ask if they have been informed of the difficulty many patients experience when they try to stop these medications. Information about withdrawal from such drugs can be readily found at reputable websites, (e.g., Mayo Clinic,

---

11. Mark Abi Horowitz and David Taylor, "Tapering of SSRI Treatment to Mitigate Withdrawal Symptoms," *Lancet Psychiatry* 6, no. 6 (2019): 538–546, https://doi.org/10.1016/S2215-0366(19)30032-X.

WebMD, or the Cleveland Clinic). As a result of these symptoms, many patients become unwilling to cease therapy with these drugs or they fail in attempts to do so.

Figure 5: Symptoms Reported Subsequent to Withdrawal from SSRI Drugs[12]

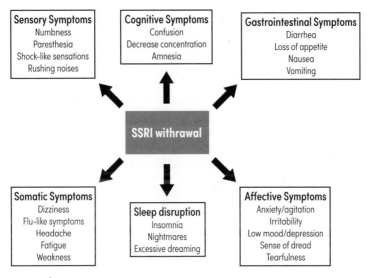

Others should not underestimate how difficult it can be for patients to stop therapy with psychotherapeutic agents, even for people highly motivated to do so. Since symptoms rapidly disappear with reinstitution of drug therapy, it is not surprising that this relief provides a strong incentive to continue taking the drug. In addition, withdrawal symptoms can mimic the syndrome for which the drug was initially prescribed (e.g., anxiety or depression), leading to a misdiagnosis of recurrence of the syndrome and resulting in unnecessary long-term drug therapy.

Strategies can be deployed to help patients who wish to cease therapy with psychotherapeutic agents. These strategies (which should only be conducted under medical guidance) include tapering the dose of the drug rather than abrupt withdrawal, a process that should occur

12. Modified from Horowitz and Taylor, "Tapering of SSRI Treatment to Mitigate Withdrawal Symptoms."

over months and not mere weeks. Studies have shown that tapering over two to four weeks is usually insufficient to prevent withdrawal symptoms.[13] It is also advisable that tapering include doses lower than the normal lowest therapeutic dose (which requires splitting the normal lowest dosage form available). In addition, beginning tapering at a time when stress in the patient's life can be minimized is advisable. The biblical counselor can be of help in this process by aiding counselees in addressing their response to the inevitable vicissitudes of life that will arise during the period of tapering the drug. Helping them deal with stress in a biblical manner can help them endure the discomfort that may arise while the drug is withdrawn.

How should the biblical counselor respond to a counselee who desires to cease drug therapy, but their physician or other medical provider advises against it? This is a sensitive matter that requires much wisdom and humility. Most counselors lack the medical expertise to make such judgments themselves and must avoid doing so. Even if they possess the appropriate medical training, the counselor is engaging with the counselee in their role as a counselor and not as a health care provider, so they shouldn't confuse their role. There are also potential legal ramifications for advising people to ignore or go against medical advice. The prudent action when faced with this dilemma is to advise counselees to respond the way we all should respond if there are questions about a diagnosis or therapy recommendation received from a practitioner: seek a second opinion by a qualified medical provider. It is inadvisable for a counselor to provide any other recommendation.

Strategies for Maximizing Counseling with Drug Therapy Recipients

While drugs can impair the ability of individuals to assimilate and act on biblical counseling, there are strategies to optimize counseling

---

13. Horowitz and Taylor, "Tapering of SSRI Treatment."

encounters while counselees are receiving acute or chronic drug therapy that reduces their ability to think clearly or results in other CNS effects. It begins by both the counselee and counselor recognizing the potential or actual impairment. A compassionate conversation can unify the counselor and counselee in the goal of getting the most out of each session.

Consider the case of a man I'll call George. I had been asked to mentor George after his formal counseling sessions had concluded. He struggled with a besetting sin, and we decided to work through a book together to encourage greater spiritual discipline in his life. Our first several meetings were productive. George came prepared and focused on the discussion. At a subsequent meeting, he appeared very distracted and was unprepared. His leg was bouncing rhythmically at a rapid rate, his gaze kept moving around the room, and he couldn't stop fidgeting with his hands. I said, "You seem very unsettled today. What's going on in your life?" Among other things, George told me he saw a new health care provider who stopped the antidepressant he had been taking for several years and put him on a completely different medication. He went on to tell how he hadn't felt quite right since the switch of medications. It was apparent to me that he was experiencing withdrawal symptoms from the abrupt medication change.

When I suggested to George that his unsettledness was likely from the switch of medications, we both recognized his unsettled state would make it hard to accomplish the goals for that meeting. Rather than frustrating both of us trying to force the issue, we talked about ways he could best manage life while his body adjusted to the medication changes. We connected by phone and texts over the next two weeks, primarily for me to give encouragement. After his body adjusted, we were able to reengage in the study with his undistracted attention.

When might the counselor suspect drug-induced deficits are occurring? First, is the counselee receiving a drug known to cause drowsiness, agitation, or other CNS effects? Second, have you observed changes in their emotional lability or their ability to focus on the content or comprehend material, which are associated with the onset of new drug therapy or dosing changes? Third, do these changes oscillate in a manner corresponding to drug dosing (e.g., one to two hours after taking the drug, when the peak effect of most drugs is observed)? This may be difficult to observe if your encounter with the counselee is once a week at the same time. Thus, open-ended questions about when they find they are most productive in doing mental tasks, like reading or home assignments, may provide the best insight.

If a counselee is suspected or clearly demonstrated to have mild impairment associated with drug therapy, steps can be taken to mitigate the impact on counseling sessions or the counselee's completion of assignments at home. Careful evaluation of the setting is a simple step. Avoiding unnecessary distractions (visual and auditory) in the room where counseling or homework takes place can help those who are struggling to focus. Air quality can also be important. We have all likely experienced the challenge of being in the discomfort of a hot, stuffy room (or one that chills our bones) in terms of our ability to focus on the task at hand. A well-lit, comfortable setting that is free of distractions can go a long way toward enhancing the ability of people to focus their attention.

The time of day and duration of counseling sessions, as well as completion of assigned work at home, can also help to mitigate the negative effects of therapy with CNS active agents. For example, we have a family member who takes a medication to treat seizures that leaves them with a brain fog for several hours each morning after their daily dose. It is best that we not try to have a serious conversation about important matters during this period of the day because the content will not be remembered nor will they be able to engage in clearheaded thinking during the discussion. While an effort of the will to overcome CNS depression causing drowsiness is debatable, the length of time a counselee seeks to do so surely influences their ability to benefit from either counsel or biblical study. The same is true for people who are experiencing the stimulant effects of a drug and having difficulty sitting still or focusing on a single task. In other words, trying to focus on one subject for sixty minutes at a time may push the limits of their ability. Shorter sessions on a more frequent basis may be the best strategy for such individuals.

Tolerance for and encouragement of movement is also a viable mitigation strategy. While a counselor might be unsettled when talking to an individual who is physically pacing, it may allow the counselee to burn off nervous energy or battle drowsiness. Individuals with back pain or spasticity in the legs may find sitting for any length of time uncomfortable. As discomfort increases, their ability to concentrate will decrease. Jesus seems to have done a fair bit of teaching while walking, and counselors may be advised to consider this as a means to help some counselees. Biblical counseling can be effective while strolling through our Father's world as well as when it occurs encased within four walls.

Resetting expectations for the length of time structured counseling will be needed may be necessary for those who have been prescribed medications that present a challenge to absorb and act on counseling. But a conscious, purposeful resetting of expectations will help the counselor avoid experiencing frustration at the pace of progress. Importantly, counselees with medication-induced impairment may need more reinforcement than others. Recognizing that this need arises through no fault of the counselee should create a higher level of patience in the counselor.

Medications and Biblical Counseling in Perspective

Drug therapy has saved untold lives and improved the well-being of many more. Antibiotics and vaccines have defanged many diseases. Other classes of drugs relieve or reduce unbearable symptoms of diseases that cannot be cured. But medications are not without their shortcomings. Among these is the cognitive impairment that can occur when drugs are used to treat a wide variety of ailments, which in turn makes mental tasks more difficult. Recognition of this effect can lead to strategies that will aid the biblical counselor in their efforts to, in the power of the Spirit, bring Scripture to bear on the hearts of those God graciously brings to them in their time of need.

TABLE5[14] Common Psychotherapeutic Drugs and Their Classifications[15]			
Indication based	**NBN – Pharmacological based**		
Indication	**Neurotransmitter**	**Mechanism**	**Drug Examples**
Antidepressants			
TCA – Tricyclic Antidepressants	norepinephrine (NET)	reuptake inhibitor (NET)	desipramine
	norepinephrine, serotonin (SERT)	reuptake inhibitor (NET and SERT)	amoxapine nortriptyline protriptyline
	serotonin, norepinephrine	reuptake inhibitor (SERT and NET)	imipramine
	serotonin	reuptake inhibitor (SERT)	clomipramine
	serotonin, norepinephrine	multimodal[16]	amitriptyline
	norepinephrine, serotonin	multimodal	doxepin
	serotonin, dopamine	receptor antagonist	trimipramine
MAOI – monoamine oxidase inhibitor	serotonin, dopamine, norepinephrine	multimodal	isocarboxazid phenelzine tranylcypromide
	dopamine, norepi-nephrine, serotonin	enzyme inhibitor	selegiline
SSRI – selective serotonin reuptake inhibitor	serotonin	reuptake inhibitor (SERT)	citalopram escitalopram fluoxetine fluvoxamine paroxetine sertraline

14. Table modified from David J. Nutt and Pierre Blier, "Neuroscience-Based Nomenclature (NbN) for *Journal of Psychopharmacology*," *Journal of Psychopharmacology* 30, no. 5 (2016): 413–415, https://doi.org/10.1177/0269881116642903.

15. Drugs are listed by generic names. Medications not included are newer drugs not previously classified by the indication-based system and, therefore, only classified using the NBN. Receptor subtypes have been omitted for simplicity.

16. Multimodal refers to drugs with more than one mode of action (e.g., reuptake inhibitor and enzyme inhibitor).

SNRI – serotonin norepinephrine reuptake inhibitor	serotonin norepinephrine	reuptake inhibitor (SERT and NET)	venlafaxine duloxetine
Stimulants			
	dopamine, norepinephrine	reuptake inhibitors and release	amphetamine methylphenidate
Antipsychotic			
Typical	dopamine	receptor antagonist	fluphenazine haloperidol perphenazine trifluoperazine
	dopamine, serotonin	receptor antagonist	chlorpromazine thioridazine
Atypical	dopamine	receptor antagonist	amisulpiride
	dopamine, serotonin	receptor antagonist	iloperidone loxapine olanzapine ziprasidone
	dopamine, serotonin	receptor partial agonist	aripiprazole
	dopamine, serotonin, norepinephrine	receptor antagonist	clozapine risperidone
	dopamine, serotonin, norepinephrine	multimodal	quetiapine
Anxiolytic	GABA	receptor agonist	alprazolam chlordiazepoxide clonazepam clorazepate diazepam flunitrazepam lorazepam oxazepam
	glutamate	calcium channel blocker	gabapentin pregabalin
Hypnotic	GABA	receptor agonist	estazolam flunitrazepam midazolam temazepam triazolam zaleplon zolpidem zopiclone
	melatonin	receptor agonist	ramelteon
Mood stabilizers	glutamate	unknown	lithium valproate

CHAPTER 10

· · · ·

A Biblical Counselor's Perspective on Psychotropic Drugs

Martha Peace, RN

Forty-plus years ago psychotropic medications were not much of an issue because there were not very many of them. Now, however, they are abundant and reproducing rapidly. Not only does that complicate the work of biblical counselors, but almost all variety of doctors are now prescribing them. Some doctors, especially some psychiatrists, are prescribing multiple drugs to a single patient.

For instance, I personally counseled a young wife and mother who came to me because she had been depressed but was on so many different psychiatric medicines she could hardly think and could not function to take care of her family. She told me about five different psychotropic medicines that she was taking. The last time she saw her psychiatrist (which was once a month), she complained about not being able to think clearly and not being able to function well. His reply to her was, "Now I know what your problem is—you have adult attention deficit disorder." He put her on Concerta, which is a stimulant medication, an *upper*, if you will. Well, talk about perking her up, it did. She knew she was on too much medicine and she was willing to come off all those medicines except Concerta. She *loved* the high that came from Concerta.

I also was recently consulted about a counseling case of a young woman who had gone to her psychiatrist because she was anxious and had trouble sleeping. Eventually, she was placed on five psychiatric medications. She became desperate and wanted to die. My counsel was for her to immediately get a second opinion from another psychiatrist. She did and was taken off all five medications, safely.

You may think the previous two examples are extreme, but they are not as unusual as we would hope. I have heard it called "polypharmacy." Many psychiatrists are using multiple medications with the same patient. Sometimes, if not often, they are medicating side effects of medicines the patient is already taking. So, a biblical counselor needs to know enough to be able to counsel someone who is apparently overmedicated and cannot think straight.

Because we need to know something about these medications, I want to give you several definitions that you may come across: the DSM, psychotropic medications, what the medical world calls "discontinuation syndrome," and black box warnings. Next, we will look at how a biblical counselor should think about these medicines and how they should respond to their counselee's questions about the medicines. Last, the counselor should be aware of basic side effects and how to explain to a counselee what they should tell their doctor when *they* and *you* think they are ready to begin safely and slowly tapering off with their doctor's help. Let's begin with some definitions.

Pertinent Definitions

The DSM is often called the psychiatrist's Bible. It provides guidelines for a psychiatric diagnosis so that the doctor can submit the justification for treating their patients when they bill insurance companies. DSM stands for the *Diagnostic and Statistical Manual of Mental Disorders*. The DSM is updated on occasion and the latest is the fifth update. The DSM gives a label to the thoughts and behavior of the patient, but it does not go so far as to declare the diagnosis an official disease. Instead of disease, they use the word disorder. However, it is interesting to read because you will notice the symptoms are not physical, but a list of the behavior and thoughts of the patient under each specific diagnosis. Biblical counselors Dr. Marshall and Mary Asher have written a book comparing the major DSM diagnosis and biblical counseling. The name of the Asher's book is *The Christian's Guide to Psychological Terms, 2nd Edition.* While reading the Asher's book, it is easy to see the differences.

Another pertinent definition is psychotropic. *Psychotropic* refers to psychiatric medications. They are thought to work by adjusting brain neurochemicals such as serotonin, dopamine, and norepinephrine. Hence, the theory of chemical imbalance causing depression. Chemical imbalance has always been a theory and now almost all psychiatrists are saying that it is a debunked theory. The psychotropic medicines are used to treat, among other things, depression, anxiety, psychosis, mania, schizophrenia, and attention deficit disorder.

One category of psychotropic drugs is tranquilizers. They calm the patient's anxiety and are medications such as Xanax, Klonopin, Ativan, and Valium. I remember from years ago that the drug companies would tout the newest tranquilizer as safe and non-addictive. They are all somewhat related to each other and one by one have been found to be highly addictive. The overall category of tranquilizers is termed benzodiazepines. Now when the drug companies come out with a new, supposedly improved version, they go ahead and warn of the addictive nature.

Another common category of psychotropic medication is antidepressants. The most common ones are the Prozac-type drugs. Since Prozac came on the market in 1988, there been many other Prozac-type medications developed. The basic thought behind these medications is to perk up a depressed patient. These medications are chemically related to methamphetamines and more distantly related to cocaine. They are stimulant drugs. The tension has been for the drug company to make an antidepressant that works but has few or no side effects. So far that has not happened, but they keep trying.

Another category of psychotropic medication is sleeping pills, which includes medications such as Lunesta and Ambien. Think of a sleeping pill as a strong tranquilizer. One of the antidepressants, trazodone, is often prescribed for sleep and/or anxiety. If a patient is taking trazodone for sleep, they would take it at bedtime. Sleeping pills are addictive so the patient may have trouble sleeping for a while when they stop taking them.

Antipsychotics are another category of psychotropic medications. They are given to people who have had a psychotic (out of touch with reality) break or are schizophrenic (see things that are not there and hear voices). Some of the antipsychotic medications are Abilify, Zyprexa, and Seroquel. Antipsychotics are difficult to tolerate because of the side effects.

Now the drug companies are advertising for patients to ask their doctor to add a milder antipsychotic medication to their antidepressant to boost the effect of the antidepressant. One of those medications is Abilify.

One additional category of psychotropic medications is mood stabilizers. They are given to patients who have been diagnosed bipolar to keep their brain calm so they will not go into a manic phase. Therefore, they take a stimulant medication such as an antidepressant *and* a mood stabilizer at the same time. Common mood stabilizers are Lamictal, Lithium, and Latuda. There is a new combination medication on the market that contains both a mood stabilizer and a stimulant drug. The name is Vraylar.

An additional pertinent definition is what the medical world calls *discontinuation syndrome* while coming off one of the psychotropic medications. I actually call it a physical addiction as often one or more of these medications are *very difficult* to withdraw from, as many thousands of patients can attest to. So biblical counselors should know how to give wise counsel to the counselee before the counselee goes back to their doctor for help coming off the medication (more on this later).

The last pertinent definition that you need to know is a black box warning. A *black box warning* is placed by the Food and Drug Administration on the boxes of medications that are especially dangerous. The warning is printed on the box of the medication and the warning is surrounded by a big black box. You really cannot help but notice it. For instance, antidepressants have a black box warning because there is an increased risk of suicide in teens and young adults who begin taking one of the medicines. If a teen is placed on an antidepressant by their doctor, the biblical counselor and the parents should be made aware of the warning and take suicide precautions for the teen.

How Should a Biblical Counselor Think about Psychotropic Medications?

First of all, do not be intimidated or overreact. Counselees are not doing anything illegal if their doctor has prescribed the medicine(s) and, by the way, doctors *are* trying to help their patients feel better. The patient may have been on the medicine(s) for years or it may be a short time. They may be experiencing side effects either way. You may think it is futile to try to counsel someone on psychotropic medications, but the Lord can certainly overcome that obstacle. Think of it this way:

> At no time are you "counseling the drug." You are always dealing with the person. He may be greatly affected by the medication, but you are still counseling him, not the drug. Even if the medication slows down his thinking process, he can still think—although it may take longer to do the counseling. But it can be done. The time will come when the issue of medication will need to be addressed.[1]

---

1. Robert D. Smith, *The Christian Counselors Medical Desk Reference* (Stanley, NC: Timeless Texts, 2004), 97.

Part of the information you will need from the counselee is what medications he or she is taking. It is not only the psychotropic medications that can cause brain fog and other side effects such as anxiety or depression, but also other medications can certainly have those effects. Examples would be seizure and blood pressure medications that cause depression. Those people who have to be on steroids perhaps for Addison's disease will likely be anxious. Hormone therapy such as birth control pills can also cause anxiety or depression. Often, when I see what medications my counselee is taking, I google the medicines to better understand the effects and side effects that my counselee may be experiencing. Very often, I never even discuss what I have learned with the counselee. But if I think it necessary, I will tell them of the possibility of the medication causing the issues, and I will send them back to their doctor to figure it out.

Do not be afraid to counsel someone on psychotropic medications. They are not a gospel barrier. God's power is far greater than any medication they may be taking. The Bible tells us about our hearts. Our hearts are what we are thinking and desiring. Don't confuse what we are thinking with our physical brains. Dr. Bob Smith answers the following question this way:

> Is a nervous breakdown a physical problem caused by some biologic problem in the brain? One important biblical and anatomical concept to keep in mind is that the human being is both material and nonmaterial. He has a physical body, which can be seen, and a spirit or soul, which is nonphysical and cannot be seen. The brain is material and the mind is nonmaterial. The mind uses the brain, but it is not the brain. The brain can be diseased and sick, but not the mind. If the brain is damaged, the mind is not sick. With brain damage, the damaged part is no longer available to the mind, and thus function is altered. But the damage

can be demonstrated. This is not a mental condition, but organic [physical] brain damage.[2]

Another issue that does not come up nearly as much in biblical counseling is the issue of chemical imbalance. While many in medicine and psychiatry are saying that the chemical imbalance explanation for depression is no longer considered valid, I still regularly encounter counselees who have been told that the source of their depression or anxiety is a "chemical imbalance." I think it important for counselors to understand a little of the history of this theory.

Basically, there are three neurochemicals in the brain that are manufactured by the brain cells and shifted out to the fluid space to facilitate impulses moving from one nerve cell to another. The chemicals are serotonin, dopamine, and norepinephrine. When there are enough of the chemicals in the fluid spaces, some will shift back *into* the cell and signal the cell to stop or slow the manufacture of the chemicals. The antidepressants change the permeability of the cell wall so that the targeted chemical cannot *shift back* in. Thus, tricking the brain cells into thinking they need to keep manufacturing and pumping out whichever chemical is targeted by the antidepressant. This category of antidepressants is called *reuptake inhibitors*.

What you end up with is a massive amount of the targeted chemical in the fluid spaces of the brain with no way to medically test if you have too much or too little. It is possible to do a brain biopsy to test for the chemical amounts, but, of course, that is not safe and doctors will not go to that extreme. So, if needed, explain to your counselee that chemical imbalance causing depression is not true. It was always a theory and now is debunked.

If you would like to read more about the antidepressants and their effect on people, there is one particular study that stands out. It is called the Star*D study and basically proves that the antidepressants do not lift the patient's mood as doctors had hoped. The patients in

---

2. Smith, *The Christian Counselor's Medical Desk Reference*, 96–97.

the study who were placed on a placebo did as well as those on an antidepressant.

So you will find that many counselees are now on antidepressants and after you have counseled them for a while, they want to come off. However, there is a significant risk of the withdrawal symptoms being so miserable that the counselee and their doctor think that their depression has returned. So the doctor places them back on their depression medication, and the withdrawal symptoms go away, thus supposedly "proving" to the counselee that they do have a physical problem with depression and need to be on the medicine for the rest of their life. As a counselor, you can help them avoid that trap.

Helping Counselees Come Safely off Antidepressant(s) Even with Temporary Withdrawal Symptoms[3]

Early in the counseling process, many if not most, of my counselees who are on antidepressant medications express a desire to come off the drug(s). The problem is they do not like the side effects. So they bring up the issue of coming off the drug(s) before I have even mentioned the topic. What I tell them is "Let's wait for a while and then when *you think* and *I think* that you are ready to come off one or more medication, I will give you some tips of what to tell your doctor. He will have to prescribe the lower doses."

But before we get to the "tips," let me give you a very brief history of psychiatric drugs.

Psychiatric Drugs Come and Go

It has always been a challenge to try and control the behavior of someone who is acting irrationally. More than one hundred years ago the psychiatric drug "of the day" was cocaine. Obviously, cocaine

---

3. This section was adapted from Martha Peace's book, *Biblical Counseling in Practice.* Special thanks to Dr. Laura Hendrickson, MD and board-certified psychiatrist, for her help and insights. Permission granted for this adaptation.

would perk a depressed patient up very quickly, but it had the unfortunate side effect of being highly addictive. Sometimes the addiction occurs with just one dose and, by the way, cocaine can cause a heart attack!

In the 1960s, the main treatments for psychiatric problems were Thorazine, Librium, phenobarbital, and shock treatments (electroconvulsive therapy). Shock treatments were very popular back then and are still used today, but to a much lesser degree. The shock treatments cause a patient to have a short-term memory loss, and the hope is that they will not remember why they were so upset and depressed. Shock treatments cause some death of brain cells. As a student nurse in psychiatric nursing, I remember assisting the doctor carrying out the shock treatments. The patient was sedated and did not feel pain, but it was a difficult procedure for me to observe.

Over the past seventy years, the psychiatric drugs have come and gone. There is a pattern that has emerged: at first the drug is touted by the drug company as safe and non-addictive. Time has told otherwise. Since 1988 when Prozac came out, we have seen the emergence of the antidepressants. It has never been established *how* these drugs lift someone's mood. However, for some people they *will* do that at least for a while, often for as little as four to six weeks.

To make matters worse, all specialties of doctors are prescribing these drugs, often misdiagnosing someone with depression whose problem is really anxiety. Also, psychiatrists in general are prescribing multiple drug therapies. As I mentioned in the opening of this chapter, it is not uncommon for one of my counselees to be on three, four, or five psychiatric medications. The problem of safely helping people come off their medications is not going away. It is getting worse and more complicated. I believe doctors are sincerely trying to help their patients and do care about them. Also, it is important to note that it is *not* a sin for your counselee to follow the doctor's orders. Even though we are *not* doctors, we do need to know a few basic things about these drugs and how to counsel our counselees about them.

Side Effects of Antidepressants

Because antidepressants are stimulant medications, it is not surprising that counselees have increased anxiety, even to the extreme of panic attacks and paranoia. These are especially noticeable the first month of a new prescription or an increased dosage. Most psychiatrists begin their patients on a low dose and gradually increase it. Some are now adding an antipsychotic medication to the antidepressant.

The antidepressants can cause sleeplessness, abnormal dreams, and panic attacks. The antipsychotics can cause one particularly dangerous side effect called akathisia. This is when the counselee experiences a severe restlessness to the point of desperation. They are agitated and suicidal. I have only seen this about four times in all of my counseling years, but it is obviously disturbing and dangerous.

I remember one counselee of mine that experienced a severe emotional reaction to Prozac, and she had been on her medication for only two weeks. She could not sleep and began to have panic attacks. She had not been previously suicidal but became suicidal. She could no longer sit still in a counseling session, but would pace back and forth, wringing her hands. Since I recognized what was happening to her, I told her what I suspected. She decided to notify her doctor that she wanted to discontinue Prozac. He agreed with her and told her to stop the medication. Afterward, she gradually began to feel better and more normal.

Keep in mind that these medicines affect all of the nerve cells in the body. Other side effects of antidepressants are tiredness, weakness, tremors, dizziness, feeling light-headed, and difficulty concentrating. Often because of difficulty concentrating, I tell my counselees to read their assignments aloud, pray, and ask God to help them comprehend what they are reading, and, if need be, read it several times over.

GI side effects are dry mouth, upset stomach, decreased appetite, nausea, and vomiting. At first, weight loss is very common, but typically over a long period of time, weight gain becomes a problem.

Sometimes people gain enormous amounts of weight when they are on antidepressants.

Most counselees experience a decreased sex drive and even impotence. Other physical symptoms can be sweating and blurred vision. I knew of one surgeon years ago that began to take Prozac but had to take himself off it because his vision became blurred. Others have trouble tolerating antidepressants because they develop abnormal heart rhythm problems. Some have hair loss, acne, dry skin, chest pain, runny nose, bleeding, blood pressure changes, bone pain, bursitis, breast pain, anemia, swelling, low blood sugar, and low thyroid activity. Obviously, not everyone experiences all of those side effects and most adjust to them after a few weeks, but as I said, antidepressants affect every nerve cell in your body. Hence, the different side effects.

Last but not least, there are the uncontrollable neurologic symptoms. Those, if they are going to occur, typically occur after a *long* time on antidepressants. Those particular side effects are called tics and tardive dyskinesia or TD. When one of these appears, the counselee may have a twitching of their face such as an eye twitch which will not stop. They also may have a drooping mouth on one side much like what would happen due to a stroke. Probably the most upsetting TDs are when the counselee cannot stop their mouth from moving in strange ways or they cannot stop their tongue from darting in and out of their mouth. Most of the time, their psychiatrist will take them off the medicines when the neurologic side effects begin to appear. Afterward, it may take several months for the side effects to go away or, in some cases, they can be permanent.

Obviously, a biblical counselor could scare their counselees to death with this list of potential side effects. That is not my intent. My intent is for the counselor to be aware of what may be happening, and it is a judgment call to perhaps explain to their counselee what *may* be happening. I think an exception would be if you think your counselee is experiencing akathisia or is suicidal. Then certainly tell them what you think may be happening and refer them right away to their psychiatrist or whatever physician prescribed the antidepressant or antipsychotic.

When the Counselee Is at Greatest Risk

The first month on an antidepressant or an antipsychotic or an increased dose places the counselee at risk. They will likely begin experiencing side effects. The most dangerous ones to watch for are akathisia, uncontrollable leg movements, anxiety, and insomnia. It would not take very long for someone already emotionally upset to feel overwhelmed and suicidal. They could very well act on those tendencies. Generally, if the counselee has been on an antidepressant for less than a month, she or he can quit taking it without withdrawal effects. Of course, they would need to consult with their doctor.

Counselors also need to be aware that antidepressants carry a black box warning. The warning is for teenagers or young adults who are at increased risk for suicide when starting to take one of these drugs. Some doctors make a judgment call that the patient is at greater risk of suicide without the medication. I would be much more comfortable with a psychiatrist making that judgment call than with other categories of doctors. Even so, when a teen or young adult is placed on an antidepressant or that antidepressant is increased, his or her family or close friends should be made aware to watch them more carefully for suicidal tendencies.

The other time period when the counselee is at greatest risk is when they are withdrawing from an antidepressant. The most common withdrawal effects from antidepressants are "anxiety, crying spells, fatigue, insomnia, irritability, dizziness, flu-like aches and pain, nausea, vomiting, headaches, tremors, and sensory abnormalities such as burning, tingling, or electric shock-like symptoms."[4] Counselees may become suicidal while withdrawing, and some of the medications are very slow to be metabolized out of the body. For instance, the *onset*

---

4. Joseph Glenmullen, *The Antidepressant Solution* (New York: Free Press, 2005), 120.

of withdrawal symptoms from Prozac could take up to twenty-five days after stopping the drug and last up to fifty-six days.[5] If a counselee did not know this, they might think their psychiatric "disease" had returned. The newer antidepressants will metabolize out of your body sooner than Prozac, but the withdrawal effects are the same.

Paxil and Zoloft are the worst offenders in terms of sheer numbers of people affected by withdrawal reactions because they are short acting and have been widely prescribed. Effexor is the worst offender in terms of the lightning speed with which it can cause withdrawal reactions—within hours of just one missed dose (no wonder doctors have nicknamed this drug "side Effexor").[6] I remember one counselee that, while slowly withdrawing from Effexor with the help of her psychiatrist, went through an absolute nightmare getting off.

The first month of taking or increasing the dose of an antidepressant and the withdrawal period are the most dangerous times for the counselee to be overwhelmed and panic. So where does that leave biblical counselors, and how can we help?

How to Help the Counselee Come off Their Medicine with Doctor's Help

First of all, I recommend you gather some data. Start with Dr. Joseph Glenmullen's fascinating book entitled *The Antidepressant Solution.* Dr. Glenmullen is a Harvard trained M.D. and board certified psychiatrist. He does use antidepressants in select patient cases, but he also has helped many to come safely off their antidepressant. His book will help you to have some knowledge of how a counselee may come off their medication safely. Also, it will help you to be able to talk to the counselee and their doctor, if necessary, in an informed way.

Even if you never talk to your counselee about their medication, research it to see what it is used for and the possible side effects. This

---

5. Glenmullen, 85.
6. Glenmullen, 88–89.

is not for the purpose of talking to your counselee about it, but if you think they may be having a side effect from the medication, you can tell them of the possibility and recommend they discuss it with their doctor. It will also help you to have an overall picture of what is happening with your counselee.

Give your counselee hope that for the Christian they *can* be controlled by the Holy Spirit. God will not give them more than they can bear (1 Corinthians 10:13). Tell them that modern medicine is a grace gift from God, and often it is very helpful with whatever we struggle. Recommend that they continue with biblical counseling so that, by God's grace, their thoughts and emotions will stabilize, and they can have *joy* in giving God glory.

Teach your counselee a biblical view of sanctification and where their feelings come from (their heart—what they are thinking and desiring). They have THOUGHTS—(then) FEELINGS—(then) ACTIONS. Keep in mind that almost all of the DSM descriptions of disorders are a list of the patient's thoughts and behaviors. Instead of being intimidated by the DSM, as biblical counselors, we help them with their thoughts (renewing their mind) and hold them accountable for their actions (loving God and loving others). Tell them they *can* honor God and show love to others in spite of how they *feel*. Ultimately, as they obey God and honor him, their feelings will improve and be replaced with the peace of God.

When your counselee and you believe they have progressed to the point of beginning to go off their antidepressant, tell them to talk to their doctor about tapering off. They should tell the doctor, "I have been receiving counseling and my counselor and I both think I am ready to begin tapering off the medication. Would you be willing to help me *slowly* taper off?" So far, in all these years of counseling, I have never had a doctor refuse, but if they did, I would want to know why because they may have a very good reason. The medical literature directs the doctor to cut the antidepressant dosage in half, wait two or three weeks, and then discontinue it. Dr. Glenmullen says that is way too fast for almost everyone! That has also been my experience with the counselees that I have had. If their doctor refuses, the counselee has the option of finding another doctor or, at least, they have the freedom in the Lord to obtain a second opinion.

Teach your counselee the possible withdrawal effects they may experience so they will not panic if they experience such things as agitation, headaches, rebound anxiety, painful electric-like zaps in different parts of their body, or feel like they have the flu. If the counselee does experience those withdrawal effects, they will be less likely to panic or be overwhelmed with discouragement as withdrawal effects happen if they know about it ahead of time and know that withdrawal symptoms will subside eventually. If the doctor increases the dosage and the withdrawal effects subside, that is proof of the withdrawal causing the symptoms. One of my former counselees felt like she had the flu and went to the doctor twice complaining of flu symptoms, but later learned it was from tapering off her antidepressant. If she had known that possibility ahead of time, it would have been easier for her.

If your counselee is having a really hard struggle with tapering off the medication, perhaps the doctor could slow down or cut down on the rate of medication taper. Sometimes this is difficult as different medications come in differing strengths. Interestingly, Prozac comes in a liquid so the taper could be in very small amounts.

Some counselees decide to take themselves off their medication. Strongly caution them against doing that! Carefully document what you told them in your counseling notes. If they insist on taking themselves off, you might want to suggest that they read Glenmullen's *The Antidepressant Solution* before they take matters into their own hands. I would be afraid for one of my counselees to take this action. They need to work with their doctor to safely and slowly taper off.

We have the good news of the gospel, and we are persuaded of the sufficiency of the Word of God. God *has* given to us "everything pertaining to life and godliness" (2 Peter 1:3). We and our counselees should come to know the grace and the power of God. We have eternal, real, concrete hope. Modern medicine is also a kindness from

God to us; but for your counselee the time may come when they are, by God's grace, emotionally stable and ready to come off their medication. You need to be ready to help them appropriately with their doctor's help.

Conclusion

Biblical counselors need to know enough about psychotropic medications to observe unsettling side effects and to suggest that the counselee consult with their doctor. They need to know enough to not be confused or intimidated with what may be happening to their counselee.

During the time your counselee is tapering off, you probably need to see him or her more often to encourage them and give them hope biblically. Neither they nor their doctor has done anything wrong or illegal, but the time may come when your counselee desires to come off the medication and leave the side effects behind. Do become informed so that you can appropriately prepare him or her to talk to their doctor.

So instead of being intimidated by the medications, as counselors we should be confident in what we do know *for certain*. And that is that we have the *sure* Word of God "restoring the soul" of our counselees (Psalm 19:7).

CHAPTER 11

ALTERNATIVE MEDICATIONS:

COUNSELING PEOPLE IN NEED OF BIBLICAL AND MEDICAL DISCERNMENT

Daniel M. Gannon, MD

At just ten years old, Joey Hofbauer died of Hodgkin's disease in 1980. Concerned about possible complications of standard chemotherapy treatment, his caregivers instead chose to administer laetrile, a natural product made from apricot pits. Joey died after three years of alternative treatments, his body riddled with cancer. Yet his caregivers claimed partial success: "Most of his body was free of Hodgkin's." (In fact, the parts of his body that were free from cancer were parts of the body that Hodgkin's does not attack.) Joey's story exemplifies the weight of making medical treatment decisions.[1]

Steve Jobs, cofounder of Apple computers, was diagnosed with pancreatic cancer in 2003. His variant was rare, and because it was diagnosed early on in the disease process, surgery offered an excellent chance for long-term survival. Although we do not know what information was provided to Jobs regarding the effectiveness of different treatments, he may have been influenced by his interest in Buddhism. He chose the alternative medical treatments of acupuncture, herbal remedies, bowel cleansings, and the "Gerson cancer diet." This diet

---

1. Paul Offit, *Do You Believe in Magic? The Sense and Nonsense of Alternative Medicine* (New York: HarperCollins, 2013), 7–22.

consists of large quantities of blended fruits, vegetables, and raw calf's liver, with daily coffee enemas to remove toxins. It also includes injections of liver extract, ozone and castor oil enemas, thyroid tablets, jelly capsules, large doses of vitamin C, and a "cancer vaccine."

After many months of these various therapies, it became clear that the cancer had spread widely. Surgery was later performed, but by then it was too late. Jobs died of what many considered a curable disease in its earlier stages.[2] On the other hand, people treated with the latest chemotherapy regimens for cancer recommended by mainstream medicine can also experience toxic or fatal complications.[3]

These scenarios demonstrate the need for biblical wisdom in making medical decisions. Though this chapter is not an encyclopedia of all possible alternative forms of medical treatment for medical illness, God's Word provides timeless principles to guide biblical counselors and those they are helping in order to glorify God and strive to become more like Jesus Christ in this arena.

What Is Complementary and Alternative Medicine (CAM)?

Before we can dive into biblical principles, we should first get on the same page about what we're talking about. What is complementary and alternative medicine (CAM)? CAM can be defined as any health care, therapy, or substance that is at variance with the dominant medical establishment within a given culture. "Alternative" refers to treatment "instead of" or without conventional treatment. "Complementary" treatment is that which is in concert with conventional medicine and is commonly known as "integrative medicine." The latter is utilized most frequently in hospitals and medical clinics.

---

2. Offit, 163–64.

3. Kulmira Nurgali, R. Thomas Jagoe, and Raquel Abalo, "Editorial: Adverse Effects of Cancer Chemotherapy: Anything New to Improve Tolerance and Reduce Sequelae?" *Frontiers in Pharmacology* 9, 2018: 245, https://www.ncbi.nlm.nih.gov/pmc/articles/PMC5874321/.

Examples of CAM include acupuncture, chiropractic care, homeopathy, naturopathy, aroma therapy, music therapy, Ayurveda, traditional Chinese medicine, herbalism, biofeedback, hypnosis, reflexology, massage therapy, Reiki, tai chi, probiotics, spiritual healing, craniosacral therapy, religious yoga, chelation, bio-identical hormones, colonics, crystals, magnets, shamanism, therapeutic touch, etc.

Some providers of alternative treatment feel a sense of competition with mainstream medicine (and vice versa). They offer persuasive arguments or may even manipulate people to choose to obtain care from them instead of from a mainstream provider. Therefore, a potential danger arises as we saw in the two stories told at the beginning of this chapter: effective treatment regimens could be abandoned in the pursuit of alternative means.

Why Do People Choose CAM?

I have identified five major reasons that people choose complementary and alternative medicine. Let's look at each of them.

1. Mainstream medicine is not perfect. If we consider its goal (to prevent or treat all disease successfully), then we could even say that mainstream medicine has a 100 percent failure rate! (Of course, we know that such an elevated goal is unattainable in any arena.) In addition, many of us can recall an encounter with a mainstream health care provider who was less than ideal. Perhaps the provider seemed uncaring, rushed, uninformed, or unhelpful. Maybe an error was made or a complication occurred from a medication, treatment, or surgery. Possibly a loved one died as a result of incompetence or an error by the health care system or provider. We may be aware of cases of health care providers' involvement in fraudulent, money-making schemes. Having one or more of these experiences can erode a person's trust in mainstream medicine.

2. "Natural and Organic" labels sound appealing, leading the buyer to conclude that these products may cause no side effects

or potential complications. However, lack of regulation means there can be uncertainty about the product's ingredients and dosage. Sometimes contaminants permeate the product.

3. CAM practitioners motivate people to pursue a healthy lifestyle. In general, CAM providers can be personable, attentive, and charismatic. They spend time with people and address their patient's lifestyle and the importance of diet and exercise. Of course, many mainstream providers also emphasize these health factors, but CAM providers often have products to sell and therefore focus on these areas.

4. CAM providers often make confident assertions, especially in gray areas for which mainstream providers are not able to provide a clear diagnosis or definitive treatment.

5. Some CAM therapies are helpful. Many conventional medications originated from herbal sources. To illustrate, some believe that Hippocrates used the leaves or bark of a willow or myrtle tree to relieve pain. The ingredients were later purified into salicylic acid (Aspirin). Other examples of effective therapies include the use of quinine found in cinchona bark for the treatment of malaria, digitalis in fox glove, anti-cancer Taxol in the Pacific yew, morphine in the opium poppy, pseudoephedrine from ephedra plants, penicillin from mold, and anti-inflammatories found in certain botanicals. Worldwide, many developing countries primarily depend on plant-based therapies.

Principles for Medical Discernment

We know that proper biblical hermeneutics is critical, and we desire to discern how to accurately interpret, understand, and apply inspired Scripture in context. The same principle applies to the world of medicine and health. We live in an age that has exploded with both true and erroneous information, along with rapid access to that data. Sifting through all of the medical options can become confusing.

The motivation of those who provide such information should be addressed—is their motivation truly altruistic, or is it personal gain? Because Christians are often the targets of false medical schemes, we must be diligent (2 Timothy 2:15). As 1 Thessalonians 5:21 says, we should "examine everything carefully; hold fast to that which is good."

When making decisions about health care, Christians must be wise as serpents and gentle as doves (Matthew 10:16). We should not be swayed by rapidly changing fads espoused by false prophets (2 Peter 2:1–3). Because the body is the temple of the Holy Spirit, Christians should strive to seek good health. Yet, we need to keep physical health in proper perspective. Paul admonishes us to remember that "physical training is of some value, but godliness has value for all things, holding promise for both the present life and the life to come" (1 Timothy 4:8 NIV).

Unbelievers know only this life and this physical body. They might fear illness and death, and therefore they may take excessive measures to obtain health. In this quest, they may search for remedies that promise physically regenerating, life-prolonging results. Alas, our opportunistic society is all too ready to offer remedies that make such claims, often at great financial cost.

So as wise stewards of our bodies, how should we choose appropriate health care options and help others to do so? Several initial factors to consider include the reliability of the evidence, drugs vs. supplements, and "truth" in medicine. In addition, several biblical principles should guide medical decisions: Christian liberty, stewardship, and the reality of the spiritual realm. In the following pages, we will look at each of these principles.

Reliability of Evidence

Any medical system should embrace scientific scrutiny. The primary motivation of health care providers should be to find truth rather than to seek fame or fortune. In an ideal world, all medical choices would be evidence-based, for science values evidence over opinion. The best evidence comes from independently funded, large, prospective, randomized, controlled, double-blinded, peer-reviewed studies, and it is further strengthened by having the studies replicated at multiple independent centers.

This ideal scenario is very expensive and time-consuming. Usually only large pharmaceutical companies can afford to test a drug in this rigorous manner because they can then patent and subsequently sell it for profit. In contrast, non-patentable drugs or therapies, such as herbals or supplements, are not as financially profitable. Most alternative medications, therefore, will not be tested rigorously to determine whether or not they are truly beneficial.

An important principle for evaluating the evidence for any medications, supplements, or other treatments, is that we cannot trust any single published study as completely representative of the truth. Any particular finding should be verified by a preponderance of studies from different sources.

Multiple less rigorous and reliable methods for testing new therapies are available, such as observational studies, cohort studies, qualitative studies, and case reports. Unfortunately, the general population is most often exposed to the least reliable evidence for medical decision-making: the testimonial.

We see this on television or hear it on radio frequently—anecdotal or testimonial evidence presented by an actor or celebrity, which is often a paid endorsement. Sometimes people love to be regarded as knowledgeable dispensers of information, even if they aren't being directly compensated. They will state with charismatic charm that the product worked for them and "you should try it too."

Even more troublesome are the medical professionals who use their medical degrees to assert credibility while promoting a supplement or therapy from which they profit financially. Often these deceivers will produce "infomercials" for radio, websites, or TV, commonly opening with true information about a medical topic (thereby gaining credibility), but then they imperceptibly move to falsified claims of miraculous cures for a wide variety of ailments. (Note the analogy to the workings of religious cults who lure people in with some truth but mix it with subtle but heretical error.) Fearmongering is one of their primary tactics—they sow distrust of mainstream medicine and promote conspiracy theories in order to sell their products (e.g., "Mainstream doctors don't talk about toxins because they've been paid off by Big Pharma; only I am willing to tell you the truth about toxins—they must be flushed out with the product that I sell").

Regulatory Oversight of Drugs

The Food and Drug Administration (FDA) is a governmental agency that regulates the safety and effectiveness of drugs sold in the United States. This organization defines drugs as "articles intended for use in the diagnosis, cure, mitigation, treatment, or prevention of disease, and articles intended to affect the structure or any function of the body (other than food)." They can be ingested, injected, or applied topically.[4]

A structured process must be followed to bring an approved product to market. The FDA reviews the new drug for safety, effectiveness, and appropriate labeling. Further, this organization assures the drug's identity, strength, quality, and purity. If the drug is approved for marketing, the FDA continues to monitor the new product, prohibiting uses that are not specified in the labeling. Some have raised concerns about the FDA approval process. Approved medications may be recalled or have a black box warning added to labeling after wide usage showed safety or risks.[5] There may also be few clinical trials with small participant numbers to establish efficacy of a product.[6] Although it is not a perfect system, it does provide some oversight.

---

4. Robert Saper, "Overview of Herbal and Dietary Supplements," UpToDate, last updated October 26, 2021, https://www.uptodate.com/contents/overview-of-herbal-medicine-and-dietary-supplements.

5. Kerry Nenn, "5 Drug Safety Issues Surrounding the FDA Approval Process," updated on November 4, 2019, https://rehabs.com/blog/5-drug-safety-issues-surrounding-the-fda-approval-process/.

6. "Problems with FDA Medical Device Approval Process Identified in New Studies," December 30, 2009, https://www.aboutlawsuits.com/fda-medical-device-approval-process-problems-7488/.

Regulatory Oversight of Supplements

For thousands of years in all major cultures, plants (herbals or botanicals) and dietary supplements have been used for medicinal purposes. Over many decades, ever-changing governmental laws and agencies have been tasked with oversight of these supplements, but there is disagreement about how to regulate these agents. Dietary supplements have been placed into a category distinct from that of drugs and are defined as products containing one or more of the following: a vitamin, mineral, amino acid, herb, other botanical, concentrate, metabolite, or extract.

Dietary supplement labels are required to present this disclaimer: *"This product is not intended to diagnose, treat, cure, or prevent any disease."* Manufacturers are allowed to market herbal products without prior demonstration of safety, efficacy, quantity, or quality, as well as to make claims such as the following: "promotes prostate health," "boosts immune system," "helps energy, focus, memory, male virility, circulation, pain, arthritis, weight loss, regeneration and longevity."[7]

While supplements such as vitamins are appropriate to use in deficiency states, they are frequently sold for chronic conditions for which conventional medicine has no cure and when no measurable parameters have proven or disproven effectiveness (such as "boosts energy" or "improves memory"). They are not proven to work, but no one can prove that they don't work! In fact, their promoters may tout supportive clinical studies even if none exist or even if such studies are invalid or results are weak.

In an effort to provide evidence-based support for the supplement industry, the government has created an agency called the National Center for Complementary and Integrative Health (NCCIH). Although government agencies do not monitor dietary supplements, if enough complications involving a supplement are reported to them, they may intervene to restrict use of that product. The FDA has established rules requiring good manufacturing practices for dietary

---

7. Saper, "Overview of Herbal and Dietary Supplements."

supplements. However, loose adherence to the regulations is common; even the inclusion of heavy metals like lead or other contaminants may occur.[8]

Herbs and other supplements are often promoted as safe because they are "natural." This concept is appealing to those who perceive nature as "benevolent and healing."[9] However, many natural elements are not safe or are unsafe for susceptible individuals (e.g., arsenic, strychnine, cyanide, dioxin, radon, ricin, gluten, poison ivy, mercury, lead, botulin, etc.). Another concern is that an inappropriate *dose* of anything may be toxic. Even water, if ingested rapidly in very large quantities, can be deadly.

Safety vs. Side Effects

Regarding safety versus side effects, the following statements apply to both natural and synthetic products:

- *Any substance that has an effect has possible side effects.* In recommended doses, side effects are rare, but not impossible. Side effects are seen more commonly in higher than recommended doses.
- A corollary to that statement is *If a substance has absolutely no side effects, it has no effect.*

Truth in Medicine

Two diagrams illustrating the truth in medicine can help us conceptualize the relative contributions of mainstream versus alternative medicine. The contributions are shown in the following way:

---

8. C. Michael White, "Analysis: Some Natural Supplements Can Be Dangerously Contaminated," *PBS,* February 2020, https://www.pbs.org/newshour/health/analysis-some -natural-supplements-can-be-dangerously-contaminated.

9. Ted J. Kaptchuk and David M. Eisenberg, "The Persuasive Appeal of Alternative Medicine," *Annals of Internal Medicine* 129, no. 12 (1998): 1061.

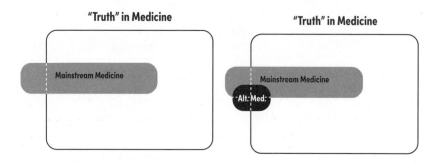

The diagram on the left contains a large white box representing the theoretical medical universe of everything that is true about our health, illness, medications, supplements, and therapies. The light gray box represents mainstream medicine relative to that which is the absolute truth. Note that a majority of mainstream medicine falls into what is true, but it does not contain all truth. There is much it does not know. Further, the gray portion to the left of the box of truth represents error not yet discovered and discarded.

The diagram on the right depicts alternative medicine as it relates to mainstream medicine and absolute truth. Note that there are four quadrants in the arena of alternative medicine: (1) shared truths with mainstream medicine, (2) shared error, (3) unique error, and (4) unique truths compared to the body of mainstream medicine. Note that the amount of knowledge contained within mainstream medicine is larger than that found in alternative medicine.

All of this is important information to consider. But how does God's Word apply to medical decision-making?

Principles for Biblical Counsel

There are five things to discuss as you counsel those considering complementary and alternative medicine. The first is the fact that as Christians we have liberty in making decisions. However, as we think about bringing glory to the Lord, we need to be careful about the reality of the spiritual realm, along with our stewardship, heart motivations, and ethics.

Christian Liberty

First, we have been granted Christian liberty in many of life's decisions (Romans 14; 1 Corinthians 8; Colossians 2:16–23). We are free to use legitimate medical means—wine (1 Timothy 5:23); isolation and hand washing (Leviticus 13:1–46); treating and bandaging wounds (Luke 10:34). In order to make wise health choices within our liberty, some principles for biblical counselors to consider follow:

1. Teach those you are helping to consider practices that align with established principles of biology, physiology, and pharmacology, with an emphasis on preventive therapies, proper diet and exercise, basic health education, and motivation for a healthy lifestyle.

2. Teach those you are helping that Christian liberty choices are guided by God's truth.

   • In Genesis 9:3, God tells Noah and his family that, "Every moving thing that is alive shall be food for you; I give all to you, as I gave the green plant."

   • In Mark 7:19, Jesus declared all foods clean. In Acts 10:9–13, Peter has a vision of a great sheet on which there were animals and creatures and birds to "kill and eat." Of this vision God said, "What God has cleansed, no longer consider unholy" (Acts 10:15).

   • First Timothy 4:3 tells us that some who fall away from the faith "advocate abstaining from foods which God has created to be gratefully shared in by those who believe and know the truth." So God gives us great freedom in enjoying what he has created for us to eat.

     Some alternative therapies may prohibit food that God allows (i.e., recommending unproven diets or treating unproven "allergies" by abstaining from certain foods).[10] As noted above, we are free to use legitimate medical means (for example, abstaining from gluten in celiac disease or avoiding red meats to decrease cholesterol in heart disease). But we recommend you encourage others to avoid practices that take obvious leaps of logic with questionable credibility.

The Reality of the Spiritual Realm

So we have freedom, but biblical freedom ends where sin begins. Where is that? People may disagree about where that is exactly, but it is clear that CAM practices that radically depart from biology and instead invade the realm of the supernatural are on the extreme end of the spectrum. These practitioners claim to manipulate invisible "life energy" in order to heal illness. Great caution is needed here! The Bible forbids seeking supernatural help from sources other than the one true God (Deuteronomy 18:10–11).

This idea of life energy was originally part of Eastern medicine. Now, a number of diverse practices, such as chi (qi) (from China), prana (from India), ki (from Japan), bioenergy, and biofield practices are based on the belief that health depends on a balanced flow of energy through the body and unblocked exchange of this energy with one's environment. Illness results from blockage of energy flow. To sense this energy field and treat for blockages, supplements or therapies must be used in order to reach a "higher state of awareness."

Practitioners presume to involve spiritual forces to heal a patient's energy field. But those who expose themselves to life energy medicine are potentially exposing themselves to real spiritual forces over which they may have little control (Isaiah 8:19–20; Deuteronomy 18:9–11; Micah 5:12). God's Word is clear: we should have absolutely no involvement with such spiritual beings or forces. Rather, we should resist them with our spiritual armor (Ephesians 6:11–13).

---

10. Stephen Barrett, MD, "British Advertising Standards Authority Criticizes Ads for YorkTest Laboratories FoodScan Test," Quackwatch, June 19, 2012, https://quackwatch.org/related/tests/yorktest.

An example of this kind of "medicine" is Ayurveda, which means "life/knowledge." In recent years, Deepak Chopra, MD, has been its main proponent. Although he is a trained endocrinologist, he has returned to his religious/medical roots from his native India. His views on health and medicine appear to be based on a modernized version of Ayurveda and Hinduism mixed with conventional medicine.

It is difficult to separate Chopra's views of health from his religious beliefs. He preaches that in order to be healthy, people first need enlightenment. He preaches that we all have the power to make reality. Once we believe this teaching, he says, we can create the health we want. He further says that if we believe that our true nature is one of perfection and complete goodness, we will be healthy.[11]

For both scientific and spiritual reasons, Chopra's teachings must be rejected. Although Chopra has become famous, discerning Christians must understand that popularity, fame, and financial success do not ensure wisdom regarding the treatment of health concerns. In fact, there is no solid evidence that Ayurveda is effective in treating any disease, and its dietary supplements have been shown to sometimes contain lead, mercury, and arsenic. The Indian Medical Association has declared this practice to be quackery.[12]

As another example of a health practice with spiritual ties, we should carefully consider the question of whether or not we should practice yoga. In the US, yoga is considered to be gentle exercise and relaxation therapy that is used to enhance strength and flexibility, reduce stress, and improve blood flow. It is frequently taught in health club classes and adult education classes, and it is used for stress management within businesses and even churches.

The word *yoga* means "union." The practice began as a spiritual exercise of Hinduism, designed to enable one to reach a meditative state, leading to enlightenment and union with the divine. In

---

11. Paul C. Reisser, David Mabe, and Robert Velarde, *Examining Alternative Medicine: An Inside Look at the Benefits & Risks* (Downers Grove, IL: InterVarsity Press, 2001), 177–78.
12. Indian Medical Association, "IMA Anti Quakery," https://www.ima-india.org/ima/archive-page-details.php?pid=291.

Hinduism, the physical positioning and breathing exercises of yoga relax the mind and body in order to bring them into spiritual harmony, enabling the flow of "prana" (the Hindu word for "life energy"). Each posture bows to a particular Hindu god. For example, the "salute to the sun" posture, which is used to begin many classes, pays homage to the Hindu sun god.

The caution, then, is to keep the spiritual roots of yoga in mind. Be wary of exposure to its religious teachings. We must remember Shadrach, Meshach, and Abednego (Daniel 3), who refused to bow to the idol even when their lives were at risk. While physical and breathing exercises may improve one's sense of general well-being, and could be practiced as purely a form of exercise with a clear conscience, when yoga is practiced as a religion with the goal of union with a "divine," this practice is antithetical to biblical Christianity.

Stewardship

As believers, we desire to make wise decisions based on faithful stewardship of what God has given to us—our bodies, our finances, and our time. To this end, when making medical decisions, we must be alert for signs of deceptive medical practices. This is not simply a matter of being smart or a savvy consumer—it is a matter of faithful stewardship. Thus, whenever Christians see the following signs, they should exercise extreme caution about investing any resources in the product or service being offered. Deceptive practitioners/organizations will

- Often use inflated words, such as "miraculous," "revolutionary," and "major breakthrough"
- Use only testimonial evidence, celebrity endorsements, and individual doctor or nurse endorsements
- Make claims of scientific support but without detail
- Refer to obscure journals, solo research, and studies never repeated
- May state "clinical studies have shown"

- Refer to obscure, unmeasurable, or broad targets, such as "boosts energy, immune system, focus, memory, virility"
- Claim to provide "support" for a specific organ (e.g., kidney, adrenal, cardiac, brain, or joint)
- Focus on toxicity issues, such as offering purification products or therapy
- Claim efficacy for a great variety of physiologically unrelated problems: "It'll cure what ails ya!"
- Offer a quick and easy fix for complex or chronic conditions
- Claim successful use for centuries elsewhere
- Proclaim widespread enthusiasm: "Many are using this product with great results!"
- Represent a conflict of interest—the discovery of a great new product (only available through this source)
- Claim that products are perfectly safe because they are "all natural" or "organic"
- Claim to be unfairly criticized by the medical establishment or regulatory authorities
- Make conspiracy claims—"something that your doctor doesn't want you to know"
- Require advanced payment (with "money-back guarantee")

A good example of an alternative medicine filled with deceptive (or deceived) practitioners and unreliable evidence is homeopathy. This word consists of two elements, *homeo*, meaning "same" or "similar," and *pathic*, referring to sickness, symptoms of sickness, or similar suffering. The practice began in the 1800s with a German physician, Samuel Hahnemann, and includes the following three primary tenets:

1. They claim that if a sickness produces symptoms, such as fever, one can treat that sickness with a substance that produces the *same* symptoms. In fact, symptoms indicate that the body's life energy is fighting the disease; therefore, to eliminate symptoms is exactly the wrong course of action to take. A substance that works to produce the same symptoms will actually promote self-healing. For example, when belladonna is given to healthy

people, it produces fever and flu symptoms, so homeopathic belladonna is used to treat colds and flu.

2. They claim that the more dilute the solution, the higher its potency. Therefore, remedies are diluted again and again in specific numeric percentages in the belief that this dilution increases effectiveness.

3. They claim that with each dilution, the mixture must be shaken in a particular manner, called "succussion," which is thought to "potentiate" the molecules. These ritualistic shakings release "the spiritual vital force" of the healing substance. Thus, more shaking releases more energy, ensuring stronger effect.

All three of these tenets of homeopathy violate verified principles of modern science. Creating similar symptoms is not logically therapeutic for the underlying disease that caused those symptoms. Greater dilution does not correlate with greater effect. (The practice of greater dilution was instituted because many of the initial elements were toxic. Dilution made the "remedy" safer since the final product is essentially only water.) Finally, there is no validity to the idea that a substance becomes more potent due to a particular method of ritualistic shaking.[13] Studies do not confirm homeopathic practices as effective; any positive results are likely related to the placebo effect or due to the passage of time.

Another area where we must exercise caution is being a good steward of the resources God has given us is in the area of vitamin supplements. It is quite easy to spend a small fortune on vitamins, which may not provide us with any benefit, and, in some cases, may even cause harm. A good example to consider is vitamin D, which is a fairly common deficiency that can be measured. The rate of deficiency is high (30 to 70 percent), particularly in climates with limited seasonal sunshine. Vitamin D is essential for many cellular activities

---

13. Michelle Dossett, "Homeopathy," UpToDate, last updated May 4, 2020, https://www.uptodate.com/contents/homeopathy#!.

of bone, muscle, nerve, and immune response; deficiency has been implicated in a variety of ailments, such as osteoporosis, childhood rickets, periodontitis, preeclampsia, respiratory infections, and even mental health problems such as seasonal affective disorder and other mental disorders. More recently, attention has been given to vitamin D deficiency as it relates to the severity of COVID-19.

Supplementation with vitamin D is appropriate if one's measured blood level of the vitamin is low. However, supplementing without deficiency makes no sense. An abundance of advertising promotes over fifty thousand available supplements. The thinking is that if something is vital, supplementing with more of that substance can only be a good thing. However, this thinking is flawed. For example, if five quarts of oil in a car engine is good, then is adding five more quarts even better? Or if thirty-five pounds of air pressure in the tires is good, then is adding thirty-five more pounds better yet?

We can appreciate the folly of the car analogy but miss the same folly regarding adding unnecessary supplements to our diets. In fact, the fat-soluble vitamins A, D, E, and K are stored in our bodies. If too much of these fat-soluble vitamins are ingested, the amount may become toxic; unexpected side effects from excess supplementation may result. Indeed, more is not always better! Effects of excess vitamin D ingestion include nausea, poor appetite, constipation, weakness, confusion, heart rhythm problems, and kidney damage.

Water-soluble vitamins (such as vitamin C) are simply excreted if taken in large amounts. Of course, in order to care for our bodies for God's glory, we must eat a balanced diet to ensure appropriate nutrition. We must be wary of so-called diet experts who spout recently discovered dietary theories or fads; we should inquire whether a deficiency of an element can be demonstrated and if the safety of supplementation has been proven. For answers to dietary questions, I would recommend consultation with a registered dietitian.

Supplementary antioxidants provide an area for caution, since they may even cause physical harm. Supplementary antioxidants have risen in popularity in recent years due to research that has revealed some important roles of antioxidants in maintaining our health. The NCCIH states that antioxidants may prevent or delay some types of cell damage. Vegetables and fruits are rich sources of antioxidants, and people who eat a diet containing these elements have a lower risk of several diseases. However, supplementary antioxidants in pill or powder form seem to represent a significantly different entity. Studies have not shown their benefit in reducing the risk of many chronic diseases. In fact, high-dose antioxidant supplements may be linked to adverse effects. For example, high doses of beta-carotene may increase the risk of lung cancer in smokers. Vitamin E supplements may increase the risk of prostate cancer and stroke. In addition, antioxidant supplements and many other types of alternative preparations may interact negatively with some prescription medicines.[14]

Heart Motivations

As we advise those who are using or considering CAM, we have touched on the need for discernment, for understanding the evidence of truth claims, for awareness of spiritual dangers, and for thinking about biblical principles of liberty and stewardship of resources. As biblical counselors, we also seek to get to the heart of the matter. We want to discuss what motivates someone's choice to use or consider CAM.

What is the person's focus? Are they putting their primary focus on extending or improving their physical health in this life, or are they putting their primary focus on doing things that will matter in the next life? In other words, are they storing up for themselves treasures in heaven or on earth (Matthew 6:19–21)? Do they fear death or physical illness? Are they yielded to God's will for their bodies or are they desperate for a cure to the point that their hope is placed in unproven claims from CAM practitioners? Even if the

---

14. National Center for Complementary and Integrative Health (NCCIH), "Antioxidants: In Depth," last updated November 2013, https://www.nccih.nih.gov/health/antioxidants-in-depth.

chosen medicine/therapy is relatively harmless, these heart issues can be drawn out and addressed.

Ethical Considerations

Some areas of CAM also bring up ethical considerations. As with the other principles, it would be impossible to address every type of CAM here, so I will simply discuss two—stem cell therapy and marijuana—that can illustrate ethical issues that can be raised by CAM. Biblical counselors would do well to help their counselees think carefully about the ethics involved in any medical decision they make.

One area of medical research that has been controversial for Christians is stem cell therapy. The term *stem cell* refers to the stem of a plant that can grow into many different "branches." Thus, it is an immature cell with the ability to grow into a variety of other cells or tissues. Within medicine enormous possibilities exists for the application of stem cell research.

While we might hear "stem cells" and think "embryonic stem cells" (with its accompanying ethical concerns), recent advances in medical research have now rendered adult stem cells much more flexible in terms of what kinds of cells they can develop into. This is of great interest for those of us who believe that life begins at conception, for this technology would preclude the sacrifice of a living embryo for the harvest of stem cells. Hence, embryonic stem cells are becoming less important as adult stem cell research continues to advance.

Adult stem cells are currently being studied for the potential treatment of much pathology, including stroke, myocardial disease, Parkinson's disease, spinal cord injuries, multiple sclerosis, damaged tissues and organs, etc. However, at the time of my writing, the only FDA-approved use of stem cells is to transplant them to restore a person's blood-forming (hematopoietic) cells. This is a very helpful component of cancer treatment, for chemotherapy kills fast-growing cancer cells but also wipes out normal blood-forming cells in the bone marrow, which are also rapidly replicating. If a stem cell transplant is available, a more potent chemotherapy can be chosen in the treatment of a wide variety of cancers as a means of eradicating more of the malignant cells (which also destroys more bone marrow cells). Stem cell transplants can then quickly restore the normal blood cell line and immune function. Unlike immune therapy, stem cells themselves do not directly kill cancer cells.

Thus, while the potential for adult stem cell research is great, at this time the representatives of the American Academy of Orthopedic Surgeons are right to caution members: "Never claim that you are using stem cells to treat any musculoskeletal condition, nor that you can regenerate articular cartilage by injection, nor that you are regenerating discs of the spine by injection. There are no products approved for that."[15]

Unfortunately, marketing is far outpacing research. Many opportunists delight in taking advantage of desperate people and lax regulations. Unscrupulous stem cell clinics are making outrageous claims to treat or cure many maladies. They charge exorbitant fees for unproven, unregulated, and uninsured therapy, making a wide variety of false claims, such as that their treatment can relieve all pain, regenerate joints, rebuild spines, cure eye and brain disease, etc. It is wise to avoid stem cell clinics that make such unsubstantiated claims. (The same warning can be applied to "exosome therapy," which claims to utilize vesicles that communicate from one cell to another regarding regenerative function.) Again, let the buyer beware!

One other area of concern for Christians is that embryonic stem cells have played a role in the development of vaccines, including the newly developed COVID-19 vaccines. Regarding the ethical considerations surrounding these vaccines, the Christian Medical and Dental Associations offers support for its acceptance based on these three principles:

1. We can "Lov[e] our neighbor by protecting them through our own vaccination."

---

15. Bruce Schnapp, "Stem Cells: Facts vs Fiction," Oregon Health & Science University, with the American Academy of Orthopedic Surgeons, on-line seminar (Rosemont, IL, November, 2020).

2. We can consider "The distance in time from an abortion connection."

3. We can remember "The fact that the vaccine does not continue to use cell lines derived from an abortion."

The organization concludes: "We find these factors considerable in mitigating the ethical concerns and opening the door to receiving the vaccines in good conscience."[16]

Another area of CAM that has significant ethical considerations for Christians is marijuana. This book includes an excellent chapter addressing marijuana, hemp, and CBD. Here I add a few additional comments pertaining to the ethics of this arena of alternative medicine.

"Medical marijuana" is an ambiguous and misused term. For decades, this idea simply referred to the use of standard marijuana, with tetrahydrocannabinol (THC), for use by those with medical conditions. Some in the public presumed that there was a special marijuana with more legitimate application for medical conditions. The name was a subtle means to promote the acceptance, legalization, and availability of standard marijuana.[17] In fact, "every single state that has legalized recreational marijuana actually legalized medical marijuana first.[18] While God allows man to use created things for his glory, man's sinful nature causes him to use creation in self-serving and harmful ways. The Bible warns against using substances that alter our minds (Proverbs 23:29–35; Galatians 5:21; Ephesians 5:18; 1 Timothy 3:3), which "is intrinsic to marijuana use."[19] At the same time, medicine is biblically commended to relieve physical problems (1 Timothy 5:23). We believe that Christians should reject recreational

16. Jonathan Imbody and Jeffrey Barrows, "Ethical Vaccines: Ready for a Shot in the Arm?," *CMDA Today* (Christian Medical and Dental Associations), Spring 2021, https://cmda.org/article/ethical-vaccines-ready-for-a-shot-in-the-arm/.

17. James Avery, *Marijuana: An Honest Look at the World's Most Misunderstood Weed* (Bristol, TN: Christian Medical & Dental Association, 2020), 62.

18. Avery, 62.

19. "CMDA Statement on Recreational Marijuana," (2019), 3, https://columbiacmda.org/documents/RecreationalMarijuanaFinalCMDA2019.pdf.

use of marijuana and only embrace its use for any obvious medical benefit.

However, currently medicinal uses are questionable. Two notable authorities on the subject state: "There is no such thing as 'medical marijuana.'" These experts are the former Surgeon General of the US, Jerome Adams, who made this statement in June 2019, and the former US Health and Human Services Secretary, Alex Azar, who made this statement in March 2018.

In more recent years, the marijuana industry has developed the ability to extensively fractionate marijuana and control how much of the more than 100 various cannabinoids are present in a product for sale. In particular, it is now possible to remove most of the THC to prevent many of marijuana's psychoactive effects. Today the term "medical marijuana" *might* legitimately be used primarily for CBD products containing low levels of THC, but there is no standard definition.

Although marijuana does have some legitimate uses, such as for cancer-associated nausea and some seizure disorders, we are being flooded with advertising for "medical marijuana" and CBD products with little solid evidence of their true effectiveness. This is a classic example of marketing outpacing science. The future may clarify that some marijuana-based products truly have certain beneficial effects, but for now, one is prudent to be wary of exaggerated claims.

Dr. James Avery has written a comprehensive book regarding marijuana, and he concludes with the following advice for the Christian community:

- Most medical conditions are best treated with FDA-approved medications. . . . Indications for prescribing marijuana are limited. . . . However, in cases where primary treatments have not been adequate . . . seek medical care from a qualified health professional who can prescribe . . . FDA-approved marijuana derivatives . . . with proper monitoring.
- Be wary of claims made about marijuana's "benefits."

- "Medical marijuana" dispensaries may include products with unknown contaminants and additives, variable amounts of active ingredients, unproven efficacy, unclear short-term and long-term problems, and unsafe packaging. This is not medicine.
- Smoking any product is never healthy.
- Be vigilant to ensure that children do not inadvertently have access to "medical marijuana."[20]

In fact, Dr. Avery's summary statements are applicable to the entirety of alternative medications and therapies.

Concluding Advice

This chapter began with the unfortunate stories of Joey Hofbauer and Steve Jobs. Each case involved the choosing of therapy that was not complementary to mainstream medicine but rather "alternative to" or "instead of" standard treatment. Certainly, the standard treatments did include potential side effects, yet they offered a reasonable chance for a cure. Presumably, the alternative treatments were chosen based on anecdotal or testimonial evidence that promised no side effects; they were natural, organic, and radical therapies that were promoted by winsome, enthusiastic, and optimistic providers. Choosing alternative therapies, along with insufficient monitoring of the disease progression, led to a lost window of opportunity to receive help. We don't know whether or not these two individuals would have survived with conventional treatment, but we do know that without it they didn't receive the best help available.

Disasters provide opportunity for those on the periphery of mainstream medicine to swoop in and take advantage of others. Sadly, medical practitioners from all fields may become involved in deceptive advertising. In December of 2020, a medical doctor was indicted on charges of selling "curative" COVID-19 treatment packs.

---

20. Avery, 156.

Recently, the College of Naturopathic Physicians disciplined some practitioners for false advertising of vitamins, booster shots, and ozone treatments purported to boost immune support or even kill the virus directly. The College of Chiropractors warned their members against marketing supplements or spinal manipulations that claimed to build immunity against the virus. And the supplement industry has promoted cannabidiol (CBD) as a "pandemic panacea" that can address all the problems that we face with COVID-19. There is simply no shortage of people willing to capitalize on other people's suffer and fears.

The following principles provide helpful guidance for discussing CAMs with your counselees:

- Be discerning. Learn about the basic workings of your body, illness, and medicine. Ask about the evidence behind medical advice given to you. Inquire about options. Be wary of dietary fads supported by testimonial advice about specific food restrictions or supplements. Seeking alternative treatments will not compromise your faith, but do not avoid proven medical therapies. Do avoid any therapies delving into the spirit world. Be a wise steward of your body for the glory of God.

- Guard against yielding to the temptation to believe marketing that is outpacing the science.

- Be wary of those who claim to provide "integrative" healthcare, but in fact provide care that is "instead of" conventional medicine. Do not discard appropriate conventional medicine while pursuing alternative treatments.

- If you are taking alternative medications, be sure to inform your primary care provider so that drug interactions can be avoided. Your local pharmacist can be a good source of counsel regarding your choice of drugs or supplement medications.

- Assess whether your care provider is willing to be part of a medical team. Beware of those who claim to find a diagnosis or cure that all others have missed.

- Seek a healthy lifestyle. Remember the importance of regular exercise and a healthy diet to avoid obesity. Pursue dietary advice from a registered dietitian. Avoid the diet fad of the day.
- Consider an analogy between mainstream and alternative medicine and the famous fable of the tortoise and the hare. Mainstream medicine is at times slow to adapt, whereas alternative medicine changes rapidly with societal interests and whims. Yet it is the slow-but-steady tortoise who wins the race against the speedy-but-wayward hare!
- Do not seek any particular treatment out of desperation or fear. Seek additional medical opinions, seek the counsel of other wise believers (Proverbs 11:14), and turn to God (Psalm 27:10 and 56:3; Isaiah 41:10 and 43:1–2; and 2 Timothy 1:7).
- Acknowledge that there is no fountain of youth. Do not make health an idol. According to Scripture, it is of some profit to seek health, but it is better to seek godliness (1 Timothy 4:8). As believers, we look forward to a future life without pain and suffering (Revelation 21:4).

An excellent and comprehensive source of information is the book *Examining Alternative Medicine: An Inside Look at the Benefits & Risks* by Paul C. Reisser, David Mabe, and Robert Velarde.

The website of the NCCIH provides commentary regarding specific alternative treatments, such as acupuncture, probiotics, antioxidants, and vitamin supplements. Whenever a counselee mentions that they are using or are considering a particular CAM, the biblical counselor would be wise to do some basic research on the substance or practice with this website. This knowledge can be used to inform further discussions and alert the counselor to any particular side effects that their counselee might be experiencing. While biblical counselors cannot make medical decisions for their counselees, they can provide a wise, Christlike voice of reason in the midst of the many competing voices in our culture that often do not have the best interest of others at heart.

CHAPTER 12

Obsessive-Compulsive Disorder (OCD):
Medical Principles and Biblical Priorities

Charles D. Hodges Jr., MD

If Jean's friends were asked to describe her in one word, they probably would say "organized!" She required order. A place for everything and everything in its place doesn't even come close to describing the life-consuming efforts that she undertook each day. Keeping things in order enabled her to keep things clean. Keeping things clean kept her from the (mostly) unspoken fear that she might harm others by contaminating them with a deadly germ.

At first it may seem as though this fear is not a great problem. Wash your hands when needed. Keep your room clean and picked up. Take your shower, and wear clean clothes. If only it ended there for Jean.

When I met Jean, she was huddled in the corner of the confer-ence room of the residential facility where I was serving as the medical director. She rocked gently and avoided eye contact. Her husband had called me a few days earlier and asked if I could help with her counsel-ing. He told me that Jean's obsessive fear that she might harm others by giving them an infectious disease had grown to the point that she could not touch their new baby.

It made no difference how much she washed her hands or what precautions she used when handling their daughter. It did not matter to her if friends and family stood by and told her that she was doing nothing that would give the child a deadly disease. Jean was paralyzed with fear, and her husband was desperate for help.

After listening to their story, I told the husband that I believed there was real hope for Jean to be helped. And this wasn't empty reassurance—I had many reasons to say that. I told him that I had heard this story before. A few years earlier, I had encountered a young woman in almost the same situation as Jean, and she was able to escape the grip of her obsessions and compulsions. Over the next eighteen months, Jean did grow and change and escape the life-consuming slavery that obsessive-compulsive disorder (OCD) had been for her since she was ten years old.

What Is OCD?

As defined by the fifth edition of the *Diagnostic and Statistical Manual of Mental Disorders* (DSM-5), OCD is a problem with both thoughts and behaviors.[1] Those diagnosed with OCD have recurrent intrusive thoughts, images, or urges, called obsessions, which result in distress, worry, and fear. They respond to these intrusive thoughts with repeated thought routines and behaviors that are called compulsions. The thinking drives them to respond in ways that they believe will give them relief or protect them from disaster. The rituals are rigid, and the person suffering from OCD believes they must be completed.

OCD typically starts in childhood or adolescence, but it is not often noticed at first. Children typically do not understand the significance of their obsessive-compulsive cycle. Adolescents are often too embarrassed or revolted by the content of their thoughts to tell anyone.

---

1. *Diagnostic and Statistical Manual of Mental Disorders*, 5th edition (Washington, DC: American Psychiatric Association, 2013), 235–37.

If left untreated, OCD continues throughout life and can cause impairment at home, work, and in all areas of life. While the intrusive thoughts and rituals may seem trivial to some, they can be devastating for the struggler. Those thoughts include the fear of contamination, fear of harming loved ones, fear of sacrilege, and fear of sexual immorality. It is important to remember that those affected do not wish to be a part of the things they fear. They do not want to commit the deeds or think the thoughts. They fear them. They do the rituals, not because they love them, but because they want to avoid the intrusive thoughts or the behavior that they fear.

Jean fit the criteria for OCD. Her problems started when she was a child, but they were neither noticed nor understood until she was an adult. Her obsessions were difficult to talk about and required her to perform rituals. She came to our attention because the perceived risk of harming her baby simply overwhelmed her.

Medical Approaches to OCD

The diagnosis of OCD is based on disclosure made by the individual and observations made by friends, family, and clinicians. The diagnostic process is subjective because there are no conclusive tests that can validate (or invalidate) the diagnosis. There is objective medical evidence that those with OCD have differences in their brains that may account for the difficulty they have in moving on from an obsessive thought. These are seen in brains scans that indicate increased activity in specific areas of the brain when OCD is present. The changes in brain activity can return to normal with counseling and treatment.[2]

Some children will develop OCD during common bacterial throat infections. It is believed that a reaction by the child's immune system is the cause. Whether or not treatment with antibiotics is useful has not been determined, but some recommend it.[2]

---

2. Michael Pichichero, "PANDAS: Pediatric Autoimmune Neuropsychiatric Disorder Associated with Group A Streptococci," UptoDate, last updated April 25, 2022, https://www.uptodate.com/contents/6031.

OCD appears to have a genetic component. Up to 20 percent of those with a first degree relative with OCD may develop the problem. The genetic basis for this is not currently understood.[3]

Treatment for OCD comes in the form of counseling, medication, surgery, and deep brain stimulation. The last two categories are reserved for those who are most affected by the symptoms. Counseling generally is in the form of behavioral therapy or cognitive behavioral therapy, which is the most helpful form of psychotherapy for OCD.[4]

While many medications have been used to treat OCD, the selective serotonin reuptake inhibitors such as escitalopram are thought to be the most useful. Medications may help reduce symptoms but are less effective if they are not also accompanied by counseling.[5] Care for OCD should start with counseling.

Surgery for OCD involves implantation of electrodes to deliver deep brain stimulation to areas of the brain thought to be the source of the problem. This is reserved for patients who have not been helped by all other modes of care and who are significantly disabled by OCD. This surgery has significant complications.[6]

A Biblical Counseling Approach

Initially, helping Jean required that she be in a place where she could be cared for by staff and counselors who understood her struggle. While this is not true for the majority of those affected by OCD, Jean simply could not function at home or anywhere. This meant that the care of her infant child was managed by extended family for a time.

---

3. *DSM-5*, 240.

4. Helen Blair Simpson, "Pharmacotherapy for Obsessive-Compulsive Disorder in Adults," UptoDate, last updated October 10, 2020, https://www.uptodate.com/contents/pharmacotherapy-for-obsessive-compulsive-disorder-in-adults.

5. Simpson, "Pharmacotherapy for Obsessive-Compulsive Disorder in Adults."

6. Damiaan Denys and Pelle P. de Koning, "Deep brain stimulation for treatment of obsessive-compulsive disorder," Uptodate.com. Literature review current through June 2022. https://www.uptodate.com/contents/deep-brain-stimulation-for-treatment-of-obsessive-compulsive-disorder.

Then, while Jean was a resident at the facility, caring for her well began with a good deal of listening.

Out of those conversations emerged a history of multiple obsessions that regularly changed. Since the age of ten, she had been playing OCD whack-a-mole. As she dealt with her current obsession, new ones would pop up. At no time did she ever have a good way of dealing with her intrusive thoughts. Checking, hand washing, and avoidance were all used at different times in the pursuit of safety. She did not want to harm others. She did not want to offend God.

Jean had become a Christian at the age of eighteen, and she was a faithful member of her church. She read her Bible and prayed on a daily basis. While she seemed certain of her salvation, at times she struggled with the thought that something she said or did would cause her to lose her salvation. She feared committing the unpardonable sin.

Changing Goals

Until the day she came to our facility, Jean had one goal in life: safety. Everything revolved around staying safe. She needed to be safe from being contaminated by any source. At times she washed her hands until they bled. She needed to keep others safe, and at times she believed that the best way to accomplish this was to simply stay away from them. If she were going to experience growth and change at all, her primary goal—safety—had to change.

Jean's desire for safety approached the level of worship. If she were to escape the bondage of OCD, she needed to be willing to change her priorities. She would have to risk feeling unsafe. Since she was a believer, a new primary goal in life was not hard to identify. Many emotional problems share the underlying issue of misplaced worship. When Christians recognize their idolatry, they become free to choose to redirect their worship.

Paul tells us in 2 Corinthians 5:9, "Therefore we also have as our ambition, whether at home or absent, to be pleasing to Him." The primary goal in the life of any believer must be to glorify God with their lives and please him. "I want to glorify God with my life more than I want to breathe" must become their new focus, rather than staying safe.

For Jean, this change in priorities would require abandoning rituals that had occupied her time and her thoughts. Those rituals dictated how she lived, and they were consuming her life. She would need to move from loving safety to loving the Lord with all of her heart, soul, and mind and loving her neighbors as she loved herself (Matthew 22:37–39). This would involve making considerable changes to both her thoughts and behavior.

Instead of being driven by her desire to be safe, Jean would need to place a higher priority on doing what the Bible said she should be doing. As Jesus says, "If you love Me, you will keep My commandments" (John 14:15). There were Scriptures that applied to the way Jean ordered her life. We would help her find them, and she would look to the Lord to help her apply them.

Despite the fact that Jean was spending her time keeping herself and her loved ones safe, the truth of the matter was that she was mostly serving herself. She would need to move away from primarily fulfilling her own desires to serving others. Following the example of our Lord, who washed the feet of the Twelve (see John 13), Jean would need to start serving others without regard to the risk; imitating Jesus's example always leads to our ultimate joy and fulfillment.

I have often said in teaching counseling, that if a counselee does not want to change their primary goal in life to glorifying God, it is not likely that they will change. Those who change that primary goal can grow and change in many other ways, as Scripture guides the way.

Four Important Aspects of Changing Thoughts and Behaviors

To help those struggling with OCD, it is necessary to approach both their thoughts and actions at the same time. Attempts to change thinking alone will often leave the counselee rocking in a corner muttering mantras. There needs to be a physically active aspect to the process of change. The goal for her response to her intrusive thoughts was to involve as many of her senses as possible while putting some part of her body in motion.

The purpose of this process was to occupy as many parts of her brain as possible in order to hamper her ability to dwell on her obsessions and to change the focus of her thoughts from obsessions to Scriptures. As our Lord said, "and you will know the truth, and the truth will make you free" (John 8:32). Merely exchanging objectionable obsessions for pleasant thoughts will fall short of the effect of biblical truth!

For Jean and those like her, changing thoughts and behaviors would be approached together. Only changing one or the other would not get to the heart of the matter. Exchanging the worship of safety for the worship and glorification of God requires a shift in both thoughts and actions.

True or not!

The first part of the process required Jean to examine her obsessive thoughts and to decide what was true and what was not. Philippians 4:8 calls us to think on "whatever is true." This would be vital to the change that needed to occur in her life.

Jean's new job was to compare her thoughts to Scripture with the help of her husband, family, and friends. Was it true that she would give her baby a disease simply by touching her child? Her doctor said no, and her husbands and friends agreed.

This process applies to any error in thought that anyone with OCD might have. Eventually, Jean would learn to make this judgment herself. It was important to help her understand that she was not making this change on her own. As a believer, she could count the power of the indwelling Holy Spirit to be her enabler in the effort. As Paul says to the Philippian church, "So then, my beloved, just as you have always obeyed, not as in my presence only, but now much more in my absence, work out your salvation with fear and trembling; for it is God who is at work in you, both to will and to work for His good pleasure" (Philippians 2:12–13). As Jean sought to change her thinking, God would be working in her to want the change and to make it!

It is a reasonable question to ask whether or not Paul's comments on the conscience apply to people like Jean. "But he who doubts is condemned if he eats, because his eating is not from faith; and whatever is not from faith is sin" (Romans 14:23). At times this was a struggle for her as she would read Scripture and wonder if she had committed the unpardonable sin or whether she had repented sufficiently to have salvation.

When obsessions come to include fears or committing or saying something vile or sinful, it may be described as scrupulosity.[7] As we dealt with Jean's religious obsession, we emphasized that her conscience on these matters was not properly informed. When her fears of losing her salvation for having an intrusive offensive thought surfaced, the aim was to have her compare that thought to the truth of Scripture and believe the truth.

Addressing the physical

The second critical aspect of this process is recognizing the physical component of OCD. Jean struggled with certain thoughts getting "stuck," so she felt unable to move away from them. She found it helpful to learn that current medical research indicates that her brain operates differently, which meant it would be harder—but not impossible—to change her thinking.[8]

When you consider the emotional impact of having an unwelcomed awful thought that you cannot get out of your thinking, the importance of the physical aspect becomes clear. Jean did not want to think her obsessions or do her compulsions. She carried enormous

7. Jennifer L. Buchholz et al., "Scrupulosity, Religious Affiliation and Symptom Presentation in Obsessive Compulsive Disorder," *Behavioral Cognitive Psychotherapy* 47, no. 4 (July 2019): 478–492, doi: 10.1017/S1352465818000711.

8. Mohammed R. Milad and Scott L. Rauch, "Obsessive-Compulsive Disorder: Beyond Segregated Cortico-Striatal Pathways," Trends in Cognitive Science, Review Special Issue: *Cognition in Neuropsychiatric Disorders* 16, no. 1 (January 2012): 43–51, https://doi.org/10.1016/j.tics.2011.11.003.

guilt for just having the thoughts. Sometimes she wondered how she could call herself a Christian and think this way. Instead of seeing herself as hopelessly trapped, knowing that there was a physical component to her struggle gave her courage to push back against her obsessions.

Paul tells us in Romans 5:12, "Therefore, just as through one man sin entered into the world, and death through sin, and so death spread to all men, because all sinned." We are not anything near what God meant us to be. The choice Adam and Eve made to sin resulted in all of us coming under the curse of sin. We are not as smart, industrious, inventive, handsome, or pretty as we might have been. And eventually we all age, wrinkle, and die.

After Jean asked herself if the stray, intrusive thought was true or untrue, and she determined that it was untrue but still struggled to let it go, she could then remind herself that the reason she could not easily dismiss it was because of her broken brain—the particular kind of Romans 5:12 consequence she suffered from as a result of the fall. This did not mean that Jean could not change her thinking. It just meant she would have to work much harder at it while others could simply move on. As I counseled Jean, she took great comfort in this thought.

When considering Jean's obsessions, it is easy to see why she devoted so much time to avoiding them. The idea that you would harm others, particularly your own child, is fearsome. Some of her obsessions were morally repulsive. Others seemed ridiculous. She could remind herself that she was not continuing to dwell on these thoughts because she wanted to do the actions. Knowing this helped her as she worked to take those thoughts captive.

Another thing that helped Jean was hearing of others' success in their struggle with OCD. Jean was able to meet with other individuals who had lived with intrusive thoughts much like her own. The idea that others had similar experiences made her thoughts less frightening. The fact that they had learned to deal with them in a less crippling way gave her courage and hope.

Seeing choices through the lens of Scripture

The third frontier for Jean in dealing with her OCD was reevaluating her compulsive responses to her thoughts. She needed to learn to accurately examine her behavior through the lens of Scripture. Part of her struggle was born of her own choices, so Jean needed to confront this fact and learn how to make new choices.

When she became overwhelmed with fears, she recognized that she often chose to respond to them by failing to fulfil real biblical responsibilities. When she chose to avoid friends and family because she feared harming them, she was not loving her neighbor as she loved herself. When she chose not to care for her child, she was avoiding her biblical duty as a parent.

When she chose to sweep the floor for four hours and spend the rest of her day rearranging her lists and washing her hands in a sort of non-religious legalism, she was consuming all of her time with activities that crowded out other God-given responsibilities. Jean had a will, and she could choose how to direct her thoughts and actions, even if it was more of a struggle for her than for others. To grow and change, Jean would need to choose to fill her scripturally defined role in life.

Finding meaning in suffering

In the final part of the process, Jean benefited from thinking through the potential value of her struggle with OCD. The value was twofold. As she turned her thinking toward the truth of Scripture, she began serving others and glorifying God with both her thoughts and actions. The OCD challenges that she overcame in order to do so made the work of the Holy Spirit in her life shine all the brighter.

The average observer could easily arrive at the conclusion that the time she spent on obsessive thoughts and rituals was simply wasted. Instead, I asked her to consider it from a different viewpoint, one that can be found in 2 Corinthians 1:4. In the introductory section of his letter, Paul says that God comforts believers *so that* they can comfort others with the same comfort that they have received from God.

Jean's struggle with OCD would not be a waste of time if she could share with others the truths she learned through those experiences that brought her comfort and helped her continue to move forward. Weary individuals dealing with obsessions and compulsions are greatly encouraged by the testimony of another person who has been where they are, but are no longer suffering to the same degree. It became Jean's privilege to come alongside others who were facing their OCD and share how God had enabled her to take her thoughts captive for Christ (2 Corinthians 10:5) and for the benefit of others.

Choosing Life!

As a believer, Jean had a considerable advantage in her struggle with OCD. Because the Holy Spirit lived in her, she had the Spirit's power to change. Paul spoke of this in his letter to the Romans:

> Do you not know that when you present yourselves to someone as slaves for obedience, you are slaves of the one whom you obey, either of sin resulting in death, or of obedience resulting in righteousness? But thanks be to God that though you were slaves of sin, you became obedient from the heart to that form of teaching to which you were committed, and having been freed from sin, you became slaves of righteousness. (6:16–18)

Having been raised to walk in new life as a believer, Jean could choose to remain a slave to her OCD, or she should choose to obey Scripture and reclaim her life. Instead of being consumed by useless rituals, she could choose to serve God and others with her time. Over the course of her counseling process, we helped Jean return to serving her family and ultimately God. Gradually, she was able to reassume the care of her infant daughter.

Changing Thoughts While Engaging in Physical Activities

As Jean confronted her obsessions, it was important for her to choose a physical activity that she could engage in as she sought to change her thoughts. In the beginning, this involved doing something with her child. Sometimes the activity was rocking her baby and singing Christian songs to her or taking her for a stroller walk while singing. These physical activities made her directly face her fear while she also worked on her thinking.

The aim was to occupy her senses as much as possible by engaging with reality while she endeavored to replace her intrusive, irrational thoughts with biblical thoughts. To be most effective, she needed to be physically active as opposed to simply sitting still and reciting a mantra. In particular, the physical activity needed to put her in situations that challenged her obsessions, rather than fed them. Scrubbing the floor while trying to tell herself that her fear of germs was unreasonable simply would not work.

She learned to sit in church or a crowded theater and not focus on the possibility of catching a disease or giving one to the stranger seated nearby. She realized that it would be difficult, if not impossible, to carry out the Great Commission if she was consumed with avoiding the world. In church, she found that taking notes during the sermon provided a useful distraction from any obsessive thoughts that might arise.

As time moved forward, Jean became more comfortable with caring for her child. When she became anxious, she would work her way through a thought process while she stayed engaged with her daughter. She would ask herself if her fear was true or untrue. Could the care she was providing her child transmit a fatal disease? Eventually she was able to tell herself that the thought was not true. After she could admit this, Philippians 4:8 reminded her that she should not dwell on things that were not true.

The Work Continues: Time and Practice

During her counseling, we did not tell Jean that there would be a day when she would never have to face an intrusive thought again. Instead, Jean was equipped to deal with "new" obsessions the way she had dealt with all her struggles during the time we counseled her. Through the counseling process, she had developed her own, biblically derived tools to use when she was faced with a new obsession.

For example, when she developed a fear that she could carry deadly bacteria into the house on her shoes because of Canadian geese that lived on the sidewalks near her home, she developed her own response. She started with simply stating that the thought was not true. She then reminded herself that she was going to spend her time dwelling on truth and not fiction. Jean continued to tell herself that this new thought/obsession could not hurt her, hurt others, or control her.

She then reminded herself of the truth found in Romans 8:28— that whatever happened to her would be for her good and God's glory. This comforted her in the midst of her struggle, along with the reminder that perfect love casts out fear (1 John 4:18). God loved her and he would not needlessly let her come to harm.

Last, Jean chose a physical activity that had nothing to do with the potential obsession. In pursuing these new thoughts and behaviors, she was genuinely seeking to glorify God instead of worshipping safety. Later on, as new potential obsessions arose, it occurred to her that they had much in common with the geese outside her house and the mess they left behind. At times, she could fend off intrusive thoughts just by asking if this was more "goose poop."

Jean's experiences illustrate that while genuine progress can be made, OCD is often a lifelong struggle. By the time most individuals seek help with OCD, they have practiced their routines for years. It should not be a surprise that they have gotten really "good" at it. As Paul tells the Galatian church, "Do not be deceived, God is not mocked; for whatever a man sows, this he will also reap" (Galatians

6:7). We not only reap what we sow, we reap more than we sow, and far later than when we sowed.

Hidden in this is really good news for everyone like Jean. She daily made the choice to continue her old OCD habits or to replace them. But as a believer, Jean could choose to respond biblically to her thoughts and compulsions. As she did so, she began to reap the fruit that the Holy Spirit bears in the life of believers. She had love, joy, and above all peace in the place where fear had lived so long.

A Word for the Counselor and the Counselee

The struggle with OCD is both challenging and rewarding. It is good to remember the value of perseverance in the process. For the counselor, Paul's advice to the Corinthians is timeless: "be steadfast, immovable, always abounding in the work of the Lord, knowing that your toil is not in vain in the Lord" (1 Corinthians 15:58). For the counselee, it is good to meditate on Paul's encouragement to the Galatians: "Let us not lose heart in doing good, for in due time we will reap if we do not grow weary" (Galatians 6:9).

Let us always keep in mind the Romans 5:12 physical difference that may be contributing to the problem. Recognizing the different physical challenges involved in resisting OCD thoughts and behaviors can be encouraging. And there is great hope when we remember that, as believers, we all can make real choices and we are empowered by the Holy Spirit to glorify God through our choices.

CHAPTER 13

SCHIZOPHRENIA:
MEDICAL BACKGROUND AND BIBLICAL PRINCIPLES

Charles D. Hodges Jr., MD

Bruce was a forty-year-old patient who came to my office because he was diagnosed as a chronic schizophrenic and needed to get maintenance medication. From a medical viewpoint, he had a few problems, including type 2 diabetes and smoking cigarettes. He was very stable and held a job; had I not known his diagnosis, I might not have suspected it. He seemed firmly connected to reality and processed questions normally.

As time passed and we dealt with his medical problems, I had the opportunity to ask him more about his diagnosis of schizophrenia. It had started in his early twenties. He would have a psychotic or delusional period and land in the hospital for treatment. Then he would routinely leave after a week or more and eventually stop his medication.

He finally reached the conclusion that it was easier to take his medicine than continue the cycle of hospitalizations. I asked him what would happen if he stopped taking it. He replied that it was only a matter of time before he would begin having hallucinations again. He had tried going off medication and experienced the same result several times before.

The Complexities of Schizophrenia

I suppose that the reason schizophrenia has become such a controversial topic for biblical counselors revolves around the real concern of identifying the thoughts and behaviors of individuals as medical problems. The concern is that if one of the DSM-5 diagnoses is a medical issue, we will be forced to identify the rest of the diagnoses in the DSM-5 as diseases that can be fixed with a pill. It is a very basic view of a complex problem, and it serves no one well.

I have practiced medicine for nearly five decades and been involved in counseling for the last three. During that time, I have encountered, treated, counseled, and cared for individuals who at times appeared to be disconnected from reality. My first encounter was when I was a child. We lived a few blocks from Central State Hospital in Indianapolis, and we passed by it often. I remember seeing patients standing behind the tall fence. I wondered why they were there.

I found the answer when I was confronted with the reality of schizophrenia in medical school. In my third year, I was assigned to a rotation on the psychiatry service. I was one of two junior students, and we split the patients on the ward between us. For the most part we were their doctors, although we had a moderate amount of supervision from a staff physician. Mostly we looked to the nurses for direction because they knew what to do far better than we did.

In my group, there were multiple schizophrenics. I had at least one who thought he was John the Baptist and another who thought he was Jesus. Their delusions sort of worked together. The main means of care was the tranquilizer chlorpromazine and conversations with psychologists or social workers. The patients would be with us for less than a week and then back out on the street. When they left, they would generally stop their medication and return in much the same delusional state. It was easy to see the whole process as an exercise in futility.

After I began to practice medicine, I continued to encounter men and women with the diagnosis. They came to my office, and I would see them in the emergency room. I did my best to help meet their medical needs. As a Christian, I would try to counsel them as best I could, but at times it seemed without much effect. Their delusions seemed impervious to reason. I couldn't convince individuals who thought they were John the Baptist that their delusions were anything but true.

Current Medical Understanding of Schizophrenia

For those in the biblical counseling movement, schizophrenia has always been a conundrum. At times, it is hard to think that the behavior of an individual may be connected to a disease process in the body, particularly if that behavior is troublesome. There is a wide range of opinions about the cause of schizophrenia and how to best care for those who suffer from it. The disagreement starts at a very basic level: Is schizophrenia a brain-based disease, or is it a spiritual problem? Or is it something in between?

Most biblical counselors view having clear pathology as the standard for calling anything a disease, including schizophrenia. In other words, for a collection of symptoms, emotions, thoughts, or behaviors to be considered a disease, there ought to be a change in the physical body that results in the change in function. And we should be able to document it.

It is important to remember that while all disease will have pathologic change causing it, we may not be able to demonstrate it. Problems like migraine headaches are recognized as a disease by most physicians, although we do not yet completely understand the underlying change in the brain that causes them. Schizophrenia is in the same position in medicine today. Most physicians and researchers would say it is a brain disease. In the past decade, we have discovered an increasing number of physical differences in the brains of individuals affected by schizophrenia. Let's consider some of them.

Defining Schizophrenia

First, it is important to understand the criteria for diagnosing someone with schizophrenia. A recent study showed that up to 50 percent of those diagnosed as schizophrenic do not actually meet the criteria for the diagnosis.[1] To qualify for the diagnosis, an individual must have experienced or displayed two of the following, one of which must be among the first three listed: delusions, hallucinations, disorganized speech, grossly disorganized or catatonic behavior, and negative symptoms such as diminished emotional expression or decreased ability to think.[2] These symptoms must have been present for a month or longer.

The Role of Genetics

As we look for the cause of schizophrenia, the role of genetics is an important aspect to address. Advances in genome-wide association studies have identified one hundred genetic areas or loci in our DNA that are associated with an increased risk of developing the symptoms associated with schizophrenia. A defect in one gene increases the risk to 30 or 40 percent. Those with this specific genetic change are in a similar situation as those who carry the gene for Alzheimer's disease—they are at an increased risk to have the problem.[3]

Although genetic inheritance appears to play a significant role in schizophrenia, it does not appear to be the sole cause as it is in Huntington's disease, a devastating degenerative brain disorder. Identical twins have a 50 percent chance of developing schizophrenia, but not 100 percent.[4] Problems during pregnancy and in the time

1. Chelsey Coulter, Krista K. Baker, and Russell L. Margolis, "Specialized Consultation for Suspected Recent-onset Schizophrenia: Diagnostic Clarity and the Distorting Impact of Anxiety and Reported Auditory Hallucinations," *Journal of Psychiatric Practice* 25, no. 2 (March 2019): 78–81, https://doi.org/10.1097/PRA.0000000000000363.
2. Robert A. McCutcheon, Tiago Reis Marques, and Oliver D. Howes, "Schizophrenia—An Overview," *JAMA Psychiatry* 77, no. 2 (2020): 201–210. A more complete version of the criteria can be found in the *Diagnostic and Statistical Manual of Mental Disorders*, 5th edition (Washington, DC: American Psychiatric Association, 2013), 99–105.
3. McCutcheon, Marques, and Howes, "Schizophrenia," 202.
4. McCutcheon, Marques, and Howes, "Schizophrenia," 202.

around birth appear to increase an individual's risk for developing schizophrenia by five times that which would be expected in the general population.[5]

The Role of the Immune System

The most interesting portion of the research has to do with the potential role of the immune system in schizophrenia. A change in a gene that affects the human immune system in the complement system (complement C4) appears to result in an increased destruction or pruning of the connecting structures in the brain called synapses. The increased destruction of brain connections (by microglia) appears to be connected to symptoms.[6] The gene defect that affects C4 was identified in a large study in 2016.[7] This study offers evidence that a physical process damaging the brain is associated with the symptoms of schizophrenia. This destructive process has been objectively documented.

In the past year, several interesting research papers and case reports have been published about this subject. I found particularly interesting a study that connects some of the dots between genetic and pathological studies. A case report published in *The Psychiatric Times* documents the history of two individuals who needed a bone marrow transplant for leukemia.[8] In one case, the individual received a transplant from a sibling who had symptomatic schizophrenia. While he was cured of his leukemia, he developed the symptoms of schizophrenia. In the second case, an individual who had schizophrenia received a bone marrow transplant from an individual who did not have schizophrenia. He was cured of his leukemia and his schizophrenia.

---

5. McCutcheon, Marques, and Howes, "Schizophrenia," 201.

6. McCutcheon, Marques, and Howes, "Schizophrenia," 203–4.

7. Aswin Sekar et al., "Schizophrenia Risk from Complex Variation of Complement Component 4," *Nature*, 530 (2016): 177–83, https://doi.org/10.1038/nature16549.

8. Brian Miller, "Immunotherapy as Personalized Medicine for Schizophrenia?" *Psychiatric Times* 36, no. 2 (February 28, 2019), https://www.psychiatrictimes.com/view/immunotherapy-personalized-medicine-schizophrenia.

What does the case study imply? Bone marrow transplants require that the individual's current bone marrow be replaced. It is the source of the cancer, and to cure the cancer, the old bone marrow must go. In essence, the individual receives an immune system transplant. It may well be the case that schizophrenia is an autoimmune disorder much like other autoimmune diseases that affect the brain.

There are other autoimmune disorders that affect the brain and can be treated.[9] If schizophrenia turns out to be caused by an immune disorder that attacks the tissue of the brain, then there is great potential that we will be able to test for it and eventually treat it. Currently, it exists in much the same realm as Alzheimer's disease, where we have a growing understanding of the pathology, but we are struggling to create drugs that cure it.

The Role of Substance Abuse

It is important to keep in mind that psychosis and schizophrenia are not the same thing. Other medical problems can include symptoms of being disconnected from reality, experiencing delusions, and hearing and seeing things that others do not. Medications as innocuous as the nonsteroidal naproxen have been known to cause hallucinations and psychosis in susceptible individuals. More commonly, prescribed amphetamines have caused psychosis in some patients. There are many medications that may potentially cause altered states of consciousness and psychosis in susceptible individuals. If anyone has hallucinations or delusions, they should be assessed by a physician right away.

Using illegal substances can also result in the symptoms of psychosis. Cocaine, crystal methamphetamine, opioids, alcohol, and marijuana are just a few examples.[10] The major concern with the regular use of these drugs is that they are all addictive or habit

---

9. Josep Dalmau et al., "An Update on Anti-NMDA Receptor Encephalitis for Neurologists and Psychiatrists: Mechanisms and Models," *Lancet* 18, no. 11 (November 2019): 1045–57, https://doi.org/10.1016/S1474-4422(19)30244-3.

10. "Commonly Used Drugs Charts," *National Institute on Drug Abuse*, last updated August 20, 2020, https://nida.nih.gov/research-topics/commonly-used-drugs-charts.

forming. Many have the potential to push a susceptible individual into a psychotic state.

Marijuana has been the subject of many publications due to the drive for its legalization both for medical and recreational use. The problem is the lack of real research that demonstrates its medical usefulness beyond intractable seizure disorders and nausea associated with chemotherapy. This does not mean that cannabis may not have any medical use. Rather, it is to say that currently no other medical use has been documented by research that would lead us to believe that the risks of using it are outweighed by the benefits. Another chapter in this book deals with this issue at length, but there is one issue that we should address.

As our laws and viewpoints on marijuana have changed, there has been an increased incidence of schizophrenia associated with the increased marijuana use. In the last five years, I have read almost every biography or memoir recording the lives of notable individuals who suffered from schizophrenia. One commonality in every case was that marijuana had played a role in the life of the struggler.

Please keep in mind that not everyone who smokes marijuana will develop schizophrenia. But the rate of incidence has increased to the point that regular marijuana use is considered a risk factor for developing schizophrenia.[11] The increased risk of developing the life-altering problems of schizophrenia should make using marijuana uninviting to anyone even if for no other reason.[12]

Brain Differences

Experiments performed on the brains of affected individuals after death have shown significant differences that may have contributed to abnormal brain function. The researchers found fewer dendritic

---

11. A. Eden Evins et al., "Does Using Marijuana Increase the Risk for Developing Schizophrenia?" *Journal of Clinical Psychiatry* 74, no. 4 (April 2013), https://doi.org/10.4088/JCP.12012tx2c.

12. Shweta Patel et al., "The Association Between Cannabis Use and Schizophrenia: Causative or Curative? A Systematic Review," *Cureus* 12, no. 7 (July 2020), https://doi.org/10.7759/cureus.9309.

spines in important areas of the brain that affect thinking. These findings are not seen in normal brains. The changes in the brain tissue would be considered pathological and support the designation of schizophrenia as a brain disease.[13]

In people currently living with schizophrenia, brain scans have been used to also identify brain differences. It is easy to be critical of how brain scans are used to support psychological diagnoses today, and I have also been critical at times. For those who are interested in reading more about the pitfalls of brain scans, see *Brainwashed: The Seductive Appeal of Mindless Neuroscience* by Sally Satel.[14] However, as time has passed, the scans have improved, and so has the information that they provide. Molecular imaging now allows researchers to look at the concentration of substances inside the living human brain. For instance, studies have been conducted to compare the concentration of dopamine in the brains of schizophrenics and control subjects.[15]

Molecular imaging has shown that dopamine is elevated in the brains of those with psychotic symptoms as compared to normal control subjects. This was true for those taking amphetamines who developed psychosis.[16] It was also true for those with schizophrenia. Among those with schizophrenia, the elevation of dopamine correlated with the level of psychotic symptoms.[17] These studies do not tell us why the levels of dopamine were elevated, but they do provide an objective way to identify differences in the brains of those with schizophrenia symptoms. Changes in brain scans appeared to be connected to problems with the ability to think. This difficulty appeared in affected adolescent patients earlier than hallucinations and delusions. In adolescent patients, brain scans done over time showed

13. McCutcheon, Marques, and Howes, "Schizophrenia," 204.

14. Sally Satel, *Brainwashed: The Seductive Appeal of Mindless Neuroscience* (New York: Basic Books, 2013).

15. McCutcheon, Marques, and Howes, "Schizophrenia," 205.

16. Lauren V. Moran et al., "Psychosis with Methylphenidate or Amphetamine in Patients with ADHD," *New England Journal of Medicine* 380, no. 12 (March 2019), 1128, https://doi.org/10.1056/NEJMoa1813751.

17. McCutcheon, Marques, and Howes, "Schizophrenia," 205–206.

changes in brain tissue. They noted that the cognitive/thinking problems appeared to be connected to significant loss in gray matter areas of the brain.[18]

One last bit of observable information comes in the form of brain wave patterns as seen with electrophysiological studies. Measured gamma brainwave activity in normal individuals has been found to differ from those with schizophrenia.[19] The differences were thought to accompany or be caused by brain damage, which resulted in a decline in the thinking ability of the patient.

Current Medical and Psychotherapeutic Treatments

Current treatment centers on reducing psychotic symptoms. Most of the medications used block the D2 receptor for dopamine in the brain and, in so doing, decrease the effects of dopamine, which appears to be involved in the psychosis. The effect of these medications can be seen today with positron emission tomography brain scans that can measure the blockade that occurs at the receptor site. A 60 percent level of blockade needs to occur to lower psychotic symptoms, but a blockade of 80 percent causes side effects to occur.[20]

The fact that we can see the area that is blockaded by the medication and the level of the blockade that is required in order to stop the psychosis is useful. This is another measurable piece of information that supports the designation of schizophrenia as a brain disease.

While current medicines can help reduce psychotic symptoms, they do not help with the declining cognitive abilities that accompany schizophrenia. Furthermore, approximately one-third of those diagnosed with schizophrenia do not respond to dopamine receptor blocking medications. However, these individuals may be helped by other medications.

One study has noted that counseling seems to benefit those experiencing psychosis due to schizophrenia. However, the study did not

---

18. McCutcheon, Marques, and Howes, "Schizophrenia," 203.
19. McCutcheon, Marques, and Howes, "Schizophrenia," 203.
20. McCutcheon, Marques, and Howes, "Schizophrenia," 206.

indicate what kind of counseling was used; it simply indicated that counseling helped the affected individual to better understand and deal with their psychotic episodes.[21]

Concluding Thoughts on Our Current Medical Understanding of Schizophrenia

What conclusions can this research lead to? We have documented several important points that would lead most of us to the conclusion that schizophrenia is a brain disease—or at least it has a significant medical/physical component. The connection between genetic defects and our immune system appears to offer a promising explanation for the damage that occurs in the brain. It may lead to the ability to validate the diagnosis with blood testing and to more effective forms of treatment.

Brain scans that can now measure the activity of dopamine offer an explanation for the psychotic symptoms. Autopsy reports on brains of schizophrenics confirm the presence of an ongoing destructive disease process. All of this information points to schizophrenia being a brain disease process, and among physicians, there are few who would disagree. It is still true that no definitive cause for the symptoms of schizophrenia has been identified. And yet, we must recognize that a great deal of research demonstrates a pathological change in the brains of those who have schizophrenia.

A Biblical Counseling Approach to Schizophrenia

Those of us in biblical counseling and medicine who provide care and counseling to individuals affected by schizophrenia should approach our care with caution and humility. Since none of us can, at the moment, definitively identify the cause and cure for schizophrenia, we should be willing to say, "I don't know." And we should suspend our judgment of those affected. James 2:12–13 is a great verse to keep

21. McCutcheon, Marques, and Howes, "Schizophrenia," 206.

in mind in these kinds of situations: "So speak and so act as those who are to be judged by the law of liberty. For judgment will be merciless to one who has shown no mercy; mercy triumphs over judgment." Withholding judgment in cases that are not clear keeps us from the grave error into which Job's friends stumbled by attempting to extract a confession of sin from him.

Help the Weak

Counselors should approach the counseling of individuals who present with the diagnosis of schizophrenia with a 1 Thessalonians 5:14 attitude: "admonish the unruly, encourage the fainthearted, help the weak, be patient with everyone."

Helping the weak starts with listening carefully to determine whether the counselee is oriented to person, place, and time. I know that some might disagree, but I have never been able to counsel someone well if they were hallucinating or delusional. Such individuals need health care.

The next important thing in helping the weak is to determine whether they are willingly coming to counseling, or whether they are there under compulsion. Motive in counseling is vital. If the counselee is only present to satisfy their family or the courts and avoid any threatened consequences, it becomes less likely that counseling will succeed. If this is the case for your counselee, you should not take this as a reason not to try, but it is good to remember this context if the counseling relationship seems to go nowhere.

In biblical counseling, we maintain that in order for a counselee to experience much benefit our counsel, they must be a believer. Without the presence of the indwelling Holy Spirt, it is not possible for any of us to comply with the imperatives of Scripture. If the counselee is not a Christian in the Romans 10:9 sense of the word, then counseling will, in great measure, be evangelism. It will require us to share the gospel while pointing the individual to the change the gospel can bring to their life.

The individual diagnosed with schizophrenia will need to grow and understand the doctrine of progressive sanctification as defined in the letter to the Ephesians. I have been a Christian since I was nineteen, and I can't say I fully understood this doctrine before I studied biblical counseling three decades later. I suspect that most who come to counseling would say the same thing.

It is vitally important that neither they nor we use their diagnosis as a reason why they should not learn and cannot change. *Schizophrenia* is not another word for ignorant. To understand this, one only needs to become acquainted with the life story of John Nash, the notable mathematician whose story was told in *A Beautiful Mind*.[22] Many, if not most, of those with the diagnosis can learn. We should also avoid excusing biblically defined sin in their lives. We do the believing individual no favor by excusing behavior defined in Scripture as sin. In fact, we do them harm as the church at Corinth did with the young believer living in sexual sin (1 Corinthians 5:1–13). We must avoid this error as we counsel.

Those who must deal with schizophrenia will need the same kind of counseling help that all of us need. They must learn to deal biblically with anger, worry, communication, problem solving, decisions, and their role as husband, wife, parent, son, daughter, brother, or sister. Many will need employment and some will need to learn a trade or pursue further education in order to be able to work and support themselves. We should help make that possible.

As with anyone who is struggling, they will sometimes need help to obtain basic essentials such as food, clothing, and a place to live. They desperately need community. The church should be a place that knows this and aims to help them find it. In the community of the church, they will need to find the kind of biblical teaching and preaching that feeds them like newborn babes so that they can grow. They will need counseling that guides them to the hope found in

---

22. Sylvia Nasar, *A Beautiful Mind* (New York: Simon and Schuster, 1998). There is also a movie about John Nash with the same name.

Scripture for anyone struggling with chronic medical problems. They will need to find a goal in life that will lead them away from despair. For any believer that goal can be found in 1 Corinthians 10:31, where Paul reminds us that no matter what we are doing, we should do it all to the glory of God.

Admonish the Unruly

As we counsel those diagnosed with schizophrenia, we need to approach any sins we see with a Galatians 6:1–2 attitude: "Brethren, even if anyone is caught in any trespass, you who are spiritual, restore such a one in a spirit of gentleness; each one looking to yourself, so that you too will not be tempted. Bear one another's burdens, and thereby fulfill the law of Christ." Paul says much the same thing in 2 Timothy 2:24–26 when he tells us to gently correct those in opposition in the hope that they would be granted repentance and come to understand the truth of Scripture. Sins need to be admonished, but in a spirit of gentleness, especially when their sins appear to be connected to the physical weakness of schizophrenia.

Patiently Encourage the Fainthearted

As we counsel these brothers and sisters in Christ and their families, they will need encouragement. Families should not be saddled with blame for their child's schizophrenia. Medically, it is unlikely that they had much of anything to do with it. The more research we do, the more this seems to be true. At the same time, we should encourage them to avoid making excuses for their child's behavior that is defined by Scripture as sin. It does not do them or their child any good to do so.

Perhaps the most important asset that any counselor should have when helping those with schizophrenia and their families is patience. In the context of schizophrenia, counselors will need the ability to patiently listen when life does not seem to make much sense. Patience may also be required when you seek to help someone recognize that getting good medical care is in their best interest, as it was with my patient Bruce. Through the long and at times challenging process of counseling someone who struggles with schizophrenia, it is vital to see the counselee as a fellow believer who needs help to grow and change and become more like Christ so that they might make glorifying God the prime directive of their existence.

Conclusions

We started by considering the question of whether schizophrenia is an outcome of spiritual problems or whether it is a medical problem, a disease of the brain that results in the symptoms of schizophrenia. We are not the first to grapple with this question. Freud considered it and decided that schizophrenia was a result of unresolved conflicts in the individual's life, usually with a parent. For him, schizophrenia was a matter of choice and behavior. In contrast, Emil Kraepelin, a German physician who is credited with identifying schizophrenia as a distinct disease in 1896, believed that schizophrenia was a biological brain disorder for which there was no cure or treatment.[23] In either case, neither of them had much success in their care for those affected.

What can we say then about the cause of schizophrenia and how to best care for those who suffer from it based on the research we have examined? First, a growing body of medical evidence supports the idea that schizophrenia is a brain-based disease. Few physicians would say anything different. At the same time, as we noted above, it is important to remember that schizophrenia is often over diagnosed. And psychosis from drug use and other diseases can certainly be mistaken for it.

23. R. F. Zec, "Neuropsychology of Schizophrenia According to Kraepelin: Disorders of Volition and Executive Functioning," *Eur Arch Psychiatry Clinical Neurosci.* 245, no. 4-5 (1995): 216–23, doi: 10.1007/BF02191800. PMID: 7578284.

Second, the more we know about schizophrenia, the more it appears to be a medical problem with spiritual implications. Many both inside the biblical counseling movement and outside would disagree. And I would admit that at this time the answer is not absolutely certain.

As a physician and biblical counselor, I believe schizophrenia will prove to be a medical problem that will eventually have a cure. That is just my opinion, although I do believe this opinion rests on a growing body of research findings. Current medical treatment for psychotic symptoms can be helpful to many, although not all. At the same time, it is important to remember that individuals struggling with the symptoms of schizophrenia will need the kind of care that comes from Scripture—as might anyone with a chronic medical problem.

This past winter, I taught on this subject for a graduate course in counseling, where I had to deal with the issue of the sufficiency of Scripture for such problems. I spent an evening in my hotel room trying to carefully word what I thought about it and what I thought the Bible said. I came up with the following:

> I am here to testify this morning that I absolutely believe that our completely sufficient and superior Savior has given us sufficient divine words in the Bible to help those struggling with schizophrenia. I also believe that God has given the common grace of physicians and medicine to be a help and comfort for the physical aspects not mentioned in Scripture.

A Word to the Counselor

Have you had the occasion to counsel and help an individual who was disconnected from reality and hallucinating? How did you respond? Do you have a physician colleague that you can consult with when you are working with individuals with schizophrenia?

A Word to the Counselee and Family

God has promised us in his Word that he will carry us through the most difficult circumstances. Are you depending on his grace to carry you through the struggle?

CHAPTER 14

. . . .

BIPOLAR DISORDER:
MEDICAL AND BIBLICAL PERSPECTIVES

Charles D. Hodges Jr., MD

Bipolar Disorder has become an important diagnosis for biblical counselors to be familiar with. Shortly after the third revision of the *Diagnostic and Statistical Manual of Mental Disorders* (DSM) in 1980, the number of individuals with this diagnosis in counseling noticeably increased. This can be attributed to the changes made to the criteria in the third edition. What had been described as manic depression became bipolar disorder 1, bipolar disorder 2, and several other variations.[1]

The criteria changes made it easier to apply the diagnosis to a growing number of patients who were being treated for depression but not improving. As a result, more individuals come to biblical counseling with the diagnosis of bipolar, and they sometimes point to it as the cause of their struggles. It is important to understand this group of diagnoses so that we can respond in a biblically compassionate way as we counsel. Because most people are diagnosed with either bipolar disorder 1 or 2, let's examine two case studies to illustrate the similarities and differences between these two diagnoses.

---

1. David Healy, "The Latest Mania: Selling Bipolar Disorder," *PLoS Medicine* 3, no. 4 (April 11, 2006): 6, https://doi.org/10.1371/journal.pmed.0030185.

Bipolar Disorder 1

George came to my biblical counseling office after a late-night trip to the emergency department of our local hospital.[2] He had been seen there because his family was concerned about his behavior. He had not been sleeping for days, and whenever someone would slow down enough to listen, George was constantly talking about a "huge" business deal that was going to make him rich! It was the opportunity of a lifetime, and anyone who invested with him would also get rich.

His family had watched in wonder when he started leaving one hundred dollars as a tip in restaurants where ten dollars would have been generous. It all came to a head when an out-of-town relative called to ask how George could afford to charter a stretch limousine to pick him up for a football game. The family said that he was currently working at a part-time job in a coffee shop. He was spending money he did not have on clothes he could not afford because he said he needed to dress well for his business.

His parents and siblings had taken him to the emergency room to get help stopping George from spending himself into oblivion. The physician and social worker in the emergency room were concerned about his behavior and arranged to have him admitted to the psych ward of the hospital where he and his empty billfold would be safe. At least there he wouldn't be able to make deals, spend money, or make other disastrous decisions for the next seven days.

George was a believer in Christ. When he wasn't in the middle of one of his high-flying episodes, he was a dependable, regular member of his church. He read his Bible daily and prayed. But when he headed into one of his exorbitant spending phases, he more or less disappeared from church.

By the time I saw George, he was again sleeping at night. And he was not talking nearly as much or as fast as he had been before his

---

2. All patients discussed in this chapter are the combination of several and are offered for illustrative purposes only; they do not represent any particular individual or their protected health information.

week in the hospital. The medication he was taking helped him sleep at night, but he was unhappy with the side effects.

A thorough medical workup revealed no other cause for George's disordered thinking and hallucinations, but his history did. This was not the first time he had been in this kind of situation; at least two times before he had had periods when he could not sleep for several days in a row. His thoughts would race, and he had difficulty staying focused on any task. As his thoughts wandered, sometimes he would come up with ideas about starting a business or investing his money in a way that he believed would make him a fortune. Then he would spend money that he did not have. During one of the episodes when George had not slept for days, he began to hallucinate.

Often these episodes resulted in George losing his job, as it did on this occasion. It left him saddled with debt for the surefire business that never materialized. His family was desperate for help. When George was sleeping and rational, he was fun to be around. But when he started to ramp up and sleep less, the family knew it was just a matter of time until George would be out of control.

After the "up" episode would come the dark "down" mood that would last for weeks. It was hard to say why, but his family was certain that he was suffering from unrestrained buyer's remorse. George and his family were hoping that I could offer them help in understanding his wild mood swings and erratic behavior.

From a physician's viewpoint, it wasn't difficult to put George in a diagnostic category. According to the DSM, George was suffering from bipolar disorder 1.

Bipolar Disorder 2

Eleanor's experience was significantly different from George's. Unlike George, she did not have periods of staying awake for days at a time. She was not gripped by grandiose thoughts of big business deals and did not indulge in excessive spending. Her pathway to a diagnosis was not through the emergency room, but through her primary care doctor's office.

Eleanor had dealt with a moderate level of melancholy for a couple of years. Nothing in life was particularly wrong or right. Notably, she and a long-term beau had recently parted ways. She wanted a ring, and he felt trapped. She was currently dating, but the fellow did not seem interested in exploring long-term attachment just yet. That left her with a growing sense of sadness. Eventually, on a routine trip to the doctor, her persistent sadness came up. Her physician found nothing unusual at her physical exam and suggested they do a series of blood tests to see if she had any physical explanation for her mood.

At a follow-up visit, the doctor explained that her tests did not show any abnormalities, and he asked Eleanor to fill out a pencil and paper test that would help them explore her sad mood. The depression self-rating scale indicated that Eleanor was moderately depressed. She had seen the television commercials that discussed depression and the medications available to fix it. Since the test said she was moderately depressed, she asked if taking medication might help her feel better. Her doctor agreed that it was possible that a medication might help, and she left the office with samples and a prescription for the specific drug she had seen in the commercial.

In a couple of weeks, the medicine seemed to be helping, and Eleanor thought she had found the solution to her struggles. While initially, the medication seemed to lift her mood, after a few months, she just seemed to not feel much at all. She did not have the lows, but at the same time, she did not seem to have any highs either. So she went back to her doctor, and this time she brought along the information for a newer medication that she had seen on television.

The newer medicine belonged to the group of medications known as atypical antipsychotics. These medications are being promoted as an add-on to first-line antidepressant medications. Her physician decided that it would be best to refer her to a psychiatrist for that type of medicine. Eleanor agreed to the referral and made an appointment.

At the appointment with the psychiatrist, Eleanor explained her situation and symptoms and answered the doctor's questions. At the end of the hour, Eleanor was asked to fill out another psychiatric test. The results, as interpreted by the specialist, indicated that she did not have the usual sort of depression. Instead, she fit the diagnostic criteria for bipolar disorder 2. The psychiatrist then told her that this diagnosis was most likely a lifelong problem and suggested that she begin taking a "mood stabilizing" medication.

Eleanor, like George, had confessed Christ as her Lord and believed that God had raised him from the dead. She was a regular attender at church—when her mood wasn't at its lowest.

Medical Background and Approaches to BPD

George and Eleanor represent the vast majority of patients that are diagnosed with bipolar disorder (BPD). Common to both BPD 1 and BPD 2 is an episode of depression.

In order to qualify for the diagnosis of BPD 1, George had to have the following experiences or behaviors in addition to an episode of depression: a distinct period of abnormally and persistently elevated, expansive, or irritable mood and increased activity or energy lasting most of the day for a week. He would meet the criteria if hospitalized.

He would also need to display at least four of the following symptoms, and they should represent a noticeable change from his usual behavior:[3]

- Inflated self-esteem or grandiosity
- Decreased need for sleep (e.g., feels rested after only three hours of sleep)
- More talkative than usual or exerts pressure to keep others talking
- Flight of ideas or subjective experience that indicates racing thoughts

---

3. The subsequent description is condensed from the criteria found in the DSM. A complete list of diagnostic criteria is found in the *Diagnostic and Statistical Manual of Mental Disorders*, 5th edition (Washington, DC: American Psychiatric Association, 2013), 124.

- Distractibility (e.g., attention too easily drawn to unimportant or irrelevant external stimuli), either reported or observed
- Increase in goal-directed activity, whether socially, at work or school, or sexually
- Psychomotor agitation with purposeless non-goal-directed activity
- Risky behavior that may have painful consequences, including buying sprees, sexual indiscretions, or foolish business investments

These behaviors must cause impairment in life or work or require hospitalization to prevent harm to self or others, or be accompanied by other psychotic features. The episode also must not be attributable to the physiological effects of a substance (e.g., recreational drugs, a medication, or other treatment) or to another medical condition.

George met the criteria with his sleeplessness, grandiose thoughts, reckless spending, distractibility, and foolish business investments. His family shared that when he took his medicine, he seemed to do well. But when he stopped, it was only a matter of time before he would be back in the same situation.

The criteria for BPD2 are similar to those for BPD1, but the threshold for meeting the diagnostic criteria is much lower. Like George, Eleanor would need to have experienced depression as defined by the DSM. She would also need to have an episode called hypomania, which is similar to the manic periods experienced by George, but less severe. Eleanor would only need to have four days of behavior that looked a bit like mania, but was not nearly as disruptive. An episode of hypomania is not severe enough to cause marked impairment in life or work or require hospitalization. If there are any psychotic features involved, the episode is, by definition, manic, not hypomanic.

The last paragraph of the BPD2 criteria is very important. It says,

A full hypomanic episode that emerges during antidepressant treatment (e.g., medication, electroconvulsive therapy) but persists at a fully syndromal level beyond the physiological effect of that treatment is sufficient evidence for a hypomanic episode diagnosis. However, caution is indicated so that one or two symptoms (particularly increased irritability, edginess, or agitation following antidepressant use) are not taken as sufficient for a diagnosis of a hypomanic episode, nor necessarily indicative of a bipolar diathesis.[4]

The important part of this paragraph is that if a counselee appears to meet the criteria for bipolar disorder while taking an antidepressant, it must be determined whether the symptoms are due to the medicine. While this would be the duty of the treating physician, it would be a reasonable question for us to ask any counselee who came with the BPD2 label. When was the diagnosis made and what medication were you taking at the time? This should not result in advice to the counselee about continuing their medication, but it could lead to the counselor conferring with the prescriber to clarify the diagnosis.

The criteria for both BPD1 and BPD2 are subjective. There are no tests that can validate the diagnosis like there are in a case of strep throat or diabetes. That does not mean that a disease process is not present. There are multiple medical diagnoses, such as migraine headaches, for which we lack a full understanding of the cause, disease process, or biophysical markers. And many times in the past we have not understood a disease only to discover that it was pernicious anemia due to a vitamin B12 deficiency.

This lack of ability to validate the diagnosis makes it likely that we may both misdiagnose or overdiagnose the disorder. This is particularly true for BPD2 because the outright manic episode associated with BPD1 is much more distinctive. Once a clinician sees BPD1, it will always seem familiar when encountered again. On the other hand, BPD2 and its characteristic hypomania could easily represent the side effect profile of any of the current crop of selective serotonin reuptake inhibitors (SSRIs), which are antidepressant medications.

---

4. *DSM-5*, 125.

Eleanor met the criteria for BPD2, but it must be taken into consideration that she was taking an antidepressant. She did have times when she felt better for a few days, but she was also more distractible and talkative. She got more done at work during these times, and yes, she did spend money that would likely end up on her credit card as long-term debt. But during these episodes, her friends just thought she looked better.

Substance Abuse and BPD

A growing concern in many countries today has been the increasing use of addictive opioids, stimulant drugs, and marijuana.[5] All of these drugs are likely to have an adverse effect on those who are prone to mania. Side effects of any of them may mimic the criteria of hypomania. Perhaps most important is the connection between regular marijuana use and psychosis.[6] The National Institute of Mental Health states that the risk of psychosis and hallucinations among those who regularly use marijuana is five times greater than among those who do not use this substance. I have cared for individuals who developed mania after using marijuana on a daily basis. Past drug use ought to be an important component of data gathering in counseling those with a history of mania or psychosis.

Medications for BPD1 and BPD2

Since I am both a practicing physician and a biblical counselor, I am often asked what I think about the role of medication in the care of those who are dealing with BPD1 or BPD2. My response as a biblical counselor is that taking medication for these diagnoses is an issue

---

5. "Key Substance Use and Mental Health Indicators in the United States: Results from the 2019 National Survey on Drug Use and Health," 15, https://www.samhsa.gov/data/sites/default/files/reports/rpt29393/2019NSDUHFFRPDFWHTML/2019NSDUHFFR090120.htm.

6. National Institute on Drug Abuse, "Is There a Link Between Marijuana Use and Psychiatric Disorders?" National Institute on Drug Abuse, April 13, 2021, https://nida.nih.gov/publications/research-reports/marijuana/there-link-between-marijuana-use-psychiatric-disorders.

of Christian liberty (Romans 14; 1 Corinthians 8). Not much is said in Scripture about it. Thus, Christians have the privilege of making the choice themselves within the confines of the rest of Scripture and taking into account how their choice will affect others.

Particularly in the case of BPD1, those who have had multiple episodes of mania may be best served by taking or continuing to take a medication. It may reduce future episodes and the disruptions that they bring. For a more in-depth discussion of this subject, see the last two chapters of my book *Good Mood, Bad Mood: Help and Hope for Depression and Bipolar Disorder.*[7]

As a physician, I would say that we all should be good medical consumers. Patients should discuss with their doctor the benefits of any medication and their concerns about side effects and then make an informed choice about whether to take a prescribed medication.

In the twenty-five years that I have been a part of the biblical counseling ministry at Faith Church, we have never taught a counselor to encourage a counselee to stop or change their medication. We have taught counselors to refer counselees back to the physician who prescribed that medication. Unless you are a licensed medical professional with prescriptive authority, you should not advise patients about their medication; you can, in fact, put yourself in significant legal jeopardy if you undertake to do so. Unless the counselee is your patient and you are licensed to prescribe medicine, you should refer the patient back to the physician who wrote the prescription with your questions and concerns.

It is not the goal of biblical counseling to see to it that all counselees stop taking medications. It is our goal to share the principles of Scripture that will enable them to grow, change, and glorify God with their lives. It is not our job to practice medicine. It is our calling to counsel from the Scripture and offer counselees the hope that can be found there.

---

7. Charles Hodges, *Good Mood, Bad Mood: Help and Hope for Depression and Bipolar Disorder* (Wapwallopen, PA: Shepherd Press, 2013).

A Biblical Counseling Approach

I once heard a wise friend say that diagnoses like BPD and schizo-phrenia require great care as we decide how to approach categorizing and counseling those who come with these diagnoses. He said there is a narrow path between dismissing the possibility that there is a medical source for their struggles on the one hand, and turning every inconvenient behavior into a disease on the other. Without taking care, we can find ourselves like Job's friends—trying to discover the sinful behavior at the bottom of every trouble. Or we can ignore the contribution our choices make to our moods and accept a neurobio-logic basis for every dysfunctional feeling. As counselors, we should work hard at staying out of either ditch.

With BPD, there are lots of opportunities to fall either way. So how do we avoid it? First, a good understanding of the differ-ence between BPD1 and BPD2 will be a great help to the counselor. Counseling may take a significantly different direction, depending on which diagnosis the counselee has received.

Although the science is uncertain, if one has seen a loved one or counselee who fits the criteria for mania in the past, it will not be hard to recognize in the future. There is a growing consensus in medicine to describe BPD as a spectrum, but the most certain end of that spec-trum is mania. As I have written elsewhere, BPD1 appears to have a physical source. On the other hand, a biological cause for BPD2 appears much less certain, and it makes up the majority of current diagnoses of BPD.[8]

In light of the ease with which depression is diagnosed and medi-cally treated today, it is just as likely that an individual who has been labeled with BPD2 simply is experiencing normal sadness as a result of significant loss. Coupled with the side effects of antidepressant medications, it is not difficult to understand how the diagnosis of BPD2 could be misapplied.

---

8. Hodges, *Good Mood, Bad Mood*, 171–72.

For years I have taught my students four principles that help us interact with DSM diagnoses. The first is that I will never call anything a disease that the Bible calls sin. In the words of Spurgeon, "Do not give fair names to foul sins. Call them what you will, they will smell no sweeter."[9] I do not call the serial adulterer a sex addict.

Second, I never call anything a sin unless the Bible clearly does. I will not apply my social preferences to others as if they carry the weight of Scripture. This covers disagreements over music, movies, dancing, card games, clothes, and a host of other things. It also includes hallucinations, unless the individual has sinfully used a substance that causes them.

Third, we should always look for pathology or a change at the cell level that explains the change in function. This requires looking at medical information or discussing the situation with a knowledgeable medical professional. What does the medical literature say about the causes for the problem you are seeing?

The fourth principle helps me distinguish between different diagnoses by grading the quality of medical evidence available to support the idea that the problem is a medical disease. I assign the research a rating of A to F. An A grade would indicate that I have very little doubt as to the reliability of the information; B would indicate that I think the information is true, but leaves room for doubt; C means that I think that the information is interesting but could go either way; D through F means I have little or no confidence that what is said in the source is reliable. For example, strep throat gets an A, and so does diabetes.

Current evidence for BPD as a medical disease is limited to the observations of physicians who care for these individuals and some genetic studies. I would grade it with a C. The observations of physicians who care for those with mania do carry considerable weight. And genetic studies do indicate an increased risk of having BPD1/

9. Charles Haddon Spurgeon, "Evening, April 7, Psalm 51:14," *Morning and Evening: Daily Readings*, Christian Classics Ethereal Library, https://ccel.org/ccel/spurgeon/morneve/morneve.

mania for those with a close relative who has experienced mania. The literature is not at all conclusive in regard to the cause of BPD1, but it does support a physiologic cause for the observed symptoms such as mania.[10]

The support in the medical literature for BPD2 is less convincing.[11] The solution to increased numbers of individuals labeled with BPD2 may be found in a better diagnosis. Those diagnosed with BPD2 are most likely individuals being treated for depression and experiencing the side effects of antidepressant medication. As I have counseled, I have found that most will be originally diagnosed with depression when they are dealing with normal sadness over identifiable loss. They are subsequently treated with medication that offers them a greater opportunity for side effects than cure. They desperately need to hear the hope Scripture can give any person who struggles with losing something irreplaceably important to them.[12]

Mercy Triumphs over Judgment

When a medical diagnosis does not have scientific literature that merits an A or an F grade, how should we approach it? And if there is no clear statement in Scripture that applies without a doubt, how should we counsel someone who has been diagnosed with it? James 2:12–13 gives us some help: "So speak and so act as those who are to be judged by the law of liberty. Because judgment will be merciless to one who has shown no mercy; mercy triumphs over judgment."

When we cannot say something for certain, then we should not attempt to make Scripture speak where it does not. And we should not make the lack of clear medical evidence say more than it does.

---

10. "The pathogenesis of bipolar disorder is not known. The etiology may involve biologic, psychologic, and social factors," according to Jeffrey Stovall, Paul Keck, and David Solomon, "Bipolar Disorder in Adults: Epidemiology and Pathogenesis," UpToDate, accessed July 14, 2022, https://www.uptodate.com/contents/bipolar-disorder-in-adults -epidemiology-and-pathogenesis.

11. Stovall, Keck, and Solomon, "Bipolar Disorder in Adults."

12. Alan Horwitz and Jerome Wakefield, *The Loss of Sadness: How Psychiatry Transformed Normal Sorrow into Depressive Disorder* (New York: Oxford University Press, 2007), 68.

A favorite phrase used by radiologists to qualify their reports is, "the absence of evidence is not evidence of absence."

In situations that lack clear direction, we should withhold judgment. We should mercifully extend the benefit of the doubt to those who are struggling. In these situations, mercy triumphs over judgment. The disciples in John 9:2 (NIV) ask the Lord the awkward question about the man born blind: "Who sinned, this man or his parents, that he was born blind?" The Lord's response was "neither!"

The blind man suffered so that God would be glorified when Jesus healed him. The disciples were quick to ascribe his suffering to sin and were entirely and grievously wrong. As we approach those who have been diagnosed with BPD1 and BPD2, we should take great care to avoid making the same mistake by saying more than we know and can actually be known.

Responsibility for Behavior

For George, the question inevitably arises as to whether or not his BPD excuses his behavior. Any of us who have counseled for a while have had counselees announce that they did X because they are ABC and that somehow, because of their diagnosis, they should be excused from responsibility for their actions.

While it is conceivable that BPD1 may make it easier for individuals to spend money they do not have or commit sexual sin, it does not cause them to do so. The money George spent was entirely his responsibility. James gives a clear description of where our sinful choices come from:

> What is the source of quarrels and conflicts among you? Is not the source your pleasures that wage war in your members? You lust and do not have; so you commit murder. You are envious and cannot obtain; so you fight and quarrel. You do not have because you do not ask. You ask and do not receive, because you ask with wrong motives, so that you may spend it on your pleasures. (James 4:1–3)

When I teach on this subject, I will ask the group, "Is George responsible for his sin? And where does his sin come from?" They almost always respond that, yes, he is responsible for sinful behavior and that it comes from his heart. As a friend of mine often says, "We do what we do because we want what we want."

As we approach those who have stumbled into sin while manic, we do well to remember Paul's words to the Galatians:

> Brethren, even if anyone is caught in any trespass, you who are spiritual, restore such a one in a spirit of gentleness; each one looking to yourself, so that you too will not be tempted. Bear one another's burdens, and thereby fulfill the law of Christ. (Galatians 6:1–2)

This is not a pharisaical exercise in "gotcha." It is one brother or sister reaching out to another who has often made a shambles of their life and harmed others. It requires humility and love for wandering sheep.

The person who is manic and knows what they are doing will be better served by counsel that calls them to accept responsibility for the sinful things they have done. There is peace to be found in repenting and asking forgiveness, which God freely offers (1 John 1:9). There is the opportunity for resolution of offenses committed against others (Matthew 5:23–24). And there is the great hope of restoration of wounded relationships (Ephesians 4:32).

Avoid Counseling the Diagnosis

During the last twenty years of teaching counseling, I have often told students that we do not counsel labels; we counsel people with problems. Instead of seeing George as bipolar, we should see him as an individual who has a medical challenge that has complicated his life. He will need counsel from the Scriptures to sort out the consequences of the behaviors he chooses. He will certainly need brother and sisters in Christ to stand around him and help him in the process of growth and change. And he most likely will need continued medical care and medication.

One consequential question involves what the biblical counselor ought to do when their counselee or friend presents in apparent mania. When a counselee presents with bizarre behavior, emotions, and thoughts, there are several important questions to answer. First, does this counselee need to be seen in the local emergency room to determine whether this behavior has a medical cause? It is beyond the scope of this chapter to list causes, but if your counselee is hallucinating, hearing and seeing things that are not heard or seen by others, they need a full emergent medical workup.

If the counselee is under the care of a physician for bipolar disorder 1 and has a history of mania, and if they express thoughts that are delusional, they need to be asked, "Do you believe these thoughts to be real?" If they tell you they believe "God is telling me how to harvest light and if you invest with me we will both be millionaires," do not hand them your debit card. Instead, call their doctor right then and arrange for them to be seen.

As a physician who treats patients with a history of recurrent mania, I know there are helpful things that family members, friends, and the church can do to help when mania occurs. Family support is critical to avoiding mania and the fallout that follows. I have worked with the families of patients who wished to be on the lowest possible dose of their medication with the understanding that if the family members started to see the symptoms of mania in their loved one, they would call me and we would manage their medicine to reduce the symptoms.

In the middle of mania, family and church both have the opportunity to come around the individual and encourage them to avoid behavior that they will grieve over later. A small group that knows the problem and is willing to spend time walking with their brother or sister can be an amazing help. This is bearing one another's burdens and fulfilling the law of Christ as Paul told the Galatians.

Eleanor's situation is a bit different. She does not fit the diagnostic criteria for BPD1, and her symptoms of "hypomania" may be due to her antidepressant. Counseling her should focus on dealing with the losses that may be contributing to her sad mood. The most important thing would be to help her move away from loss recovery and instead begin wanting to glorify God with her life more than she wants to breathe.

A Word to the Counselor

Does your current data gathering process give you the information you need to help an individual who comes to you with the diagnosis of BPD? If not, how can you improve it?

Do you have a relationship established with a physician with whom you could discuss a difficult case? Do you ask your counselees' permission to discuss their case with their physician in a printed release form before it is needed? These things may prove useful when a counselee is struggling.

A Word to the Counselee

There is great hope to be found in the Scriptures for those who must deal with chronic medical problems. While good health is always in the picture, the primary goal for anyone who lives with illness is to glorify God in the way they respond to it. What opportunities does God give us to "work out our salvation" (Philippians 2:12) in the way we live as patients?

CHAPTER 15

Post-Traumatic Stress Disorder (PTSD):
Rewriting the Narrative to Include Hope

Mark Buono, MD

Hannah was born into a family that worshipped Satan. At the age of four, on the day of her younger brother's birth, her father showed her how babies were made by raping her. This began a fourteen-year series of events that involved sex trafficking and sexual abuse at the hands of her father and his brothers. Hannah suffered at the hands of evil men for years.

Hannah came into our lives when my wife served as a mentor at a women's residential treatment center. During Hannah's third phase of treatment, she was to live with a Christian family. She lived with us for two years, and during that time, she joined our church. Our family came to know her struggles well. She had developed multiple personalities to try to protect herself, depending upon the situation. For example, if someone was trying to hurt her, she became very submissive to avoid being killed. Today Hannah struggles with sleep disturbances because she dreams of these terrible events.

She often cut herself in an attempt to control the pain and try to bring herself back to the present moment. She can feel, smell, and taste things that occurred in the distant past. She sometimes loses her grip on reality and becomes less able to distinguish what is real and what is imagined around her. Her physician says that at times she becomes psychotic with a gross impairment in reality testing, which is a technical way to say that the past and present can become indistinguishable for her.

She believed that she was stupid and worthless, as her young soul had been given that identity physically, emotionally, verbally, and spiritually through gaslighting. Before coming to Christ, she had become a dysfunctional person for whom basic life tasks such as cooking, eating, showering, and putting gas in her car were impossible as she moved in and out of reality and in and out of actual horrific situations.

Hannah attempted to control her world with obsessive and compulsive behaviors. Hannah overanalyzed every small detail—such as a slight frown or glance—for deeper hidden meanings and intentions. This hypervigilance occurred in almost every interaction and kept her from developing normal trusting relationships. Large crowds and noisy environments were terrifying to her because trafficking commonly happened in these types of settings. She sought to control and analyze everything in an effort to make sense of life by using her words to play one family member against another if she imagined one person was becoming a threat to her. She would often dream about her pastor, his wife, her deacon, and his wife. In the dreams, they (trusted individuals) were doing horrible acts to her. Sadly, this was the result of fourteen years wherein those who were supposed to be trusted authorities in life (her own mother and father) were the principal ones perpetrating evil.

Eventually, God graciously brought a Christian police detective into her life. After he learned of her situation, "Detective Ninja" (as she likes to call him) helped her escape from this environment and assisted her in getting into a Bible-based women's residential treatment program. There, Hannah came to understand the reality of the gospel in her life and how God would change her through his Word.

Today, she continues to struggle with daily reminders of her past life before Christ, which can show up in her physical sensations, her thoughts, and her dreams. Yet daily, even hourly, she battles to cling to the truth of the gospel, to cling to Christ, and to rest in the new life he has given her. Hannah is a true living testimony of God's mercy and grace. She is a follower of Jesus Christ. The one who was lost now serves Christ. The biological daughter of one of the most wicked men on earth is a productive member of society and a follower of Christ!

Medical Diagnosis and Physical Symptoms

Hannah came to our residential treatment program with a diagnosis from a secular center of post-traumatic stress disorder (PTSD). Since the traumatic events she experienced occurred during ages three to eighteen and occurred repeatedly, she meets the criteria of complex post-traumatic stress disorder (C-PTSD).[1] In addition to the symptoms of a person having had a onetime traumatic event, Hannah and others with C-PTSD can have emotional instability and major relationship challenges. Since the foundation of all healthy relationships should be trust, those suffering from years of trauma struggle to believe that anyone (even God) can be trusted or be safe in a relationship.

A person is diagnosed with PTSD based on the criteria listed in the *Diagnostic and Statistical Manual of Mental Disorders*, Fifth Edition (DSM-5). The reader may wish to read the criteria as a whole in an article posted by Brainline.org.[2] For brevity's sake, I've listed in the next few paragraphs some of the most prominent criteria. The following signs and symptoms need to present for at least one month, and the individual must be over six years of age. The criteria for PTSD include the following:

> Exposure to actual or threatened death, serious injury, or sexual violence in one (or more) of the following ways: by directly experiencing, witnessing, or learning of these terrible events.

---

1. *The Diagnostic and Statistical Manual of Mental Disorders*, Fifth Ed., (Washington, DC: American Psychiatric Association, 2013).

2. BrainLine, WETA Public Television, Arlington, VA, https://www.brainline.org/article/dsm-5-criteria-ptsd.

The presence of recurrent, involuntary, and intrusive distressing memories and dreams of the traumatic events. The individual may experience dissociative reactions or flashbacks in which the individual feels or acts as if the traumatic event(s) were happening again. They may lose contact with the situation around them.

They may suffer severe or prolonged emotional distress when exposed to events, people, and places that symbolize or resemble part of the traumatic event(s). The individual may have a marked physical reaction to situations that resemble a part of the original traumatic event.

Those affected will avoid putting themselves in situations that are similar to their past trauma. They will avoid memories, thoughts, and feelings associated with the events or situations that arouse distressing memories, including people, places, conversations, activities, or objects.

Those affected by PTSD will also see changes in their moods and in their thinking. They may not remember important aspects of the event. They many also suffer with persistent, exaggerated thoughts about themselves. They may see themselves as irreparably broken and struggle with guilt and shame over the events. They may blame themselves for what has happened to them and to others. They struggle with a negative mood and often distance themselves from those who love them.

Activities which used to bring them enjoyment are neglected. People, places, activities that have brought them joy and happiness no longer offer them any comfort. Social isolation becomes a significant risk.

Those affected will often develop hypervigilance, hyperreactivity and a sometimes irritable demeanor. There is potential for physically aggressive behavior in response to situations that remind them of their prior trauma. Sleep disturbances are common. Dreams and nightmares may result in the individual getting very little restful restorative sleep.[3] Hannah exhibited many of these symptoms; for example, she struggled with hypervigilance, sleep disturbances, and nightmares.

Patients may also experience dissociative symptoms in which they feel disconnected from themselves and from reality. Hannah was helped with her dissociation by friends who surrounded her with support. They would remind her of what was real when she would begin to disconnect.

To meet the criteria for PTSD, the person's symptoms have to result in significant problems at home, school, work, and other aspects of life. In addition, the disturbances in the thinking and behavior cannot result from the use of medication or other substances. Hannah certainly met these criteria; there was not an aspect of her life unaffected by her symptoms of PTSD.

PTSD patients often seek isolation and have a desire to bolt—or run away—when recalling events from the past. Their facial expressions often display fear or sadness when they are reliving past events, despite joyous present circumstances. I observed this in Hannah during Christmas Eve present opening, and I learned that it was a trigger for her because past, large gatherings had led to abuse situations.

Experiencing these kinds of triggers led to Hannah withdrawing and feeling a desire to be alone or run. If Hannah did remain present in triggering situations, such as large gatherings, she would not only have odd facial expressions, she would also make comments such as "Are you mad at me?" or "Did I do something wrong?" Those present would always answer, "No! *You* did nothing wrong."

Changes to Neuroanatomy and Neurotransmitters

Not only did Hannah suffer mentally from the abuse that she experienced, it also affected her physically; she often experienced symptoms

---

3. Curtis Solomon, "Counseling Post-Traumatic Stress Disorder," Association of Certified Biblical Counselors, October 24, 2019, https://biblicalcounseling.com/resource-library/essays/counseling-post-traumatic-stress-disorder-plotting-the-course/.

of stress such as sweating, dilated pupils, and rapid breathing. Sometimes she appeared to be in catatonia, a physical state in which she did not or could not move. This typically would occur after a triggering stimulus took her mind back to a former horrific event.

As we consider how to help someone in Hannah's situation, it can be beneficial to deepen our understanding of the structure and function of our brains. There has been ongoing investigation using magnetic resonance image brain scans to examine both aspects of our brains.[4]

Brain scans of PTSD patients reveal that different anatomical features develop as a result of the horrific events they have experienced. For example, PTSD patients show a decrease in the physical size of their hippocampus (a brain region important for memory and learning), in their left amygdala (which processes emotions) and in their anterior cingulate cortex (which is involved in impulse control and decision-making).[5] There are actual physical differences in these areas of the brain in individuals who suffer from PTSD after a traumatic experience.

The brain is a "plastic" organ designed by God to adapt to its environment, so it can change both anatomically (structure) and physiologically (function). By way of example, you may have heard the expression "he's in the groove." This has been used to describe a baseball pitcher who is throwing strikes every time. He's "in the groove." If you examined the brain of a professional baseball player, you would find an actual "groove" in the cerebellum not seen in the rest of us. This means that our brain structure can change as we respond to various life circumstances. However, this does not mean that our brain cannot be reshaped. Later in this chapter, we will see that we can retrain our brains and think according to what Scripture says.

---

4. A. M. Parker et al., "Posttraumatic stress disorder in adults: Epidemiology, pathophysiology, clinical manifestations, course, assessment, and diagnosis," *Critical Care Med.* 43, no. 5 (May 2015): 1121–29.

5. Parker et al., "Posttraumatic stress disorder in adults."

Not only does the structure of our brain adapt to our experiences, but the function of our brains can also be altered. As our bodies respond to traumatic events, norepinephrine is present in our brains in high concentrations; norepinephrine is a hormone and neurotransmitter that elevates cerebral activity. This can perhaps explain the hypervigilance and sometimes profound responses to triggers that occur in those suffering from PTSD. These individual's systems are always in the "on" state, and the wires are hot.

At the same time, another class of hormones called glucocorticoids may be involved in PTSD. Glucocorticoids affect memory and anxiety, and they may cause high blood pressure, elevated blood glucose levels, obesity, muscle weakness, increased appetite, gastrointestinal tract irritation, sleep disruptions, and more.[6] Glucocorticoids are a part of our bodies' stress response, and in PTSD, that stress response is frequently and strongly activated. Hannah struggled with these effects as well.

Treatments: Medications and Therapy

Therapeutic treatments for PTSD include cognitive behavioral therapy, prolonged exposure therapy, and eye movement desensitization and reprocessing (EMDR) therapy.[7] PTSD is also treated with various types of medications, which may or may not be combined with therapy. These medications include alpha-1 receptor blockers such as prazosin, dopamine receptor blockers such as Risperdal, GABA receptor agonists (benzodiazepines) such as Ativan, and tricyclic antidepressants, such as Amitriptyline. First, I will discuss medications, and then I will examine the various therapies.

---

6. Parker et al., "Posttraumatic stress disorder in adults." Also see M. C. Deak and R. Stickgold, "Sleep and Cognition," *Wiley Interdisciplinary Reviews, Cognitive Science* 1, no. 4 (2010): 491–500, https://www.ncbi.nlm.nih.gov/pmc/articles/PMC5831725/.

7. R. J. Ursano, et al., "Practice Guidelines for the Treatment of Patients with Acute Stress Disorder and Post-Traumatic Stress Disorder," *American Journal of Psychiatry*, 2004:161:3; *Clinical Practice Guideline for the Treatment of PTSD, American Psychological Association*, Guideline Development Panel for the Treatment of Posttraumatic Stress Disorder in Adults, February 24, 2017; https://www.apa.org/ptsd-guideline/ptsd.pdf.

Medications

Nearly every psychiatric medication available has been used to help those who struggle with PTSD. None have been particularly or consistently curative, but patients may experience relief from some of their symptoms. Current recommendations for the medical treatment of PTSD can include of antihypertensives, dopamine blockers, benzodiazepines, and tricyclic antidepressants

Hannah's symptoms lasted for over a decade and led to functional impairment and social isolation. These debilitating symptoms all occurred while she was on no medication. At first, she refused medication because often drugs were used to gain access to her physically and mentally when she was being raped or attacked. As she grew weary, she sought out medical doctors who were also trained biblical counselors. These physicians made judicious use of some medications. These medications provided some short-term benefits, such as allowing her rest and sleep, and they served as temporizing measures that allowed Hannah time to process events biblically.

Antihypertensive—Prazosin

Prazosin is an older medication that blocks receptors in the brain (and elsewhere in the body) called the alpha-1 adrenergic receptor. It has been found to be useful for individuals who struggle with nightmares and resultant sleep disturbances. It may work by blocking the receptor sites stimulated by our adrenal gland hormones, epinephrine and norepinephrine.

Blocking these sites will prevent the rapid heart rate that occurs when our adrenal glands produce the hormones associated with our "fight or flight" response to perceived threats. Nightmares such as those Hannah suffered from would cause this outpouring of adrenal hormones and result in her sleep being fragmented. This medicine offered her, and has offered others in the same situation, some relief. Being able to sleep is important for our mental and physical health, so although this medication does not directly address the underlying causes of PTSD, suppressing its sleep-disrupting symptoms can be very beneficial, especially for short-term use. One side effect can be postural hypotension or feeling light-heated upon standing suddenly. When Hannah experienced this, her dosage was adjusted slightly.

Antidepressants

The most commonly prescribed medications for those affected by PTSD are antidepressants, including selective serotonin reuptake inhibitors (SSRIs) and selective serotonin/norepinephrine reuptake inhibitors (SNRIs) and tricyclic antidepressants (TAD). They may offer some symptom relief for the individual who suffers with PTSD, but they are not a simple one-a-day solution for all PTSD symptoms.

Hannah found some benefit in taking a medication in this class. One of the side effects is sedation, which is why these meds are often chosen, as a way to help with sleep. Their mechanism of action is not clear, and like all medicines, they have undesirable side effects. TAD can also cause dry mouth, which can be self-limiting but quite both-ersome. Anyone who is thinking of taking an antidepressant should have a detailed conversation with the prescriber concerning the benefits and side effects.

Dopamine blockers

Antipsychotic medications commonly used for PTSD include risperidone (Risperdal), quetiapine (Seroquel), and olanzapine (Zyprexa). Current medical thinking is that the patient suffering from PTSD has elevated dopamine levels, which can overwhelm his or her brain and result in hallucinations and psychosis. Antipsychotic medications are thought to act by blocking dopamine receptors, thereby diminishing dopamine's effects on the central nervous system. This results in a decrease in psychosis and hallucinations, while simultaneously causing nighttime sedation to help with sleep.

These medications have significant side effects—such as tardive dyskinesia—that should be discussed with the prescribing physician. Patients should carefully weigh the side effects and benefits before making a decision about taking them.

Benzodiazepines

Benzodiazepines are most commonly used for PTSD patients who have trouble sleeping due to terror or bad flashbacks. These are helpful in the short term to enable the sufferer to get some rest so they can think and process the waves of memories that assault them each day. A rested mind is better able to process realty. Often extreme interrogations used by different militaries around the world (and used by Hannah's parents) include sleep deprivation to break down the person's reasoning ability. There is a time-dependent decay in cognitive functions as sleep deprivation increases.[8] Continual use of this class of drugs should be avoided as the body develops tolerance requiring increasing doses. Regular use can lead to habituation. Consequently, the therapeutic effect diminishes at the same dose, requiring higher and higher dosing to achieve the same effect. As these are scheduled medications under tight regulation by the Drug Enforcement Agency, large dosing scripts can raise the level of scrutiny for the physician and the patient.

Exposure Therapies and Cognitive Behavioral Therapies

Psychological therapies for PTSD are many and varied, but they basically fall into one of two categories: cognitive behavioral therapy (CBT), and exposure therapy.[9] These treatments seek to modify the patient's understanding of and belief about the danger they suffered in the past. The goal is to change the narrative associated with the trauma. Hannah still uses some of the techniques she learned, such as journaling the memories. Writing them out helped her process her whirlwind of thoughts.

---

8. Deak and Stickgold, "Sleep and Cognition."

9. Ursano, et al., "Practice Guidelines for the Treatment of Patients with Acute Stress Disorder and Post-Traumatic Stress Disorder." Also see *Clinical Practice Guideline for the Treatment of Posttraumatic Stress Disorder (PTSD) in Adults,* American Psychological Association, *Guideline Development Panel for the Treatment of PTSD in Adults Adopted as APA Policy* February 24, 2017; (https://www.apa.org/ptsd-guideline/ptsd.pdf.)

Cognitive Behavior Therapy

This form of therapy can involve meeting and talking with a psychologist (PhD) or psychiatrist (MD). Commonly, the latter only treat using medications, rather than cognitive behavior therapy (CBT). As described by PTSD Clinical Practice Guideline,[10] the core principles on which CBT is based are

Psychological problems are based, in part, on faulty or unhelpful ways of thinking.

Psychological problems are based, in part, on learned patterns of unhelpful behavior.

People suffering from psychological problems can learn better ways of coping with them, thereby relieving their symptoms and becoming more effective in their lives.

Interestingly, each of these principles are not original with CBT. They can be found in Scriptures, which are at the core of biblical counseling (Ephesians 4:22–24). The sufferer is often not thinking or acting biblically in response to the trauma they have experienced. Hannah demonstrated a remarkable resilience in her ability to hourly rethink and act biblically—not bolting, not running—as reminders of her years of horror reappeared in smells, visuals, or just noise in the room. In biblical counseling, Hannah learned to rehearse truth, rely on Christ, and go to the throne of grace when struggles occurred. These practices helped Hannah to relieve her symptoms and become more effective in her life.

Exposure Therapy

Exposure therapy seeks to have a patient/sufferer face their fears. This form of behavior therapy is thought to desensitize the person and dull the effect of the inciting stimulus by overexposure. With no foundation upon which to stand being offered, this psychological tool

---

10. *Clinical Practical Guideline*, American Psychological Association.

leads nowhere. Hannah has utilized a crossover between exposure therapy of sorts and CBT. As a new memory of trauma surfaces, she will write out the memory in detail and then discuss and process the events through the lens of Scripture.

How a Biblical Perspective Can Help with PTSD

What can biblical counseling offer Hannah? Many describe PTSD as a "normal response to an abnormal event." It seems very reasonable to think that Hannah would find herself right in the middle of that statement.

There was nothing normal about the things that happened to her. She experienced a horrific way to grow into adulthood. Her multiple personalities and defensive responses revealed a woman who was scared, spiritually alone, and hopeless. The problems, behaviors, and defensive manipulations she brought to the residential counseling facility were enormous. She was the product of years of gaslighting.

So what does Scripture offer that medication and secular counseling do not? I remember my mentor Dr. Smith raising these questions for consideration: Who put you in this situation? Where is God in your thinking on this? These excellent questions can prick the conscience and bring realignment of the circumstances and events toward scriptural truths. Scripture is for teaching in part, and we see that Psalm 39 and Psalm 88 demonstrate that we can cry out in frustration to the Lord. He's okay with that as even our complaints are to the Lord and lead to a deeper relationship with him. All things—good and bad—can be reflected upon in terms of their Creator. What follows are things that I have seen to be helpful to those who struggle with PTSD. The order they come in is not particularly important, except for the first.

Hope Through Listening!

Offering people hope starts with listening. It is often difficult for those affected by PTSD to talk about the terrible things they experienced. As we seek to help them, we should make it easy for them to speak. This environment is best created by establishing trust and by asking good questions. Good questions are the key and often seek to understand the heart behind the comments. Dr. William Osler, who is in great measure responsible for how physicians in the United States are educated, would tell students and residents that "if you let a patient talk long enough, they'll tell you what's wrong."

In a world where the average doctor visit is down to eight minutes, the counselor who listens well and long gives hope. The counselee may say things such as, "You are the first person who listened to me." Do not be in a rush to speak or to diagnose or to offer solutions. Many secular programs go through a checklist, render a diagnosis, and administer a pill.

Offering Hope Through the Love of Christ

When I counsel individuals who are facing illness and suffering, John 11 offers real hope. It is a familiar story to all who hear the name of the main character, Lazarus. We know that Jesus loved Martha, Mary, and Lazarus and that he often stayed with them. When Lazarus became ill, the sisters sent word for Jesus to come quickly and help. Instead, he came four days later, after Lazarus was already dead and in the tomb. In John 11, we see Jesus tenderly listen to Martha and Mary, weep with them, and then raise Lazarus from the dead.

Four important points for the sufferer give hope. The first point is that Jesus KNOWS. From the text we read that Jesus knew all about Lazarus. The second point is that Jesus had a PLAN. The text reveals that he certainly had a plan for Lazarus and his sister's suffering. In John 11:14–15 (NIV), Christ says, "Lazarus is dead, and for your sake I am glad I was not there, so that you may believe."

Third, we also know that Jesus CARED. Jesus wept with Mary and Martha over Lazarus. He cared about them and their suffering. And last, Jesus ACTED on their behalf.

I have often pointed struggling counselees to this picture. I have told them that Jesus knew, planned, cared, and acted for Lazarus.

And I've told them that Jesus knows, plans, cares, and will act on their behalf as well. There is great hope in that.

Hannah found great comfort in the story. For the first time in her life, she could see that someone knew and cared about her. She could trust that God had a plan for her life and was acting on her behalf.

Find Meaning and Hope in the Sovereign God

Those who struggle with PTSD may benefit from studying the life of an Old Testament figure that had enough adverse experiences to have given him PTSD. As you read Genesis 37–50, Joseph suffered repeated traumatic events at the hands of others.

First he was hated by his brothers, in part because of the multi-colored coat that his father Jacob had given him. When Jacob sent Joseph to check on his brothers one day, they plotted to kill him, but instead threw him into a pit and sold him to a passing caravan. While working as a slave for his Egyptian owner, Potiphar, God blessed everything Joseph did and he was promoted to chief steward. In the process, Potiphar's wife decided Joseph was attractive and began daily sexually harassing him. Eventually, when Joseph refused her advances, she accused him of attempted rape.

That resulted in Joseph being thrown into prison, where once again, God prospered all that he did. Eventually, Joseph is running the prison, yet the butler promptly forgets him when an opportunity arises to help him be freed. It would be two more years until Pharaoh has a dream and the butler remembers Joseph and tells Pharaoh about the young man who interpreted his dream. Then, in short order Joseph gets a bath, clean clothes, interprets Pharaoh's dream, and becomes prime minister of Egypt.

How did Joseph survive all these hardships without any record of PTSD? When God promised Joseph that the sun, the moon, and the eleven stars would bow down to him, God meant it. And Joseph believed it. Joseph may not have always understood it, but he eventually came to understand God's *sovereignty* over his life.

When Joseph's brothers came to him after the death of Jacob, fearful for their own lives, Joseph comforted them and then gave the precursor to Romans 8:28–29. Joseph told his brothers, "'Do not be afraid, for am I in God's place? As for you, you meant evil against me, but God meant it for good in order to bring about this present result, to keep many people alive. So therefore, do not be afraid; I will provide for you and your little ones.' So he comforted them and spoke kindly to them" (Genesis 50:19–21).

In this passage, Joseph seems to understand that if his brothers had liked him, they all would have starved to death in Canaan. The pathway from the pit to the palace in Egypt was difficult at best, but through it, God intended to preserve Joseph, his father, his brothers, and their families. Joseph serves a small role in preserving the line through which God would send his Son, our Savior Jesus.

It may have taken Joseph twenty years to get there, but at the end, he understood that God was acting sovereignly in his life. And he no doubt took great comfort in it. The biblical narrative does not give any indication that Joseph suffered from PTSD. It does state that he remembered the promises of God revealed to him in the dreams of his younger days. This may very well have helped Joseph either avoid PTSD-like behaviors or arrive at the conclusion he states in Genesis 50:20.

Hannah eventually found comfort in this as well. In our women's residential treatment program, the ladies go through three phases. During phase three, the ladies live for six months in a Christian home. Our family has had several girls live with us during phase three. Hannah was one of these ladies, and she's never left! Many, many godly women have come alongside Hannah over the years. In working through many memories and anniversaries, she has come to see God's plan in all this, which has offered healing to her soul. This is Genesis 50:20 in action! Hannah has worked through the work-book *Mending the Soul, Understanding and Healing Abuse* by Steven

R. Tracy.[11] The following questions from this workbook have served well to process thoughts and memories and look at the guilt and the shame and the lies:

1. Type out the memory or event.
2. What are the lies you were told or believe?
3. Do you think the memory is completely out?
4. Are you having any pain or other flashes/pictures/strong emotions indicating there may be more to think/talk through?
5. What lies were told or implied in this memory? What is true?
6. Are you holding any unnecessary guilt about this event?
7. Are you accepting another person's responsibility?
8. Did the abuser convince you of anything about yourself in this event, especially anything that is not true?
9. What attributes or characteristics of God can you focus your mind on after working through this memory?
10. What verses can you cling to by faith right now?
11. How can you see the goodness of God in this memory?
12. What are appropriate thoughts and emotions you should have about this memory? Are you purposefully shutting them off?
13. What are some things you can do today to help move forward and focus on biblical priorities?
14. Is there anything in this memory that I am confused about?
15. Are there any conclusions I drew about myself or this situation that are upsetting to me?

Once trust has been established and after writing the events out, the sufferer can then process the trauma by talking about the events out loud. This puts another believer in the conversation and helps the counselee to understand how the Lord views these circumstances.

The path her life took was horrific. No other word fits the events. Only time will tell the part that God has for Hannah in his plan, but she is confident that there is a part in his plan.

---

11. Steven R. Tracy, *Mending the Soul: Understanding and Healing Abuse* (Grand Rapids: Mending the Soul Ministries, January 1, 2015).

Changing the Destination

Many other things are important to helping those who struggle as Hannah did. It almost goes without saying that it is important to determine whether or not the counselee is a Christian. In counseling, it makes all the difference in the world for the direction counseling will take.

As Jay Adams was known to teach, biblical counseling is primarily aimed at believers. In truth, the only way to permanently change in life (which also has an eternal impact) requires us to be "in Christ" (2 Corinthians 5:17). Helping those outside the faith is an opportunity to share the gospel of grace with them in the hope that in time they will confess Christ as the risen Lord.

Once inside the faith and with the indwelling Holy Spirit in their lives, real change can begin. An amazing amount of encouragement can be found for the believer struggling with PTSD. Paul tells us in his letter to the Philippians "for it is God who is at work in you, both to will and work for His good pleasure" (2:13). No Christian is ever on his own when facing the need to change! "We are his workmanship, created in Christ Jesus for good works" (Ephesians 2:10). What God intends for us to do, he will enable us to do.

Purpose

Not long ago I heard a sermon by Tim Keller on suffering.[12] He talked about the two things that he thinks are essential for an individual to survive PTSD: purpose and the need to learn to trust others again.

Purpose is important for any believer, and it became an organizing principal in Hannah's life. On her darkest days of trauma, the only purpose she could see in life was to be abused by those who should have protected her. The idea of trust was equally difficult.

---

12. Tim Keller, "Gospel in Life, Questions of Suffering," January 6, 2008, Redeemer Church, New York City.

Children will trust almost any reasonable adult. Hannah had learned to trust no one.

For Hannah, purpose would come from the same place it does for all believers in Christ. As Paul told us in 2 Corinthians 5:9, our goal and ambition are to be pleasing to him. Hannah was taught that our purpose is to glorify God, to love him (Matthew 22:37–39), to obey him (John 14:21), and to serve others (John 13:5–17). When difficult memories came up daily, Hannah would write to her supporting text group. In doing this, she was asking for prayer, and also she was making her brain remember to think in ways that brought glory to God by seeking out what was true. She would look for ways to serve others to obey and trust that YAHWEH was good. These motives for living were part of her biblical training that she relied on to get through a memory.

Until Hannah confessed Christ as her Lord and Savior, her main purpose in life was to survive. Safety became the object of her worship. After her salvation, the sentence that became the foundation for her purpose is "I want to glorify God with my life more than I want to breathe."

Someone to Trust

Helping those like Hannah to build trust in God and others is a challenge. There are many places in Scripture that can be used to their benefit. Paul offers much help in his letter to the Romans. Here are a few of the insights found there.

Paul starts by telling the struggler that in Christ, they are no longer under condemnation (8:1), which includes the self-condemnation that those with PTSD might struggle with as they often blame themselves for their troubles. In verses 9–12, he tells us that we are no longer under obligation to continue living as we did in the past. Non-biblical responses can be replaced with biblically informed ones.

In verses 14–16, Paul reminds weary, suffering believers that we are the children of God—although we were born into a spirit of slavery that leads to fear, we have been adopted. Verse 18 tells us that our suffering will be worthwhile, and verse 26 reveals that the Holy Spirit is praying for us. As Hannah and others like her struggle, the Holy Spirit is interceding for them. When we do not even know what we need to ask for, the Holy Spirit does, and he is asking on our behalf!

Romans 8:28–29 are familiar to most, and they were vitally important to Hannah. They told her that God knew about her suffering and intended in the long run to use it for her good. God would use her struggles to grow and change her into the image of his Son. Verses 31–39 are a comfort to all believers who face struggles. For Hannah, the idea that she would never be alone in facing her PTSD was a great comfort. There is great assurance that as sons and daughters of the King we are invincible; only until and when God's plan for each of our lives is complete will we leave this earth. Until then, we can be bold for the Lord in all that we do. At first it was difficult for Hannah to trust God because she had been gaslighted for sixteen years. Trust is gained in teaspoons but lost in wheelbarrows. For a person such as Hannah suffering from C-PTSD, it will take years of fellowship with caring Christian men and women to begin to learn to trust again. It is through the body of Christ that Christians are used as instruments to help those suffering to trust in God and to come to love Jesus.

Dealing with Fear

Among Hannah's PTSD symptoms, flashbacks were the most distressing. Sights, smells, sounds, situations, sleep, dreams, and nightmares all offered her the opportunity to relive the horrors of her past. The things we see and experience with all our senses are indelibly recorded in our brains. They remain with us for as long as we live and can think. The primary emotion that surfaces during remembrances is fear and a fight or flight response. In Hannah's case, since she had been gaslit, the option to fight was trained out of her. Her default mode and response to the terror and fear that often grips her is to bolt, to run, to hide, to escape. Fear became her master years after the events of the past were over. To help her see the truth of 1 John 4:9, we assisted her by offering new training—training in how to think biblically and trustfully about her memories. By doing so, she has come to learn that love does indeed cast out fear, as she has come to see the love of Christ and to love Jesus more.

While the pictures we have seen do not change, the narrative attached to them can. For Hannah, flashbacks told her many things. They most frequently told her that she was worthless, useful only to be abused. In counseling, she learned to change the meaning she attached to the visual and sensory memories. One tool we used has been called the "propeller drill."

A sailor with PTSD put the drill together as he struggled with flashbacks after watching a fellow mechanic walk into a whirling airplane propeller on the deck of an aircraft carrier.[13] The sailor and five others were sprayed with the man's blood. He experienced a flashback of the event whenever he was sprayed in the face with water mist, and it devastated him.

The message that he attached to the vision was that something awful had happened and that it could happen to him. The flashbacks made life very difficult. Eventually, the sailor became a Christian and settled on a strategy to deal with the flashbacks. It consisted of four true statements that he would remind himself whenever he experienced the vision.

1. This vision is not real.
2. This vision cannot hurt me.
3. Whatever God has for me now or in the future will be for my good and his glory (Romans 8:28–29).
4. Perfect love casts out fear (1 John 4:18).

The sailor recounted how, at first, he would need to use that construct twenty-five times a day, but over time, the number decreased. If you met him today, he would tell you that he still has the vision, but that the emotional distress attached is gone. He succeeded in

---

13. Dr. Charles Perry was a helicopter mechanic on the USS *Roosevelt* during the Cuban missile crisis.

changing the meaning attached to the vision. Hannah found this drill and others like it useful as she worked to change the meaning associated with her flashbacks.

Worry and Fear seem to go hand in hand for most of us and certainly for those who struggle with PTSD. To be concerned about things we can change can be a normal part of life. On the other hand, worry about health, possessions, and food is defined by our Lord Jesus as sin. "Do not worry then, saying, 'What will we eat?' or 'What will we drink?' or 'What will we wear for clothing?'" (Matt. 6:31). It is the result of a split mind. When worrying, one struggles with trusting one's own strength versus trusting Christ. Worry should be confessed and repentance embraced by instead thinking on what Paul instructed in Philippians 4:8. Fear is rooted in a disbelief of love—a disbelief that self-sacrificial love exists. When a person is fearful, the gospel makes no sense to them. The cross seems to be a tragedy instead of the greatest accomplishment in history. There are many good resources to help those who struggle with repetitive fearful thinking. See chapter 12 on obsessive-compulsive disorder or further suggestions. Matthew 6 and Philippians 4 also offer substantial guidance.

Forgiveness

The counselee with PTSD will need to deal with many important areas over time. Depending on the nature of the trauma experienced, a biblical understanding of forgiveness will most likely be essential. While there are many different views on when or if individuals such as Hannah should forgive those who have harmed them, most would agree that believers are obligated to extend forgiveness to repentant individuals who ask for it (Matthew 6:9–15). Withholding forgiveness from those who ask brings into question our belief in the forgiveness granted to us by Christ's sacrifice. Our duty to forgive does not determine the nature of the relationship one might have in the future with those who caused the harm. In other words, if Hannah were to forgive those who abused her, that does not mean she needs to allow them to be part of her life. Sin has consequences.

Moving

When asked why PTSD did not become the major factor in determining the rest of his life, the sailor said that he chose to move on. Paul's words moved him forward. "Brethren, I do not regard myself as having laid hold of it yet; but one thing I do: forgetting what lies behind and reaching forward to what lies ahead, I press on toward the goal for the prize of the upward call of God in Christ Jesus" (Philippians 3:13–14). Hannah found that she also needed to move forward in life, away from the hurts in her past.[14] In John 21:3, the apostles are waiting to again be with the risen Christ. While waiting for what the Lord has planned next for them, Peter says, let's go fishing. The point here is that it is far easier to steer a moving object than a stationary one.[15] The example is that in trying to ride a bike it becomes far easier if the bike is rolling. So, also, with us. Be busy working unto the Lord. Scripture states in Proverbs 16:3 "Commit your work to the LORD and your plans will be established" (ESV). Do something and then God will reveal the plans for your life—not vice versa.

These truths from God's Word can give hope and action steps for those with PTSD and C-PTSD. They do not have to be paralyzed or ruled by fear, they can be productive. And in doing so, Scripture promises that the Lord's plan for their lives will be established despite the evil they have seen or experienced. What a comfort and truth to think on!

The Continuing Mission

Civilians and soldiers alike benefit from the renewed sense of purpose that comes with serving others.[16] We love Christ because he died for

---

14. Richard G. Tedeschi, "Growth After Trauma," *Harvard Business Review*, July–August 2020.

15. Skip Heitzig, EXPOUND sermon series on the Gospel of John, March 9, 2017, Calvary Church Canada.

16. Yoram Barak, "Lifelong Posttraumatic Stress Disorder: Evidence from Aging Holocaust Survivors," *Dialogues Clin Neuroscience* 2, no 1, March 2000: 57–62.

our transgressions. We demonstrate that we love him by following his commands (John 14:21). In Matthew 22, Christ boils all the law down to two imperatives: loving God and loving others. Serving others can enable Christians to put their own struggles in perspective. Hannah found mission and purpose in helping others who struggled.

Time!

Helping individuals with PTSD is not a short-term project. It will take time. Joseph had nearly twenty years to consider the things that happened to him. Hannah is many years into her journey, and she is making progress daily. After she left the residential facility, several caring families became the source of love, support, and biblical guidance that her biological family should have provided.

Outside the residential facility, she has the support of the local church, her small group, and her deacons and pastoral staff. She continues to receive counseling through a church counseling ministry. Much like the sailor, she still deals with flashbacks, dreams, and memories, but unlike before, she now has scriptural tools to deal with them.

A Word to the Counselor

PTSD presents significant challenges for the counselee and counselor, but they are not insurmountable. Encouragement for both can be found in the commitment God makes in the Scripture to help believers grow and change. The words of 2 Chronicles 7:14 were written to believers. The promises come about if we take four actions: humble ourselves, pray, seek his face, and repent. If we do these things, God promises to the nation of Israel (and to us) that he will hear, forgive us, and heal our land. How awesome is our Creator God!

Paul's epistles are filled with examples of how to pray and what to think about. He prays a beautiful prayer for the Ephesian church in chapter 1:15–23. This is our example of how and what to pray. Paul does not ask for the struggles to go away, he does not ask for pain to be removed; he instructs us instead to seek a deeper faith and belief in Him who saved us. Victory is measured by our faithfulness! Praying to the Lord for a PTSD sufferer in this fashion can be so refreshing and different and be a balm for a body and soul that has most likely never prayed like his before. In the Lord's prayer, in John 17, Jesus prays for himself, his disciplines, and us! (verses 20–21). This is helpful to recall—especially when suffering.

Paul tells us that the believer is currently engaged in a battle and that in the process, "We are destroying speculations and every lofty thing raised up against the knowledge of God, and we are taking every thought captive to the obedience of Christ" (2 Corinthians 10:5).

A Word to the Counselee

Anyone who has confessed Jesus Christ as Lord and has believed that God has raised Jesus from the dead has the gift of eternal life (Romans 10:9–13). And, if that weren't already enough, God promises to make us able to live in a godly way, despite our circumstances. It is indeed God who works in us, both to will and to do his good pleasure. The Christian who is engaged in changing the narrative associated with the pictures in their memory can have confidence in God's empowerment (Philippians 2:13; 4:13, 19). Trauma and evil are real aspects of living in a Genesis 3 world, and those aspects have been brought to the front door of the PTSD sufferer. Often, as the psalmist declares in Psalm 73, the evil ones appear to go unpunished. Victims of evil and trauma can know that the Lord is just and that evil will be dealt with (Romans 12:19; Hebrews 10:30). The promise of justice can offer comfort to the PTSD soul. When the PTSD also has included gaslighting, as in Hannah's case, the idea of justice rarely comes to mind. In this latter case, focusing on what to think on (Philippians 4:8), who God is (2 Chronicles 7:14), how we were loved first (1 John 4:9), and that we always have an invitation to the table with Christ

(Revelation 3:20) can be our truths and lampposts now and forever. These are refining fires—not consuming ones—that last for a lifetime but to which the truth of God's Word can offer hope and peace.

CHAPTER 16

PREMENSTRUAL SYNDROME (PMS):

MEDICAL BACKGROUND AND BIBLICAL HOPE

Dan Wickert, MD, and Erin Ramirez, DO

Lauren felt so guilty. She couldn't believe she had snapped at her husband Dave and yelled at the kids . . . again! She sat in the shower crying, unable to move for fear that she would have to face one of her family members. It was just so embarrassing that this kept happening. She normally felt like she could hold it all together, but for about eight days every month, things just unraveled.

Lauren was thirty-two and had been married to her college sweetheart for almost ten years. Dave was an engineer and had landed his dream job after graduating. While they didn't go as often as they would like, Dave and Lauren loved hiking and squeezed in workouts when they could. Lauren loved kids and taught fifth grade at the local public school. They also had beautiful eight-year-old twin girls and two boys who were ages five and three. They lived in a nice neighborhood, and Lauren sang in the church choir. She had the life that she had prayed for, and she knew how blessed she was.

But life was stressful too. She worked hard as a teacher. Lauren was invested in her students and even volunteered to help coach soccer after school. Although she wasn't the best cook, she attempted to make home-cooked meals most evenings. And between ballet practice for the twins and the activities her boys were starting to get interested in, she tried to keep their home clean. She always had a partially completed to-do list and consistently lay awake at night remembering something that she had forgotten to put on the list.

Despite all of life's stressors, she was truly happy. However, one week a month, she felt as though she became a different person. It seemed that one minute she was just fine, and the next she was in tears for no reason at all! Her children's voices, which she normally loved to hear, irritated her. She just felt so angry, which lead to her repeatedly yelling and making everyone around her miserable.

Although Lauren knew that God didn't promise life would be easy, she just couldn't see a way through this monthly problem. In her mind, she knew that trials were a way to help draw her to God. But her heart struggled to remember this truth when she knew her period was coming again. The week before her cycle she would begin to feel anxiety rising in her chest that she just couldn't shake. She would recite 2 Corinthians 4:17–18 before trying to start her day: "This light momentary affliction is preparing for us an eternal weight of glory beyond all comparison, as we look not to the things that are seen but to the things that are unseen" (ESV).

Lauren regularly worried about how she would plan meals, pack kids' lunches, grade papers, and still have the energy to make love to her husband. But during the week before her period, she felt so tired that she could barely keep her eyes open through dinner. Her breasts hurt if a child hugged her too tightly or even when she changed her clothes. At times she even had to call out from work due to feeling terrible crampy pain and fatigue. She hated how she felt during this "longest week of the month" and wished that this wasn't something women had to put up with. Since Lauren didn't want to continue in this pattern for the next twenty years, she decided to get help.

Medical and Psychotherapeutic Approaches to Premenstrual Syndrome

Premenstrual syndrome (PMS) is a combination of physical and behavioral symptoms that occur in the second half of a women's menstrual cycle. These symptoms occur nearly every month and affect many aspects of a woman's life. Most women have some mild symptoms associated with their cycles. But when these symptoms cause problems economically or socially during the five to eight days before their period, they are defined as PMS.[1]

A woman's cycle is divided in half. The first half is the follicular phase and starts with bleeding. The second half, or luteal phase, starts with ovulation and lasts until menses begins again. PMS symptoms begin in the luteal phase and typically resolve within a few days of bleeding. The most common behavioral symptoms are mood swings, irritability, food cravings, and sensitivity. The most common physical symptoms are bloating, fatigue, headache, and breast tenderness.[2]

Symptoms of PMS are usually experienced by the time a woman reaches her early twenties, but they can occur any time in a woman's life. There are no lab tests or physical exam findings associated with PMS, so the diagnosis is made based on symptoms. It is often helpful for patients to maintain a journal to ensure that their symptoms are associated with their period. While the cause of PMS is unknown, it is thought that women with PMS have an abnormal response to normal changes in their hormone levels. It is believed that PMS is triggered by changes in ovarian steroids and serotonin.[3] The role of vitamins or minerals in causing PMS has been inconsistent. There is

---

1. P. M. O'Brien, et al., "Towards a Consensus on Diagnostic Criteria, Measurement and Trial Design of the Premenstrual Disorders: The ISPMD Montreal Consensus," *Arch Womens Ment Health* 14 (2011): 13.

2. M. G. Munro, O. I. D. Critchley, I. S. Fraser, FIGO Menstrual Disorders Committee, "The Two FIGO Systems for Normal and Abnormal Uterine Bleeding Symptoms and Classification of Causes of Abnormal Uterine Bleeding in the Reproductive Years: 2018 Revisions," *Int J Gynaecol Obset* 143 (2018): 393.

3. P. J. Schmidt, et al. "Differential Behavioral Effects of Gonadal Steroids in Women with and in Those without Premenstrual Syndrome," *N Engl J Med* 338 (1998): 209.

some evidence that magnesium levels may be lower during the cycle of women with PMS.[4]

Women who are experiencing symptoms associated with their cycle should be evaluated by their doctor to rule out other illnesses. Thyroid disease can be ruled out by a blood test and physical exam. Assessment for an underlying psychiatric or mood disorder, including depression, can be performed. If symptoms are more severe, premenstrual dysphoric disorder (PMDD) may be diagnosed. PMDD can be associated with difficulty concentrating and feeling overwhelmed, irritable, hopeless, and on edge. In its most severe form, PMDD has been associated with an increased risk of suicidal thoughts and attempts.

Medical treatment for PMS depends on severity of symptoms. If symptoms are fairly mild, exercise and stress reduction can help decrease symptoms. Some herbal supplements, such as chasteberry, have been proven to reduce some PMS symptoms.[5] Other treatments might attempt to improve the negative thoughts or feelings that can occur with PMS. A psychotherapist can try to help the patient identify and correct maladaptive beliefs. Psychotherapy can help women to learn coping mechanisms such as meditation, relaxation exercises, or stress management to better handle their symptoms. Using cognitive therapy, a therapist can try to aid in symptom reduction and improved functioning.[6] When symptoms are more moderate to severe, prescription medication may be indicated. A selective serotonin reuptake inhibitor (SSRI) is a common medication used to treat depression. This class of medication can be taken intermittently during the luteal phase of the menstrual cycle or continuously if symptoms require it.

---

4. D. L. Rosentstien et al., "Magnesium Measures Across the Menstrual Cycle in Premenstrual Syndrome," *Biol Psychiatry* 35 (1994): 557.

5. M. Diana van Die et al., "Vitex agnus-castus extracts for female reproductive disorders: a systematic review of clinical trials," *Planta medica* 79(7), 562–75. https://doi.org/10.1055/s-0032-1327831.

6. Judith S. Beck, *Cognitive Behavioral Therapy: Basics and Beyond*, 2nd ed. (New York: Guilford Press, 2011), 391.

All women should carefully consider the many treatment options available. Some options address specific physical symptoms, such as pain medications for cramping. Each treatment option has different efficacy rates and potential side effects. Others aim to reduce all symptoms for a more prolonged period, like continuous birth control pills, which might be prescribed for six to nine months to eliminate periods during that time frame. Even if they are not prescribed to eliminate the period altogether, typical use of oral contraceptive pills (which still allow for a monthly period) can decrease the hormonal fluctuations that accompany a menstrual cycle, and therefore potentially reduce symptoms.

A Biblical Counseling Approach to PMS

As biblical counselors, it is important to remember that it is not our role to play physician in the counseling room. Many of the women who will present for counseling have already been evaluated and treated for PMS. They come in for counseling because the medical treatments may not have provided the desired relief they are seeking. If they have not sought medical care, we would always recommend referral to a medical professional to evaluate other possible disorders or abnormalities that might be present (like thyroid disease). The temptation to provide medical advice might be even stronger when the presenting issue is something relatively common, like PMS, rather than something that is clearly outside our expertise, such as cancer. At the same time, we must acknowledge the suffering, pain, and discomfort—both physical and psychological—that may occur with any of our counselees' physical illnesses. In particular with PMS, it is helpful to keep in mind that not all women experience the same symptoms or even the same degree of symptoms from month to month. This is important to remember—not everyone has the same symptoms or challenges each month. Our role as biblical counselors is to help those who are suffering to process their thoughts and desires, grow in their understanding of God and themselves, and discern how to act in a way that is honoring to God. Philippians 2:13 says, "for it is God who is at work in you, both to will and to work for His good pleasure". This includes times of pain and suffering brought on by PMS—God is working in us both internally and externally to conform us to his image.

Just as in any biblical counseling session, it is important to first gather data to understand what the individual is thinking and desiring before beginning to offer them counsel from God's Word. Each of the following themes that might come up when working with a counselee who struggles with PMS includes both a questioning aspect and an instructional aspect.

As we begin the process of gathering data, it is important to slowly and carefully ask questions that encompass when the problems started, what else was going on in their life at that time, what symptoms are they experiencing, whether the symptoms are the same each month, what people situations or events worsen or improve the symptoms, what treatment strategies have they tried and how successful have they been. Some specific questions include the following:

- How do they respond to people or events during the time of their PMS each month?
- Are there any common responses that occur each month?
- When that time of the month comes, what are they fearing, worrying, or wanting? Do they just want everyone to go away and leave them totally isolated?
- What is the response of family, friends, church members, and coworkers during that time each month?

As in the story of Lauren, how does she handle the embarrassment or shame that is repeated? How does she mentally process before and after the events of those five to eight days each month? Did she think it was outside of her ability to control those responses of yelling and making everyone miserable?

A biblical counselor should first seek to understand their counselee's view of God. How do they fit God into these five to eight days each month? What is her opinion of God during those days? Is her opinion of God influenced by the experience with her own father? Do they see and understand that God is good, even in the midst of their PMS? Or do they see God as unkind and unfair because he allows them to have this particular problem to this particular degree? Your counselees might say that of course God is good, while displaying contrary attitudes in answering careful questions. Psalm 25:8a says, "Good and upright is the Lord" (ESV). In the midst of suffering, it is easy to forget this truth. Practical homework assignments can help encourage them to remember that God is good. For example, you could assign your counselee to list every day three ways that God is good, even on the days when the struggle with PMS is at its most intense. Remember to continue gathering more information with each session. She may not be willing to share important details until there is a trusting relationship. It is very challenging for a counselee to open up to the ugliness that resides inside. By spending time asking questions and listening, you as the counselor are building a relation-ship of care and trust with a better ability to tailor the truth, hope, and encouragement found in God's Word.

After spending the time to begin to understand the details and answers to the questions above and your counselee's view of God, trials, and suffering, it will be important to begin discussing truth from God's Word to give hope and encouragement. We will look at a number of truths that could be used in cases like that of Lauren at the introduction to this chapter.

An important facet of God's goodness is his providence. I like Jerry Bridges's definition of providence in *Trusting God*. He defines providence as "God's constant care for and absolute rule over his cre-ation for his own glory and for the good of his people."[7] Note the absolute terms in this definition: constant care, absolute rule, and all creation. God's constant care and absolute rule applies even in the struggles associated with PMS, and they are always—without reserva-tion or question—for his glory and our good. Let that sink in, and, at

---

7. Jerry Bridges, *Trusting God* (Colorado Springs: NavPress, 2016), 13.

the appropriate time, let that sink in for the person who is struggling with the symptoms of PMS. We often think that if a hardship is for God's glory then it certainly cannot be for our good. Conversely, we wonder, *If it is for my good, then how could it be for God's glory?* Yet this definition clearly communicates that both elements are always bound together. You cannot separate one from the other. What an incredible hope and assurance we have when we feel awful: there is a purpose for our infirmities. It is always for our good and for God's glory even when it is challenging to compute how that could be. According to Romans 8:28–29, "good" is for me to become more like Jesus. Meanwhile, the "glory of God" is giving a God-honoring response to a watching world, friends, coworkers, and family, even in the midst of difficulty.

Some counselees might struggle with the fact that PMS does not affect every woman to the same extent or with the same symptoms. The question might be asked, "Could God have allowed me to be one of those who don't experience monthly PMS symptoms or who experience them only to a very mild degree?" Of course the answer is that he could have. But the follow-up to your counselee's question is "Did he?" For those experiencing significant symptoms, the answer is clearly no. The third question is "Why not?" Although it may take some time to get here, we must go back to our definition of God's providence—it is always for my good. According to Romans 8:28–29, the good in view here is to help you become more like Christ. Becoming more like Christ includes, for example, bearing the fruit of the Spirit (Galatians 5:22–23). This isn't always the kind of good we most want, but it is what we most need.

A second concept that can be helpful to discuss is the time-limited nature of the suffering your counselee will experience from PMS. In a lifetime, PMS does not start until menstrual cycles begin in the teen years, and it will resolve with menopause when periods stop. Within a month, it lasts about five to eight days. And ultimately, all of our sufferings will end when we are united with Christ in heaven. You might have your counselee meditate on the rich passage of 1 Peter 1:3–10:

Blessed be the God and Father of our Lord Jesus Christ, who according to His great mercy has caused us to be born again to a living hope through the resurrection of Jesus Christ from the dead, to obtain an inheritance which is imperishable and undefiled and will not fade away, reserved in heaven for you, who are protected by the power of God through faith for a salvation ready to be revealed in the last time. In this you greatly rejoice, even though for a little while, if necessary, you have been distressed by various trials, so that the proof of your faith, being more precious than gold which is perishable, even though tested by fire, may be found to result in praise and glory and honor at the revelation of Jesus Christ; and though you have not seen Him, you love Him, and though you do not see Him now, but believe in Him, you greatly rejoice with joy inexpressible and full of glory, obtaining as the outcome of your faith the salvation of your souls.

Our consideration of this passage is never meant to dispute or minimize symptoms of any medical condition or any problem or challenge we face. It is not saying that the symptoms don't matter or don't hurt or don't create emotional challenges. But it is reminding us that our hope is a living hope, one that comes from the resurrection of Jesus Christ. It's amazing to talk about rejoicing in the midst of discussing trials and distress. And it is helpful to read the phrases "if necessary" and "for a little while" in these verses—they point us to the reality that there is a goal that is more important than the problem. The goal, as articulated in this passage, is proving our faith so we can bring praise, honor, and glory when Jesus returns. Our rejoicing is ultimately all about our salvation.

Finally, no matter what the presenting problem might be, in biblical counseling we must always return to the cross. It's at the cross that we see the ultimate sacrifice and victory over sin, which was accomplished by Jesus's death and resurrection. J. D. Greear states,

Jesus on the cross was drinking the cup of God's wrath against our sins. As God's wrath was coming toward us Jesus stepped to the cross. He took the cup of God's wrath. He drank it to the dregs. He turned it over and set it down on the table and said it is finished. Jesus was humiliated in your place. He was accused in your place. He was condemned in your place. He was defiled in your place. He was abandoned in your place. He was beaten and accused in your place. Jesus did not just die for you he died instead of you. . . . Since he has done that for me, of course I can trust that he has not forsaken me in my pain and is using my pain for his good purpose. That doesn't mean that I won't still go through pain at times. I may not understand everything that God is doing in my pain, but the cross proves to me that he cares and proves to me that he is in control. I may not know what some painful thing in my life means, but the cross shows me what it cannot mean. It cannot mean that God has abandoned me or lost control. If God saved me from my greatest condemnation—my sin— then he won't abandon me in my struggles either.[8]

The cross and resurrection are the ultimate reminder and hope when we consider the problems and struggles associated with PMS. He will not abandon your counselee, and he has not lost control, even though at times it may feel like both of those statements are true. The cross and resurrection also provide each believer with our primary reason to hope and find assurance that we can rejoice in with joy. Does knowing this take away the pain and anguish? No. However, it can help your counselee have the right perspective about how she should view this season in her life as she struggles with PMS, and it can help her respond in ways that will bring praise and honor to Jesus.

---

8. J. D. Greear, "Punished for Me," session four of *Easter*, Rightnow Media, 2021, https:// app .rightnowmedia .org/en/content/details/477705.

Up to this point we have discussed Lauren's story, followed by the physiology and possible medical treatment options available. Some people will have mild symptoms and will not seek medical care, and others will have improved enough with medical care that they do not seek further care or counseling. Others who have not improved to the degree they desire will present for biblical counseling. We have started to unpack what gathering data could look like, some questions to ask, and some areas of her life and family dynamics to unpack. We have begun to teach her truths about God, trials, and suffering to give her a God-focused perspective and mindset. In essence, we have followed Ephesians 4:22–24: "That, in reference to your former manner of life, you lay aside the old self, which is being corrupted in accordance with the lusts of deceit *[the hard work of gathering data and uncovering those corrupting deceitful strong desires]*, and that you be renewed in the spirit of your mind *[truth about God, trials, and suffering]*, and put on the new self, which in the likeness of God has been created in righteousness and holiness of the truth" (italics added).

Now comes the practical work that requires creativity and adaptability to develop plans and strategies to be righteousness, holy, and truthful like God in the presence of a renewed mind, even in the midst of the struggle with PMS.

In this case there is not one standard answer, solution, or strategy that solves every problem. In Lauren's case a number of issues were discussed. For one week a month she feels like a different person, but in reality at her core she isn't a different person. Her identity has not changed. She remains "in Christ," secure, accepted, and beloved. Yes, the emotions and feelings may be different, but what is she consistently telling herself before and during the time frame of PMS symptoms? A helpful resource for Lauren would be *Gentle and Lowly: The Heart of Christ for Sinners and Sufferers* by Dane Ortlund,[9] with chapters on how Jesus is able to sympathize and deal gently with you, never casting

---

9. Dane Ortlund, *Gentle and Lowly: The Heart of Christ for Sinners and Sufferers* (Wheaton, IL: Crossway, 2020).

you out. Reading and rereading these reminders each month will help to keep a correct mindset and maintain a God-centered focus.

Lauren's anger and yelling at those around her should be further examined and understood. A counselor could ask her, "What about activities or words makes you so upset that you yell at people? Is there a consistent pattern?" This would be a great time to incorporate her husband and even potentially the children into counseling. There may be certain things that her husband does that she usually tolerates, but which set her off that week each month. What would/could/should be a godly loving response from a loving husband? Does her husband or family help Lauren to lighten her load each month, or do they just roll their eyes and say, "There she goes again!" Can her husband and even children learn to be more loving and accepting—and helpful? What does that love look like in specific concrete terms in this household? How could they help with household chores and packing lunches instead of expecting mom to do it all? Is there medical care that could improve her pain, fatigue, possible bloating and weight gain each month? Counseling can provide the experience of uncovering creative solutions for each unique situation.

The challenge is not to dismiss, discount, or minimize Lauren's symptoms and feelings. Instead the goal is to maximize the hope and encouragement found in being God's child. Instead of focusing on "that time of the month" with life revolving around all the problems, could it be a time of crying out to God for his mercy and grace that is always promised in abundance? All the symptoms don't go away; they are just not the primary focus during that one-to-two-week time frame each month. Yes, seek medical care and treatment, but also battle each month to maintain the goals of pleasing God and becoming Christlike even when life is challenging.

A Final Word to the Counselor

Why would God bring someone into your life asking for help with PMS? *Why me?* The purpose is to grow and stretch you. You may find this unpleasant and challenging. You may be stretched to know more in depth and detail the truth of God's Word. You may need to read and understand the abundance of good resources available to help people in the middle of their struggle and to develop practical strategies for their particular struggles that point them to God. He is always there.

A Word to the Counselee

This chapter is not about disputing or minimizing your symptoms or problems. Instead, this chapter is about maximizing the hope, truth, and answers when we see God as Ephesians 1:18 says, with "the eyes of your heart." Be willing to think carefully about changing your thoughts, attitudes, and actions for the glory of God.

· · · ·

CHAPTER 17

Postpartum Depression:
Medical Background and Biblical Hope

Dan Wickert, MD, and Jocelyn Wallace

Awareness of postpartum depression has been increasing in recent years, both among secular mental health professionals and among biblical counselors, and with good reason. It can put immense pressure on young families, affect parental adjustment and newborn development, and result in great suffering. This chapter was written collaboratively to provide medical background (by Dr. Dan Wickert) on postpartum depression and to illustrate from a personal story (by Jocelyn Wallace) how postpartum depression can develop and be ministered to through biblical truths and the support of the local church.

A Personal Story of Postpartum Depression

The story of my (Jocelyn's) experience with postpartum depression begins in April 2002. My husband and I had recently celebrated five years of marriage after having weathered a few turbulent growing years. On April 23, 2002, I was twenty-seven weeks pregnant with our first baby, just about ready to enter the last twelve weeks of my pregnancy.

I was also working full-time in a Christian ministry running a faith-based (although wholeheartedly integrationist) transitional housing facility. I had been working there for the past five months, and I was on a quest to clean it up. My first months were all about helping the ministry transform through the application of biblical counseling. I had gone through biblical counseling training at my church and was on fire for the authoritative and sufficient Word of God being applied to hurting people's lives.

On that day, so many years ago, I got up and went into work just like any other day. It was a particularly hard day at work since a woman with a psychiatric diagnosis had gone off some meds cold turkey and, as a result, had out-of-control behavior and was threatening to kill herself. By the end of that long day, I was a shaky mess. Police had been involved, and my client had to take a trip to the psychiatric hospital. On top of that, I didn't feel well. My stomach hurt really, really bad. When the excruciating pain didn't get better, my doctor's office advised me to get to the hospital immediately.

Being the strong woman that I was, I drove myself to the hospital since my husband was at school—or at least I tried to until I realized that I couldn't. I stopped in a nearby town and had my friend drive me the rest of the way. I felt like I was dying, but I was pretty sure that when I got to the hospital, they would roll their eyes at me and say, "You silly first-time mother, just go home and go to sleep and everything will be fine."

However, in the next two hours, every definition of normal in my life was rewritten. I went from being obliviously and innocently excited about our first baby to finding out from the doctor that I had twenty-four to forty-eight hours to live unless they got the baby out. I didn't know what was going on, but I knew that I was very sick.

I had never been to a birthing class, had never toured the hospital, and I had no idea that a twenty-seven-week-old baby could even survive outside the womb. They gave me steroids to make the baby's lungs mature more quickly, and they were going to try to keep the baby in as long as possible. But according to Dr. Wickert, the baby had to come out within the next day or two.

The next twelve hours were a blur. I remember seeing my husband ushered out into the hallway and noticing his terrible reaction to the doctor's news, seeing the numbers on my blood pressure monitor and realizing they were high enough that I could have been having a stroke, throwing up repeatedly, writhing in pain, calling my parents who were at the burial service for my grandmother who had died only two days before (after a three-year battle with colon cancer) and telling them that they should probably make the thirteen-hour trip to be with us as soon as possible. As they drove all night long, my mom, who was a hospice nurse, kept getting updates from the nurses at the hospital about my blood counts and liver panels, and I knew she was panicking because they were bad. She was worried that I might die before she got there to see me one last time.

Finally, I was stabilized, and the next day they wheeled me to the operating room where Dr. Miller cut me open and pulled out my tiny little 1-pound 13-ounce baby, who had been born twelve weeks early in order to save both of our lives. An NICU team was standing there waiting to put her on a ventilator. I felt like death warmed over, and I just wanted to go back to two days prior, when everything was innocent and fine. I was sent to recovery, and I spent every ounce of energy I had trying to stay awake, desperately trying to wiggle my toes so I could leave that recovery room and go see my baby.

They wheeled me to my baby's side in the NICU, and I almost threw up as I looked at my baby and realized that I didn't even recognize her to be human. She was so tiny and was lying under a see-through plastic blanket that covered her entire body, including her head.

A machine was breathing for her, and all I could think of was that she looked like a pound of hamburger that you buy from the store on a Styrofoam tray wrapped in plastic wrap. She looked like an ugly little red rat. What kind of a mother is revolted by the sight of her own baby?

Next I was wheeled into my room, where I went through the motions in a big, black fog. I visited the baby through pictures, and then finally when I was allowed to leave the room, I went and saw her for the first time after that horrible first post-surgery visit.

She was all hooked up to wires, lying under a plastic blanket, and she screamed and screamed and screamed. I looked at her and told myself, *Don't you dare start loving her, because when she dies you will not be able to handle it.* I told my husband I was going to hold her loosely in case God decided to take her. He got angry at me and said, "No we're not . . . we're going to fight for her. We're going to beg God to let her live."

All I could do was cry because I could not imagine letting myself love her and being able to handle that much grief when I lost her. It was easier to just not love her, and what kind of terrible pathetic mother didn't love her baby? Everyone says, "You look at your baby, and you instantly feel a surge of love." That was baloney. I looked at my baby, and I felt nothing but pity.

All of my dreams were ruined. I wanted to have a wonderful pregnancy and look adorable in those cute little maternity clothes. I wanted to have a natural birthing experience, where I embraced my true womanhood and pushed out a baby and then got up and washed the dishes without even a shot of pain relief. I wanted to nurse my baby with the wind blowing my long blonde hair as butterflies wafted in the distance through sunlit daisy fields.

But instead, I was in NICU, surrounded by machines beeping all around me and alarms going off and nurses rushing to babies and parents crying. I couldn't even comfort my own baby. Every time I touched her, she screamed. I wasn't a cute, pregnant girl, I was monstrous and sick and puffy; my own parents didn't even recognize me when they saw me in the hospital. Breastfeeding wasn't a glorious spiritual experience. It was terrible. I was afraid of *everything*. I was afraid my baby was going to die. I was afraid I was going to pass out or throw up when I went to visit her because being in the NICU made me nauseous.

On top of that, I still had a business to run. I took two weeks off to recover from the surgery, but then I went back to work because I only had six weeks of maternity leave. I needed to save some of it for when the baby got out of the hospital. So, for the next two months, my life became a flurry of driving thirty miles to work, thirty miles to the hospital, thirty miles home, thirty miles to work, thirty miles to the hospital, thirty miles home—until I finally just moved into Lafayette and slept at a friend's house.

My husband and I juggled work, driving, seeing each other, updating our parents with the baby's progress, dealing with the baby's illnesses and setbacks, and simply trying to remember to eat, until finally the doctors said it was time for her to come home. I was so afraid to leave the hospital. We knew the nurses could do anything. We had seen them resuscitate one of the other babies there while we were visiting our baby, and we knew we would never be able to do that at home.

For the next three months we took care of her at home, and we managed. Things began to feel a little normal, but then during our first big car ride (about ten hours long), I began to feel unwell. In fact, I felt a lot like I did when I was in the hospital originally. I felt light-headed, short of breath, and panicky. Then, while we were at my parents' house, it became evident that their marriage was truly terribly broken after years of warning signs and worrying.

While in their home, I had my first full-blown panic attack, only I didn't know what it was. I just knew I felt like I was going to die, and six months earlier when I'd felt like that, I actually did almost die. During the drive home, I had panic attack after panic attack for ten hours straight. For anyone who has ever experienced one, you know the extreme physical effects they can have on your body. On that entire drive home I was on the phone with my doctor's office, trying to figure out what was happening.

We finally got home, but the next few months were marked by more horrible, overwhelming panic. I was so terribly, terribly sad. I was starting to understand that my parents' marriage—a pastor and his wife—was really and truly broken, which left me questioning things that no "good Christian girl" should ever be questioning. I couldn't handle my doubts so my sadness was mixed with shame.

My life became completely overwhelmed by darkness. I woke up sad and went to bed sad. I was so extremely tired all of the time. The baby was up every two hours to eat, and at six months she was still only eight pounds. I was worried that I couldn't make enough milk for my baby. I felt like I couldn't do anything right. There was no joy in my life, and, as a Christian, that is never supposed to happen. I felt ashamed that my life was falling apart, and I didn't know how to get it back together. I felt guilty, embarrassed that I didn't know how to be a good mom or a good daughter to a mom who was also falling apart. And I felt inadequate, unable to take care of this special baby when I couldn't even take care of myself.

My thoughts were constantly going to "what ifs." *What if my baby had cerebral palsy? What if she had a brain bleed? What if the baby's heart monitor went off in the middle of the night and I didn't hear it? What if she died? If my baby died, would I ever be able to handle that much grief? What if the baby died and then on top of that my husband died? What if my baby died and my husband died and then my mom died? What if I found myself completely and desperately alone? What if the rest of my life was this dark? What if it never got better? What if I had fifty or sixty or seventy more years of this panicky darkness always shrouding me?*

I started envisioning what my life would look like if all of those "what ifs" happened. I could picture myself sitting in the front row of church with a tiny little baby casket in the background, holding my dead baby's body, grieving all by myself. I could see myself drowning in a grief that was so horrible and terrible that it almost killed me. I could picture the grief so terrorizing my life that I ended up committed, sitting curled up in the corner of a psych ward, sucking my thumb, rocking back and forth, with no husband, no mother, completely and utterly alone. Eventually, every fear, every "what if" question led me to that picture of my future.

I would wake up in the morning, exhausted, and scream to God in my head, *Why didn't you just let me die in my sleep last night? Aren't you merciful? Why won't you let me out of this terrible existence?* And then I would get up and trudge through another miserable, panic-filled day so full of crying that I couldn't even do anything but sit at my desk at work and stare. Every day was the same. My mind was full of questions that I didn't think I was allowed to ask of a God that wasn't kind enough to just kill me.

And *none* of this should have been happening. I was a Christian. I was a biblical counselor, for Pete's sake. I was a maverick, cleaning up a ministry and righting wrongs, fighting for justice for the oppressed. I was helping people change. And this wasn't allowed to happen.

Christians *don't* fall apart. Christians don't get depressed. Christians don't get so stressed out that they forget how to walk up the stairs. Christians don't start being afraid to use scissors around their baby because they have delusions that the scissors might fall onto the baby and cut the baby open and they can picture the baby's guts falling out all over the place. Christians don't imagine their baby's funeral. Christians don't find hope in a little pill that promises to take their depression and anxiety away. Christians don't go to the emergency room for panic attacks. Christians don't doubt God. Christians don't beg God to kill them.

So there must be no reason to live. My whole life had been dedicated to being a Christian . . . and being a good one. I was strong. I was brave. I had grown up as a missionary kid in a third world country. If this is how God treated strong, brave, courageous Christians, then what point was there in being alive? I knew my alternative to being alive with this much suffering, and that was being dead and waking up in heaven. I knew where I was going, and it wasn't worth staying on earth and fighting this hard each day only to wake up the next day and have to do it all again. All I could think about was that I needed out. I needed God to just let it be okay for me to die.

But he never let it happen.

I couldn't hurt my husband and my mom and my tiny little daughter by doing it myself so I just kept on existing. Kept on waking up day after day for months and months and months, living panicky moment after panicky moment, begging God to just put me out of my misery. Why would he have saved my life in the hospital just to make me so miserable that I wished I could die?

And I never told anyone—especially the people at church. I never asked for weekly biblical counseling because Christians do not suffer this way. They don't bring trials on themselves like this. They are strong and brave and obedient and they smile and fight on, and they do not let feelings run their lives. No one knew what was happening, except for my husband and my mom, and even they didn't know how bad it was inside my head. They just knew it was bad and that I needed help—and that we were never, ever, ever, *ever* having another baby, *ever*. I never wanted to go through anything like this ever again.

Medical and Psychotherapeutic Approaches to Postpartum Mental Disorders

What hope does the medical and psychotherapeutic community offer to a woman in Jocelyn's situation? The focus of this medical discussion is multifaceted. First, be aware that there are multiple degrees of severity associated with the postpartum state. As biblical counselors we would always encourage the new mother to follow up with their own medical professional to rule out or to identify any other medical conditions that could contribute or worsen the severity of her symptoms. As biblical counselors we always want to assess and take necessary steps to protect the mother and her newborn infant. This may involve incorporating additional family and church members, along with medical professionals, in order to protect the safety of the newborn infant mother and father. Certainly, severe forms of depression and psychosis should incorporate medical professionals who can make decisions regarding medications and even hospitalization if necessary. The medical community generally breaks postpartum mental disorders into three categories primarily based on when they occur and their severity: postpartum blues, postpartum depression, and postpartum psychosis. Although I (Dr. Wickert) will provide a brief overview of each, the focus of this chapter will be on postpartum depression because it is the one that biblical counselors will see most frequently.

Postpartum Blues

Postpartum blues is a transient condition characterized by mild and often rapid mood swings that peak around five days after delivery and typically resolve within two weeks. Because it is so transient, most biblical counselors will not see mothers in this state. When a new mother is experiencing postpartum blues, she may quickly shift from elation to sadness, as well as display increased irritability and anxiety. Tears and crying spells will be more frequent. She may find it more difficult to concentrate, and she may also suffer from insomnia.

In addition to being transient, postpartum blues is quite common. Approximately 40 to 80 percent of postpartum women will develop symptoms of postpartum blues within two to three days after their delivery. No clear cause has been identified, although fluctuating hormones post-delivery are suspected to play a role. Although all women experience hormonal fluctuation, some women may be more sensitive than others. The risk factors for postpartum blues include a history of depression, depressive symptoms during pregnancy, a family history of depression, mood changes associated with menstruation or oral contraceptives, as well as stress about child care.

Postpartum Depression

In contrast, postpartum depression is not as transient as postpartum blues, lasting for at least two weeks or more. To be diagnosed with postpartum depression, a new mother must meet the criteria for non-pregnancy-related depression. For specific criteria about non-pregnancy-related depression you can refer to chapter 5 about depression or refer to the *Diagnostic and Statistical Manual of Mental Disorders* (DSM-5) for diagnostic criteria of Major Depressive Disorder. Additionally, postpartum depression typically begins within the first month of delivery and, like other forms of depression, results in clinical changes in sleep, energy level, appetite, weight, GI function, and libido. Mothers struggling with postpartum depression report feeling anxious, angry, irritable, guilty, overwhelmed, and afraid of harming themselves or their baby. This condition is frequently unrecognized and underreported, but the estimated prevalence is between 5 and 9 percent.

Like postpartum blues, no specific hormonal cause has been consistently identified as the causative agent, although research has looked at estrogen, progesterone, thyroid hormones, testosterone, cholesterol, and cortisol levels as potential contributors. The risk factors for postpartum depression are similar to those for postpartum blues: having a personal history of depression prior to pregnancy, experiencing marital conflict, suffering from stressful life events, living with lower socioeconomic status, and lacking social support.

Postpartum Psychosis

Postpartum psychosis is the most severe condition of the three disorders, characterized by disturbances in an individual's perception of reality. When a new mother is experiencing postpartum psychosis, she will have delusions, hallucinations, and disorganized thoughts. It typically begins within two weeks of delivery, although it can occur at a later date as well. Postpartum psychosis is also the most uncommon condition, with a prevalence of only 0.1–0.2 percent.

Similar to postpartum blues and depression, the etiology of postpartum psychosis is unknown. The risk factor for postpartum psychosis is having a personal history of psychosis or bipolar disorder, a family history of psychosis, or having recently stopped taking lithium or other mood stabilizers.

When a biblical counselor meets with a new mother suffering from one of these postpartum disorders, the point of knowing these three categories is not to attempt to diagnose the counselee, but rather to note that in any case, the cause of their suffering is unknown. Furthermore, the currently known risk factors for these conditions are primarily not medical in nature, but are rather social or psychosocial issues.

Another conclusion from the discussion of the medical categories is the association of social or psychosocial issues that are commonly seen in postpartum disorders. This is another reminder of the importance of gathering data. In listening, understanding, and helping individuals, biblical counselors are gathering data at every opportunity. We never know everything about a person or their situations. Later in this chapter we discuss common recurrent themes that should be investigated throughout the counseling sessions.

Biblical Counseling Principles for Postpartum Mental Disorders

What hope can a biblical counselor offer to a woman in Jocelyn's situation? The biblical counselor's primary tools are biblical truth and the loving support of Christian community. The remainder of this section will provide principles and guidelines to help biblical counselors apply these two tools to the specific situations of the women they counsel.

Begin with Gathering Data

As can be seen in Jocelyn's story, each woman's experience of pregnancy, labor, delivery, and postpartum recovery/newborn care is unique. Layered on top of these differences are the unique expectations and fears that each woman brings to motherhood, as well as the many different ways she can interpret what happens to her.

This underscores the importance of carefully gathering data about your counselee's specific experiences and the meaning that she has attributed to them. Most women will not have had the specific medical struggles that Jocelyn had, but no matter how minor their physical suffering or disappointments might seem, recognize that there is real suffering involved. Many Christian women, like Jocelyn, believe that their negative feelings about pregnancy, labor and delivery, or motherhood are wrong, and, therefore, they try to pretend that they don't exist.

The first step a biblical counselor must take is to draw out and listen to each woman's emotions and walk with them through the valley of the shadow of death. In addition to hearing her emotions, it is helpful to learn about her expectations and desires going into pregnancy. On the one hand, there are many difficult aspects of pregnancy and motherhood that women are completely unaware of before they enter into it. On the other, there is a strong cultural emphasis on empowerment and choices that, if taken to extremes, can give women unreasonable expectations about what is in their control or what might happen during their pregnancy or labor and delivery.

For example, if a woman is committed to a vaginal delivery, she might not feel just disappointed that she needs a C-section, but completely devastated or betrayed if she has one. Although a vaginal delivery is a positive goal because it is typically better for both mother and child, at the same time it is unfortunate that many women are not reminded that medically necessary C-sections are a mercy that have saved countless lives, including Jocelyn's and her daughter's.

In addition to gathering data about their expectations, it is also helpful to gain an understanding of their theology of suffering. Do they believe that Christians should be exempt from pain or severe medical challenges? Do they understand that even a devout Christian's body is subject to the curse of the fall? What do they believe about themselves and their rights? Is having children primarily about fulfilling their own needs or desires?

As you listen to your counselee, take note of any recurring themes. These might include feeling overwhelmed or experiencing fear (typically fear of failing as a wife or mother), suffering from lack of sleep, pressure to go back to work (if present, is it coming from the mother, father, employer, or someone else?), financial struggles (is the loss of the mother's income or unexpected medical bills causing financial hardship?), and problems with extended family (are any of them antagonistic toward the pregnancy or one of the new parents? Or are they simply unavailable, whether due to physical or relational distance?).

As you serve your counselee, pay close attention to the "what if" questions that surface. Those questions will give you a window into her heart and will help expose the fears that are really driving her. Recognize that this data gathering process may be a difficult experience. It can be difficult to hear of the suffering that women have gone through, especially if all of your prior experiences with pregnancy or childrearing have been largely positive. It also might be difficult to hear your counselees' negative emotions toward their children and their ungodly interpretations of their experiences. However, it's important not to display any revulsion for the ugliness that might come out during your counseling session; remember, it is most likely just as difficult (if not more so) for your counselee to honestly express these thoughts and feelings as it is for you to hear them.

Connect Biblical Truths to the Specifics of Her Experiences and Struggles

When you have heard and understood what your counselee has gone through and how she's making sense of her experiences, the most important things you can do are praying with and for her. When we pray, we proclaim that God is with us and cares about every detail of our lives. We also avail ourselves of the help that God says is ours when his children cry out to him. Help her draw near to the God who cares for her.

In addition to prayer, you can help women suffering from postpartum depression by encouraging them with hopeful Scripture passages, such as Romans 8:31–39 and 15:13 and Isaiah 26:3–4 and 41:10. And, depending on what you learned during your data gathering process, you can point her to Scripture passages that speak to her specific struggles, whether she is feeling overwhelmed (1 Corinthians 10:13; James 1:2–4), pressured to work (Colossians 3:23–24), or fearful about finances (Hebrews 13:5–6). Many Psalms can also bring hope as you help her learn how to work through her thoughts and feelings before the Lord (consider, for example, Psalms 13, 17, 23, 27, or 42).

Along with pointing her to specific passages of Scripture, it is imperative that you help your counselee learn how to interpret her life and her struggles in light of the gospel. Jocelyn needed to learn that the gospel spoke to her need not only for salvation from God's wrath but also her suffering, sanctification, and growth as a believer. She needed the gospel to allay fears that God would be angry and judge her for having honest questions about his providence and prudence. She needed to be reminded that her identity in Christ made her welcome to approach a Father who cared for her and her family and to seek his grace and mercy that could help her in specific moments of need. The truths of the gospel also allowed her to let others know that she was needy and could use their practical help. The gospel taught her to love her fragile daughter the way Jesus had loved her and to sacrifice to serve her in ways that demonstrated Christ's compassion and care. The gospel taught her to give up self-protection and embrace self-sacrifice and to seek satisfaction in her relationship with Jesus alone.

Many people struggling with depression, postpartum or otherwise, are also struggling to see any good purpose for their life. Biblical counselors can help reorient their counselees by reminding them of what Scripture says about their purpose and by helping them think creatively about how they can live in light of that biblical purpose, given their specific circumstances. Jocelyn needed to learn that God had created her to love him and be satisfied with his love alone, and that the closeness of that relationship would result in knowing and emulating him more fully. Out of that relationship she learned to embrace his mission for her during her years on the earth, being abundantly productive for his glory and others' good and allowing God's righteousness and justice to influence her activities in her spheres of influence even in circumstances that were challenging. When Jocelyn lacked a clear awareness of God's creation purpose for her, she was tempted to create alternate purposes that would give her an identity she thought would satisfy her, like having a certain kind of childbirth experience or portraying herself a certain way. As she learned that her identity in Christ was more important than any earthly identity, it freed her to live out what was already true because of her union with Christ, instead of needing to create ways for her life to have meaning according to what she had determined was valuable.

Last, a nearly universal topic to address will be your counselee's understanding of her suffering. Part of your task as a biblical counselor is helping your brothers and sisters in Christ learn how to interpret the hardest parts of their lives in light of the truth of Scripture. I (Jocelyn) have found it helpful to use an eight-part pattern originated by Robert Kellemen in his book *God's Healing for Life's Losses* to aid counselees in practically work through their suffering in a biblical way:

1. Candor—Courageously tell the truth about my external and internal suffering.
2. Complaint—Frankly and vulnerably express to God my pain and confusion over how he could allow such evil and suffering.
3. Cry—Humbly, in faith, ask God for help based upon my acknowledgement that I can't survive without him.
4. Comfort—Experience the presence of God in the presence of suffering, which plants the seeds of hope that I will yet thrive.
5. Waiting—Trust God's future provision without attempting to provide for myself what only God can give.
6. Wailing—Long for heaven but also live passionately for God and others while I am still on earth.
7. Weaving—Entrust myself to God's larger purposes and good plans.
8. Worshipping—Want God more than I want relief. Walk with God in the dark because he is the light of my soul.[1]

These are, of course, not an exhaustive list of ways to connect biblical truths to the specifics of your counselee's postpartum depression, but hopefully they will provide you with a launching point as you consider how to bring biblical truths to bear in helpful ways.

---

1. R. W. Kellemen, *God's Healing for Life's Losses: How to Find Hope When You're Hurting* (Winona Lake, IN: BMH Books, 2010).

Identify Practical Means to Demonstrate God's Grace Through the Body of Christ

Ask your counselee's church family to help her in practical ways, especially if her extended family does not live nearby or is unable or unwilling to provide this kind of practical care. This could include dropping off meals, providing childcare, helping out with housework, and offering to watch her baby while she sleeps. Churches would do well to consider how to create coordinated efforts to support and mentor all young mothers in their local community, regardless of whether or not they struggle with postpartum depression.

In addition to providing practical care for mothers, churches can minister to new fathers, a journal article entitled "Postpartum Depression in Men" states the condition is not well understood, with a frequency of 8–10 percent usually within the first three to six months after delivery, but possibly occurring up to a year after delivery.[2] A second journal article entitled "When Fathers Begin to Falter: A Comprehensive Review on Paternal Perinatal Depression" discusses the negative impact on the marital relationship, along with challenges in family and parental functioning.[3]

Not only can fathers also suffer from postpartum depression, they are likely struggling with how to respond to their wife's suffering. A new father might feel hopeless because he has tried "everything" and his wife hasn't gotten better. A biblical counselor can help a new father in this situation learn to helpfully support his wife and have reasonable expectations for what "better" might look like and how long it might take her to get there. Husbands whose wives are struggling with postpartum depression might also be tempted to cope by engaging in unhelpful or even sinful behaviors, such as working long hours to be away from home or indulging in various forms of

---

2. Jonathan R. Scarff, "Postpartum Depression in Men," *Innovations in Clinical Neuroscience* 16, no. 5–6 (2019): 11–14.

3. Antonio Bruno et al., "When Fathers Begin to Falter: A Comprehensive Review on Paternal Perinatal Depression," *International Journal of Environmental Research and Public Health* 17, no. 4 (February 2020): 1139.

escapism. These are also areas where a biblical counselor can provide guidance and support. Even though the wife may be the only family member coming in for counseling, a biblical counselor would do well to also meet with the husband.

A Conclusion to a Personal Story of Postpartum Depression

The remainder of my (Jocelyn's) story can be summed up in these two verses:

> "You shall remember all the way which the LORD your God has led you in the wilderness these forty years, that He might humble you, testing you, to know what was in your heart, whether you would keep His commandments or not. He humbled you and let you be hungry, and fed you with manna which you did not know, nor did your fathers know, that He might make you understand that man does not live by bread alone, but man lives by everything that proceeds out of the mouth of the LORD." (Deuteronomy 8:2–3)

Although my time in the wilderness of postpartum depression often felt unbearably hard, now that I'm on the other side of it, I can see that this experience was the best thing I could have ever gone through. Just like the Israelites, I was humbled. I was tested. I had the opportunity to see what was in my heart—and it was ugly, disgusting sin, not the righteousness that I had supposed was there. This experience revealed to me in a new way the truth of the gospel—I have been saved by God's grace alone, not by my own merit. I am completely dependent on God's provision of grace and mercy for every aspect of my life, both now and on into eternity.

My struggles were a combination of hard circumstances and my responses, which certainly revealed my heart. The difficult circumstances were life altering, and I needed to understand God's comfort and care. As I processed those events, I was also able to see heart patterns of self-protection, self-centeredness, and fearfulness. God absolutely delivered on 2 Corinthians 9:8, where he promises that his grace is sufficient, but like Jonah 2:8 says, when I clung to my worthless idols, I forfeited a lot of the grace that could have been mine. As I learned to identify and reject patterns of sin in this period of life, God gave me his grace to handle this hard time of suffering.

Like many people, I clung to these idols because I didn't understand who God really is. Going through postpartum depression helped me learn more about God's character. He is not appalled by my honest questions, even my questions about his sovereignty and prudence. I am not the first person, nor the last, to ask these questions, and God is big enough to handle them all.

When I finally looked at God with naked honesty, I saw that God is good and he only does good (Psalm 119:68), even if that includes allowing me to have a preemie baby, health problems, and postpartum depression. God was providentially unfolding the events of my life for his glory and my good. I didn't arrive at this insight in a moment; reading and rereading *Trusting God* by Jerry Bridges during this hard season helped me learn and believe this truth. If God could have prevented my suffering but didn't, that doesn't make God unkind—it proves his supremacy and wisdom.

In addition to learning more about who I am and who God is, I needed to grow in my understanding of *why* I exist. During times of immense suffering, if we don't know our purpose, then we won't have a reason to live. I am so thankful that at some point in my life I had memorized the first part of the Westminster Shorter Catechism: "What is the chief end of man? The chief end of man is to glorify God and enjoy Him forever." This thought helped me get out of bed in the morning, but it also confronted me with the realization that I had no idea what it meant. I began to find new energy and a sense of purpose in realizing that I could spend the rest of my life figuring out how to glorify and enjoy God—and I would still have more to learn.

Through all of this, the Word of God became even more precious to me. Although the Bible is a tool that can help us learn how to live well, it is far more than that. It is also God's love letter to me, describing how he's going to continue to pour out his loving-kindness on me, his beloved child, forever. And, because he loves me, he has taught me in the Bible the best ways to live, the paths I can walk in to find true joy, peace, and contentment.

This realization, along with the other lessons that my time in the wilderness of postpartum depression taught me, helped me to finally recognize and reject my false gods because I could see how they were nothing compared to the one true God. My particular idols included self-protection (I even went so far as to avoid loving my daughter to keep myself safe), believing I would find satisfaction in something other than what God had given me (longing for the perfect pregnancy, or, later, longing for escape through death), and upholding my image as a strong and courageous Christian woman who only had stable, positive emotions, who never struggled to obey, and who never needed anyone else's help. These idols were cruel, insane masters. They wanted me dead, and they wanted my death to be slow and torturous. But God is a kind master who sacrificed Jesus to purchase me and make me his slave; his yoke is easy and his burden is light. The idols controlling other women in the throes of postpartum depression might be quite different from mine, but we all need to learn to see them for what they are, and we all need help to demolish them.

I learned to face my sadness and fear by reading good books written by godly authors, meditating on Scriptures and teaching that showed God's love for me and sovereign wisdom over the intricate affairs of my life, and allowing myself to be more vulnerable and authentic in my marriage and local church. There were good books that dealt with anxiety, worry, and fear that proved to be valuable resources in learning how to evaluate and adjust my thinking to be more honoring to God. *Trusting God* by Jerry Bridges[4] helped me see the many reasons God is worth trusting with the intimate details of my life. As I learned to share my thoughts with my family and friends

---

4. Jerry Bridges, *Trusting God* (Colorado Springs: NavPress, 2008).

from church, I learned that much of what was overwhelming me had been faced by other new mothers before me, that my concerns were normal, and that Scripture offered effective solutions. As I learned to be authentic and vulnerable instead of isolating myself in fear, I found godly advice that helped in practical situations and willing servants that intervened when I needed it. We had never been parents before, and we were relatively newly married. There was so much that we did not know about how to love God and obey him in the reality of family life. Learning to work as a team, supporting each other when our new reality was overwhelming, drew us together as a couple and taught us how to be even more unified. As I learned that my struggle was revealing a lot of things in my heart and in my life that were good to work through, I was able to be excited about the ways I was growing, instead of overwhelmed by everything that was changing and challenging.

A Word to the Counselor

My experience with postpartum depression revolutionized how I thought about biblical counseling. Prior to my own journey through the valley of the shadow of death, I was passionate about helping people change. I still am, but now I view biblical counseling primarily as helping another soul suffer well when God calls them to walk through difficult trials. My job as a counselor isn't to simply give my counselees the "four principles of this" or the "three rules of that" and give them fifty things to do. If that's all I have to offer, then it is simply behavioral change. My job as a counselor is to *love* my counselees, to sacrifice to serve them at the most terrible times of their lives, and to suffer with them while they grow in their understanding of God, themselves, and this world we live in. I probably say a lot of the same things I used to say, but I do it completely differently. I think it's probably the difference between being passionate about theories and philosophies and compassionate about real people who are suffering.

The women you work with who are struggling with postpartum depression will likely feel hopeless, helpless, and overwhelmed with cares. The greatest hope you can give a struggling woman is the confidence that Jesus Christ is with her in her struggles and is using them to help her know and love him better, and that the benefits of that will far outweigh the pain of her suffering. Additionally, there will be real ways her local church can help as the family adjusts to adding another member—like providing meals, maintaining the home and keeping up on laundry, or babysitting so she can rest and recover from childbirth.

In many ways, women struggle after childbirth because there are questions and concerns during this adjustment that are normal and healthy and will most likely include both a body and soul component. Counselees need to be reassured that their concerns are common and have been thought through before (1 Corinthians 10:13), and there is nothing new going on with their family that others have not faced before or that Jesus will not help with. Counselees will also be helped as you remind them that every concern is complicated by lack of sleep, physical adjustments after childbirth, and relational changes as each new member is added to the family.

Connecting both the mother and father with mentors who can walk through this adjustment and provide on-the-job training to the new parents could be extremely beneficial. Both parents will be blessed to have spiritually minded and experienced mentors or counselors that they can openly talk with as new concerns arise, fears are faced, or needs surface. Teaching this couple to rely on the love and support of their local church during this major life adjustment will be a blessing to both the church and the family and will provide practical one-another ministry that glorifies Jesus and accentuates the gospel.

Bringing new life into the world has many risks, and it is likely that postpartum mothers will need to process some portion of that life-altering experience with people who love both them and the Lord. Be aware that traumatic birth experiences or near-death experiences for the mother or child are very statistically likely to result in some form of postpartum difficulty as the adrenaline wears off and the realities of those experiences settle in. At some point in counseling, it is wise to lead the conversation toward helping a counselee process any life-threatening experiences.

A Word to the Counselee

As hard as it might be to believe, I am thankful every day for the gift of eighteen months of postpartum depression. I would never trade this horrible experience for a life without it because through it I learned to trust what the psalmist says: "You have dealt well with your servant, O LORD. . . . It is good for me that I was afflicted, That I may learn Your statutes" (119:65, 71). You're most likely not here yet. Let my story just encourage you to keep seeking answers. Keep going to God with all of your thoughts and feelings, no matter how evil or terrible you fear they might be. If you do, I believe that you will find the one true God at the end of your honest questions. Resist seeking refuge in anyone or anything other than Christ.

> I sought the LORD and He answered me, and delivered me from all my fears. They looked to Him and were radiant, and their faces will never be ashamed. . . . Oh taste and see that the LORD is good; how blessed is the man who takes refuge in Him! . . . The eyes of the LORD are toward the righteous and His ears are open to their cry. . . . The LORD is near to the brokenhearted and saves those who are crushed in spirit. . . . The LORD redeems the soul of His servants, and none of those who take refuge in Him will be condemned. (Psalm 34: 4–5, 8, 15, 18, and 22)

CHAPTER 18

SUICIDE AND THE GOD
OF ALL COMFORT:
HELPING SUICIDAL COUNSELEES AND THEIR
LOVED ONES DRAW NEAR TO GOD

Daniel Dionne, MD

When we consider the topic of suicide, the biblical counselor will encounter two possible scenarios: you will most likely be meeting with someone who is expressing suicidal ideation or sadly you might be called upon to meet with grieving family and friends after a suicide. It's no wonder that most counselors feel overwhelmed and unqualified to handle this subject. The stakes are so high, and the misery is so deep. One will think first, *Who can I call that knows more than I do about how to handle this situation? I might mess this up!*

But when your counselee is thinking suicide is their only hope, or you need to go to the home of someone who has just lost a loved one to suicide, remember that this is a God-designed opportunity for you to practice what Paul says in Galatians 6:1–2: "Brothers, if anyone is caught in any transgression, you who are spiritual should restore him in a spirit of gentleness. Keep watch on yourself, lest you too be tempted. Bear one another's burdens, and so fulfill the law of Christ" (ESV). There is very little time for you to research this topic as you sit across from this counselee or as you drive to a friend's house. It is "go" time! Of course, every situation is different, but hopefully this chapter will give you the tools to move into these situations and help you be a good friend to these suffering people.

The Suicidal Sufferer

Bob is a forty-five-year-old man who has been attending my church for fifteen years and has recently signed up for biblical counseling. He has four children, has been told to move out of the house, and the elders are helping his wife get a legal separation. He has a habitual gambling problem and has lost his job for trying to embezzle funds from his employer. He is currently being investigated by the police for his actions, is not sleeping at night, and is drinking large amounts of alcohol while living in a rented hotel room. The leadership at our church has "told it to the church" as outlined in Matthew 18:17, and Bob is desperate for help. I am a counseling elder at our church and a physician, and he has asked to meet with me.

During Bob's first counseling appointment, I found out how much he is drinking, that he is not sleeping well at night, and that he fears he might be going to jail in the next couple of weeks. He says he is a Christian and that he "prayed the prayer" at age twelve, but he has not been attending church for some time and does not have any accountability or relationships with other Christian men. It is difficult to tell if he is truly repentant or just despairing over the consequences of his sinful choices. He is fearful and miserable and tells me that he sees no way out of his situation and that he has purchased a handgun at a local pawnshop. He is angry with the elders and with his wife. What should I do and say next?

The Suffering Survivor

Rick and Chelsea are also forty-five years old and have attended my church for fifteen years. They have three grown children and have recently become empty nesters. Their youngest daughter, Tiffany, grew up in our church and attended our youth group until she was a junior in high school, but stopped because she needed more time to do homework and sports. She was a high achiever in school and got a prestigious scholarship to an Ivy League school on the East Coast. In our city she was a big fish in a small pond, but when she got to college, the competition was fierce and she struggled to keep her grades up. She almost didn't return after winter break, but then she decided to give it one more try. She started losing weight, was unable to sleep, and would not return her parents' texts and attempts to communicate. When she failed her first midterm exam, she wrote a letter to her family and jumped off a bridge. When my wife and I heard the news, we called Rick and Chelsea and asked them if we could come be with them. They have tearfully accepted our request, and we are driving to their house. What should we do and say next?

Medical Facts and Suicide Statistics

Nearly 45,000 people commit suicide every year in the United States, and about 800,000 per year worldwide. It is the tenth leading cause of death in the US and fourteenth leading cause worldwide. In the US, most successfully completed suicides are a result of firearms (50 percent), followed by hanging (25 percent), and then drug overdose (15 percent). Twice as many men are successful in their suicide attempts compared to women in the US. Among the 1.4 million suicide attempts in the US each year, 3 percent are successful.

How does it start? It typically begins with a thought called "suicidal ideation." Of those that have a suicidal thought, 33 percent of them will go on to make a plan, and 55 percent of those with a plan will go on to make an attempt. When a person does not have a plan, there is only a 15 percent chance that they will make an attempt. It is estimated that in the US every year, 4 percent of the population has suffered from suicidal thoughts, so this is a significant problem involving a fairly large number of people. Besides the differences in the sexes, there are also differences in age groups. Young people between age eighteen and twenty-five are five times more likely to attempt suicide than any of the older age groups. Also a large number of men over the age of seventy-five successfully commit suicide.[1]

Risk factors include race, education, previous suicide attempts, and psychiatric diagnoses like schizophrenia, depression, anxiety, and bipolar disorder. Other factors that can increase suicide risk include alcohol and substance abuse, being single or part of a sexual minority, and a history of military service. The greatest common denominator in all these cases is hopelessness. Those who are suffering from some sort of physical or emotional pain often reach a point of despair where suicide seems like a logical option. Dr. Jay Adams taught that when a counselee is suicidal and has come to the conclusion that his life is useless, it is important to take his conclusions seriously. He or she has concluded that the world would be better off without him or her. Those considering suicide are painfully aware of how miserable their life is, but their choice of suicide is the wrong solution. God has a much better, hope-giving solution for the counselee's miserable condition.

Biblical counselors know that this world is full of suffering as a result of the fall and its effects on our planet and all of humanity. We also suffer from the consequences of our own sinful choices. We try our hardest to solve these problems with our own worldly wisdom— and sometimes it seems like we might actually be successful—but ultimately without our Savior Jesus Christ, there is no reason to be hopeful. So what can a biblical counselor do when they learn that their counselee is contemplating suicide?

---

1. These statistics and more can be found at Jennifer Schreiber and Larry Culpepper, "Suicidal Ideation and Behavior in Adults," UpToDate, September 1, 2022, https://www. uptodate.com/contents/suicidal-ideation-and-behavior-in-adults. Also see "Suicide Data and Statistics," Centers for Disease Control and Prevention (CDC), June 28, 2022, https:// www.cdc.gov/suicide/suicide-data-statistics.html.

Counseling the Suicidal Sufferer

Proverbs 20:5 says the best way to get to know someone is to ask good questions and to be a good listener. As you are getting to know your counselee and trying to build a connection, you will be asking about their current life situation and digging deeper so you can understand their heart. If your counselee is miserable, they might start to say things like, "the world would be better off without me," or "I wish I had never been born." Whenever I hear these kinds of statements, my first response is to wonder if the person is suicidal and to consider if I need to ask them directly. I know that if they say yes, the rest of the counseling session and perhaps the next few hours or days are going to be focused on this problem. This is where you need to know that *God has brought you to this moment in his sovereignty to address these wrong thoughts with your counselee.*

Counselors often worry that if they bring up the topic of suicide, they are going to put wrong ideas into a person's head. Experts agree that this is not the case, and that most times the counselee is grateful to have you talk with them about the thing that is foremost on their mind. If a person has decided to take their own life and is completely determined to be successful, they will not give hints like, "I wish I had never been born." They will just go ahead and commit suicide. The person that makes these statements is giving you an opportunity to explore this subject with him. You need to take this person seriously and say something like, "You must be in a lot of pain to think that suicide would be a good choice for you. May I ask you some questions?"

The following questions will help you assess how serious your counselee is so you can get them the kind of support they need:

- Have you ever tried to commit suicide before, and if so, how?
- Do you have a plan or have you been planning to end your life?
- How would you do it?
- Where would you do it?
- Do you have the means (drugs, gun, rope) that you would use?

- Where is it right now?
- Do you have a time line in mind for ending your life?

These are hard questions to ask, but they will tell you a lot about where your counselee is in the process. As a physician I have often needed to ask my suicidal patients, "Do you think you would ever follow through on these thoughts?" I have often heard them say no because they consider it a sin or they know how much it would hurt their loved ones. I usually consider this to be a good sign and ask them to let me know if these thoughts become more troublesome. And, of course, stay alert to any signs that they are still thinking about and considering ending their life.

Prioritizing Next Steps to Provide Practical Help

When counselees seem to be in immediate danger of following through on their plan, you need to call out for help. This is when you tell your counselee that you are very concerned and you ask if you can call some people to help. Don't ever try to help someone who seems to be in imminent danger of suicide all on your own. The following is a list of people you should consider asking for help:

- Parents
- Spouse
- Friends
- Siblings
- Small group leader
- Pastor or elder
- Another biblical counselor
- The police

If your counselee is comfortable with you making those calls, then your first priorities are to

- Be sure they are not left alone.
- Be sure someone removes the gun, rope, drugs, or other planned tools for their suicide and puts them in a safe place.
- Be sure family, friends, and church body gather around the counselee to provide love and support.

If your counselee becomes agitated and wants to leave, then your first priority is their safety. In your community, the safest place to take them is the emergency department of your local hospital, where they can be assessed by physicians and psychiatric professionals to see if they need to be kept in the hospital for a few days. This could take the form of a voluntary or perhaps involuntary detention.

Many counselors worry that if they take their counselee to the hospital, they will get stuck in the secular mental health system. In reality, if medical professionals think your counselee is in grave danger of self-harm, they will keep your counselee safe, give them medication for sleep, and give their family and friends a few days to figure out how to help once your counselee has been discharged. There is very little actual "counseling" during these hospitalizations, so you don't need to worry that they will be exposed to lies that will be spiritually harmful. The suicidal person thought their life was horrible, but after spending a couple of days separated from their everyday routines, they may be ready to approach their problems with a better perspective. I always encourage counselors not to consider a hospitalization as a "failure" of biblical counseling. It is a tool you can use to keep your counselee safe while the church rallies to help them.

If you haven't already, you should also find out about other available resources in your community. If there is a mental health system, you and your counseling ministry should ask them to talk to you about how they assess and prevent suicide. Find out if they have a local hotline that you can call for help. They can instruct you if you should take a suicidal counselee to the emergency department yourself or whether you should call 911 and get the police involved. Our counseling ministry was able to do this, and we generated a document to help counselors when this emergency situation occurs. In addition to a safety plan, it contains a large number of Scripture references to give comfort and encouragement to the suicidal sufferer. I have included that document at the end of this chapter, and you may use it or adapt it for your counseling ministry.

Should I Have My Counselee Sign a Suicide Contract?

In the past, a suicide contract was considered a helpful tool to keep a suicidal person safe. This is no longer an acceptable practice even in the secular world, as contracts have not been found to be preventive. Today's secular programs are promoting a "safety plan" instead.

Bringing Biblical Truth, Hope, and Comfort to the Suicidal Sufferer

Your counselee is ready to come home from the hospital, and you have a group of people surrounding your counselee who are aware of the problem. Or your counselee was not hospitalized because you discerned that your counselee's suicidal thoughts did not pose an immediate threat to their life. In either case, now the counseling begins. As biblical counselors, we want to know where suicide is mentioned in the Bible. The topic of suicide is found in five different places:

- Saul falls on his own sword in 1 Samuel 31:3–5.
- Ahithophel hanged himself in 2 Samuel 17:23.
- Zimri set the king's house on fire and died in the fire in 1 Kings 16:18.
- Judas hanged himself in Matthew 27:3–5.
- Abimelech asked his armor-bearer to kill him after a woman crushed his skull with a millstone in Judges 9:54.

The Bible does not use the word *suicide*, and does not call suicide a sin, but it does not paint the men in these examples in a good light either. So the biblical counselor will not be able to take their counselee to a chapter and verse forbidding this choice (other than the sixth commandment, "You shall not murder"). But God's Word is full of truth that will restore hope, so that suicide does not seem like a logical choice for the suffering counselee.

Discerning the Primary Sources of Their Suffering

Dr. Nicholas Ellen likes to break the core issues of suicide into two categories. Category one is "the external pressures of life." When a person is experiencing overwhelming troubles, like losing a job, experiencing health problems, or living with the consequences of someone else's sin, they may not see a way out and become hopeless and then suicidal. Saul, Ahithophel, Zimri, and Abimelech all had shameful things happen to them and chose suicide to escape the potential for suffering or disgrace. Category two is "the internal pains of the heart," where the suicidal person is trying to escape the guilt they feel over unrepentant sin.[2] Judas Iscariot would be an example of this category. There are other "pains of the heart" that might cause someone to consider suicide. We will discuss depression in more detail below.

It will be helpful for you to determine which category your counselee fits into. If they do not have a godly theology of suffering, they will lose hope. Almost every person I see in counseling is suffering in some way. They have tried everything they know to stop the pain, but are now crying out for help.

So after you have spent a good amount of time listening to their story and asking follow-up questions, you will want to spend time showing your counselee all the ways that God sovereignly uses suffering for our good and his glory. I love how Romans 8:29 (ESV) says that God is using all things to conform us "to the image of his Son." James 1:2–4 promises that we can count our suffering all joy, because the end result is that we are "perfect and complete, lacking in nothing" (ESV). Hebrews 12:3–11 promises us that God lovingly disciplines (trains) us so that we get "the peaceful fruit of righteousness" and that we get to "share his holiness."

You will also want to remind counselees that God has compassion for them in their suffering. Isaiah 42:3 says, "A bruised reed he

---

2. Nicholas Ellen, "Understanding and Dealing with Suicide," Association of Certified Biblical Counselors, July 15, 2020, https://biblicalcounseling.com/resource-library/conference-messages/understanding-and-dealing-with-suicide/.

will not break, and a faintly burning wick he will not quench" (ESV). In Luke 22 Jesus is in the garden of Gethsemane, crying out to God in his emotional agony. Because of what Jesus experienced, Hebrews 4:15 says, "we do not have a high priest who is unable to sympathize with our weaknesses, but one who in every respect has been tempted as we are, yet without sin" (ESV). Going through passages such as these will help your counselees know the heart of God for them in the midst of their pain.

When your counselee is suicidal because of "internal pains of the heart," you will need to discern if they are actually believers. If they are unbelievers, they may be suffering the consequences of guilt for their rebellion against God and need to hear the hope of the gospel. They need to understand that each of us has a soul that will live forever, and they need to be certain of where they will spend eternity. The reality is that most suicidal people do not actually want to die; they just believe that death will put an end to their present suffering. If they are not believers, their torment is just beginning if they do not repent and submit their life to Christ before their death. Dr. Stuart Scott encourages us to "warn her, yes, warn her" about the eternality of the decision to commit suicide. If our counselees put their faith in Jesus, their problems will not instantly disappear, but with help they can face them in Christ.

Your counselee may be a believer who has no assurance of their salvation because they have been acting like an unbeliever for so long. They need to be encouraged to repent and humbly draw near to the Lord as described in James 4:8.

Your counselee may be a believer who has become very discouraged by their current suffering and needs to be reminded that our hope is only in Jesus and that he lovingly calls us to take his yoke on us and rest as described in Matthew 11:28–30. Each counselee is an individual, and you will want to take the time to listen to their story so that when you speak God's Word to them you don't sound like one of Job's friends.

Addressing the Role of Depression in Suicidal Ideation

The word *depression* means different things to a secular counselor and a biblical counselor. The DSM-5 is often considered the psychiatrist's "bible." They will check to see if their patient/client has a number of criteria to meet the qualifications for a diagnosis of Major Depressive Disorder. One of those criteria is "Recurrent thoughts of death, recurrent suicidal ideation without a specific plan, or a suicide attempt or a specific plan for committing suicide." When their patient/client is suicidal, they will almost always give them the diagnosis of Major Depressive Disorder.

The Bible does not actually use the word *depression*, but biblical counselors might call depression "disordered sadness," as described by Dr. Charles Hodges in *Good Mood, Bad Mood*.[3] Dr. Ellen's criteria for suicide mentioned above are similar to the first two used by Dr. Wayne Mack in *Out of the Blues*,[4] where he lists three specific causes for depression: refusal to deal with sin and guilt, mishandling a difficult event, and having unbiblical standards.

Depressed people often have a very hard time thinking clearly. They get into mental ruts and have a hard time breaking free. As the counselor, you will need to have a long-term strategy for walking alongside your counselee while you point them to the hope they have in Christ and waiting for the Spirit to work.

Your counselee may have gotten into a serious rut where suicide is their best "hope" for relief from their suffering. Sometimes your counselee will have so much trouble thinking clearly that you and their physician agree that medication can be helpful for a time. If your counselee comes home from the hospital on medication, it might be helpful to continue until your counselee is stabilized. The biblical counseling world has many great resources to help your

---

3. Charles D. Hodges, "Depression or Sadness: Two Ways to Consider the Diagnosis," in *Good Mood, Bad Mood: Help and Hope for Depression and Bipolar Disorder* (Wapwallopen, PA: Shepherd Press, 2012), 61–64.

4. Wayne Mack, "Why Do People Get Depressed?" in *Out of the Blues, Dealing with the Blues of Depression and Loneliness* (Bemidji, MN: Focus Publishing, 2006), 37–57.

counselee start thinking more clearly and to restore their hope in our gracious Lord Jesus. See a list at the end of this chapter for some of my favorites.

Counseling the Suffering Survivor

When you are called to visit the survivors of a recent suicide, you will need to consider a few principles in preparation. First of all, it is helpful to remember that this is an amazing privilege. This is an opportunity to obey Christ's command in Galatians 6:2 to "bear one another's burdens, and so fulfill the law of Christ" (ESV). In the following paragraphs, I will refer to those who are still alive as the "survivors." I will refer to the one who committed suicide as the "victim," but this is not to imply that they were innocent in the process because they do bear responsibility for their sinful choice.

Preparing for the First Conversation

Have you ever been at the scene of a medical emergency? Someone is on the ground, and everyone is scurrying about. All I have to do is say, "I am a doctor!" and the crowd parts and makes a way for me to the patient. They believe I have something to offer, and I am welcomed into the fray.

Have you ever been at a crime scene? I hope not, but in all the movies it is dark and there are flashing lights, sirens, reporters, crowds, and some burly police officers guarding the scene behind the bright yellow tape. Our hero steps forward, the police glare at her, but then she pulls out her wallet and shows her badge. The police part like the Red Sea, and she walks in, ready to contribute!

What about you? You have been called to comfort the survivors of a suicide and everyone is wondering why you are here. Dr. Kevin Carson says Romans 15:14 is your badge![5] Paul says to the Roman

---

5. Kevin Carson, "Care After a Suicide," Association of Certified Biblical Counselors, 2019 Annual Conference, Plenary Session 4, Southlake, Texas, November 12, 2019, https://biblicalcounseling.com/product/2019-annual-conference-suicide-self-harm-and-scripture/.

believers, "I myself am satisfied about you, my brothers, that you yourselves are full of goodness, filled with all knowledge and able to instruct one another" (ESV). He is talking to fellow believers, which is why he calls them "brothers." He says they are full of goodness. This is the kind of goodness that is a fruit of the Spirit. These are believers that are mature, godly, and have the fruits of the Spirit. The fact that someone called you to be there means you are already a mature believer that is bearing fruit. What kind of knowledge are you full of? You are full of truths about our Lord, and you are ready to admonish or instruct others. The word *instruct* here is from the Greek word *noutheteo*, the very word that started the biblical counseling movement fifty years ago!

Jesus shows us how to comfort those that are grieving by the way he treated Mary and Martha after Lazarus died. He listened patiently, let them ask him hard questions, and even wept with them because he truly felt their grief. Job's friends came and sat with him for seven days while he grieved, and they were a comfort to him until they opened their mouths and started speaking. When you open your mouth, you will want to ask good questions (Proverbs 18:13). You may not even know the person who died, so a good place to start is to ask the survivors what they remember about the victim. As you ask questions, you will likely find out if the victim was a believer and what their faith was like. You will hear all sorts of statements, receive all kinds of questions, and witness a wide spectrum of emotions as you sit and listen. Keep listening, and pray that God will give you wisdom when it is time to speak.

Responding to a Survivor's Hard Questions

We biblical counselors think a lot about what it means to "speak the truth in love." The reality is that often hearing the truth can be painful, and our motives always need to be that a person is restored to God and restored in their relationships with others. The problem with suicide is that the survivor does not get the opportunity to be restored with the victim. People that commit suicide were listening to lies and not focusing on the truth. We are reminded in 2 Corinthians 11:3 that the devil tries to lead us "astray from a sincere and pure devotion to Christ" (ESV). In John 8:44 Jesus called the devil "a murderer . . . and the father of lies" (ESV). Anyone who contemplates suicide is believing the lie that death will end their pain. The one who commits suicide actually ends up playing right into the devil's schemes. Those that survive the suicide of a loved one are also susceptible to a long list of lies that may discourage them and cause them to despair. Julie Gossack has written a wonderful book where she describes five suicides in her own family and all the lies that attacked her. I highly recommend this resource, which is listed below.

Is suicide a sin?

Suicide is a sin because only God decides when a person is born and when they die. People in pain often make choices that they think will relieve their pain but are disobedient to God's instructions for how we are to live. As you will see, it is important to understand suicide as a sin because God's Word has so much to say about how we should respond to the one who has sinned against us. A person who commits suicide disobeys God's command "You shall not kill." When someone decides to take their life, they are not trusting God with their situation but instead choosing to take matters into their own hands. You may get an opportunity to show the survivors that suicide is always a wrong choice. You can also comfort them by reminding them that God always forgives our sins when we repent, and yet he often lets us live with the consequences of our sins. God can forgive even the sin of a self-murder, and if the victim was truly a believer, we can be comforted that his spirit is with the Lord.

In a similar vein, survivors might wonder if the sin of suicide is unforgivable and whether they will ever see the victim again or whether they have gone to hell. Although some believers may think that suicide is an unforgivable sin, there is no Scripture reference to support that teaching. Jesus teaches in three of his Gospels that the only unforgivable sin is blasphemy of the Holy Spirit. Several New

Testament passages teach that all of a believer's sins are forgiven (Romans 8:1, 38–39; Philippians 1:6). If it seems the suicide victim was a believer, you can comfort the suffering survivor that their loved one is now with the Lord, is forgiven, feels no pain, and is in their right mind and at peace.

This is also a great opportunity to try to discern if the survivor has trusting faith in Jesus. If the suicide victim was not saved and went to hell, that is tragic for all eternity. These funeral services are usually the saddest of all if the survivors do not have the comfort of knowing they will see their loved one again. If the survivors do not take the opportunity to trust Christ, that is even more tragic (Ezekiel 18:4; Matthew 7:23; John 15:6). Just as in every counseling situation you will want to determine whether your counselee is saved and has the indwelling Holy Spirit, the same is true here. You want to and need to give hope, and the hope of the gospel is what we have to offer the suffering survivor. In your desire to encourage and give comfort, you will be tempted to make statements about whether someone was a believer or not. But keep in mind that it is not up to you to judge anyone's salvation or their relationship to the Lord. The Bible teaches us that we only have one Judge—God himself. He is the one that will discern hearts, not us (James 4:12), and the character of God is our ultimate comfort.

Is it okay for me to be angry?

Your counselee may be feeling anger toward the one who committed suicide, and that is not necessarily a wrong feeling. The victim acted selfishly and sinfully, which hurt those left behind. Because the victim has inflicted pain on the survivor, the survivor may be tempted to respond sinfully. The emotion of anger itself is not a sin; even our Holy God gets angry. The problem is that we humans often start with anger and then go on to respond sinfully. Hopefully you will get an opportunity to walk alongside the survivor and encourage them not to do that. "Be angry and do not sin . . ." (Ephesians 4:26 ESV).

Will I ever be able to forgive them?

Bitterness is something that happens to our hearts when we choose not to forgive someone that has wronged us. Your counselee may need to be warned not to allow their heart to become bitter toward the suicide victim. In essence, each survivor has been sinned against by the victim, and each survivor needs to come to a place where they can forgive the victim. Of course, this cannot happen face-to-face like in a normal reconciliation, but it is possible to have a heart of forgiveness toward the offender as described in Matthew 18:21–35. When I truly understand all that Jesus has forgiven me of, my only response can be to forgive those who have hurt me.

Is it my fault they died?

Guilt is an appropriate emotion to feel when we have sinned. A survivor may be racked with guilt, wondering if there was something that they could have done to "save" their loved one. *Guilt* is a word that should be attached to a sin or an offense. A person might *feel* guilty, but what they are experiencing is false guilt. In the case of suicide, what they are actually feeling is regret. No matter how guilty your counselee may feel, God shows throughout the Bible that each person is responsible for their own sin (Ezekiel 18:20; Romans 14:12). You may need to repeatedly remind the survivors that they may have regret and wonder if there was something else they could have done to prevent the suicide, but God does not hold them responsible. You will likely get an opportunity to explore the "what ifs" that are running through their minds. They may have even committed sins against the victim before the suicide, but those offenses did not *make* the victim commit suicide.

Should I just kill myself too?

Statistics show that often when one person commits suicide, others around them will choose suicide to end their suffering. We see this among families and even in schools. Your counselee may believe the lie that they are doomed to make the same mistake that their loved one made, especially if the person who committed suicide was a parent. That is absolutely not true. Suicide in families is not an inherited genetic trait on a certain chromosome. It is a personal sinful choice. The survivor has the freedom to renounce the lies that may make them feel doomed to repeat the cycle.

Where is God in all of this?

Whenever you are in the counseling room, you will encounter suffering, and you will need a strong theology of suffering to help encourage your counselee. The survivor may be struggling with some of the following lies:

This is more than I can take!

God didn't have anything to do with this awful situation!

God was wrong to let my loved one die!

My loved one's suicide has ruined my life![6]

God's Word has answers to all of these lies, and you will need to help your counselee learn to put off those lies, renew their mind, and put on the truths that will give hope and comfort. This will not happen with one visit; it may take months or years for the suffering survivor to be at peace with God. For an encouraging list of passages to give comfort, see "Stabilizing Truths for Noisy Souls" by Jim Berg.[7]

A Final Word about Biblical Hope

If your counselees, whether they are suicidal or survivors, have not put their faith in Jesus and submitted their lives to him, there is no ultimate hope for them. But as long as there is life, there is hope! Your primary goal is to make sure they see the truth of the gospel because knowing Jesus as their Savior and Friend will give them hope for the future. As you come alongside your counselees in their overwhelming grief, the only thing you have to offer is our Lord Jesus Christ. And he

---

6. Julie Gossack, "A Smorgasbord of Lies and the Truth of God's Word," in *Hope Beyond Despair: Finding Truth After a Loved One's Suicide* (Bemidji, MN: Focus Publishing, 2017), 22–37.

7. Jim Berg, "Stabilizing Truths for Noisy Souls: The Knowledge of God," in *Taking Time to Quiet Your Soul* (Greenville, SC: BJU Press, 2005), 4–5.

is more than enough. For believers, promises like 2 Corinthians 1:3–4, James 1:2–4, and Romans 8:28–29 can be immensely comforting.

Dr. Paul Tautges says about Isaiah 43:2, "Comfort from God does not only come to us after our trial has come to an end, or after we have accepted that it may never end (in this life), but rather, the comfort of God's presence is with us during our times of grief and loss. The realization of God's presence is not determined by our emotions, but by embracing scriptural promises by faith, promises like the one quoted above."[8] Encourage your counselee not to wait until he "feels" like God is with him. He needs to focus on God's promises to realize that God is with him in the middle of his suffering.

Suicide is the natural conclusion to despair. God is the supernatural source of hope that removes despair and makes all things new!

---

8. Paul Tautges, *A Small Book for the Hurting Heart: Meditations on Loss, Grief, and Healing* (Greensboro, NC: New Growth Press, 2020), 151.

Suicide Prevention and Protocol

(Adapted from Faith Biblical Counseling Center, Faith Bible Church, Spokane, WA)

Questions to Ask if You Suspect Suicidal Tendencies

A common belief is that asking questions may encourage people to act or put ideas in their minds. The research does not support this notion, and the risk of NOT asking these questions is too great. *You must have the courage to ask these questions* directly and compassionately and then be willing to respond accordingly (please know that any "yes" answer will initiate the "Next Steps" below). It is always better to err on the side of caution and contact others or refer them to someone for professional and/or medical intervention. That is *NOT* a counseling failure; it is often a necessary and responsible decision.

Here are a series of questions to ask to screen someone for suicidal tendencies.[9]

I want to care for you well and make sure you're okay. Can I ask you some direct questions?

1. In the past few weeks, have you wished you were dead?
2. In the past few weeks, have you felt that you or your family would be better off if you were dead?
3. In the past week, have you been having thoughts about killing yourself?
4. Have you ever tried to kill yourself?

If yes, how? _____

_____

When? _____

_____

If the individual answers YES to any of the above, ask the following question:

---

9. Adapted from the ASQ Suicide Risk Screening Toolkit, from the National Institute of Mental Health (NIMH), https://www.nimh.nih.gov/research/research-conducted-at-nimh/asq-toolkit-materials. If you do eventually call a local or national hotline, you can indicate you used the questions from this tool.

5. Are you having thoughts of killing yourself right now?

O Yes   O No

If yes, how/where would you do it? _____

_____

Do you have the (drugs, gun, rope, car, bridge, etc.) that you would use? _____

Where is it right now? _____

_____

NEXT STEPS:

- If counselee answers "No" to all questions 1 through 4, screening is complete (not necessary to ask question #5). No intervention is necessary (*Note: clinical judgment can always override a negative screen*).
- If patient answers "Yes" to any of questions 1 through 4, or refuses to answer, they are considered a positive screen. Ask question #5 to assess how clear and definite their suicide ideation might be.
  - "Yes" to question #5 = acute positive screen (*imminent risk* identified)
    - Counselee requires a full mental health evaluation.
    - Counselee cannot leave until evaluated for safety.
    - *Keep counselee in sight.* Remove dangerous objects from the room. Call doctor, clinician, hotline, or 911.
  - "No" to question #5 = non-acute positive screen (*potential risk* identified)
    - Counselee requires a brief suicide safety assessment to determine whether a full mental health evaluation is needed. Patient cannot leave until evaluated for safety.
    - Call doctor, clinician, hotline, or 911.

Protocol for Caring for Someone with Suicidal Tendencies

If the counselee is found to have suicidal tendencies based on the assessment on page 1, you MUST call the suicide hotline immediately. *Affirm your love and care for them, your desire to help, and your appreciation for their transparency. Seek to persuade them to engage in the process, but do not seek to restrain or detain them. Call 911 if they refuse to stay.*

1. (Insert your local number here) (24/7 Regional Crisis Line), or 911, National hotline 1-800-273-8255

   Call one of the above hotlines in the session, ask to speak with a mental health professional, put the phone on speaker, and *have the crisis hotline screener ask the questions and make the assessment.*

   _____   _____   _____
   Name of Screener   Date   Time

   The crisis screener will give you direction as to your next steps. Stay with the counselee if at all possible. Record the instructions given to you by the crisis screener.

   _____

   _____

   _____

   Collaborate with the crisis screener to develop a safety plan. The steps you will be directed to take will likely include, but not be limited to, elements of the following:

2. If the crisis screener doesn't recommend a hospital evaluation (calling 911 or transporting to the ER in your city) make sure that they are passed personally to someone so that they will not be left alone. Ask them, "Who is the person you trust the most?" Have them contact this family/friend/etc. in your presence (if they won't, then do it yourself). If you do transport someone yourself, it is best not to do so alone.

3. Call a pastor/elder of counseling (or any other church leader you can reach), and strategize whether it is possible to structure care and secure the counselee's commitment to be transparent and involved relationally in the life of the church (fellowship, accountability, care, etc.).

4. Attempt to make whatever arrangements are necessary to remove the things they have considered using to harm

themselves (i.e., remove guns, ropes, drugs, vehicles [keys], etc., from wherever they will be staying). Also have access removed to things that may increase risk (alcohol, drugs, etc.).

Tell them what you're doing, and why: *"It is best for us to remove things that you might use to hurt yourself as soon as you can. If we do this, it will be harder to harm yourself if you find yourself under stress or having thoughts of killing yourself."*

Scripture to Give Hope to the Suicidal

Valuing Man/Life Because Everyone Is an Image-Bearer

The grounds for forbidding murder and punishing the murderer is that it is a crime against the image of God—it is equivalent to destroying God's image, not just your own!

Genesis 9:6: "Whoever sheds the blood of man, by man shall his blood be shed, for God made man in his own image" (ESV).

Exodus 20:13: "You shall not murder."

God's desire to not have his image denigrated is so strong that he says it is the basis for forbidding us from even *wishing* evil on others.

James 3:8–9: "But no human being can tame the tongue. It is a restless evil, full of deadly poison. With it we bless our Lord and Father, and with it we curse people who are made in the likeness of God" (ESV).

The Desire and Design of Death Is of the Devil

John 10:10: "The thief comes only to steal and kill and destroy. I came that they may have life and have it abundantly" (ESV).

2 Corinthians 10:5: "We destroy arguments and every lofty opinion raised against the knowledge of God, and take every thought captive to obey Christ" (ESV).

1 Peter 5:8: "Be sober-minded; be watchful. Your adversary the devil prowls around like a roaring lion, seeking someone to devour" (ESV).

God Desires the Preservation of Your Life and Your Loyal Service

Psalm 33:18–19: "Behold, the eye of the LORD is on those who fear him, on those who hope in his steadfast love, that he may deliver their soul from death and keep them alive in famine" (ESV).

2 Thessalonians 2:16–17: "Now may our Lord Jesus Christ himself, and God our Father, who loved us and gave us eternal comfort and good hope through grace, comfort your hearts and establish them in every good work and word" (ESV).

God Is Seeking to *Do* Something Through Your Affliction

Romans 5:1–5: "Therefore, since we have been justified by faith, we have peace with God through our Lord Jesus Christ. Through him we have also obtained access by faith into this grace in which we stand, and we rejoice in hope of the glory of God. Not only that, but we rejoice in our sufferings, knowing that suffering produces endurance, and endurance produces character, and character produces hope, and hope does not put us to shame, because God's love has been poured into our hearts through the Holy Spirit who has been given to us" (ESV).

2 Corinthians 1:3–4: "Blessed be the God and Father of our Lord Jesus Christ, the Father of mercies and God of all comfort, who comforts us in all our affliction, so that we may be able to comfort those who are in any affliction, with the comfort with which we ourselves are comforted by God" (ESV).

Hebrews 12:11: "For the moment all discipline seems painful rather than pleasant, but later it yields the peaceful fruit of righteousness to those who have been trained by it" (ESV).

1 Peter 5:6–8, 10: "Humble yourselves, therefore, under the mighty hand of God so that at the proper time he may exalt you, casting all your anxieties on him, because he cares for you. Be sober-minded; be watchful. Your adversary the devil prowls around like a roaring lion, seeking someone to devour. . . . And after you have suffered a little while, the God of all grace, who has called you to his eternal glory in Christ, will himself restore, confirm, strengthen, and establish you" (ESV).

God Longs to Hear You and Be Your Ultimate Source of Hope and Peace

Psalm 34:17–19: "When the righteous cry for help, the LORD hears and delivers them out of all their troubles. The LORD is near to the brokenhearted and saves the crushed in spirit. Many are the afflictions of the righteous, but the Lᴏʀᴅ delivers him out of them all" (ESV).

Psalm 55:22: "Cast your burden on the Lᴏʀᴅ, and he will sustain you; he will never permit the righteous to be moved" (ESV).

Psalm 62:5: "Yes, my soul, find rest in God; my hope comes from him" (NIV).

Psalm 71:5: "For you have been my hope, Sovereign Lᴏʀᴅ, my confidence since my youth!" (NIV).

Isaiah 26:3–4: "You keep him in perfect peace whose mind is stayed on you, because he trusts in you. Trust in the Lᴏʀᴅ forever, for the Lᴏʀᴅ Gᴏᴅ is an everlasting roc" (ESV).

Philippians 4:6–7: "Be anxious for nothing, but in everything by prayer and supplication with thanksgiving let your requests be made known to God. And the peace of God, which surpasses all comprehension, will guard your hearts and your minds in Christ Jesus."

Additional Resources

Berg, Jim. "Session 2—Stabilizing Truths for Noisy Souls: The Knowledge of God." Essay in *Taking Time to Quiet Your Soul*. Greenville, SC: BJU Press, 2005, 4–5.

Carson, Kevin. "Care After a Suicide," Association of Certified Biblical Counselors, 2019 Annual Conference, Plenary Session 4, Southlake, Texas, November 12, 2019, https://biblicalcounseling.com/product/2019-annual-conference-suicide-self-harm-and-scripture/.

Ellen, Nicholas. "Understanding and Dealing with Suicide," Association of Certified Biblical Counselors, July 15, 2020, https://biblicalcounseling.com/resource-library/conference-messages/understanding-and-dealing-with-suicide/.

Gossack, Julie. "Chapter 3: A Smorgasbord of Lies and the Truth of God's Word." Essay in *Hope Beyond Despair: Finding Truth After a Loved One's Suicide*. Bemidji, MN: Focus Publishing, 2017, 22–37.

Hodges, Charles D. "Chapter 5: Depression or Sadness: Two Ways to Consider the Diagnosis." Essay in *Good Mood, Bad Mood: Help and Hope for Depression and Bipolar Disorder*. Wapwallopen, PA: Shepherd Press, 2012, 61–64.

Mack, Wayne. "Chapter 3: Why Do People Get Depressed?" Essay in *Out of the Blues, Dealing with the Blues of Depression and Loneliness*. Bemidji, MN: Focus Publishing, 2006, 37–57.

Powlison, David. *Grieving a Suicide: Help for the Aftershock*. Greensboro, NC: New Growth Press, 2010.

Powlison, David. *I Just Want to Die: Replacing Suicidal Thoughts with Hope*. Greensboro, NC: New Growth Press, 2010.

Schreiber, Jennifer, and Larry Culpepper. "Suicidal Ideation and Behavior in Adults." UpToDate. Wolters Kluwer Health, February 2021.

Scott, Stuart. "Handling Suicidal Threats," Association of Certified Biblical Counselors, 2019 Annual Conference, Breakout Session 1, Southlake, Texas, November 12, 2019, https://biblicalcounseling.com/product/2019-annual-conference-suicide-self-harm-and-scripture/.

Welch, Edward T. *Depression: Looking Up from the Stubborn Darkness*. Greensboro, NC: New Growth Press, 2012.

CHAPTER 19

Marijuana and CBD:

Navigating the Medical, Legal, and Spiritual Issues Involved

Daniel Dionne, MD

You may have noticed in the last few years that there are more and more billboards advertising marijuana. While standing in the checkout line at your local pharmacy, you may see products that contain cannabidiol (CBD) being displayed. If my pharmacist is selling it, could it be dangerous? If it is no longer illegal in my state, can it be wrong to use it?

If my counselee is using these chemicals, what should I say and do in our counseling sessions? In this chapter, we will start with a few case histories. Then we will cover the medical facts about marijuana and CBD, followed by the legal issues, and finally the heart issues for your counselee.

Four Stories

Mark is a fifty-five-year-old Christian man who has worked in the medical field and is married to a nurse. They are both believers, and they have three children. He is my patient and I see him about once a year. About five years ago, he had sudden onset of burning pain all over his body from his chest down to his feet. It was agonizing and unrelenting, and the specialists diagnosed him with transverse myelitis. There has been no cure and no improvement in his misery. His neurologist has tried everything to give him some relief, but he had to go on permanent disability because he could no longer do his job or sleep at night. He confessed to me that he was smoking marijuana during the day and every night in order to get a little sleep. One of their children got into trouble with prescription pain meds years ago, so they have some nightmare-like memories about opioids. His neurologist offered to prescribe opioids for him, but his wife is terrified for them to have those drugs in their home. We live in a state where marijuana is legal for recreational and medical purposes, but he feels guilty and conflicted about whether using marijuana is right for him as a believer.

Zach is a fifteen-year-old boy who goes to my church, and his parents have taken him to his youth leader, horrified that he is smoking marijuana every day. He has started skipping classes at school, is flunking out of his advanced placement classes, and is hanging out with other young people that are not heading down a good path. He has started stealing from his parents to pay for his marijuana, and he does not seem to feel guilty about his behavior. He argues that marijuana is legal and that everyone else is doing it. He says his parents put way too much pressure on him and they need to lighten up. He argues that God created marijuana on the third day of creation, and didn't he say that everything he created was "good"? His parents are with him in the church counseling office, and they are desperate for me to help them and to rescue their son.

Evan is a twenty-nine-year-old lawyer who is married and has one child. He and his wife met in college and started attending church after their baby was born. He has smoked marijuana twice weekly on the weekends since his college days. He has a good job, has no criminal record, and he can buy good quality marijuana down the street at one of the legal marijuana shops. His wife, Amber, worries that smoking marijuana is a sin and wants him to meet with me for biblical counseling regarding his marijuana use. He says he only needs a few "hits" to get high, and how can this be any worse than drinking alcohol? He has lots of Christian friends who use alcohol, which seems to be acceptable in some Christian circles.

Sally is a seventy-year-old lady who comes for her yearly Medicare wellness visit. As we review her medication list, I learn that she is using topical CBD oil on her hands. She has arthritis in her finger joints, and ibuprofen just does not seem to help. She explains, "My kids bought this for me and insisted that I try it." I asked if it helps, and she replied, "I think so. What do you think about CBD, doctor?"

Botany and Biochemistry

Cannabis is a genus of plants that includes three varieties: sativa, indica, and ruderalis. The scientific name for marijuana is *Cannabis sativa*. "Marijuana" refers to all the parts of the sativa variety, the leaves, stalks, seeds, resins, etc. The main ingredient is THC (delta 9-tetrahydrocannabinol). Today's marijuana has been engineered to have higher concentrations of THC, between 5 and 20 percent. The second most common ingredient is CBD (cannabidiol), and its concentration can be variable. Marijuana grows like a shrub and needs to be in a hothouse. Hemp is also known as "Industrial Hemp," and is a different variety of Cannabis sativa. It was outlawed in the US in the 1930s, but is now legal again in several states. It has been grown for thousands of years and can be used for rope, textiles, and many other functions. Hemp contains minimal amounts of THC, 0.3 percent, and higher concentrations of CBD. Hemp grows outdoors in fields and can reach twenty feet in height.

Because hemp is in the same family as marijuana, it has been considered a controlled substance and has been an unacceptable agricultural crop in the US. The Hemp Farming Act of 2018, which was part of the 2018 Farm Bill was signed by former President Trump on December 20, 2018, changed hemp from a controlled substance to an agricultural commodity, making it easier for farmers to get loans to grow hemp and allowing them to get federal crop insurance.

Now that marijuana has become legal in many states, it can be purchased in very potent forms to be smoked or concentrated oils/tinctures to consume orally. It can also be ingested as edibles in the forms of brownies, gummies, lollipops, and drinks. CBD, which can be produced from either marijuana or hemp (but is primarily made from hemp in the US), has also become immensely popular.

Medical Properties

Although previously thought to be mostly just a hallucinogen, in the 1970s physicians discovered that marijuana seemed to relieve some of the pain and nausca associated with chemotherapy given to cancer patients. This led to the production of a tablet called Marinol that contained man-made THC, the active ingredient in marijuana. This was the beginning of the thinking that marijuana could be used for medicinal purposes. More recently, CBD has been thought to be helpful for pain relief and as a sleep aid. There is some research that shows it can be helpful for patients with multiple sclerosis, while a pure CBD product called Epidiolex is used for treating a rare type of seizure disorder seen in a small number of children.

These days, people are advertising it for almost every possible problem. Manufacturers put it in cosmetics and encourage you to give it to your pets to calm them down. There is even less science about how to safely prescribe CBD to patients. People assume the CBD they are buying is pure, but there is usually a little THC in it. In a worst-case scenario, a person using CBD does a urine drug screen for work that turns up positive for THC; the employer assumes they are using marijuana, and they get fired!

Are There Safe Dosages?

Because hemp and marijuana have been illegal for many years, very little pharmaceutical research has been done to determine what dose of THC or CBD can be helpful and for what conditions. If people check the internet to learn more about the benefits of marijuana, they will find a myriad of websites and venders raving about their product. All of their claims are what scientists call anecdotal. A person might claim that rubbing CBD on his hands took away his arthritis pain, but there is no scientific evidence that can tell us that CBD oil in a certain dose will help a certain percentage of patients that suffer with arthritis. For example, 400 mg of ibuprofen two or three times a day can help for arthritis pain, but more than 2400 mg per day seriously increases the risk of kidney and liver damage. Doctors know this research and are comfortable giving advice about the pros and cons of using ibuprofen. Patients want to know what their doctors think about marijuana and CBD, and doctors want clinical studies to back up their opinions. In order to get good research, usually a pharmaceutical company needs to spend millions of dollars to see if their new drug is beneficial and safe for patients. Because the marijuana and CBD industry has exploded and so many people are willing to buy it without good science, I am not sure that any of that research will ever be done.

Are the Medical Effects Dangerous?

Is marijuana dangerous? Yes, it can be. The number of people going to emergency rooms yearly because of marijuana is escalating. Marijuana intoxication causes many motor vehicle accidents, and it is very difficult to prove that a person is intoxicated because the blood levels drop so rapidly. Marijuana can cause hallucinations, delirium, collapsed lungs, and acute heart attacks in young people. Children are also accidentally ingesting marijuana products that are sold as gummies, brownies, and soft drinks.

I frequently tell my friends and patients, "Marijuana makes you stupid," based on studies that show decreased cognitive function in those that use it regularly. As a medical professional, I never advise my patients to use it, but I find that my patients begin using it without consulting me. I say, "Just because it is legal, does not make it good for you." I cannot be exhaustive about all the negative effects of marijuana in this chapter, but I will try to hit the highlights.

Adolescents face particular dangers when they use marijuana. They have an increased risk of developing schizophrenia when they get older.[1] When adolescents use marijuana, they have decreases in learning, memory, and attention, but it seems to eventually return to normal days to weeks after cessation. At this time there is evidence that use of marijuana leads to decreased academic function, unemployment, decreased income, and impaired social functioning.[2] Teens that use marijuana are more likely to spend time with peers that are not doing well academically and are skipping school and getting into trouble.[3] In addition, twenty-one is the legal age for marijuana use in all states where it is legal, so underage users are committing a crime.

Impaired Functioning

Research suggests that two to three "hits" of marijuana (two to three mg of THC) is enough to cause a person to become impaired, which is the equivalent of drunkenness.[4] When five to twenty mg of THC is ingested, it will impair attention, concentration, short-term memory, and executive functioning. Higher levels can cause nausea, panic attacks, and psychosis. Because THC takes so long to clear out of the body, the impairment caused by marijuana may last for days to weeks. A systematic review of neuroimaging studies of adult cannabis users showed reduced volume of an area of the brain called the

1. Susan H. Gage, Matthew Hickman, and Stanley Zammit, "Association Between Cannabis and Psychosis: Epidemiologic Evidence," *Biological Psychiatry* 79, no. 7 (2016): 549–556, https://doi.org/10.1016/j.biopsych.2015.08.001.

2. National Academies of Sciences, Engineering, and Medicine, "Health Effects of Cannabis and Cannabinoids: The Current State of Evidence and Recommendations" (Washington, DC: National Academies Press, 2017), Chapter 11.

3. Center for Behavioral Health Statistics and Quality, "Results From the 2016 National Survey on Drug Use and Health: Detailed Tables" (Rockville, MD: Substance Abuse and Mental Health Services Administration, 2017), Table 1.34B, https://www.samhsa.gov/data/sites/default/files/NSDUH-DetTabs-2016/NSDUH-DetTabs-2016.pdf.

4. George Sam Wang, "Cannabis (Marijuana): Acute Intoxication," UpToDate, last updated November 30, 2021, https://www.uptodate.com/contents/cannabis-marijuana-acute-intoxication/print.

hippocampus. Functional MRI studies showed decreased neuronal activity in certain parts of the brain as well.[5]

Cannabis Use Disorder

When someone is using marijuana daily, it might affect multiple areas of their life to the point where they could be diagnosed with cannabis use disorder. When you interview your counselee about their marijuana use, look to see how many of the following criteria they meet from the fifth edition of the *Diagnostic and Statistical Manual of Mental Disorders* (DSM-5):

1. Cannabis is often taken in larger amounts or over a longer period than was intended.
2. There is a persistent desire or unsuccessful efforts to cut down or control cannabis use.
3. A great deal of time is spent in activities necessary to obtain cannabis, use cannabis, or recover from its effects.
4. Craving, or a strong desire or urge to use cannabis.
5. Recurrent cannabis use resulting in a failure to fulfill major role obligations at work, school, or home.
6. Continued cannabis use despite having persistent or recurrent social or interpersonal problems caused or exacerbated by the effects of cannabis.
7. Important social, occupational, or recreational activities are given up or reduced because of cannabis use.
8. Recurrent cannabis use in situations in which it is physically hazardous.
9. Cannabis use is continued despite knowledge of having a persistent or recurrent physical or psychological problem that is likely to have been caused or exacerbated by cannabis.
10. Tolerance, as defined by either of the following:

---

5. D. A. Nader and Z. M. Sanchez, "Effects of Regular Cannabis Use on Neurocognition, Brain Structure, and Function: A Systematic Review of Findings in Adults," *Am J. Drug Alcohol Abuse* 44, no. 1 (2018): 4–18.

      a. A need for markedly increased amounts of cannabis to achieve intoxication or desired effect.

      b. Markedly diminished effect with continued use of the same amount of cannabis.

  11. Withdrawal, as manifested by either of the following:

      a. The characteristic withdrawal syndrome for cannabis.

      b. Cannabis (or a closely related substance) is taken to relieve or avoid withdrawal symptoms.[6]

How to specify current severity:

Mild: two to three symptoms

Moderate: four to five symptoms

Severe: six or more symptoms

Quitting

Many daily marijuana users will experience some withdrawal symptoms if they decide to quit. "Cannabis withdrawal is manifested by a constellation of signs and symptoms occurring within one week after abrupt reduction or cessation of heavy and prolonged cannabis use, including irritability, anger, anxiety, depression, and disturbed sleep."[7] Fortunately, people do not die from marijuana withdrawal and do not need to be hospitalized. They do not need medications to help withdrawal symptoms, but they will need lots of support in that first week when they are sleepless and irritable.

Legal Issues

Cannabis is the third most commonly used psychoactive substance on the planet, behind alcohol and tobacco. It is used by an estimated

---

6. David A. Gorelick, "Cannabis Use Disorder in Adults," UpToDate, Table 1, last updated December 16, 2021, https://www.uptodate.com/contents/cannabis-use-disorder-in-adults.

7. Udo Bonnet and Ulrich W. Preuss, "The Cannabis Withdrawal Syndrome: Current Insights," *Substance Abuse Rehabilitation* 8 (2017): 9–37, https://doi.org/10.2147/SAR.S109576.

two hundred million individuals worldwide.[8] The marijuana industry was able to get a foothold in America by first convincing people that it could be used for medicinal purposes. After marijuana became medically legal, it was not long before it was accepted for recreational purposes. Every election year in the US, more states legalize marijuana for a number of reasons. Some states argue that decriminalizing it will help cut costs to the criminal justice system. Other states are making it available for medical purposes, while some are making it legal for recreational purposes to access some of the revenue it generates. At the federal level, the United States still classifies marijuana as a "Schedule 1 Drug," putting it in the same category as heroin, LSD, and ecstasy, meaning that "it has a high potential for abuse, no currently accepted medical use in treatment in the United States, and a lack of accepted safety for use under medical supervision."[9] It is hard to say when the federal government will legalize marijuana. At the time of this writing it is possible to use marijuana in a state where it is legal, but to be breaking the law at the federal level.

The US Drug Enforcement Administration considers CBD extracted from hemp to be legal as long as there is a concentration lower than 0.3 percent THC in the hemp. If CBD comes from marijuana, it is still considered illegal. Each state has different rules for how much marijuana is considered illegal. Less than one ounce for personal use is legal in many states. If someone possesses more with the intent to sell it, the penalty can be fines of $10,000 to $15,000 and prison time of between one and ten years. There are no states where marijuana possession below age 21 is permissible.

If a marijuana user causes an automobile accident, it can be very hard to prove they were intoxicated. A urine tox screen may be positive for up to a month after marijuana is used, but the blood level drops quickly after just an hour. A blood level that is admissible in

---

8. United Nations Office on Drugs and Crime, "World Drug Report 2021."

9. "Department of Justice/Drug Enforcement Administration Drug Fact Sheet: Marijuana/Cannabis," United States Drug Enforcement Administration (2020): 3, https://www.dea.gov/sites/default/files/2020-06/Marijuana-Cannabis-2020.pdf.

court can be difficult to obtain, unless the police can get the driver to a hospital quickly enough to draw a blood sample while it is still elevated.[10]

What about the Heart?

Hopefully these first few pages help you understand the scientific, medical, and legal issues associated with marijuana and CBD. But now you are sitting across the table from a person or a family that has a real-life situation that seems to justify the use of these substances. So let's go back to our four stories and see if they can help us explore different types of heart issues. Then let's find out what the Bible has to say to guide you and your counselee in their situation.

Physical Suffering

Mark has true and significant physical suffering. He appears to really have genuine faith in the Lord Jesus, and he is trying to be a godly man and a godly husband. He can no longer work so they must rely on his wife's job for the income they need to supplement his disability checks. He feels guilt and shame that he is smoking marijuana to get relief from his pain, but it does seem to help. He does not appear to have any other viable options. If he takes prescription pain medicine from his neurologist, he will develop a tolerance to it and may require higher and higher doses to control his pain. He does not want to trouble his wife with opiates after what they went through with their child. His neurologist has tried everything else. While important to address Mark's concern about whether his marijuana use is a sin, we need to begin by discussing God's view of our physical suffering.

10. Marijuana-Impaired Driving A Report to Congress, NHTSA, July 2017, https://www.nhtsa.gov/sites/nhtsa.dot.gov/files/documents/812440-marijuanaimpaired-driving-report-to-congress.pdf.

Theology of Suffering

There are several different types of suffering. It can be emotional, relational, spiritual, or physical, and rarely is there just one dimension in someone's life. What starts out as a physical injury to a neuron, which sends an attention-getting message to the brain, can quickly affect the person's emotions and cause them to cry out in spiritual pain and wonder, *Where is God in this situation?*

We want to have a biblical view of all kinds of suffering so we know how God views our suffering. First, the Bible shows us that all medical illnesses are a result of the fall (Genesis 3:15–19). God's Word is filled with examples of people that God allowed to suffer. The apostle Paul had some type of affliction that may have been a medical problem, and he begged the Lord to remove it from him. God's reply in 2 Corinthians 12:9 was, "My grace is sufficient for you, for my power is made perfect in weakness" (ESV). God has a wonderful way of using physical suffering to cause us to draw near to him. When we are in the middle of physical suffering, suddenly we are not distracted by the peripheral issues in our lives, and we are able to keep our eyes focused on him. When we suffer, God promises that he will not waste it, and that he will comfort us in all our afflictions. Psalm 119:67 (NIV) says, "Before I was afflicted I went astray, but now I obey your word." And verse 71 says, "It was good for me to be afflicted so that I might learn your decrees" (NIV). He also promises that he will use us to comfort others in the future (2 Corinthians 1:4–8). When we take our suffering to Jesus, he can mercifully empathize with us and comfort us in our pain. Hebrews 12:3–11 offers lots of comfort and hope when it tells us that God lovingly disciplines us for our good. This is not the kind of discipline we get when we have done wrong, but the kind of training that a coach uses to make an athlete stronger. God promises us two things when we suffer in Hebrews 12. In verse 10, he says we get to share in his holiness. Verse 11 says that our suffering yields the peaceful fruit of righteousness. So we can encourage those with physical suffering that God uses it to make us more like his Son Jesus.

Is Using Medication for Suffering Biblical?

If God can use physical suffering to grow me and glorify him, would it be wrong for me to take medication to relieve that suffering? God's Word does endorse the use of oral and topical medications for the relief of suffering, and in biblical times those passages are usually referring to alcohol, strong drink, or salves and ointments. Some of those passages are Proverbs 31:6; Isaiah 38:21; Luke 10:34; and 1 Timothy 5:23. Other than the verses from Proverbs 31, there are no passages about medication for pain relief. In the twenty-first century, medical science can almost always offer ways to relieve physical suffering, but nearly all of them have risks or side effects to consider. Mark had tried all that medical science had to offer, and he had found that medical marijuana worked best. He had learned that if he smoked it during the day, his THC levels went up in his bloodstream too quickly and he tended to be more intoxicated. If he ate a marijuana brownie at bedtime, he could sleep and wake up in the morning without a hangover and then tolerate his pain all day. Their marriage seemed better, and they seemed to be more united as a couple. So he was using marijuana for a medical purpose that did not appear to be dangerous to his relationship with his wife, his family, or the Lord.

Youthful Dangers

Zach was raised in a Christian family, and his parents were rightfully terrified at his behavior. Because Zach did not seem to be a believer, I mostly warned him about the physical dangers of marijuana use. I explained that regular cannabis could affect his cognitive function and decrease his chances of doing well academically or even diminish future employment opportunities. I explained there are physical dangers associated with marijuana use, and even increased potential for psychiatric problems like schizophrenia. I showed him how he met several criteria for cannabis use disorder and that he would be considered to have a problem even by secular people not associated with his parents' church. I reminded him that although recreational marijuana is legal in our state, he is breaking the law until he is twenty-one years old. I showed him that God's Word tells us not to be intoxicated and that his actions were not pleasing to God. Then I spent several sessions going over the gospel with him, making sure he understood what God's Word says about our sin, how our sin separates us from a relationship with God, and that Jesus could offer much more joy and pleasure than getting high with his friends.

Counseling the Parents

I counseled Zach's parents like one would counsel any parent who is concerned about their teenager. Paul Tripp teaches us that when our children disobey us, we can choose to be offended by their rebellion or we can thank the Lord that he has just given us a glimpse of the child's true heart condition.[11] If a child is not saved, why wouldn't he look to marijuana as a form of pleasure and foolishly give in to peer pressure? Zach's parents needed help knowing how to lovingly keep showing him how wonderful the Lord is, even while he was being foolishly sinful and perhaps even making choices that would ruin his life. Often when counseling a child that may not be saved, we spend a lot of time helping their parents remember how to be faithful as described in Ephesians 6:4. Zach also likes to annoy his parents by quoting Genesis 1 where God calls "all things good." We will discuss that passage further in the next story, but right now, Zach is behaving like a fool, and the Proverbs are full of warnings for the fool. These passages teach us how to respond to a fool with wisdom, as in Proverbs 26:4–5.

My Story

Thankfully, our good God is in the business of continually rescuing perishing people from their predicaments. I was much like Zach when I was sixteen, and God brought me to the place where I was

---

11. Paul David Tripp, *Parenting: 14 Gospel Principles That Can Radically Change Your Family* (Wheaton, IL: Crossway, 2016), 19, 206.

so miserable in my sin that I chose to recommit my life to the Lord. I needed to say no to marijuana, and I needed to stop associating with my old group of friends. In his faithfulness, God helped me to walk away from that lifestyle and avoid all kinds of frightening consequences. The biblical counselor will lovingly help the parents to grow in their faith and trust in God, and the counselor can help them learn how to be better ambassadors for Christ to their child. The biblical counselor can also lovingly warn the fool that is trapped in the marijuana lifestyle.

Marijuana Intoxication

Evan claims to be a believer who does not seem to see anything wrong with using marijuana. Clearly, his marijuana use is bothering his wife, while his child is too young to see Daddy's behavior as being a bad witness. He knows Christians who use alcohol responsibly and likens his marijuana use to being on the same level as alcohol. He and his wife were attending an evangelical church that did not have a counseling ministry, and his wife found us online. In a sense, Evan was dragged to counseling by his wife; he had not sought it himself. I learned that he was secretly hoping I would agree with him and that this would get him off the hook with his wife. Like most lawyers, he loved to argue and was quite talkative, so I needed to keep bringing him back to task. I used a helpful book called *Can I Smoke Pot?* to guide our conversations. I found this book, which was written by Tom Breeden and Mark L. Ward Jr., to be an excellent resource.[12]

Mark and I needed to discuss the topic of intoxication. We looked at marijuana and compared it to alcohol, which is addressed in God's Word. You may feel that good Christians should not use alcohol under any circumstances, or you might believe it is possible to use alcohol responsibly as a believer and still honor the Lord. Passages in

---

12. Tom Breeden and Mark L. Ward Jr., *Can I Smoke Pot? Marijuana in Light of Scripture* (Minneapolis, MN: Cruciform Press, 2016).

Scripture say it can be used to enjoy life (Psalm 104:15). Jesus made wine himself (John 2:1–11), and drank wine himself, and promised we would drink it together in his Father's kingdom (Matthew 26:26–29). Paul encouraged Timothy to use it for medicinal purposes (1 Timothy 5:23). So the Bible seems to describe the possibility of using wine without getting intoxicated.

Intoxication Prohibited

The Bible has a lot to say about intoxication in the Old and New Testament. It is called drunkenness and is condemned in Genesis 9:21; 19:30–38; Proverbs 23:20–21, 30–35; Galatians 5:19–21; 1 Timothy 3:3; and Titus 1:7. These passages show examples of what happens when a man becomes drunk. Proverbs describes what an intoxicated person is like. Galatians condemns drunkenness in a long list of other sins, and when Paul describes the qualifications for an elder, he prohibits drunkenness. Romans 14:20–22 tells us not to cause our brother to stumble, and 1 Corinthians 6:12 says we should not be dominated by anything. So while the occasional glass of wine seems to be permissible in Scripture, intoxication and alcohol addiction are clearly prohibited.

I explained to Evan that each time he used marijuana to get high, he was in disobedience to God's prohibition against drunkenness. Ultimately the question was, can I use marijuana and please God? Breeden and Ward's *Can I Smoke Pot?* asks a similar question: "Can a Christian smoke pot for God's glory?"[13]

If your counselee realizes that his use of marijuana is the same as "drunkenness," you will want to use some of the same biblical counseling resources that are available for alcohol and drug addiction to help your counselee see how they have been using marijuana in a sinful way. There are many heart issues to address, but God is our hope. He gives us a new identity in Christ, so that Paul could say

---

13. Breeden and Ward, 5.

to the Corinthians in 1 Corinthians 6:11, "such were some of you" (ESV).

God Created Marijuana

First we looked at Genesis 1:12 and 1 Timothy 4:4–5 (NIV) which says, "For everything created by God is good, and nothing is to be rejected if it is received with thanksgiving, for it is consecrated by the word of God and prayer." Breeden and Ward spend a whole chapter explaining why we need to be able to understand that "everything God made is good for its intended purpose."[14] My conclusion with Evan was that there must be good purposes for marijuana, but that is not the same as saying all purposes of marijuana are good.

Putting Others First

Then we spent time in Scripture looking at the subject of how we relate to others. First, I focused on how we think of others. Romans 14:20–23 and 1 Corinthians 8:13 both talk about not causing a brother or sister to stumble. Was Evan's marijuana use confusing other believers? If his marijuana use was hurting his wife, then that was harmful to her. We spent considerable time looking at what the Bible says about how we treat others. Six of the Ten Commandments are about our horizontal relationships with others. Philippians 2:3–4 says that we need to spend more time caring about what is good for others than about ourselves, and when that seems really hard, the next six verses remind us that is just the kind of sacrificial love Jesus showed us. Ask your counselee if their marijuana use is hurting another believer or their witness for Christ.

Authorities in Our Lives

Then we spent time looking at all the authorities that God has put over us. Every human struggles with embracing the concept of living under the authority of others. The first authorities that God

---

14. Breeden and Ward, 19.

puts in our lives are our parents. Ephesians 6:1–3, Exodus 20:12, and Colossians 3:20 each discuss the blessings of obeying our parents and the consequences if we do not. They tell us that it will go well with us and that it pleases the Lord. These were passages that I used when counseling Zach, who was still supposed to be under the authority of his parents. These did not go very far with Evan, but he is a parent now and will be soon embracing the importance of these passages. Ask your counselee if they are disobeying their parents by using marijuana, and ask them what the Bible says happens when we don't obey our parents.[15]

Employers

The next authority in our lives is often our employer. Ephesians 6:5 says to "obey your earthly masters," and Colossians 3:22–25 says,

> Bondservants, obey in everything those who are your earthly masters, not by way of eye-service, as people-pleasers, but with sincerity of heart, fearing the Lord. Whatever you do, work heartily, as for the Lord and not for men, knowing that from the Lord you will receive the inheritance as your reward. You are serving the Lord Christ. For the wrongdoer will be paid back for the wrong he has done, and there is no partiality. (ESV)

I asked Evan if his employer knew that he used marijuana and whether or not it was prohibited in his employee manual. He did not have to do urine drug screens in his workplace, and as long as he did not show up to work intoxicated, he was not likely to get into trouble with his employer. The authority of his employer did not seem to apply to him or get his attention while we were meeting. Ask your counselee if their employer forbids the use of marijuana and if so, what does God's Word say about them not submitting to this authority in their

---

15. Breeden and Ward, 20.

life? God may allow them to lose their job as a consequence of their choices.[16]

Pastors and Elders

God has also put pastors and elders in places of authority in a Christian's life. Hebrews 13:17 says, "Obey your leaders and submit to them, for they are keeping watch over your souls, as those who will have to give an account. Let them do this with joy and not with groaning, for that would be of no advantage to you" (ESV). Ask your counselee if her pastor, elder, or growth group leader would be concerned if he heard they were using marijuana for recreational purposes. Ask them what God's Word says about causing our spiritual leaders concern. We should all want it to be a joy for our spiritual leaders to shepherd our souls.[17]

Governing Authorities

Next, God has also ordained governing authorities over us. Titus 3:1, 1 Peter 2:12–17, and Romans 13:1–7 all have something to say about those authorities, and there are consequences when we disobey them. For the teenager, it is always illegal in any state in the nation. For someone over twenty-one, their state may deem it legal for medicinal or recreational purposes. This believer may justify their marijuana use as "legal" and therefore not feel they have violated their conscience. With Evan, I did point out that the federal government considers it illegal. He had taken a course in law school about the constitution and thought he knew more about it than me. That did not convince him, but I encourage you as counselors to probe your counselee's heart with this information. God's Word tells us what to expect when we break the laws of the land. Ask your counselee if they can disobey the federal government in good conscience. Zach did not express concern about the federal law, while

---

16. Breeden and Ward, 20.
17. Breeden and Ward, 20.

Mark had a soft enough heart that he wanted to please God with his conduct.

Case Closed

Over the weeks that we counseled, Evan started to see changes in his relationship with the Lord. He was hearing good teaching weekly, being discipled by people who loved Jesus, and learning to study God's Word and develop a healthy prayer life. Pleasing God was becoming important to him, and this is what ultimately convinced him that he could joyfully give up this habit and stop getting intoxicated. Since he was not using marijuana daily, he was not addicted to THC. As he stopped using, thankfully, he did not have to experience any effects of withdrawal.

My Kids Made Me Use It

What about Sally? She did not come to me for counseling, but she does wonder what I think about CBD. Is CBD dangerous? Probably not, but we do not have good long-term studies to tell us what to expect five or ten years from now. Many of my patients say they tried it and stopped using it because it did not help.

What should you advise? If your counselee is using some form of CBD, the best thing you can do is ask what they are using it for and whether they think it helps. Ask them if their doctor knows they are using it and whether or not their doctor approves. If your counselee is using it for pain, you might want to ask about their view of physical suffering. Some people are very defensive and will say, "What's the big deal? It does not contain THC!" If they are using it to sleep, I suggest you explore why they have sleep issues because this can sometimes be due to spiritual problems. It is going to be difficult to be dogmatic on CBD, but you might be able to learn more about your counselee's heart if you ask a few questions.

Conclusion

If you are a biblical counselor, most of the time your counselee is not going to have marijuana use as their presenting problem. It may show up in their Personal Data Inventory, or it may come up as you are getting to know them. It probably won't be the first thing you need to address with them, but eventually you will want to find out more about why this person uses marijuana and what heart issues are behind this behavior. The second half of this chapter has been all about heart issues and biblical answers for those issues.

Because our society is changing so rapidly and marijuana use is not always illegal, it may be difficult for you to appeal to their conscience. If your counselee is using it for medical purposes, you will want to discern your counselee's theology of suffering and help them to draw near to God in the way they deal with their pain. If your counselee is a rebellious youth, you may find it more helpful to come alongside the hurting parents and shore them up in their understanding of biblical parenting. Dr. Charles Hodges loves to say of 1 Corinthians 10:31, "Do you want to please God more than you want to breathe?" Your goal with your counselee that uses marijuana to become intoxicated is to use God's Word to lead them to the point where they want what God wants for them. Finally, for the person using CBD, asking their motivation may lead you to further discussions about their physical pain or causes for sleep problems.

If you are the counselee talking to a biblical counselor about your marijuana use, please do the hard work of getting to know the God who created marijuana and called his creation "good." God is taking you on a journey with a very specific destination. As you come to know your good Creator better, you will arrive at a place where you can honestly answer the question, "Does God consider marijuana to be good for me?" When you care more about pleasing God than about your next breath, you will find the way to give him glory in this matter.

CHAPTER 20

Dementia:

Comforting the Sufferer and the Caregiver

Matthew Rehrer, MD

The two women who sat across from me in my counseling office were clearly related—they shared many features and mannerisms. Sadly, I could also see that today they came in with a shared fear.

About a year ago, Alice had begun to suspect that something was wrong when her mom, Joann, started to misplace things like her keys. Joann, who was seventy-six years old, lived by herself as a widow. Around the same time, Alice also had observed that her mom was repeating stories in the same conversation and forgetting to pay bills.

Despite these concerns, the mistakes were attributed to old age. Finally, one night Alice waited anxiously for her mom's arrival, while Joann, who lived less than five minutes away, was uncharacteristically late. She was lost in her own neighborhood. A neighbor recognized Joann's car and directed her back to her own house. When Alice shared her concerns with Joann, at first Joanna tried to dismiss them, but eventually she agreed to go see her doctor.

Alice accompanied her mom to the doctor's visit that day. Joann recounted the recent mishaps while Alice filled in the details. Next, the doctor administered the Montreal Cognitive Assessment. This cognitive test is scored on a 30-point scale and is designed to capture subtle cognitive deficits.[1] Joann stumbled her way through drawing a clock and recalling objects to receive a score of 21, which indicated that she had significant cognitive impairment. After a physical exam, the doctor recommended blood testing, a computed tomography (CT) scan of her brain, and an electrocardiogram (EKG) to check the health of her heart. The doctor did not mention the word *dementia*, but these tests were ordered to evaluate for it.

What Causes Dementia?

Dementia is a brain disease that can be brought on by a variety of causes leading to serious cognitive impairment.[2] Cognitive impairment manifests in difficulty learning new things, remembering past things, and making decisions in everyday life. Joann's tests were ordered to evaluate for different types of dementia, especially types that may be improved with treatment. The blood tests look for vitamin B and thyroid deficiencies, as well as infectious causes like human immunodeficiency virus (HIV) and syphilis.

The brain scan rules out normal pressure hydrocephalus (NPH), subdural hematoma, and stroke. NPH occurs when the ventricles (fluid spaces) in the brain become enlarged, which can cause dementia, gait problems, and urinary incontinence. Subdural hematoma shows up on a CT scan as blood between the brain and the skull from trauma to the head, typically due to a fall. Vascular dementia can present after a stroke or as a stepwise cognitive decline from underlying blood vessel disease in the heart or brain. The symptoms will stay the same for a while and then suddenly decline and worsen. An EKG screens for heart arrhythmias like atrial fibrillation, which increase the risk for strokes.

1. Ziad S. Nasreddine et al., "The Montreal Cognitive Assessment, MoCA: A Brief Screening Tool for Mild Cognitive Impairment," *Journal of American Geriatric Society* 53, no. 4 (2005): 695.

2. John Swinton, *Dementia: Living in the Memories of God* (Grand Rapids: Eerdmans, 2012), 39.

Other causes of dementia, like Lewy body disease and frontotemporal dementia, do not have specific tests, but possess unique features that doctors use to identify them. Lewy body disease produces visual hallucinations and rigid, slow movements, whereas frontotemporal dementia affects speech and behavior. Last, the most common cause of dementia is Alzheimer's disease, which is estimated to be responsible for up to 80 percent of dementia cases.[3] Research on Alzheimer's disease continues to explore whether or not different biomarkers like Aβ protein, tau protein, and Apolipoprotein E can be used to definitively diagnose Alzheimer's disease. These tests have not yet been validated but will possibly prove helpful in the years to come.[4] Presently, doctors rely on the National Institute on Aging and Alzheimer's Association (NIA-AA) criteria to diagnose Alzheimer's disease.[5]

These criteria seek to distinguish Alzheimer's disease from other kinds of dementia, but this is difficult because not everyone's disease has the same symptoms or progresses in the same way. To make things even more complicated, a dementia sufferer might have a mixture of symptoms because they suffer from two different types of dementia. With dementia, do not assume that once you have known the experience of one dementia sufferer, you know them all.

It is also important to distinguish dementia from delirium. Delirium is a change in cognition from baseline that develops over a much shorter period of time (hours to days). Delirium most commonly results from a medication, infection, or intoxication. Besides delirium, depression might also present similarly to early dementia. Some of the symptoms overlap, such as social withdrawal, poor sleep,

---

3. "2020 Alzheimer's disease facts and figures," *Alzheimer's & Dementia* 16, no. 3 (March 2020): 391–460, https://doi.org/10.1002/alz.12068.

4. Clifford R. Jack et al., "NIAA-AA Research Framework: Toward a Biological Definition of Alzheimer's Disease," *Alzheimer's & Dementia* 14, no. 4 (2018): 535, https://doi.org/10.1016/j.jalz.2018.02.018.

5. Guy M. McKhann et al., "The Diagnosis of Dementia Due to Alzheimer's Disease: Recommendations from the National Institute on Aging-Alzheimer's Association Workgroups on Diagnostic Guidelines for Alzheimer's Disease," *Alzheimer's & Dementia* 7, no. 3 (2011): 263, https://doi.org/10.1016/j.jalz.2011.03.005.

and memory decline. When someone presents with these symptoms, the doctor will consider the possible presence of depression.

Dementia Statistics

Alice and Joann returned to the doctor's office to learn what the tests found. However, in Joann's case, the blood tests, CT scan, and EKG did not reveal any specific diagnosis. Based on the NIA-AA criteria, Joann was diagnosed with Alzheimer's dementia. Joann joined around 5.7 million Americans who suffer from dementia.[6] With an aging population, the number of dementia sufferers is projected to double over the next twenty years.[7] Combined with 18.4 billion volunteer caregiver hours provided by around 16 million Americans, dementia is relevant both to sufferers like Joann and caregivers like Alice. The disease is not just prevalent but also prolonged as dementia sufferers live on average ten years following diagnosis. Shockingly, around 20 percent of spousal dementia caregivers die prior to the dementia care recipient.[8]

Progression of Dementia

Over the coming months after her diagnosis, Joann's frustration began to escalate as her world grew smaller and closed in on her. As her memory slipped away, she would hit her head with her fists to try to jar the memories loose. She was embarrassed by memory mistakes that popped up, and she wanted to avoid situations that might expose her deficiencies. Eventually, she stopped going to

---

6. Centers for Disease Control and Prevention, "At a Glance: Alzheimer's Disease," last updated June 6, 2018, https://www.cdc.gov/aging/publications/aag/alzheimers.html.

7. Centers for Disease Control and Prevention, "U.S. Burden of Alzheimer's Disease, Related Dementias to Double by 2060," last updated Sept. 20, 2018, https://www.cdc.gov/media/releases/2018/p0920-alzheimers-burden-double-2060.html.

8. Joseph E. Gaugler et al., "Caregivers Dying Before Care Recipients with Dementia," *Alzheimer's & Dementia: Translational Research & Clinical Interventions* 4, no. 1 (December 2018): 688–693, https://doi.org/10.1016/j.trci.2018.08.010.

church, for the former place of comfort had now become a place of consternation.

The progression of dementia varies by type of dementia and stage, but studies provide a framework for a typical pattern. For Alzheimer's, the Global Deterioration Scale provides an average duration for mild dementia of two years (requires assistance in complex tasks), for moderate around four years (requires assistance with dressing and bathing), and for severe around two years (speech declines and mobility lost).[9] Other types of dementia will typically show a faster decline. The decline can be hard to predict, and it weighs on the dementia sufferer and caregiver.

Treatments for Alzheimer's Dementia

As Joann's disease progressed, her doctor discussed treatment options. There is no cure, but medications offer varying degrees of help. The first class of medications is called cholinesterase inhibitors. These medications work by increasing certain neurotransmitters in the brain that help carry messages from one neuron to another. These medications may potentially slow down the disease; however, they have a high rate of side effects so those taking them need to be carefully monitored.[10] Vitamin E also provides some potential modest benefit to slow disease progression, but studies are mixed. Since the supplement is relatively safe with few side effects, vitamin E might be started.

When dementia progresses to a moderate stage, memantine might be added. Memantine represents another class of medications that works to regulate a different neurotransmitter. Memantine produces

---

9. B. Reisberg, S. H. Ferris, M. J. de Leon, and T. Crook, "The Global Deterioration Scale for Assessment of Primary Degenerative Dementia," *American Journal of Psychiatry* 139 (1982): 1136–39.

10. Noll L. Campbell et al., "Adherence and Tolerability of Alzheimer's Disease Medications: A Pragmatic Randomized Trial," *Journal of the American Geriatrics Society* 65, no. 7 (2017): 1497–1504, https://doi.org/10.1111/jgs.14827.

fewer side effects. While it might be neuroprotective, improvements have been small and remain unproven.[11]

Aducanumab is a newer medication approved for the treatment of Alzheimer's dementia. It attacks amyloid plaques in the brain thought to contribute to Alzheimer's dementia. However, it is still early and the benefits remain controversial.[12]

On this doctor's visit, the doctor started her on a cholinesterase inhibitor and vitamin E as her dementia was still mild.

Medications to Avoid in Dementia

Almost as important as the medications to take are the medications *not* to take. The doctor reminded Alice and Joann to be careful not to use antihistamines (such as Benadryl) and sleep aids (such as NyQuil). These medications lead to confusion and an increased risk for falls. Medications for overactive bladder and benign prostatic hypertrophy (BPH), a condition with an enlarged prostate gland, carry similar concerns. When they are prescribed, the patient needs to be closely monitored. It is important to always communicate about medications or conditions with all medical professionals involved in the dementia sufferer's care.

Counseling Dementia Sufferers

After leaving the doctor's office, Joann continued to spiral into the depths of depression—mingled with anxiety. The lack of a cure combined with the growing sense of loneliness began to weigh heavy. She did not want to burden her family, especially Alice. She was slowly

---

11. P. Raina et al., "Effectiveness of Cholinesterase Inhibitors and Memantine for Treating Dementia: Evidence Review for a Clinical Practice Guideline," *Ann Internal Medicine* 148, no. 5 (March 4, 2008):3 79–97, doi: 10.7326/0003-4819-148-5-200803040-00009. PMID: 18316756.

12. "FDA Grants Accelerated Approval for Alzheimer's Drug," US Food and Drug Administration, https://www.fda.gov/news-events/press-announcements/fda-grants-accelerated-approval-alzheimers-drug, accessed March 20, 2022.

transitioning from being a caregiver to a care receiver as she regressed back to childhood dependence.

At this low point, Alice urged her mom to seek help from the counseling provided at the church. With dementia sufferers, the tendency can be to slowly pull away from the church community at the very time when that community is most needed. Alice and Joann sought out counseling as they looked for help to deal with the overwhelming and uncertain future. Each looked down the future path as caregiver and care receiver with fear.

As a counselor, the tendency may be to go right to the caregiver for specific information about the past year since she will be able to give the most details. However, it is important to directly address the dementia sufferer and involve them in the conversation to reinforce their dignity and acknowledge the value they add to the conversation. The method and types of engagement will change as the disease progresses. You cannot counsel or care for someone with early-stage dementia in the same way that you would someone with late-stage dementia.

Draw Out the Heart by Starting with the Familiar

To help draw Joann into the conversation, we initially focused on finding out how she was doing in the immediate present. Dementia erodes our ability to communicate emotional, physical, and spiritual needs. A dementia sufferer might need help not just expressing these needs, but also understanding what these needs are. "The purpose in a man's heart is like deep water, but a man of understanding will draw it out" (Proverbs 20:5 ESV). As our memory fades, the water deepens. To reach the waters of the heart, the rope must be lengthened through time and patience.

In counseling, another way to draw out a dementia sufferer is to help them find familiarity in older, more accessible memories. Many with dementia will recall childhood stories with surprising clarity because these areas are not affected early on. After I asked Joann about her childhood home, she brightened as she remembered walking down the main street of her small hometown with fondness. We spoke about her childhood church, and then the conversation transitioned to her present church. We talked about why it was hard for her to attend. At this point, Alice added that some of Joann's friends had been checking in on her. Joann started to tear up and said, "What if my friends stop coming to visit? I am worried that I will be forgotten."

Address the Fear of Forgetfulness

Joann expressed her fear that not only would she forget others, but that they would forget her. Memory provides meaning and maintains identity. Author Jeffrey Arthurs writes, "If we have no memory, we are adrift, because memory is the mooring to which we are tied."[13] As dementia progresses and memory's moorings loosen, fear sets in as you "lose the ability to tell one's story."[14] Joann feared not just that she would lose her story, but that others would also forget to tell her story.

At this point, compassion bubbled up within me for Joann, who was burdened by this fear. Joann needed hope; she needed to be reminded of the Savior who kisses away the fear of dementia with his promises.[15]

Find Hope in the Memory of God

As the three of us sat in a moment of silence, Alice looked at her mom and said, "Mom, don't forget God remembers you." Alice spoke wise words. As Joann's memory slipped away, God's memory remained like an anchor. As the moorings of memory loosened from the dock, the anchor held the boat securely underneath the water, tethered to the perfect memory of God.

First, we opened and read together Psalm 139:1–12 to look at God's perfect memory. David marvels at the omniscience of God who

---

13. Jeffrey Arthurs, *Preaching as Reminding* (Westmont, IL: InterVarsity Press, 2017), 1.
14. Swinton, *Dementia*, 22.
15. Charles H. Spurgeon, "Psalm 71," *The Treasury of David*, vol. 1 (Nashville: Thomas Nelson, 1984), 212.

is intimately "acquainted with all my ways" (v. 3 ESV). Even when memory fails and my knowledge of God wanes, he knows me better than I know myself. "God can still relate to a person even if his or her ability to relate to God (or to other people) appears lost."[16] His omniscience surpasses my knowledge even when my memory is fully functional.

David goes on to speak of God's omnipresence. God is everywhere, and is as high as the heavens and as far as "the uttermost parts of the sea" (v. 9 ESV). You cannot wander away from him intentionally or unintentionally. God knows you personally, and he knows where you are positionally. This knowledge is not cold and confined, but wrapped in compassion and care. God does not simply use his knowledge to convict you of your shortcomings, but to care for you in those shortcomings. This care is best expressed through his promises.

Through God's perfect memory, his promises spring forth in Christ. "For all the promises of God find their Yes in him" (2 Corinthians 1:20 ESV). Dementia is a result of living in a fallen world, a world that is broken from the presence of sin. The earth now sits under the curse that brings disease and death to all mankind. Through his grace, God made a way of salvation from sin through his Son, Jesus Christ. Through his death and resurrection, Jesus conquered sin and death. The promises secured by Christ need to be recounted, especially in the face of dementia.

Review the Promises We Have in Christ

Joann, Alice, and I walked through these applicable promises together. We turned to Romans 8:38–39, which reminds us that nothing (including dementia) can separate us from God's love. This promise reiterates the security Joann has in Christ. Salvation is not lost when she forgets the gospel story. Rather, dementia reinforces that salvation rests in God's memory, not in our forgetful minds. Jesus

16. Stephen Sapp, "Hope: The Community Looks Forward," in *God Never Forgets: Faith, Hope, and Alzheimer's Disease,* ed. Donald K. McKim (Louisville, KY: Westminster John Knox Press, 1997), 94–95.

promised that "this is the will of him who sent me, that I should lose nothing of all that he has given me" (John 6:39 ESV). God sought you out when you were a lost sheep and purchased you with the precious blood of Christ. Trust in the One who will keep you to the end.

Hope extends from the present to the future when all things will be made new. As one author expressed it, "I will trust in God, who will hold me safe in His memory, until that glorious day of Resurrection, when each facet of my personality can be expressed in the full."[17] The resurrection of Christ ensures the resurrection of his children. We now have victory through Jesus Christ (1 Corinthians 15:54–57). Joann will still feel the sting of losing her memory on this earth, but it will not last beyond this life because her body will be raised imperishable, no longer ravaged by the effects of the disease of dementia.

Finally, God promises that our suffering is limited (2 Corinthians 4:16–18). Joann's physical body and mind were suffering from her dementia, but the years that she will suffer on earth will be momentary compared to eternity with Christ. Focusing on the temporal is overwhelming, but not when it is viewed in light of eternity. In many regards, dementia helps loosen the grip we have on this world. Suffering reminds us that there is something better to come than this present world, and "we groan, longing to put on our heavenly dwelling" (2 Corinthians 5:2 ESV).

Joann's fears represent the feelings of many others who fear dementia. In fact, dementia is now the most feared diagnosis in the United States, even more feared than cancer.[18] For Christians, "God's promises are as a fountain, never emptied, ever overflowing, so you may draw from them, and they shall be still as full as ever."[19] Counseling encouraged Joann to draw comfort from the promise of

---

17. Christine Bryden, *Dancing with Dementia: My Story of Living Positively with Dementia* (Philadelphia: Jessica Kingsley Publishers, 2005), 153.

18. MetLife Foundation, "What America Thinks: MetLife Foundation Alzheimer's Survey," February 2011, https://www.metlife.com/content/dam/microsites/about/corporate-profile/alzheimers-2011.pdf.

19. Charles H. Spurgeon, *Gleanings Among the Sheaves* (New York: Fleming B. Revell, 1869), 110.

security in Christ, the hope of resurrection, and the limits of suffering. God always keeps his promises; his memory never fails.

Practical Tips for Helping Dementia Sufferers

Counseling provides biblically based care for the soul. Encourage a mild dementia sufferer to continue to daily read the Bible with its promises. Ask about favorite Bible verses that your counselee could write down in a book or frame to place around their home. As memory slips, consider moving toward audio options for Scripture intake.

Play favorite songs and hymns that provide peace through familiarity and comforting truths. Music accesses a part of memory that is preserved even in late-stage dementia. Music acts as a key "that can unlock emotions, feelings, and recollections that would otherwise be inaccessible,"[20] and it serves as a calming presence in a confusing and changing world.

A dementia sufferer should be encouraged to tell others about their diagnosis. Let others come alongside and bear the burden. When Christians do not forget the dementia sufferer, they further cement the promise that God also does not forget. With Alzheimer's dementia, Joann might benefit from joining a support group. However, support groups and close involvement might not be helpful for all types of dementia, like frontotemporal dementia, which strongly affects behavior. Community organizations also provide resources and programs that should be explored.

As your counselee's memory progressively worsens, communication will be progressively hindered. Early and open communication is necessary. A key first step is to establish a durable power of attorney (DPOA) with an advanced directive. The DPOA needs to be the person who knows the dementia sufferer the best and is able to express their wishes. The DPOA and dementia sufferer should sit down with the doctor to fill out a POLST (Physician's Order for Life-Sustaining Treatment). Available in most states, a POLST is a medical order

20. Swinton, *Dementia*, 250.

signed by a doctor to give direction to other medical professionals about the patient's end-of-life decisions regarding CPR, ventilators, and artificial nutrition (feeding tube).

This important discussion should take place when the dementia sufferer is still able to make decisions. Unfortunately, many delay these conversations and then arrive in the emergency room in critical condition. This places distressed family members in a position where they have to make difficult decisions at the worst time. Making end of life decisions together prior to a crisis is a loving act that allows the caregiver to be at peace about implementing decisions.

Conclusion

With Joann, the first visit to the counseling office opened up the conversation so she could express her fears. These fears were addressed through the Word of God and the hope of his promises. Joann left with a plan to write down Bible verses that brought her hope and frame a few to place around her room. Joann and Alice also planned to sit down together and put together a memory book with childhood photos and captions of memories. The path over the coming years would prove challenging, but God was present, along with the church that provided counsel and friendship.

A couple of years passed, and Joann's dementia progressed. The time arrived for Joann to move out of her home of forty years and live with Alice and her family. The decision to move was hard on Joann as she left the comfortable familiarity of her home, but the move was also hard on Alice. The next sections of this chapter will address the challenges that a caregiver might face as the effects of dementia worsen.

Counseling the Caregiver

In many ways, Alice fell into the typical demographics of a dementia caregiver. According to an article in *Journals of Gerontology* in September 2020, "Daughters provide the majority of unpaid hours of care for those with dementia (39%), followed by spouses (25%), sons (17%), and other family and friends (20%)."[21] Alice joined about 25 percent of dementia caregivers who are in the "sandwich generation"—those who care for their loved one with dementia while also caring for children under eighteen years old.[22] Alice and her husband had two children, both in high school. Similar to Joann and Alice, the majority of caregiving happens in the home as 80 percent of those with dementia live in a traditional community setting.[23] Even though caregiving for those with dementia is common, that does not mean it is easy.

Around the time that Joann moved in with Alice and her family, Alice started to receive individual counseling. The burdens were growing, and so the opportunities to counsel and encourage Alice were growing. Unfortunately for many caregivers, opportunities to step away to receive encouragement and counsel may be limited. In Alice's case, her husband worked during the day but would help in the evenings and weekends. Be flexible and willing to offer alternatives to in-person meetings. Recognize that many caregivers of those with late-stage dementia are unable to leave. Just like a dementia sufferer's world shrinks around them, the same may be said for the caregiver. In fact, the needs of a caregiver are often forgotten in the face of the overwhelming needs of the dementia sufferer.

When Alice arrived for counseling, she looked exhausted. Alice sat down across from Sandy and me. Sandy was a counselor and a friend who knew Joann and Alice well. After praying, we began to hear from Alice about how things were going. Initially, Alice painted a bright picture focused on her son's baseball events. Her oldest son's

---

21. Brenda C. Spillman et al., "Change Over Time in Caregiving Networks for Older Adults with and without Dementia," *Journals of Gerontology* 75, no. 7 (September 2020): 1563–72, https://doi.org/10.1093/geronb/gbz065.

22. Centers for Disease Control and Prevention, "Caregiving for a Person with Alzheimer's Disease or a Related Dementia," last updated October 30, 2019, https://www.cdc.gov/aging/caregiving/alzheimer.htm.

23. Judith D. Kasper et al., "The Disproportionate Impact of Dementia on Family and Unpaid Caregiving to Older Adults," *Health Affairs* 34, no. 10 (2015): 1642–49.

team reached the championship game a week ago. Alice quickly added that she was glad her husband had taken a video to share with her. She had been unable to attend because she stayed home with Joann. The family tried to take Joann to a game earlier in the season, but the crowd and noise had panicked her. Alice took her home that day and had not taken her to a game since.

Challenges Caregivers Face in Performing Daily Activities

When asked what a typical day looked like, Alice started to describe the different daily activities that dominated it: bathing, dressing, and eating, which all required supervision and assistance. Everything took longer. Joann was still able to walk around with a cane, but she would shadow Alice around the house and try to stick close to the one person that kept her oriented. When Joann was not nearby, Alice's mind would subconsciously start to think through a safety checklist, such as wondering whether or not the stove was turned off. The subconscious list would continue at night. She thought, *What if Mom wanders out of the house and gets lost? What if she gets up in the night and falls and is on the ground all night?*

Challenges Caregivers Face at Night

A well-rested caregiver would find the daytime challenges draining, but the night issues compound these challenges. Sleep disturbances are common in dementia, and thus they are also common for the caregiver. Some types of dementia, like Lewy body dementia, affect sleep earlier on, while Alzheimer's dementia affects sleep in the later stages.[24] Poor sleep should prompt a visit to the doctor as a number of causes can contribute to the problem.

The doctor will assess for restless leg syndrome and breathing problems like sleep apnea, and review the sleep environment. A sleep problem might be related to alcohol, tobacco, or caffeine intake. The

---

24. Donald L. Bliwise et al., "Sleep Disturbance in Dementia with Lewy Bodies and Alzheimer's Disease: A Multicenter Analysis," *Dementia and Geriatric Cognitive Disorders* 31, no. 3 (2011): 239–46, https://doi.org/10.1159/000326238.

medication list will be reviewed. Antihistamines (such as Benadryl), decongestants (such as Sudafed), diuretics, or benzodiazepines commonly alter the sleep cycle. Finally, the doctor will perform a physical exam with a particular focus on checking for any pain. As dementia advances, the dementia sufferer might struggle to communicate pain with their words. The doctor and caregiver should look for grimacing, groaning, and labored breathing, among other signs; these signs can be evaluated using the pain assessment tool for dementia (PAINAD).[25]

Once other causes have been addressed, it is possible that dementia is disrupting the dementia sufferer's sleep/wake cycle and circadian rhythm. The disruption of the circadian rhythm is closely tied to sundowning.[26] Sundowning occurs when the sun goes down, and it manifests with changes in behavior like agitation, delusions, and hallucinations. A dementia sufferer may transform from peaceful in the daytime to pacing back and forth at night. To understand the burden of caregiving, a counselor should ask direct questions of the caregiver about sundowning and nighttime, as many underreport these symptoms.[27]

The counselor should also be aware of the possibility of delusions with paranoia or hearing voices since one-third of those suffering from severe Alzheimer's suffer from delusions.[28] Delusions can be particularly distressing to a caregiver as the dementia sufferer might suspect or even accuse them of things like stealing. If delusions and other behavioral concerns are present, the counselor should also ask about the safety of the caregiver with specific questions such as the

---

25. Victoria Warden et al., "Development and Psychometric Evaluation of the Pain Assessment in Advanced Dementia (PAINAD) Scale," *Journal of the American Medical Directors Association* 4, no. 1 (2003): 9–15, https://doi.org/10.1097/01.JAM.0000043422.31640.F7.

26. Ladislav Volicer et al., "Sundowning and Circadian Rhythms in Alzheimer's Disease," *The American Journal of Psychiatry* 158, no. 5 (2001): 704–11. https://doi.org/10.1176/appi.ajp.158.5.704.

27. George M. Savva et al., "Prevalence, Correlates and Course of Behavioural and Psychological Symptoms of Dementia in the Population," *The British Journal of Psychiatry: The Journal of Mental Science* 194, no. 3 (2009): 212–19, https://doi.org/10.1192/bjp.bp.108.049619.

28. M. S. Mega et al. "The Spectrum of Behavioral Changes in Alzheimer's Disease," *Neurology* 46, no. 1 (1996): 130–35, https://doi.org/10.1212/wnl.46.1.130.

following: Do you feel safe in your home? Have you ever been hit or kicked? Many times, physical harm will be hidden as the caregiver does not want to get the one they care for in trouble or lose the opportunity to care for the dementia sufferer. The counselor is able to serve as a guide in trying times.

If there is no significant distress or harm, the first approach to poor sleep will involve non-pharmacologic interventions like implementing outdoor activities to increase sunlight exposure or incorporating music into the daily routine. Training might also be available to improve communication and care. If the behavior problems persist or are severe, then medications will also be discussed. Each class of medication represents benefits and risks that need to be assessed. Commonly prescribed medications include antidepressants and atypical antipsychotics. Sleep problems[29] and behavioral problems[30] are common and concerning, and both lead to an increased likelihood of the need to place a dementia sufferer in a care home.

As a caregiver, Alice experienced some of these challenges because Joann struggled to sleep through the night. She would wake up to use the bathroom but then wander through the house. On one occasion, Joann tripped over the pet cat but caught herself on the nearby couch. Alice followed her doctor's instructions to remove clutter, replace slippery rugs, and add night-lights. In the counseling office, Alice began to express how she felt like things were only getting worse, despite following all the doctor's instructions. Just that morning, Joann threw her breakfast at the wall. No one was hurt, but the outburst frightened Alice. As Alice spoke, her voice rose in anger: "I cooked her favorite breakfast for her even though I was tired, and this is how she thanked me! I want someone to cook me breakfast and give me a break!" Alice felt under-rested, underappreciated, underwater, and angry.

---

29. C. P. Pollak et al., "Sleep Problems in the Community Elderly as Predictors of Death and Nursing Home Placement," *Journal of Community Health* 15, no. 2 (1990): 123–35, https://doi.org/10.1007/BF01321316.

30. N. Scarmeas et al., "Disruptive Behavior as a Predictor in Alzheimer Disease," *Archives of Neurology* 64, no. 12 (December 2007): 1755–61, https://doi.org/10.1001/archneur.64.12.1755.

The Need to Comfort the Caregiver

When counseling a caregiver, gentleness needs to encapsulate any encouragement offered for perseverance in caregiving. Alice knew she needed help and even asked, "Can you remind me why I am doing this again?" Sandy and I opened our Bibles and began to walk through the biblical and noble reasons that Alice cared for her mom.

First, the Bible commands us to provide care for our families. By her sacrifices, Alice was following the command to "Honor your father and your mother" (Deuteronomy 5:16a). In the New Testament, Paul reiterates, "But if a widow has children or grandchildren, let them first learn to show godliness to their own household and to make some return to their parents, for this is pleasing in the sight of God" (1 Timothy 5:4 ESV). Finally, Christ provided an example to follow as he cared for his mother Mary even from the cross by charging John to watch over her (John 19:26–27). Alice imitated Christ in the sacrificial service she now provided for her mom.

Second, the command to honor and care for our parents broadens to include all human beings. All have value, including those with the most severe dementia, because all are made in God's image. The world measures value by usefulness, but God measures value by his likeness. "Then God said, 'Let us make man in our image, according to Our likeness'" (Genesis 1:26). God established value in the creation of the first man and woman, but this value extends to every human being who is formed and woven together by God (Psalm 139:13). Dr. Benjamin Mast adds, "The reason that people warrant love is not that people are so lovable in themselves, but that love is the appropriate way to treat those in God's image."[31] Jesus came to earth "not to be served but to serve, and to give his life as a ransom for many" (Matthew 20:28 ESV). In caregiving, you are called to serve like Christ but not to save like Christ. When you are serving the least of these, you are actually serving Christ himself (Matthew 25:39). What a powerful

---

31. Benjamin Mast, *Second Forgetting: Remembering the Power of the Gospel During Alzheimer's Disease* (Grand Rapids: Zondervan, 2012), 85.

reminder of the value of service: you are serving the King by serving one of his image-bearers (Ephesians 6:7).

Remember God Supplies Power and Rest

Alice needed encouragement to "not grow weary of doing good" (Galatians 6:9 ESV). Perseverance is not encouraged by just a pat on the back. God graciously provides the power to fuel endurance through his love (Romans 5:3–5) and through people lifting you up along the way. God supplies all your needs through his strength. Isaiah reminds those who "grow weary and tired" "will gain new strength; they will mount up with wings like eagles, they will run and not get tired, they will walk and not become weary" (Isaiah 40:30–31).

Alice could not do this on her own. She could not just dig deeper and push harder. She needed help from outside of herself. It is in this place of dependence that Christ's words ring true, "Come to Me, all who are weary and heavy-laden, and I will give you rest" (Matthew 11:28). Rest in the arms of the Savior and rely on him. It is here that a counselor can point the caregiver like Alice back to Christ, to help draw her gaze away from self and fix her eyes on Jesus (Hebrews 12:1).

Practical Tips for Helping Caregivers

Counseling anchors the caregiver into the comfort of God's Word but also offers practical ways to help. Caregiving limits personal time for Bible reading. Counselors can help caregivers explore creative ways to make sure that their daily Scripture intake continues, even with the added pressures of providing care for a dementia sufferer. One option for Alice may be to incorporate Bible reading into her caregiving by reading to Joann and playing worship songs that Joann knew. Alice also wanted to try to pray with her mom and make it a part of their routine. Sandy and I encouraged her to write down praises and answers to prayer that she could pull out again to reflect on in dark times.

For Alice, the church served a vital role in providing support and stepped in to help in many ways. Many times caregivers see outside help as a last resort. The church community needs to offer help early on and not wait to be asked to help. Explore different ways to free the caregiver to attend church in person. Check in to see how they are doing. The church may have a program for assistance, but these ways of providing love can be naturally fostered as the church seeks ways to show love to one another.

Assistance is also available outside of the church through community-based programs. Respite programs offer support to caregivers in a variety of ways, from picking up groceries to housecleaning and preparing meals.

The day may arrive where other options for physical help need to be pursued. In-home caregiving services should be brought in early, even if only for an hour a week, to allow the caregiver and dementia sufferer to become familiar with each other and ensure a good fit before more intensive help is needed. Help should gradually increase over time. Also investigate the best available options for assisted living or skilled nursing. Research the costs and know the waiting lists. The financial toll throughout the course of dementia escalates, especially during the later stages, and additional help may not be covered by insurance.

The emotional toll also rises as many caregivers experience guilt and feel weak because they need outside assistance. If at some point you had said you would never put your loved one in a skilled nursing facility, discuss these options with your loved one early on to free yourself of any promises because you do not know how the disease will progress. Your desire might be to do everything you can to care for your loved one at home, but the disease might reach a level that makes it physically unsafe to do so. You love them and want to do what is best for them, and what is best might conflict with what you desire or had originally promised.

Conclusion

Alice left counseling that day with a sense of relief, not relief that all of her challenges had been removed, but rather a sense of relief that came from knowing God would supply all her needs. She did not need to be a savior but a servant. Over the coming years, Alice would need reminders of the promises of God to find comfort in God's care as she provided care.

Joann and Alice both represent many who face the trials of dementia. The dementia sufferer and caregiver share burdens and fears but also share future hope in Christ. The groaning of the past and present from the effects of sin and suffering will one day be redeemed in future glory (2 Corinthians 5:1–5). Until that day comes, God supplies his abundant grace through Christ to help bear the burdens.

CHAPTER 21

· · · ·

Sleep Disorders:
Medical Background and Biblical Guidance

Lee Edmonds, MD

On the surface, Sarah has what seems like the perfect life. Her life includes a wonderful husband of ten years, along with two beautiful and healthy children. What more could she ask for? Despite appearances, in recent years, she has felt more stressed. The stress makes it seem like life is just too much to bear. Some days are so overwhelming that she wishes to just run away.

Her parents are aging, and she feels the guilt across the 823 miles to their home. Sarah tries to call every day. The calls are often long, unpleasant, and burdensome. If she skips a day, she feels like a "bad daughter," and the guilt is stifling. Mom really could use more help in caring for Dad as his dementia deepens. Frequent trips to visit are just not possible with Sarah's responsibilities at home and church.

While Tom, her husband, is supportive, he just does not seem to really understand. Some days the misunderstanding leads to open conflict with harsh words and even resentment. Some evenings they go to bed having not spoken. These nights leave her feeling misunderstood and unloved. Morning will often come with seemingly no sleep.

These sleepless nights have been increasing in the past year, along with a sense of numbness and despair. Sarah finds herself exhausted during her busy day of homeschooling her children. "I just wish I could take a nap," but there is no time during the school day. After school come sports teams for the kids and dinner preparation, not to mention the call to Mom and Dad.

By bedtime Sarah is exhausted, but when she closes her eyes, it seems her mind comes alive—alive with regrets of today and worries for tomorrow. Her short-tempered remarks to her children during the school day begin to haunt her. Next her thoughts move to,

> *If only I could get more help for my parents; after all, they deserve better. Deserve better, yes, I also deserve a better husband who helps more and kids who listen better. Listen better, yes, God listens, but he never answers. Answers, yes, maybe my doctor could give me answers as to why I feel so overwhelmed. Overwhelmed, yes, I just feel so overwhelmed, if only I could get some sleep! When will it all end? No one can help me; maybe I will end it myself!*

It has been observed that sleeplessness, hopelessness, and suicidal ideation are bedfellows. As a biblical counselor, how can you help Sarah? Are her problems physical or spiritual?

Medical Background

Sleep is essential to human life. Sleep can be described as brain food. With no sleep, humans become increasingly confused and out of touch with reality (psychotic).[1] Lesser degrees of sleep disruption or deprivation also have negative effects on humans.[2] It is these negative

---

1. J. J. Ross, "Neurological Findings After Prolonged Sleep Deprivation," *Archives of Neurology* 12, no. 4 (1965): 399–403.
2. Namni Goel et al., "Circadian Rhythms, Sleep Deprivation, and Human Performance," *Progress in Molecular Biology and Translational Science* 119 (2013): 155–90, https://doi.org/10.1016/B978-0-12-396971-2.00007-5; Namni Goel et al., "Neurocognitive Consequences of Sleep Deprivation," *Seminars in Neurology* 29, no. 4 (2009): 320–39, https://doi.org/10.1055/s-0029-1237117; Siobhan Banks and David F. Dinges, "Behavioral and Physiological Consequences of Sleep Restriction," *Journal of Clinical Sleep Medicine* 3, no. 5 (2007): 519–528; Gabriel Natan Pires et al., "Effects of Acute Sleep Deprivation on State Anxiety Levels: A Systematic Review and Meta-Analysis," *Sleep Medicine* 24 (2016): 109–118, https://doi.org/10.1016/j.sleep.2016.07.019.

effects that often contribute to the issues under review in the counseling room. Sleep loss leads to changes in learning, concentration, mood, and a reduction in a person's general sense of well-being. What exactly makes sleep essential is still not understood. However, by observation and study of people, many things have been discovered regarding sleep.

A better awareness and understanding of the biology of sleep can help us avoid some common errors or pitfalls with regard to getting better sleep. Let's look at some of those details.

- *Sleep is best done in the dark.* Melatonin, a hormone with far-reaching health effects, is secreted during sleep in the dark.[3] If possible, sleeping at night is preferable. If you must sleep during the day, try light-blocking curtains. If a dark bedroom is not available, eye patches can create darkness to improve sleep.

- *Human biology has a rhythm.* This biologic rhythm (circadian rhythm) centers on the 24-hour day/night cycle. Our bodies function best when we stay in synchrony with the daily rhythm.[4] Activity, sleep, and meals are best done on a recurring daily routine. The brain has an "internal clock," which knows the difference between 3 p.m. and 3 a.m. This clock can reset; if not, we would need to always live in the time zone of our birth. However, we cannot ignore our clock and still sustain good sleep/wake function. Jet lag and shift work are two common examples of how our rhythm's link to the day/night cycle can be lost. Until our rhythm is restored, we will have an acute awareness of the negative effects of being out of synchrony with our internal clock. Sleep is best done at the same time each day to maintain the biologic rhythm to life. Our rise time is the most important and powerful element

3. H. J. Lynch et al., "Entrainment of Rhythmic Melatonin Secretion in Man to a 12-Hour Phase Shift in the Light/Dark Cycle," *Life Science* 23, no. 15 (1978): 1557, https://doi.org/10.1016/0024-3205(78)90583-0.

4. J. Aschoff, "Human Circadian Rhythms in Activity, Body Temperature and Other Functions," *Life Science Space Results* (1967): 159–73.

anchoring sleep to the local time. Frequent shifts in the timing of sleep, especially rise time, are not healthy.

- *The longer wakefulness is maintained, the greater the urge, need, and tendency to sleep.*[5] This can be referred to as sleep debt. Afternoon naps reduce the debt and can affect the upcoming night. "Power naps," if needed, should occur eight hours after the routine rise time. They must be limited to only twenty to thirty minutes, in order to not to interfere with the debt needed at bedtime. When both the internal clock is ready to sleep *and* the debt is sufficiently high, better sleep ensues.

- *Sleep is best done in comfortable states.* We should feel comfortably well-fed, have a comfortable temperature, perceive a comfortable and secure environment, and have a comfortable and unstressed state of mind. Sleep is difficult when wet, cold, hungry, or in danger. Physical danger is not the only issue. Mental danger is commonly referred to as stress. Stress is a common reason for difficulty sleeping.

- *Medication and drugs can affect sleep.* Caffeine reduces the urge to sleep and stay asleep. Alcohol's metabolites disrupt rapid eye movement (REM) sleep. These need to be avoided if one is struggling to sleep. Our brain is involved in sleep, and the brain has and is affected by chemicals.

The above simple measures of sleep hygiene are helpful in obtaining good sleep. How can one judge the quality of their sleep and recognize if there is a problem? Quality sleep is best recognized by two simple tests.

Test 1: Awaking in the morning feeling refreshed and ready for the day is a sign of good sleep. The goal of sleep is to adequately restore our body and mind for a new day. Using

---

5. J. K. Wyatt, "Chronobiology," in *Principles and Practice of Pediatric Sleep Medicine*, 2nd ed., ed. S. H. Sheldon et al. (Philadelphia: Elsevier, 2014), 25.

multiple snooze alarms is actually a warning that something is wrong with our sleep.

Test 2: Healthy sleep provides the ability to stay awake during passive midday activities, such as listening to lectures, reading, or driving. Daytime unintentional lapses into light sleep, such as "nodding off," suggest a problem.

If either test 1 or 2 is positive, it suggests two possibilities. One is simple: insufficient daily time is allotted for sleep. During the initial interactions of data gathering, ask a counselee to walk you through a usual day, hour by hour, from one morning to the next. This exercise can be enlightening in many ways. Things will be indirectly revealed that the counselee never recognized as important, unique things of which the counselor may never have known to inquire. You will discover how their gift of time is allotted. Is there time to feed the brain with sleep, feed the soul with Scripture, feed the body with food and maintain it with exercise, and feed their family relationships? Where is the resource of time consumed? Busy schedules, late-night TV, and social media are a few ways that time is squandered. For some, a lack of understanding or self-discipline frequently contributes to inadequate time for sleep. Like much of biology, sleep varies across the age continuum, with unique problems at every age. (See the section entitled "Sleep in Older Adults.") Adults need approximately seven to eight hours of sleep. Young adults (adolescents) need eight to nine hours of sleep.[6] Time management can prove to be very helpful.

Sleep in Older Adults

With age come many social and biologic changes which can affect sleep. As one ages, sleep can become more difficult to initiate. Sleep

---

6. N. F. Watson et al., "Recommended Amount of Sleep for a Healthy Adult: A Joint Consensus Statement of the American Academy of Sleep Medicine and Sleep Research Society," *Journal of Clinical Sleep Medicine* 11, no. 6 (2015): 591.

398 The Christian Counselor's Medical Desk Reference

is also more fragile, with a greater frequency of arousals. In addition, with aging comes the potential for many new health problems that can affect sleep quality and quantity. These problems may include menopause and accompanying hot flashes, arthritis, heartburn, urinary issues, heart disease, and lung disease, as well as aches and pains from injuries. These medical problems reduce sleep quality and can increase daytime sleepiness.

Social change is also significant in older adults. Retirement creates opportunity for poor sleep hygiene habits. Time management issues may result in irregular schedules, afternoon napping, or even excessive time in bed. These habits may reduce the quality of sleep, resulting in complaints of daytime sleepiness and naps. While brief twenty-minute power naps can be helpful, longer naps are not recommended. Structured day, night, and meal schedules can be helpful with sleep success in the older adult.

It has been observed that the need for eight-hour nights decreases as one ages. Mild alterations in sleep, such as brief naps or shorter nights, are normal with advancing age. Sleep can serve as a barometer of other life issues. Very chaotic or abnormal sleep/wake patterns in an older adult is a warning sign of possible underlying social or biologic problems. At all ages sleep is linked to biology as well as psychosocial issues.

Adolescent Sleep (Phase Delay)

A common presenting problem in a sleep clinic is the adolescent who is unable to get out of bed in the morning for school. Parents and school officials are very frustrated by tardiness and sleeping in morning classes. Once sleep apnea or other sleep disorders have been excluded, delayed sleep phase is the most frequent cause of this problem.[7] Delayed sleep phase is a term referring to a circadian rhythm

---

7. American Academy of Sleep Medicine, *International Classification of Sleep Disorders*, 3rd ed. (Darien, IL: American Academy of Sleep Medicine, 2014), 191.

delay. Simply put, in delayed sleep phase syndrome, bedtime has been repetitively delayed, which results in the inability to sleep at the desired earlier bedtime.

Phase delay in young adults is rooted in the fact that adolescents do not perceive themselves to be sleepy at bedtime. A contributing factor is evening screen time (social media or movies), which engages the young mind long past an appropriate bedtime. Sleep commences too late to be adequate when the morning alarm rings. Sleeping in late on the weekends reinforces the delay in the sleep/wake timing. The late weekend rise time, seen as catching up on sleep, anchors the teen to an alternate time schedule. Monday morning awakenings are very difficult if one lives on the East Coast while following the sleep schedule of a Hawaiian.

This is best corrected by a disciplined and regular rise time seven days per week. Avoiding evening screen time or other activities that can delay bedtime must be enforced with the help of parents. Late evening screen time not only delays bedtime, but exposes one to blue light at the wrong end of a sleep cycle. Morning light, activity (exercise), and food upon arising all help anchor the circadian rhythm to local time.

Sleep Disorders

In addition to time management, the second contributor to daytime sleepiness is an actual sleep disorder. Most folks with a sleep disorder never realize this is the reason for the lack of morning refreshment. Several common sleep disorders can make refreshing sleep unattainable. Let's look at some of them.

Obstructive Sleep Apnea

In years gone by, it was thought that sleep was deep and restful when one "sawed logs" at night. It turns out that snoring is the tip of the iceberg for a very common problem known as obstructive sleep apnea (OSA). Due to frequent micro arousals and low oxygen,

OSA steals from people at night. It reduces their energy, ambition, short-term memory, and emotional reserves, along with other effects. Unfortunately, OSA also increases the risk of high blood pressure, heart disease, stroke, and premature mortality.[8] OSA affects approximately 20 percent of US males and 10 percent of females. Excess body weight is a significant risk factor, but more important is the hallmark snoring.

As humans relax into sleep, muscle tone declines, including those in the upper airway or throat. This reduction in muscle tone allows for tissue vibration, which we call snoring. People do not snore while awake, but rather during sleep, making them personally unaware of the hallmark sign. The term *apnea* means to stop breathing, but cessation of breathing is often not present and is not required. OSA should be considered in any habitual snorer, especially with any sleep complaints such as frequent awakenings, restlessness, frequent urination, or gasping. Daytime symptoms include the routine symptoms of sleep deprivation, such as short-term memory loss, irritability, sleepiness, or reduced libido (sex drive). Daytime symptoms may be part of the reason for obtaining counsel.

If OSA is suspected, a sleep evaluation should be given serious consideration. This includes a detailed medical and sleep history, as well as a physical examination. The final test is a polysomnogram (sleep study). This might be conducted at home or in a sleep laboratory. It monitors sleep and breathing to assess for OSA.

OSA, when discovered, is most often treated with positive airway pressure (CPAP, APAP or BiPAP). This comes from a machine that generates air pressure. It requires the patient to wear a small facial mask through which air enters the upper airway. This air then creates an air splint to stop snoring and keep the airway open during sleep. During the first several weeks of treatment, sleep is often disrupted MORE by this treatment, causing some patients to abandon

---

8. T. D. Bradley and J. S. Floras, "Obstructive Sleep Apnoea and Its Cardiovascular Consequences," *Lancet* 373, no. 9657 (2009): 82–93.

the therapy before the benefits begin. Just like riding a bike, it is not fun on the first day, but after people learn to ride, they do not turn back.

In overweight patients, weight loss is also needed, but it is not always curative for OSA. There are other benefits from weight reduction, given that excess weight increases the risk of OSA as well as diabetes, high blood pressure, cancer, and arthritis.[9] Other treatments for OSA are available for the right candidate. An oral device similar to a sports mouth guard to help maintain the airway during sleep is helpful in more mild cases of OSA. Hypoglossal (tongue) nerve stimulation with implanted pacemakers is also an option in select patients.[10] There are currently no effective medications for OSA.

Narcolepsy

The term *narcolepsy* is sometimes incorrectly used to describe a person who is sleepy, but it is actually a very specific sleep disorder involving the brain. A person with narcolepsy actually has a loss of brain cells that manufacture hypocretin.[11] Hypocretin turns REM sleep off during the day. Without this compound, a narcoleptic is typically profoundly sleepy and may experience additional symptoms. One additional symptom is a loss of muscle strength in emotional states such as laughter, fear, or anger. This loss of muscle power is called cataplexy. The symptoms of narcolepsy can be disabling, with significant personal effects like loss of employment, loss of relationships, and motor vehicle accidents. If narcolepsy is suspected, a complete evaluation by a sleep specialist is required in order to make an accurate diagnosis and assure proper treatment.

---

9. F. Xavier Pi-Sunyer, "The Obesity Epidemic: Pathophysiology and Consequences of Obesity," *Obesity Research* 10 (2002): 97S–104S, https://doi.org/10.1038/oby.2002.202.

10. Peter R. Eastwood et al., "Treating Obstructive Sleep Apnea with Hypoglossal Nerve Stimulation," *Sleep* 34, no. 11 (2011): 1479–1486.

11. American Academy of Sleep Medicine, *International Classification of Sleep Disorders*, 146.

Nightmares

Most people remember an occasional dream. There is no way to know if dreams occur unless the person upon awakening reports a memory. Many dreams disappear like a mist with only fragments remaining, unless captured in the first moments of consciousness. The content of the dream and the extent of immediate wakefulness contribute to the extent of memories. Also, actively writing down the dream immediately upon awakening increases the memory. Likewise, very unpleasant content is disturbing and is often more easily remembered. Unpleasant dreams are called nightmares.[12]

As is discussed under insomnia, life events do affect how well we sleep. Poor or fragmented sleep has more transitions between sleep to wake, increasing the opportunity for dream recall. Similarly, tumultuous wake events can impact the content of our dreams. Post-traumatic stress disorder (PTSD) is an example of events contributing to nightmares.

Some medications are associated with an increase in nightmares—in some cases medication use causes nightmares, and in other instances it is the withdrawal of medications. Beta blockers, common blood pressure and heart medications, have a strong association with nightmares. Withdrawal of antidepressant medications has also been linked with increased frequency of nightmares.

In non-medication induced nightmares, treatment is mostly directed at lifestyle management. In other words, improving daily life improves sleep. Improved sleep generally means fewer nightmares. Recurrent or frequent nightmares are best seen as a dashboard light that something is wrong with life while awake.

Insomnia

Insomnia—not being able to sleep when given the proper opportunity—is a common complaint at a medical visit, as well as in the

---

12. American Academy of Sleep Medicine, *International Classification of Sleep Disorders*, 258.

counseling room. The human desire (and need) to put one's head on a pillow and awake refreshed makes insomnia unpleasant or frustrating for the person experiencing it. It can affect all ages, including children, but is more prevalent in older age groups.

Insomnia is divided into two categories. Acute insomnia is of less than three months duration and commonly has an identifiable cause. The causal events are often major life events (death, divorce, social upheaval, etc.). Chronic insomnia is defined as difficulty initiating or maintaining sleep at least three nights per week for at least three months. Acute insomnia is estimated to affect about 30 to 35 percent of the population, while chronic insomnia affects about 10 percent. Chronic insomnia is more common in females. It is also common in people in need of and receiving counseling. Insomnia is linked to suicidal thoughts when the sufferer experiences a sense of hopelessness.[13]

The first goal in evaluating insomnia is to gather information regarding the circumstances of sleeplessness. Could there be an easily reversible cause? Causes such as pain, medication side effects, poor sleep habits (see above), or a medical illness can be identified. The medical problems which may contribute to insomnia are numerous and common. Heart disease, lung disease, sleep apnea, or hormone abnormalities like hyperthyroidism or menopause are just a few possible contributors to the complaint of insomnia. If no primary cause for the sleeplessness is uncovered, the labels of either acute insomnia or chronic insomnia are applied based on chronicity of the problem.

Both acute and chronic insomnia require daytime effects by definition. Please note that these daytime effects are also seen in other sleep disorders. Recognizing these effects in a counselee is a tip-off that a sleep problem may contribute to the reasons for counsel. The daytime effects might include the following:

- Fatigue
- Impairment in attention, memory, or concentration

---

13. Woosley et al., "Hopelessness Mediates the Relation between Insomnia and Suicidal Ideation," *Journal of Clinical Sleep Medicine* 10, no. 11 (2014): 1223–30, https://doi.org/10.5664/jcsm.4208.

- Impaired social, family, occupational, or academic performance
- Mood disturbances or irritability
- Daytime sleepiness
- Reduced motivation
- Concerns about or dissatisfaction with sleep[14]

Medications can induce sleep for acute or chronic insomnia. However, medication is not recommended as the first-line approach, especially for chronic insomnia. Over-reliance upon medication can result in increased dependency upon medication and the risk of side effects from that medication.

It has been shown that cognitive behavior therapy specifically for insomnia (CBT-I) has more lasting effects at controlling chronic insomnia than medication.[15] CBT-I provides important education regarding the biology of sleep (refer to the previous section on the biology of sleep). This information improves the counselee's understanding of sleep and preparation for a good night's sleep. However, this educational component of sleep biology alone has *not* been shown to be helpful in reducing insomnia. CBT-I also includes secular counseling to change how people think about sleep *and* other issues of life. In both acute and chronic insomnia, this counsel regarding life skills helps the sufferer achieve better sleep.

Medical study has unwittingly recognized that humans are more than just chemical machines in need of more chemicals (medications). Rather, CBT-I works with immaterial aspects of people such as expectations, security, goals, purpose, and relationships. It is these aspects of being human that medication cannot alter, but have immense effect on peaceful sleep.

---

14. American Academy of Sleep Medicine, *International Classification of Sleep Disorders*, 21–22.

15. S. Beaulieu-Bonneau et al., "Long-Term Maintenance of Therapeutic Gains Associated with Cognitive-Behavioral Therapy for Insomnia Delivered Alone or Combined With Zolpidem," *Sleep* 40, no. 3 (2017), https://doi.org/10.1093/sleep/zsx002; G. D. Jacobs et al., Cognitive Behavior Therapy and Pharmacotherapy for Insomnia: A Randomized Controlled Trial and Direct Comparison," *Archives of Internal Medicine* 164, no. 17 (2004): 1888.

The medical model of health is incomplete. It can be likened to using morphine alone for a broken leg. While pain relief may help, it does not address the real problem of the fractured bone. As biblical counselors, we understand that although CBT-I can be helpful in addressing sleep problems, it is an incomplete solution because it does not address root issues of the heart.

Counseling a Person Suffering from a Sleep Disorder

A biblical anthropology recognizes humans are both material and immaterial. Some sleep disorders, such as OSA and narcolepsy are principally bodily (material) problems. Medical care is essential in dealing with these bodily disorders. However, as with any medical disorder, heart issues of noncompliance, discouragement, and even hopelessness can arise. As biblical counselors, we focus on these immaterial heart issues of any medical illness. Insomnia is a difficulty centering more on our immaterial, rather than material. This falls within the purview of biblical counseling and will be the focus of our remaining discussion.

Let us begin by examining an important night, the night of Jesus in the garden of Gethsemane from Matthew 26:36–41 (NIV).

> Then Jesus went with his disciples to a place called Gethsemane, and he said to them, "Sit here while I go over there and pray." He took Peter and the two sons of Zebedee along with him, and he began to be sorrowful and troubled. Then he said to them, "My soul is overwhelmed with sorrow to the point of death. Stay here and keep watch with me."
>
> Going a little farther, he fell with his face to the ground and prayed, "My Father, if it is possible, may this cup be taken from me. Yet not as I will, but as you will."
>
> Then he returned to his disciples and found them sleeping. "Couldn't you men keep watch with me for one hour?"

he asked Peter. "Watch and pray so that you will not fall into temptation. The spirit is willing, but the flesh is weak."

What can be gleaned about sleep from this passage? Scripture is indirectly informing us that humans are not just chemical machines. We are not switched into the off position at bedtime for sleep to commence. Based on Scripture, as well as the common human experience, we know an occasional sleepless night comes with being human. We all have concerns and worries. At times, these concerns might lead to thoughts in the night that inhibit sleep. What we do with these thoughts is very important. Recall that Jesus once slept in the bottom of a boat in a storm while the disciples were awake and terrified (Matthew 8:23–25). Conversely, Jesus was awake in the garden of Gethsemane while the disciples slept.

Jesus, in a time of sleeplessness caused by the great sorrow and burden of facing the cross, went to the Father in prayer. Trust has a calming effect on the soul. As Isaiah 26:3 (NIV) says, "You will keep in perfect peace those whose minds are steadfast, because they trust in you."

As with Jesus in the garden, personal sin is not required to experience insomnia. Scripture is replete with references to the human experience of life called sleepless nights (Psalms 6:1–10; 42:3; Daniel 6:18). Often sleeplessness is the result of the implications of death and decay from the general curse of sin under which the whole world is living (Romans 8:18–25).

But the consequences of personal sin with resultant difficulties such as guilt, remorse, or worry, may also result in insomnia. A biblical counselor must exercise wisdom and discernment, unlike Job's friends (Job 4:6–9) who misjudged the situation and assumed personal sin to be the core issue. Sin should always be considered, but not always be assumed.

The fact that Jesus experienced sleepless nights should be a comfort to us and our counselees. What Jesus did through that long night of sorrow and horror can also point the way forward for us when we experience sleeplessness. He prayed continually—telling his real sorrows to his heavenly Father and ultimately submitting his will to his Father. He asked others to pray with and for him (although sadly the disciples were "exhausted from sorrow" and not keeping watch with him).

Likewise, we might pray and deepen our commitment to the Father's will for us, asking that his "will be done on earth as it is in heaven." Excessive focus on self and our sleep is not the solution to the problem of insomnia. In the garden, during one of Christ's great hours of need, he maintained his focus upon the Father and above all things, doing the Father's will. Taking our eyes off ourselves and focusing on our love for God and others is important (Matthew 22:37). During a wakeful night, consider what we might do in the night and in the coming morning to please the Lord. Do we need to mend a relationship, forgive another, or meet another's need?

The Psalms provide many examples of how we can spend this time awake on our beds:

- "Be angry, and do not sin; ponder in your own hearts on your beds, and be silent" (4:4 ESV).
- "On my bed I remember you; I think of you through the watches of the night" (63:6 NIV)
- "Let his faithful people rejoice in this honor and sing for joy on their beds" (149:5 NIV).
- "In the night, LORD, I remember your name, and I will keep your law" (119:55 NIV).
- "At midnight I rise to give you thanks for your righteous laws" (119:62 NIV).

When the sleepless night arrives, one must never allow lack of sleep to be an excuse to sin. When Jesus was in the wilderness (Matthew 4:2), both hungry and undoubtedly tired, he did not find it an occasion or excuse to sin. One must be vigilant not to permit the issues of our bodily biology to push our soul into disobedience.

It is wise though to anticipate challenging daytime situations after a poor night's sleep and plan and pray accordingly to avoid temptation. Such plans might include asking for help from family and friends and/or off-loading responsibilities. These same changes can be helpful not only to prevent sinful responses following a night of sleeplessness, but also key in reducing stress to aid in preventing another sleepless night.

Let us return to the introductory scenario of Sarah. She admits that her stress levels are leading to chronic sleeplessness and even hopelessness. Recall that hopelessness associated with sleeplessness has been observed to be associated with increased suicidal ideation. Sarah is hurting and needs help quickly.

It is paramount to ensure Sarah has no plan of self-harm (suicide). If there is any hint of self-harm, she should not be left alone, and she needs immediate help to guarantee her physical safety. This may require the involvement of the health care system. If necessary, physicians can legally hospitalize someone to protect them from plans of self-harm. If Sarah has no intent of self-harm, at minimum she needs to have a medical examination. In extreme situations like Sarah's, medication may help her obtain adequate sleep to begin to make changes.

As mentioned, Sarah knows stress is causing harm, but she may not accurately understand the source of her stress. She, like many, may think it a combination of biology and situation, while neglecting the role of her own heart. The biblical counselor's role is to bring the truth of Scripture to her mind while the Holy Spirit uses it to "judge the thoughts and attitudes of the heart" (Hebrews 4:12 NIV). Change only comes after a need for change is realized.

The end of this chapter contains a chart which may aid a sleepless counselee to gain insight. It can be employed as homework. This heart work needs to be combined with application of the biologic factors of human sleep discussed in the section on medical background.

In Sarah's specific case, here are some areas in need of exploration over weeks of counseling and coming alongside to help her troubled and stressed heart.

- Sarah is expressing desperation. Asking counselees about self-harm has *not* been associated with an increase in suicide, but rather can bring extra help before the event. Actual suicide does not have a second chance for intervention.
  - Sarah needs immediate help to keep her physically safe. This might mean employing medical resources to ensure her safety. Short-term use of medication may be appropriate to allow the sleep her body requires.
- Could Sarah obtain more local help for her parents?
  - Coming alongside Sarah to find additional measures to aid her parents may seem like social work, but is part of the counselor's role. Helping to connect her parents with friends and the church in their community will be useful. Even exploring new assisted living options for Mom and Dad is a realistic view of the future.
- Is Sarah's guilt real or imagined regarding her parents?
  - The biblical understanding of responsibility and guilt regarding the decisions of family members is often difficult. Arriving at an accurate balance of trusting the sovereignty of God, our personal role, and their role needs discussion.
- Does Sarah have realistic or unrealistic expectations of her role as a wife, homeschool mother, daughter, and church member?
  - Marriage requires a leaving and cleaving that needs to be explored in this situation. The discussion of a possible child-centered home is also an area which may need to be addressed. Sarah may have an imbalance between her roles of wife, mother, and daughter.
- How well is Sarah communicating with the people in her life: her husband, children, and parents?
  - Helping Sarah to use the principles of biblical communication for improving her relationships with her husband, children, and parents could improve her situation. Poor communication is often at the root of stressful relationships.

- Are there issues of the marriage bed that are being poorly communicated, executed, or expected?
  - The area of sexuality is often poorly communicated and therefore contributes to marital stress. Marital stress is a major contributor to insomnia. Recognizing the need to make personal change, not spousal change, is key to stress reduction.

Remember, the night is really part of a day. There is no single solution to improve sleep. No special Bible verse, tea, or activity will guarantee sleep. Sleep is a product of a life. Chronic sleeplessness suggests there is an opportunity to grow in our relationship with Christ. This growth changes our life and therefore our sleep.

A Final Word to the Counselor

Sleep is very important to daily function as a human. Sleep exists at the cross section of both our material body and immaterial soul. The body affects the soul, just as the soul affects the body. Similarly, our day affects our night, just as our night affects our day. A wise counselor will explore the entire 24-hour day of the counselee to gain insight and offer truth to help another live as God intends.

Our sleep does not define us, but it is a part of our biology. As with all areas of biology, people have different strengths and abilities. Some people sleep well; others face nightly challenges. People should not neglect or idolize sleep. Like all of life, sleep will have seasons of ease and times of increased struggle. We must discern what is to be accepted and what can be improved. As we counsel those who are struggling with sleep, keep in mind that all searching and changing needs to be done for God's glory because that is the reason we exist.

Weekly Sleep Log and Quiet Time Aid							
Week of _____	**Mon.**	**Tues.**	**Wed.**	**Thurs.**	**Fri.**	**Sat.**	**Sun.**
What time did you go to bed?							
About how long for you to fall asleep?							
How many times did you wake up?							
What time did you get up to stay?							
If awake, what was occupying your thoughts? ***							

Daily Quiet Time Questions

***How can the truth of Scripture be applied to your wake thoughts of last night?

Is there anything I must do today, which will honor Christ, in regard to my wake thoughts last night?

What things can I do today to strengthen at least one of my many relationships?

CHAPTER 22

APPLYING THE PRACTICE OF BIBLICALLY BASED MEDICINE TO RHEUMATOLOGY

Jim Halla, MD

This section's goal is to help biblical counselors recognize some of the physical problems related to rheumatology and how those symptoms can affect a counselee emotionally and spiritually. Throughout the section, I refer to a series of papers I offer my patients to help them thrive spiritually even with difficult—and in some cases unresolvable—physical symptoms. Those papers can be accessed via my website: https://jimhalla.com/.

Patient Presentation

Patient 1: Ms. Brown is a twenty-four-year-old single woman, a recent college graduate, and a new elementary school teacher. She is here because of aches and pains, fatigue, and recently a facial rash. She just had a positive lupus test and wonders what it means. She says to me, "All of this is so new."

She has always been active and is excited about her new job. She is part of a Bible-believing church and sings in the choir. But she does not think she can continue all of her activities unless she gets help. She tires easily, and her joints ache. She knows other people with lupus and wonders what her life will be like now.

Before her diagnosis, she was healthy and rarely went to the doctor. She worked hard to get into school, keep up with her studies, keep her scholarship, and stay active in church. "Now this," she said to me. "How will I keep going and succeed?" Fatigue is a major concern for her.

Her parents, boyfriend, and her church are concerned and praying for her. On examination, she complained of pain on palpation of her joints, had mild puffiness over her knuckles, and presented with a facial rash (a butterfly distribution) going across the bridge of the nose. We eventually made the diagnosis of systemic lupus erythematosus (SLE).

I explained to her that I give every new patient a series of papers that give basic facts and principles about many conditions, including a group of diseases called the connective tissue diseases (CTD). The papers are designed to help the person get victory in the problem. I don't define "victory" as the disappearance of disease, although it is certainly my goal to heal physically as much as possible. But true victory occurs as we function as a true Christian oyster: the believer is not passive but uses the irritation/hard times (and good times) as a means to make the pearl of Christlikeness.

The believer puts off self and self-pleasing and puts on what pleases and honors God. Being functional to the degree that the person can is one example. The person relies more and more on God and on his truth and faithfulness. It's important to present this message empathetically, not as an easy fix, but as an ongoing process of going to the Lord with all of our troubles and trusting him to help us love him and love others in the midst of trials. The message is counterintuitive and countercultural. But it is biblical!

Patient 2: Ms. Smith, a thirty-five-year-old married woman, has been in good health, but now she has multiple concerns. Over the past three years she reports increasing hours of morning stiffness, trouble getting up and getting things done, decreasing function, and fatigue.

She is discouraged. The tempo of her discomfort has picked up recently, and ignoring it has not helped. A variety of medications have not helped.

She says to me, "I need to get back to my usual self. They are so many people depending on me." Feeling physically impaired is a new experience for her, and she asks with an anguished look, "What will happen with and without treatment?" Pain and fatigue are her constant companions. Both affect her thinking and she struggles with fear, worry, discouragement, and anger. It will be very important to help her understand the linkage between her thoughts, desires, emotions, and her physical discomfort.

Physical examination shows that she has synovitis in multiple swollen joints—warmth, reduced mobility and function—but no deformities or nodules. After completing the examination, I share with her the working diagnosis of polysynovitis, which I define as more than four joints inflamed. Further, I tell her that rheumatoid arthritis (RA) is the most common disease that causes synovitis. The goal of treatment is to stop the synovitis—to stop the "fire from burning." She says that she is beginning to understand.

She wants to know what happens now. I have a decision to make. I can simply keep things in the physical realm and focus on her presumed RA. Or I can take the situation as an opportunity to minister to her as a whole person. I chose the latter since this is part of the practice of biblically based medicine and counseling. She liked my choice. The nonphysician biblical counselor has a similar choice. You would certainly want counselees to see a physician, but you can still take the opportunity to help them depend on God during trouble.

She tells me that her husband would have been there at the appointment, but she likes to do things herself and he has work to do. I realize that I need to know her as a person. I am not treating RA but am treating God's image-bearer who has RA! This is a fact both the physician and the counselor should keep in mind.

She is a Christian, but she wonders why God is allowing this and why he hasn't answered the many prayers for her. I asked her the nature of the prayer. She shares that she and her family and friends are praying for healing. I asked her what answer she would accept. She did not reply to that question, but these are good questions for a counselor to ask.

Patient 3: Mary is a sixty-two-year-old married woman, a retired nurse. She came to the office with complaints of all-over-pain, fatigue, good and bad days, and "going nowhere fast." The duration of her symptoms has been about two decades. She told me that she hurts from her head to toe, but mostly along the spine: from the scapular areas (shoulder blades) to her lumbar area and buttocks. Fatigue was a constant companion, but she did not describe joint swelling or redness.

She told me that she felt like life was "the pits." She didn't think that her attitude pleased God, but she didn't know what else to do. She had been given a label of fibromyalgia (FM) and depression. Medications were prescribed, including psychotropic drugs. She reported that they did not make her feel better. Rather, she felt like she was in black hole—a long, dark tunnel with no way out. She said she was down and almost out.

She wanted to make sure that she had the proper diagnosis, and she wanted help. She told me that pain worsened when she overdid or underdid, and when her thoughts and desires focused on "doing everything like I used to." She hoped to return to her former status but just wanted out. As a believer, she knew God was in control *but* . . . she stopped with *but*. She could not think of any redeeming purpose in her life.

I asked her how I could help. She told me that listening was a good start. She wondered if I would be any different from others. On physical examination she had important negatives. Her joint and muscle examinations were normal. There was no evidence of synovitis and only mild changes of osteoarthritis in several hand joints. She did complain of pain when I palpated certain area of her body (so-called trigger points).

I completed the initial work by ordering radiographs and laboratory testing. I gave her some homework—the series of papers I give every new patient (mentioned earlier). The papers review the spectrum of rheumatic diseases and help probe the person's thoughts and desires. They gently introduce the patient to the beauty and value of a biblical approach to life.

Patient 4: Mrs. White is a forty-year-old married woman who presents with an array of symptoms and a three-year diagnosis of chronic fatigue syndrome (CFS). She wants to know how she can get better. She had been healthy until this chronic fatigue began. It is an overwhelming fatigue and exhaustion such that she just wants to stay in bed. It's as if she is drained of energy.

The problem began after a nonspecific illness that she called a virus: a sore throat and some swollen lymph nodes in the neck. Her doctor gave her medication and analyzed her blood work, which was normal. Since that time her life has changed dramatically. Fatigue is her constant companion, often accompanied by pain and crampy sensations. In cataloguing her symptoms, she includes problems focusing, although she remembers many specific details.

She goes to bed fatigued and awakens fatigued. It's all she can do just to get out of bed. But often she can't and she doesn't. I ask what would happen if she got up anyway. She doesn't know. If her house was on fire, she thinks she could get out, but she hopes that does not happen.

She explains that it is hard to concentrate because of her preoccupation with the fatigue, both wishing it was gone and the preoccupation with pacing herself. The sore throat, headache, and enlarged nodes have not recurred. She won't move around or exercise, saying it is too hard. When she engages in physical exercise and mental activity, such as praying and Bible reading, she feels more fatigued. However, she does listen to people talk and watch them on the internet. She says she tries to do things around the house but says she can't accomplish much. Her husband does almost everything. She believes he is getting tired of it all. Also, it is hard for her to be intimate with him—a concern that has not been addressed.

She says she "listens to her feelings" because that is all she can do. Dizziness worsens with getting up and down, and sleep is not refreshing. I ask what her last thought and desire is before falling asleep and what her first thought and desire is upon awaking. She responds, "To get to sleep," and "Why do I have to get up?"

She knows that there is much written about CFS, but she is wearied of reviewing articles, seeing doctors, and hoping for improvement. She wants to know what she should do, but she doesn't know how I can help except to make it go away. I asked how she has responded to God. She said she was praying but that her problem (CFS) has remained.

Her physical examination was normal. I gave her papers that I give every new patient/counselee. It includes a questionnaire to fill out, and we will review it when she returns. She said she appreciated my interest, specifically that I asked questions and listened for her answers.

Summary of Findings

Although these four women had different medical diagnoses, they shared many things in common. Their symptoms were similar, although signs differed. Complaint of pain and fatigue were as common as was the desire for relief. Specifically, while two of the women were diagnosed with immunological-mediated diseases (RA and SLE), the other two diagnoses were labeled chronic pain conditions (FM and CFS).

Several facts stand out and are noted in the following list:

1. Even though the term *autoimmune* is a long-standing and common term, I believe it is preferable to refer to such rheumatic diseases as RA and CTD as *immunological mediated*. The immune system is active, but there is little evidence that it is "attacking" itself. In fact, certain proteins that are helpful

in the diagnosis of these diseases—such as rheumatoid factors and antinuclear antibodies—are not uncommonly found in the blood of normal people where they do not induce disease.

2. Pain is a common complaint. The figures are staggering. Various reports state that 10–20 percent of the United States population has back or neck complaints each year.[1] The number has only increased! However, pain is a symptom, not a sign. A symptom is subjective—it is what the person feels and even experiences and communicates to the physician. The statement "I hurt" is a symptom. It is not verifiable. The statements "I hurt and my joint is swollen" (assuming it is!) present both a symptom and a sign—an objective finding. The complaint of pain is common especially in the rheumatologist's office. A physical examination helps the patient and physician sort out the difference between a symptom and a sign. Symptoms or signs or both are present in various rheumatic conditions.

3. As the case reports indicate, a thorough history and physical examination helps the physician differentiate between arthritis (a problem with the joint that may be inflammatory such as RA or degenerative such as OA) and soft tissue rheumatism, which originates from non-inflammatory irritation of the soft tissue as opposed to the hard tissue (bone and joints) for any number of reasons. Soft tissue rheumatism is quite common and can be classified as:

   a. local (tendonitis and bursitis);
   b. regional (myofascial problems that are thought to emanate from muscle, ligament, and or tendons); and
   c. generalized (such as fibromyalgia that is reported to occur in up to 5 percent of the United States' population).[2]

---

1. John Klippel, *Primer on Rheumatic Diseases*, 13th edition, Arthritis Foundation, 2008.
2. Klippel, *Primer on Rheumatic Diseases*.

A Further Word about So-Called Pain Conditions

How do these facts regarding the body—the outer person—relate to the whole person? Where does the inner person (the heart) fit into the practice and receiving of medical care?[3] How does true science and the Bible intersect to help both the doctor and the patient get victory in their problem?

It is mandatory that the rheumatologist know his stuff—rheumatology—so he can function as God's kind of rheumatologist. But he must know biblical truth and how to bring that to himself and the patient. Biblical principles abound that help doctor, patient, and family get victory *in* the problem, not necessarily *out* of it! Good theology and good medicine are linked. Both are fundamental for and to the practice of biblically based medicine and counseling.

Similarly, the biblical counselor will address the whole person. Biblical truth rightly applied is not some adjunct or temporary last-gasp measure. God's truth sets people free. It is not a guarantee that bodies will be healed in this life. But helping patient, doctor, and counselor function as trustworthy biblical stewards of God's providence always brings hope, joy, and comfort.

All four of the patients discussed experienced similar symptoms: fatigue and bodily pain. These symptoms are often associated with such terms as having a *lower quality of life*. Patients describe, either voluntarily or in response to data gathering, a difficulty in daily living. Performing routine and necessary tasks that used to be carried out with little effort now require much effort and stamina. Sometimes the mountain seems too high, the hole too deep and dark, and the road too long, hard, and lonely. In response, the person takes upon himself or herself a new identity—that of a suffering victim. Suffering and victimhood then take center stage. A downward spiral of thoughts and desires ensues: discouragement, fear, giving in, and giving up.

---

3. See Jim Halla, *Being Christian in Your Medical Practice, True Competence in Medicine* (Greenville, SC: Ambassador International, 2012); Jim Halla, *How to Be a God-Pleasing Patient: A Biblical Approach to Receiving Medical Care* (Greenville, SC: Ambassador International, 2020).

Sadly and commonly, the person's eyes and heart are on the problem and not the God of the problem.

It's important to begin by giving counselees an opportunity to express their fears, worries, and frustrations. Common concerns include uncertainty regarding the final results of medical tests, worries about finances, and dread of impending trouble, including the loss of caring for others and themselves especially in the ways they are accustomed. Often these are called *quality of life* issues—I think incorrectly. These patients and their families have *inner-man issues* that come to the surface in the context of physical problems. Some may call these *spiritual struggles*. In reality, the whole person—inner and outer man—is to be considered as a whole.

These issues involve a person's thoughts, desires, and actions—in both the body, brain, and the heart. Therefore, the physician and counselor must help uncover the person's thoughts, desires, and actions in both the inner and outer man. Unfortunately, many call these *struggles* without defining the term. Most often the term *struggles* are a description of the person's unfavorable response to God's providence.

A good way forward is to help the person understand such passages as Romans 8:28–29 and 2 Corinthians 4:16–18 and 12:7–10. A proper focus on God ensures that the person will develop a proper focus on self and the problem. This, in turn, facilitates the patient to function as God's kind of patient.[4] Life is simplified, and improvement often follows.

Patients in either group (rheumatism or arthritis) often describe themselves as having little pleasure. Joy may be replaced by bitterness. Routine activities are now burdensome. Many keep moving because they bottle up their pain and feelings. These are *roadrunner types*. Others are couch potatoes: they sit and often brood. This dynamic of *increase* (thoughts and desires that focus on the bad) and *decrease* (a decline in physical function while thoughts and desires are rampant)

---

4. Halla, *How to Be a God-Pleasing Patient.*

is often compounded by irritation, frustration, anger, and bitterness. Their focus is horizontal and often not controlled by a proper vertical (God-ward) reference. This is an area where medicine and biblical counseling meet and can be a great benefit to the patient.

An Overview of Rheumatic Diseases

What follows is a simple way to get some idea of the magnificence of God as Creator and Controller (Psalms 19, 139; Romans 8:28–29). God has designed the human body marvelously and wonderfully. Science has given us information about the body's immune system. It is a complex protective system that involves a myriad of cells, neurochemicals, and neuropeptides that serve as signals alerting the body that help is needed. These cells have a number of functions, including producing antibodies aided by so-called helper and suppressor cells, priming cells for removal of proteins from the circulation, facilitating cell to cell interactions that help in this removal, and generally functioning as a cleanup crew. This system must have been in the garden of Eden, but since there was no sin or sinners, there was no disease. After sin (Romans 5:12–14; 6:23), the immune system was "turned on" to do its job of protection.

However, in some people the immune system has become a problem. How so? Initially, cells did not attack the body or its constituents. However, in the 1960s a blood test called the *rheumatoid factor* helped in diagnosing patients with RA. The key is not the presence or absence of the antibody, but how much is present and its correlation with the patient's symptoms and signs.

In the 1970–1980s, a blood test termed *antinuclear antibody* was detected in a high percentage of patients with Systemic lupus erythematosus (SLE). This added to the idea that diseases such as RA and SLE were "autoimmune." Somehow the body was attacking itself.

All the above is to say that it is better to think of such diseases as RA and the connective tissues diseases such as SLE, Sjogren's syndrome (SS), progressive or limited scleroderma (PSS and LSS), polymyositis

(PM), and dermatomyositis (DM) as whole-body diseases. The disease can involve any number of organ systems. Moreover, they have a number of antibodies serving as markers for diagnosis. Their presence also can help in understanding how these diseases manifest. This information helps inform the biblical counselor as he or she speaks with the person and the physician.

Figures vary regarding the frequency of these entities. RA is common, especially in women between age twenty and forty, but it can occur at any age. SLE is a disease that affects women much more than men and it tends to be a younger age group. SLE is more common in Black and Hispanic populations.

Thankfully, many of these rheumatological diseases have specific features and accompanying blood tests and radiographs that simplify the diagnosis. There are times when symptoms (subjective information such as what the patient tells you about fatigue, pain, and feverishness) and signs (what a patient has on physical exam) can be similar and mimic another disease. However, as I have learned, one aspect of being a God-honoring rheumatologist is knowing my stuff! I like to convey that information to both the counselor and the patient.

Symptoms and Signs

To that end, I discuss the difference between symptoms and signs. I reflect on specifics. Patients often present with nonspecific features: fatigue, pain, stiffness, and just not doing well. Joints may be involved specifically with swelling or complaints of pain. On physical examination, I look for evidence of the disease in the joints, skin, muscle, lungs, and internal organs such as the liver or spleen. A proper history and physical examination is important. I want the patient to know that I have heard and understand them. Those two facts don't necessarily mean that I always agree with them. I need more data to confirm or refute my impression and their impression. Fortunately, the laboratory and its results and proper radiographs can aid in this endeavor. Certain simple labs are helpful in distinguishing between inflammatory (RA and CTD) from noninflammatory conditions.

These include a complete blood count (CBC) and a sedimentation rate, which is a measure of inflammation.

Good Stewardship

Both patient/counselee and physician/counselor should be aware that good stewardship is a biblical principle. It involves seeing and not seeing a doctor and the motivation for each decision. It is wise to see a physician when there is joint swelling, especially if accompanied by redness and warmth. So-called systemic features (fever, weight loss) also should be investigated. Symptoms and signs related to other organ systems such as the skin, lungs, gut, kidney, and nervous system warrant some type of attention.

Treatment

I discuss treatment after I am satisfied the person understands that God has them where he wants them and he has not deserted them. I want them to know that neither will I—we are in this for the long haul, but we are not alone. However, some people never move to relying on God's grace and wisdom. Rather they focus on the difficulties of the situation and depend solely on treatment modalities, including medications. They fail to acknowledge several things: (a) a proper diagnosis is a gift as it directs both patient and physician; (b) medications are God's gift to be used for his glory; (c) and proper stewardship of the whole person is an attainable goal and always blessed by God in some form and fashion.

Several of the pain papers I share with patients address the classification of rheumatic diseases:

1. Soft tissue rheumatism, localized and generalized;
2. Arthritis that is noninflammatory, such as osteoarthritis, which often has a mild inflammatory component, with inflammatory RA being the prototype;
3. Connective tissues disease, including SLE, SS, PSS, LSS, PM, and DM.

Moreover, the papers address a patient's thoughts and desires and their link to feelings. Often the patient (and all of us) chase feelings—having good ones and avoiding bad ones—such that God is either used or ignored. In those cases, self is on the throne. Sadly, the person as a whole person—body and soul, inner and outer person, is not addressed. This can result in the patient missing aspects of care that can be very helpful to them.

I have heard it said by many physicians and pastors that the doctor's office is not a place of theological activity. People don't say it quite like that, but that is what they mean. That is a sad commentary on Matthew 22:37–40; 28:18–20. The whole world is God's classroom. Loving God and my neighbor means helping people view life, self, and God's providence (circumstances) from God's perspective. Being God's kind of physician means knowing truth—biblical as well as knowledge of the body and diseases—and using it properly. We are to share God's truth that is most appropriate for the person in their situation, given their spiritual maturity and willingness to listen and learn. Truth is not a club or hammer; it is God's tool to be used for his glory and the good of his people.

This is true for the biblical counselor. He must not focus only on the heart but take the whole person into consideration. All physicians need to be taught proper theology and all biblical counselors would benefit from being familiar with at least some aspects of medicine!

In the initial visit, both the physician and the biblical counselor need to address the following:

1. Becoming familiar with the patient and their condition. I always explore their thoughts and desires in some form and in varying depths.
2. Helping them to familiarize themselves with me and my approach to the practice of rheumatology.
3. Conveying several things: I know my specialty, I will listen, and I expect them to listen and to learn, which is defined in a variety of ways.

Follow-up visits are built on that initial visit. Hopefully, they begin to understand that I am treating the whole person. Patience and perseverance are necessary for both them and me.[5] Those traits are two pillars of success. Some people would let me pray with them, and I asked them to pray for me. The initial visit was important, but follow-up visits were more so. Those who familiarized themselves with the material I sent home with them were the ones who stayed with the "program."

I bring biblical truth into the conversation to the degree that I can. Some patients are not interested. Others are intrigued, and still others are very accepting. I practice medicine as I counsel, asking questions and moving inwardly. The two are linked. The idea is not to give a sermon or even evangelize. Rather, I would bring biblical truth that was appropriate for that person given their situation, their level of spiritual maturity (unbeliever, believer, growing believer), and their willingness to hear and do. I have a captive audience at least initially, but some want no part of the beauty and grandeur of biblical truth. Others embrace it, sometimes slowly, and are able to enjoy the body they have even if it is not the best. That last statement is a theological mountain for many to climb. But climb it we must—the patient, often the family, and the physician/counselor!

Medications in Perspective

A word regarding treatment is appropriate. This is always a loaded question. The medical profession has a number of medications for almost anything. God has graciously allowed researchers to discover a number of effective medications for these diseases and many others, and they benefit us all. Some medications have a proven track record, and others are new.

Many of the newer medicines seem to be more effective, but they certainly cost more! In some of these diseases, the "oldies" (such as

---

5. More about this concept can be found in *Endurance: What It Is and How It Looks in the Believer's Life* (Greenville, SC: Ambassador International, 2012).

Plaquenil (hydroxychloroquine) for SLE and Enbrel for RA) are still good choices. Drugs work in a variety of ways, which is exciting in itself. In the area of SLE, several new drugs are available, each with a different mechanism of action. They can affect the entire person and disease or only a specific aspect of the disease. Skin involvement in SLE is especially sensitive to hydroxychloroquine, but at the same time, it has shown total body benefit for every SLE patient irrespective of the overall picture.

All medications have potential side effects, but, depending on the disease, deciding not to get treatment also carries a risk. The key is wise stewardship designed to please God. I remember one patient who had RA for fifteen years or so. She was only on a low dose of prednisone. Some people don't think any dose of prednisone is safe; however, that was not my major concern. She had refused other disease-modifying drugs because prednisone was so cheap and the others so expensive and because she was better and fearful of side effects. She announced, "I am just fine." However, her physical exam gave a different story, as did her husband who came but sat in the room without saying anything. Her physical exam showed evidence of active arthritis—both wrists and her knuckles were swollen (the term is *synovitis*). She had active RA; her disease was not under control. I asked her the reason she had come to see me. She told me she wanted me to say it was okay for her to continue as she was. She had told me she was a Christian.

I summarized her situation as follows: you have active, uncontrolled RA, and God has provided medications that can potentially help. I asked her the reason she toyed with God and rejected a potential gift. She told me she had not considered such as a scenario. To her husband's joy, she agreed to take a remission-inducing agent.

I wondered if she had talked with her pastor or if she had consulted a biblical counselor. Hopefully, both would have gently but firmly helped her embrace good stewardship. Moreover, I wonder how her other doctors had approached her.

This principle also works the other way. Some patients, including believers, will take any and every medication in order to get relief.

Their mantra is *for me, by me, and to me.* That believer has no idea that God is their God and that they belong to him. They miss the beauty and joy of pleasing God simply because he is God and deserves to be pleased. I often use Romans 8:28–29 in this situation. I have learned to use it gently, but firmly. It is heavy theology. When patients pursue stewardship with a mindset described in Romans 8:28–29 and 2 Corinthians 4:16–18, life is simplified.

Outcomes

The four patient's stories that opened this chapter were among those who decided to continue the combination of medical care and biblical counseling. All of them faced discouraging symptoms and problems that came with their diagnosis. What follows is a short summary of the course of their care and their response to the adversity of their disease.

1. Ms. Brown came with the diagnosis of SLE. She had been healthy, had a new job as a teacher, and had a fiancé, and her life changed dramatically. She was not medically informed and even though a believer, she was not schooled in a biblical response to God and his providence. That latter point is crucial in helping this young lady get victory. Victory was not in her vocabulary, only relief.

As I gathered data it was easy to discern her significant fear and worry. I knew that those responses were considered normal for persons with this problem or any problem that is a significant stressor. The problem with overwhelming fear and worry are that they tend to take God out of the picture, or at least obscure the promise of victory in the midst of trouble. The question before me was how best to present biblical truth and which aspect. I wanted to help her, but how? As a physician-counselor, I had the advantage of knowing something about SLE. I needed to teach her facts about the disease and her response to it. Her response to it was a response to God. That is heavy theology for anyone, especially a twenty-four-year-old. She said she had never thought of it that way. Moreover, she understood victory only one way: pain relief or, even better, no SLE.

She had read the pain resource I had given her and said she better understood the disease and the role of her thoughts, desires and behavior in terms of symptoms. She was a young believer and had a church family. She did pray, but it was only for relief. She was willing to read homework assignments addressing hope and endurance,[6] and she was also willing to read Romans 8:28–29. She began to understand that addressing things including SLE God's way had its own rewards. She was strengthened in the inner person and consequently in the outer person.

2. Mrs. Smith, a young married lady and the mother of three children now has RA. What was she to do? She was thankful that the diagnosis was an obvious one. From her perspective, it seemed surreal. What did she do to cause this or to deserve this? She was a Christian; she prayed regularly and had a caring husband. But she wanted to know how she would make it through this trial. We discussed her view of God, problems in general, and her RA in particular. We explored the Bible's view of victory and her journey from start to finish. She envisioned the journey would be far too long: the hills too high, valleys too deep, and no light along the way. She wondered how she would make it as a wife and mother. What would happen to her body?

She was eager to gain victory. But the term and concept were new to her. She said she understood that sometimes she knew that her response to her condition aggravated the complaints of pain and fatigue. She was glad to hear that she could not think and desire herself out of pain and fatigue or into RA. She was happy to know that her thoughts and desires were linked to feelings, including pain and fatigue.

Mrs. Smith was maturing and beginning to understand she was not a victim but a victor in Christ. Romans 8:35–37 became a solid foundation for her. She began to change her approach to her disease, to herself, and to her husband and to her family

---

6. My homework is based off of my books: *Endurance: What It Is and How It Looks in the Believer's Life*, and *Out of the Maze: A Covenantal View of Hope*.

More than that, she was changing her concept of and approach to God. The book of Job became a refuge for her.[7] Job never received an answer to his initial "Why" questions. He did get an audience with God, but on God's terms not his! Job, who was portrayed as a winner early in life (Job 1–2) came to understand that God always had him. He had no right to demand an accounting from God. Job did get some answers to his questions and even his demands of God. He did get a restored body, but he received more: his relationship with God was deepened. He became intimate with God in a way that he did not think was possible.

Mrs. Smith began to actually count her blessings in the midst of trouble. She began to understand that her God had not left her or forsaken her. She drew strength, courage, and humility from these truths.

3. Ms. Mary came to me with a diagnosis of chronic pain syndrome. What a burden!! The phrase is more of a description than a diagnosis! Thankfully she recognized that fact. She had been labeled with a chronic pain syndrome and she had an agenda. She wanted relief, reasons for her situation, and a body like she had before the symptoms started. She did not believe there was much hope in achieving victory.

When meeting patients or counselees, I follow the same pattern gathering data (I want to know the person hopefully from the inside out); discerning the problem (I want to know from the person's perspective what she is thinking, wanting and doing or not doing); listening and learning where she is in terms of the problem and her relationship with the Triune God; and giving hope in part by introducing her to a new definition of hope and giving homework building on the time spent together. In this situation we had a head start on the homework because she had answered the questions reading the first four pain papers.

---

7. For more about the book of Job, see my book, *The Book of Job: God's Faithfulness in Troubled Times* (Greenville: Ambassador International, 2022).

In the office, I had laid the groundwork in terms of diagnosis. She understood the difference between soft tissue rheumatism and hard tissue rheumatism, which is arthritis of some type. She was ahead of the game, so to speak. She was also a believer and that changed everything. Her identity in Christ had not impacted her thoughts and desires in terms of her response. She was at a crossroads in her life, a spiritual crossroads that affected her whole person. She had a problem, and she could not get rid of it. She told me she was used to getting what she wanted, especially if she just worked hard enough. Now she was not in control, and she was upset at the unfairness of her situation.

Ms. Mary was eager to "get better"—by that she meant *pain-free*. However, by God's grace she came to understand early at least five facts: (1) Pain is one problem, and her response to it is another. (2) Her response to her situation may actually be playing a role in why she hurts. (3) She was beginning to view herself in a different light: she was not in control. (4) The term *victory* was a new one and she could not believe that victory was possible given her problems. (5) Hope should be defined differently than her initial definition.

These were major breakthroughs! Not only did she articulate them, but she was willing to share them. She was on her way to being a learner! I had spoken the truth of Scripture into her life. She grew in her willingness to listen, to be taught, to change, and to grow in spiritual maturity. I saw her as one willing to stay the course, hear and heed truths about God and herself, and change her view of victory and hope. She told me she was pleasantly surprised that I, both as a doctor and counselor was willing to listen and take her seriously. She had been cared for initially in a completely secular approach, and she had found it lacking. Now she was interested in what God had to say.

History-taking and gathering data is in one sense ongoing. It is essential if the patient/counselee is going to make progress. Mary began to open up about anger, resentment, and bitterness. I knew those responses existed because of her frustration with her diagnosis and symptoms. At first, she maintained she had a right to be the way she was. However, as she read Scripture, her understanding changed by the Holy Spirit. We focused on such passages as Romans 8:28–29; 2 Corinthians 4:16–18; Hebrews 12:1–3; and 1 John 3:1–3. She began to embrace slowly but surely a good God in the midst of trouble. She decided that pleasing God was far better than complete pain relief. She told me she still hurt but pleasing was a blessing. She began to embrace life as a Christian oyster: using what was an irritation to make the pearl of Christlikeness. She says she still has pain, but pleasing God was joy in itself (2 Corinthians 4:16–18).

4. Ms. White carried a diagnosis of chronic fatigue syndrome. She reported that she was a mess and did not like it. Fatigue was her constant companion, and a sedentary life was her lot. She had no hope of regaining what she had lost. But she said she understood inactivity was not good for her. I was able to give her credit for understanding how God made us body and spirit. She did articulate that she "felt trapped in her body." Eventually, she expressed the idea of wondering, even demanding, what is God doing. At that point, she had opened the door to discuss God and his control. She wondered how God fit in and reported that she had lost the will to pray. She had not gotten what she asked for.

I asked her what she wanted, and she said relief. The door was opened a little wider. I asked how her approach to her problem had been a blessing and benefit to her. What had it accomplished? She said it was the best she could do and at least she passed the time. I asked her if she willing to hear the "better way." She cautiously said yes. She was facing the long-term prospect of having something she did not like. I was helping her to reexamine her approach to it and to God.

The going was slow. She could not believe that hard things were from the hand of God. Why me and why now? With that we turned to the cross. The cross answers all the "Whys" that anyone could ask about God, self, others, and life. Predictably, it was still slow going. The cross is countercultural and counterintuitive especially for someone with chronic symptoms. We looked at 1 Corinthians 1:18–31.

Verse 31 summarized one aspect of the beauty and wisdom of the cross: the believer is something in Christ. That plus 2 Corinthians 5:17 (the believer is a new creature in the new creation) were key passages to help reorient herself. She had a new identity in Christ and therefore a new perspective, goal, and purpose in life. The Holy Spirit would her recall these truths as she focused on pleasing God. She was to take captive one thought and one desire at a time (2 Corinthians 10:3–5; Philippians 2:3–5; 3:7–11). She was cautiously optimistic.

Conclusion

People are not under their circumstances but are in the hands of the Triune God who made them, saved them, and indwells them. Once they acknowledge this truth, they begin to develop thoughts, desires, and behaviors that are linked to who they are in Christ. Victory comes *in* the situation, not *out* of it. An added benefit follows Proverbs 3:5–8 (NIV):

> Trust in the LORD with all your heart and lean not on your own understanding; in all your ways submit to him, and he will make your paths straight. Do not be wise in your own eyes; fear the LORD and shun evil. This will bring health to your body and nourishment to your bones.

This and other nuggets of truth from Proverbs amplify the connection and linkage of the inner person (heart, mind, spirit, or soul) and outer person (body, including the brain) (Proverbs 12:25; 14:30; 15:13, 30; 16:24; 17:22).[8] Our thoughts and desires are present in the outer person (brain) and the inner person (heart). Each affects the other. These thoughts and desires are linked to feelings and these three produce action or inaction.

---

8. See also my book, *True Competence in Medicine: Practicing Biblically-Based Medicine in a Fallen World*, self-published, jimhalla.com.

Every patient is called to be a good steward of their whole person—their body and their inner person. The Christian physician is to be a blessing to the patient, but being a blessing must be defined God's way for his glory! As a biblical counselor, you are also called to be a blessing to your counselees. Lord willing, this chapter will help you to wisely and kindly help counselees with these issues.

CONTRIBUTOR BIOS

Editor: Charles D. Hodges Jr., MD, is a family physician and biblical counselor who serves as the Executive Director of Vision of Hope and is a counselor and instructor at Faith Biblical Counseling Ministry. He is the author of *Good Mood, Bad Mood: Help and Hope for Depression and Bipolar Disorder* and is a contributing writer for *Caring for the Souls of Children*. He and his wife, Helen, have four children, thirteen grandchildren, and one great-granddaughter.

Mark A. Buono, MD, PhD, is an assistant professor of anesthesiology at Indiana University. He is also the West Central Region director of anesthesia services at Indiana University and the Chief of the Medical Staff. He has a MS and PhD in chemical engineering from Kansas State University and attended medical school at the University of Michigan in Ann Arbor. His training in anesthesiology was at the University of Pennsylvania. He is an ACBC certified counselor.

Daniel Dionne, MD, went to Medical School at George Washington University in Washington, DC. He and his wife, Kelli, live in Spokane, Washington, where he has practiced primary care internal medicine for thirty-two years. He became ACBC certified in 2016 and enjoys teaching on medical subjects for ACBC. He serves as the lay elder of biblical counseling at Faith Bible Church. He and Kelli have raised three children who are all married, and they enjoy their six delightful grandchildren. In his free time he loves bicycling, woodworking, music, reading, and travel.

Lee Edmonds, MD, is an associate clinical professor of medicine, Columbia University. Lee attended Jefferson Medical College in Philadelphia, with advanced training in pulmonary, critical care and sleep medicine at the Mayo Clinic. He is chief of pulmonary and sleep medicine at Bassett Healthcare in Cooperstown, New York. He is an ACBC certified counselor and teacher.

Daniel M. Gannon, MD, practiced orthopedic surgery in Bozeman, Montana. He has served as an elder and biblical counselor at Grace Bible Church. He enjoys archery hunting, biking, horseback riding, and motorcycling. He and his wife have been active in teaching on medical issues for ACBC.

Pamela Gannon, RN, MABC-FBS, is a speaker for ACBC on medical issues with her husband, Dan. She enjoys hospitality, hiking, and horseback riding in the mountains of Montana where her family resides. She is coauthor of *In the Aftermath: Past the Pain of Childhood Sexual Abuse.*

Jim Halla, MD, now retired following four decades in full-time practice of rheumatology, continues to minister and champion the practice of biblical-based medicine and counseling. His writings include *Pain, The Plight of Fallen Man, Being Christian in Your Medical Practice,* and *How to Be a God-Pleasing Patient.* He is an ACBC certified counselor.

Martha Peace, RN, is a biblical counselor to women at her home church, Faith Bible Church, in Sharpsburg, Georgia. She has been a certified counselor since 1989 and has written several books including *The Excellent Wife, Attitudes of a Transformed Heart, Precious Truths in Practice,* and *Biblical Counseling in Practice.* She and her husband, Sanford, have been married for fifty-six years. They have two children, twelve grandchildren, and five great-grandchildren.

Gordon "Chip" Phillips, MD, MABC, has served as a missionary surgeon in Amazonas, Brazil, for twenty-seven years, where he oversees the Amazon Baptist Hospital and teaches biblical counseling at conferences and seminaries. He is also an ACBC certified counselor. Chip and his wife, Laurie, have been married for thirty-five years and have five children and one grandchild.

Erin Ramirez, DO, is a board-certified obstetrician and gynecologist at Franciscan Alliance in Lafayette, Indiana. Erin attended Kansas City University of Medicine and Biosciences and completed her residency at Ascension Genesys Hospital through Michigan State University. She serves as the president of her OB/GYN group and the medical director at Franciscan Health Hospital. She enjoys teaching and spending time with her husband and children.

Matthew Rehrer, MD, is an emergency medicine physician in the San Francisco Bay Area and author of *Redeeming Memory*. Matt and his wife, Kara, live in California with their three kids. They attend Northcreek Church, where Matt serves as an elder and staff member.

Craig Svensson, PharmD, PhD, is Dean Emeritus and Professor of Medicinal Chemistry & Molecular Pharmacology, Purdue University College of Pharmacy, and Adjunct Professor of Pharmacology & Toxicology, Indiana University School of Medicine. He is the author of *When There Is No Cure*, *The Painful Path of a Prodigal*, and *Breaking the Grip of Addiction*.

Jocelyn Wallace is an ACBC certified biblical counselor, as well as a teacher and conference speaker, and has served as the director of both a women's transitional home and a faith-based residential treatment center for girls. She is the author of the minibooks *Anxiety and Panic Attacks: Trusting God When You Are Afraid* and *Helping Children with Body Image*. Jocelyn and her husband, Brian, have two daughters.

Daniel Wickert, MD, practiced OB/Gyn for thirty years before taking his current position as vice president of medical affairs in Franciscan Health Western Indiana in Lafayette. Dan is a member of Faith Church, where he coteaches a Sunday morning adult Bible fellowship. He counsels and teaches with Faith Biblical Counseling as well as with ACBC.